Go...
in ...
con...
adu...
Eve...
eas...

...
to i...
witl...
con...
asse...

...
opn...
syst...

-
-
-
-

-

This...
and...
sabl...
Con...
trea...

Sim...
Adolescent Psychiatry, University Hospital, Oslo, Norway. A Yorkshireman
by birth and inclination, educated and trained in Cambridge, London and
Edinburgh, he now lives in Oslo.

Coping and Complaining: Attachment and the Language of Dis-ease

Simon R. Wilkinson

The author has received support from the Norwegian
Non-fiction Literary Fund

Brunner-Routledge
Taylor & Francis Group

HOVE AND NEW YORK

First published 2003 by Brunner-Routledge
27 Church Road, Hove, East Sussex BN3 2FA

Simultaneously published in the USA and Canada
by Brunner-Routledge
29 West 35th Street, New York, NY 10001

Brunner-Routledge is an imprint of the Taylor & Francis Group

Copyright © 2003 Simon R. Wilkinson

Typeset in Times by Keystroke,
Jacaranda Lodge, Wolverhampton
Printed and bound in Great Britain by
TJ International Ltd, Padstow, Cornwall
Cover design by Sandra Heath

British Library Cataloguing in Publication Data
A catalogue record for this book is available from the British Library

Library of Congress Cataloging-in-Publication Data
Wilkinson, Simon R.
  Coping and complaining : attachment and the language of dis-ease /
Simon R. Wilkinson.
    p. ; cm.
  ISBN 1-58391-169-3 (hbk. : alk paper)—ISBN 1-58391-170-7 (pbk. :
alk. paper)
  1. Clinical health psychology. 2. Sick–Psychology. 3. Adjustment
(Psychology). 4. Attachment behavior.
  [DNLM: 1. Sick Role. 2. Attitude to Health. 3. Object Attachment.
4. Physician–Patient Relations. WM 178 W687c 2003] I. Title.

R726.7 .W556 2003
616'.0019—dc21   2002153909

ISBN 1-58391-169-3 (Hbk)
ISBN 1-58391-170-7 (Pbk)

For Ioan and Helga

Contents

Boxes

Preface

> Books are good enough in their own way, but they are a mighty blood-less substitute for life.
>
> Robert Louis Stevenson, 'An Apology for Idlers'

When I first moved to Norway I was taught Norwegian in classes for foreigners. There were about fifteen different nationalities present, and we were grasping at the possibility of talking with each other, about what it was like being in Norway. We got nowhere for a long time. The only spoken language that we had in common was the concrete language of 'this is a chair', 'stand/sit'. When the only language being spoken was Norwegian, the chair, or the teacher's example, was needed to ensure that we understood what was required. Feelings about being in Norway could not be on the agenda as we had no words for these hidden 'blips'. Feelings sprang up on our internal screens, and were visible for others to guess at through our facial expressions and body posture. We were unable to use words to reflect on and cope with them. We did not share a cultural way of interpreting and responding to our expressions.

Learning a foreign language in one's mature years does not mimic the process a young child uses to learn a language. Nevertheless it brings forcibly home the difficulties in developing a vocabulary for conveying subjective states, be they joy or discomfort. People have very different styles. Some want us to know of their aches and pains before we feel we have really got to know them, and even then they may lay it on thick. Others are very self-contained and tell us afterwards about the discomfort they had. Yet others seem to balance things in a different sort of way, checking out whether they could share their difficulty, but not being too reticent to try to make use of another to help them cope. In keeping with these stereotypes, their body postures may either scream at you with their aches, hide them from view, or be one way they peep out, so that others get a chance to show their sensitivity to the distress. You cannot read all the participants on the language course in the same way, although signs of emotional distress appear to be reasonably universal when they are visible.

Besides the strain of adapting to a new country, there can arise other forms of internal discomfort such as illness. These can be more critical to convey to others, but have been even less researched. There is no prospective research programme looking at the effects that episodes of childhood illness have on people developing ways of telling others about their being 'poorly'. We nevertheless need to understand how it is that some people develop variations on the styles mentioned above. These issues are central to effective communication between an ill person, and their carer. And it is *effective* that is the key word for the patient. I will therefore be presenting hypotheses that are based on generalisations from the literature as regards the development and presentation of emotional discomforts, adapted to what is known about health and illness behaviour.

In this book I attempt to avoid a dichotomy between constitutional and environmental factors. I present hypotheses and theory based on the developmental research, which emphasises that brain development is dependent on continuing feedback from the environment, genes being turned on in particular contexts. I will only rarely use 'psychosomatic' in this book, although issues around understanding asthma (classically regarded as a psychosomatic illness) will be included to illustrate points. I see the use of the term 'psychosomatic' as a relic from Cartesian duality. All illness has bodily and minded components.

I am interested in presenting an overview that can generate fruitful working models for those meeting illness. Working models are part of the same ideas I present when describing attachment strategies in Chapters 4–6. The theory being presented has to make sense, and be integrated with our common-sense views about how we relate. The work concerning children has also to be coherent with the models we have of ourselves. There should be no distinction between ourselves as readers and the subjects we talk to/work with. The usefulness of looking at working models is that they can help us explore the processes that are hypothesised to generate behaviour.

The theory being presented is generative of new ways of formulating research issues. The validity of the theory will be tested through making clear predictions, which are testable. The research has not come far enough to present data that can confirm the picture being presented, but it has proved useful in understanding patients in a variety of settings. My hope is that the data will be coherent with the internal models of practice that are currently held, and in that way facilitate integrating new knowledge into daily practice. The book's usefulness will be evaluated on whether it has been helpful, not so much on whether it has been right.

An understanding of memory systems is beginning to inform research in several fields, and especially attachment theory. Theories of development need to be particularly mindful that all learning has to be accommodated in memory, and so the way of understanding memory has to be coherent with the changes one encounters during development. Research into development, and brain function, including memory, has led to many different hypotheses, which have not all been tested out. There is a danger when a group of authors use one another's references and refer to one another's hypotheses, that the hypotheses will be reified to facts about development. Small errors become exaggerated. The ideas are not being checked out in relation to what is seen. This is especially likely in the current situation where attachment behaviour is being looked at differently by different theoreticians, who are interpreting observations differently. There are fundamental differences here that need to be resolved. One system of classification can say a child is secure, and another insecure. Some differences relate to how we view deviance from an hypothesised ideal. Is it evolutionary adaptive, or pathology? Is there an ideal 'secure' attachment of the B strategy, or is the choice of name unhelpful because it leads to the hypothesis that it should be the aim (compared to aiming for an 'insecure' strategy). I have had to take a stand as regards whether I will continue with 'secure' as a description of one of the attachment strategies, and have decided that I need to break with tradition, as a few other researchers in the field have begun to do. I will though point out the alternative terms being employed to describe the various attachment strategies.

Making our attachment strategies available for conscious reflection will facilitate further hypothesis development. Conscious reflection influences the outcome of emotional processes. I hope that illness and disease will not be quite the same after you have read this book.

Acknowledgements

Over the course of the last seven years I have had the pleasure of being trained by Pat Crittenden in the use of several measures of attachment behaviour and strategy. Discussion of her thinking has played a very helpful part in the development of my own ideas. I need to ensure that she only gets credited with the best ideas presented here, whilst I am responsible for the rest, and any inadvertent mistakes in the presentation of her dynamic-maturational model of attachment.

I received assistance from St John's College, Cambridge, England, during the writing of this book, and have been able to make generous use of the University of Cambridge's library facilities. My employers at The Centre for Child and Adolescent Psychiatry, Oslo, Norway, supported me throughout. Our librarians there have been invaluable. Many other colleagues have given advice and encouragement along the way for which I am very grateful.

Abbreviations

A, B, C and DX attachment patterns and strategies are not abbreviations, but codings for designation of attachment type. In this book they are not used as codings for personality types unless specifically identified as such.

AAI = Adult Attachment Interview
ACTH = Adrenocorticotrophin hormone
ADHD = Attention Deficit Hyperactivity Disorder
BMI = Body Mass Index
EBM = Evidence Based Medicine
GP = general practitioner
HPA axis = hypothalamic–pituitary–adrenal axis
ICD-10 = International Classification of Diseases, version 10
IBS = irritable bowel syndrome
IL-1 = Interleukin-1
LTP = Long-term potentiation
NHS = National Health Service
PAA = Preschool Assessment of Attachment
PKU = Phenylketonuria
PTSD = Post-traumatic Stress Disorder
RAP = recurrent abdominal pain
SSn = Strange Situation
Ul/tr = Unresolved loss/trauma
VIP = very important person – used as a shorthand for those people on whom patients depend when they are hoping for comfort. It includes parents, close colleagues and health professionals, but may also include dangerous people.

Chapter 1

'I'm ill; you're sick'

An infant crying in the night:
An infant crying for the light:
And with no language but a cry.
              Alfred, Lord Tennyson *In Memoriam* (pt. LIV, st.)

Pamela was going to have her fourth birthday party in the afternoon.
But just now she did not feel like getting out of bed, and coming down
for breakfast. All her parcels were waiting downstairs. There was
not much time to spare. Soon her father would be taking her to the
nursery. Various thoughts whipped through their minds. Was she
going down with the flu? Granny had had that a week ago. Was
she too excited and troubled by a churned-up tummy? Was she
worried about coping with the celebrations planned in the nursery?
Was it the sort of thing that meant that one of them had to stay at
home with her? Was she ill, or upset, or both – and did it matter? Had
she been too late to bed the night before?

This book is for and about patients, and that should mean just about all
of us at some time or other. It presents a way of understanding how people
learn to complain about their suffering so that they can cope as well as to
be expected. This involves understanding how they come to discriminate
between different sorts of dis-ease, which includes complaints caused by
disease and the suffering of being ill at ease. In order to understand this
I will show how the behaviour we see amongst adult patients develops.
This starts with looking at how parents respond to their sick infants, and
the infant's primitive complaining – crying. Their crying evolves so that
they are heard helpfully, given the competencies of their parents.
Everyone develops their own preferred 'language of dis-ease', their ways

of making known that something is not right, both what they say and how they 'say' it. The way they have been looked after has led to things being different; if some behaviour is ignored there will be less of it, and more of other behaviour, or, as we say, the behaviour has been shaped. Pamela's lack of tears does not mean to say that she is not in pain.

Illness threatens people's sense of security. Getting somebody to listen to complaints is urgent and essential, especially when young. If Pamela had cried it would have alerted those nearby – crying demands attention when something unpleasant is going on. The problem is trying to answer the crying with that magic solution, which can soothe the infant as soon as possible. Only later might the child be able to manage on her own, and learn how to soften the impact of the dis-ease through self-regulating of the discomfort. Parents respond to children's distress in a variety of ways, which will have consequences for how children subsequently manage more or less on their own.

The likely causes of distress are everyday discomforts of hunger, loneliness, a wet nappy – and illness cannot be ruled out. Until babies have developed self-soothing strategies they can cry for a long time. The parents' expectations of the likelihood of illness affect how tense they get – especially if the disease can be lethal (a meningitis outbreak in the neighbourhood for example). Each sign of a rash is then looked at with an anxious gaze until it has been distinguished from the everyday rashes of childhood illnesses. Parents cope with this time of maximal uncertainty very differently. Parents are more or less attuned to their children's suffering while they are thinking about the cause. This usually means trying to identify precedents (what did Pamela eat the evening before?), and interpreting children's emotional states in the light of how much they have invested in carrying through what was planned for the rest of the day – the consequences of being sick. A patient's emotional state is part of the suffering. People who suffer can lay claim to being 'patients' (based on its Latin root – *patior*, to suffer or bear). I use 'patient' throughout this book in this prime sense of a person who is suffering, and not in relation to a patient role.[1]

Cries do not start off being distinct signals for specific discomforts. We used to think they did, but current research suggests otherwise (Barr, Hopkins, Green, 2000). Cries rapidly become extended into recurring bouts, which take on their own form, possibly initially related to associated breathing patterns.[2] When crying takes a form, it invites 'translation' (Hoffmeyer, 1995a).[3] A pattern has become a sign for those looking after the child. This is like the ticking of a watch, which we hear as having a pattern over and above the regular ticking – when we have fever the ticking pattern can take on dramatic qualities. The significance depends on the culture – witness the Japanese saying that crying children grow well.

Crying is one starting point for a language of dis-ease. Languages are used to share our internal states with others, our thoughts, and to ask others to do things. There is a vocabulary we use, and various non-verbal signs – the bowed posture, the holding of the head, the grimace, the tone of voice (the prosody). In discussion non-verbal modifiers accompany the verbal emphasis, but in relation to our internal discomfort the primary channel is the non-verbal. Words and behaviour develop through how discomforts and diseases are responded to when people are children.[4]

In order to understand how illness talk or discourse proceeds, it is necessary to start with the suffering person – the discomfort. The subjective experience is part of how the person is, and cannot be distinguished from what is happening in their body. The next step is to add in the semiotic bit – how people interpret ill people, and they recognise their own state, such that they can self-referentially say – 'I am ill'. In this tangle grows the 'language of dis-ease'.

The etymological origin of disease is the basic state of dis-ease – being ill at ease. Understanding the link between dis-ease and illness behaviour involves understanding the nature of emotions, and how illness becomes discriminated from the discomforts of other negative emotions. It is as if there are primary primitive undifferentiated emotional states (Siegel, 1999: 125–126), corresponding to my use of dis-ease, which are subsequently differentiated into either emotional states with distinct characteristics, the conventional feelings of anxiety, anger and frustration, or feelings of illness. A lot has been written on emotions and their place in development, but the close relationship between the origins of languages for conveying emotions and feelings of illness has not been given attention. Research into the emotions helps unravel this important central process concerning the origin of the feeling of being ill.

Understanding the initial primary background emotion of dis-ease provides a common thread to understanding the mind–body unity of bio-, psycho-, social processes in medicine. From day one the cry as a signal of dis-ease can be interpreted as if it represented an emotional or somatic discomfort, or a mixed aroused state, a sign of illness or stress, or both. These distinctions are made on the basis of the carers' repertoire of what might be 'up' with their baby, and how they have evaluated the infant's circumstances. Dis-ease is in the minded body; it is psychosomatic.

The newborn baby has learnt a lot already (Bateson, Martin, 1999: 20). Parents have also learnt a lot about their baby; they have interpreted their baby's movement patterns during pregnancy (Zeanah, Keener, Stewart, Anders, 1985) and ascribed a personality to the unborn child. Many biases of interpretation will already be in place. After birth the security of the womb will never be repeated. Parents relate to the baby's smiles and grimaces, babbling and other noises, and the child experiences threats to its existence in new ways. The immediate demand when the baby cries is to find out what is up, and check on the baby's safety.

'Talk' between an ill child and parent can feel particularly complicated at 3 a.m., and almost as difficult for adults when they want their doctor to understand and comfort them in a busy surgery. The participants' particular developmental histories give clues as to why a consultation is such a complex process. Through exploring how people learn to complain effectively about states of dis-ease, it becomes understandable how doctors and patients get into a mess when talking with each other – and how complicated it can be trying to improve matters.

For discussions with ill people to be as helpful as possible, it is necessary to operate with assumptions about what is likely to be helpful. 'Working models' about what partners, children or patients are likely to need tend to guide what to do. Such working models are taken for granted, and assumed to be shared. It is illuminating to see what happens when people have different models, or, as with an infant and parent, only one has the model and the other has not yet heard that she is supposed to have the same one. People try both to get something and give something in some sort of crazy two-step. Dancing is fun when both partners dance the same steps to the same tune, and avoid each other's toes. Working models are a key concept in attachment theory. They are used to integrate information from brain development, psychology and ethology to explain how children generally make sense of how people are likely to respond. Children and their parents are making inspired guesswork about each other – inspired by previous experience.

These guiding expectations bring order to relationships. It is impossible to be totally naïve. People live in a world full of best guesses, where their previous experience and ideas about what the current situation entails determine what they say and do. People have private ways of defining what they mean when they try to convey that they are possibly ill. People say they are 'under the weather', 'fairly' or 'crook' for example. These are vague terms for those not versed in the local variations of how phrases are used. It is not possible to give a concrete definition of a subjective state. 'Fairly' (from Wensleydale, England) can mean both well and poorly, depending solely on intonation; it can invite discussion, or exclude further comment, depending on how it is said. Social scientists have tried to define the usage of words so as to limit misunderstanding. Here I will use 'illness', 'disease' and 'sickness' in these narrower ways. These do not necessarily correspond to the ways they are used informally.

Illness

Dis-ease corresponds closely to what is referred to as *illness*. When infants are ill, they are dependent on others recognising their discomfort in order to be comforted. Their primary difficulty lies in their subjective state of discomfort. Their parents will have to distinguish states of illness from discomfort secondary to changes in natural body states, tiredness and hunger, and from psychological discomfort, such as feeling lonely. Parents employ a variety of strategies in order to settle fractious children, depending on how they have attributed causes to the children's difficulties. Parents are often not immediately aware of where they get inspiration from as to the cause of the children's subjective distress. It is often preconscious.[5] Piet Hein, the Danish polymath, conveyed the dilemma rather nicely in one of his 'prose grooks': 'Subjectivity is reading a sundial – using a pocket torch!'[*]

The first requirement of a crying infant is to get control over/reduction in their disorganised aroused body state, their 'dis-ease'. For this they depend on someone else's help initially. By the time children get to Pamela's age they can usually soothe themselves. In contrast to what we believed until recently, infants whose parents respond particularly rapidly to their crying are those who can come to take a longer time to learn to soothe themselves. It is as if children need to have parents who enable them to experience that they can sort things out themselves by being a bit slower off the mark (Van IJzendoorn, Hubbard, 2000). Parents need to modify their perspective about speed of response in line with the growing skills of their infants.

Discomfort, when caused by a disease, gives rise to 'illness'. First the dis-ease has to have been labelled as illness. Illness is used for the child's *subjective state* of discomfort, when that is believed to be caused by disease. People feel that they are ill. I have described elsewhere how family processes around ill children enable them to take the first steps in using their personal dis-ease language (Wilkinson, 1986, 1988). Discerning illness is difficult, and ambiguous dis-eases, which may have

---

[*]   Piet Hein © prose grook reproduced with kind permission from Piet Hein a/s, DK-5500 Middelfart.

a somatic, psychological or mixed foundation are discussed specifically in Chapter 7.

The following definition of illness covers its use by three-year-olds: 'Something counts as illness if it affects an important dimension to the child's relation with a significant other person, and is labelled as illness' (Wilkinson, 1988: 77). People learn about their feelings of illness, as well as emotions, in relationships. Something must have happened to alter the quality of the relationship, which made a difference to the parent–child, and the child was told he was ill. It was the best guess at the time. An exception to the rule is illustrative:

> A lawyer, who had serious problems with his back, was bedridden at home. His four-year-old son did not regard him as ill. The most important thing that this father did with his son each night was to read him his bedtime story. This ritual was unaffected by his back problem. Father was not ill from the child's point of view.

In summary, illness is a subjective state of discomfort attributed to a disease or disorder. The discomfort is not regarded as being primarily dependent on what is happening around the child. People who are ill are patients.

Sickness

The person suffering feels illness, whereas others decide that someone is sick. For adults, sickness is used for someone who is unable to fulfil a social role by virtue of having a disease. An 'expert', be it parent or nurse, comes to the decision that a child 'has' something. Parents say to children, and patients subsequently say themselves, that they have caught 'it' (whatever 'bug' is going around) – rather than focusing on their own symptoms, their illness. The sickness becomes externalised as a thing, divorced from the subjective dis-ease. Pamela's parents decide if she has caught 'it' – the flu which granny had.

'Sickness' is used when a state of dis-ease is *attributed* to someone. The use of the terms 'illness' and 'sickness' translate as, 'I'm ill; you're sick.'

To say that a child is sick depends on the carer noticing that their relationship to the child has altered (the complement of the definition of illness for the child given above). The early parent–infant interactions lead to children learning about illness through parents attributing sickness. The role quality present in the adult definition of sickness is present in terms of the *pattern* of mother–child relationship having altered. Illness and sickness are complementary. As illness is not distinguished without the associated attribution of sickness, there is a complicated mix here between illness and sickness that has not always been clear in the adult sociological literature.

The importance of this illness/sickness distinction can be illustrated in relation to a condition being treated in child psychiatry called hyper-activity. A child with hyperactivity and low attention can have a condition diagnosed as attention deficit hyperactivity disorder, ADHD (according to the American diagnostic system), or hyperkinesis (according to the diagnostic system of the World Health Organisation). Teachers, the experts on disorder in the classroom, can then attribute a disorder to their pupils, to explain why they do not attend in their class and race around. They can be said to have defined the pupil as 'sick' in this terminology. The pupils do not necessarily experience themselves as ill. They seldom do. They rightly say 'I do not feel ill', where teachers say 'you are sick'. They are not patients with suffering in the illness sense, but can have a sickness.

Can doctors and/or psychologists (somewhat culturally defined as to who are qualified to define the pupils' disorder), confirm the school experts' designation of sickness? With sickness supported, certain 'rights' fall to patients – issues of responsibility for actions are revised on the analogy of other sicknesses, such as influenza, which can lead to children being excused their daily chores.

Disease and disorder

Disease specifies the pathological biological processes which can give rise to a state of dis-ease rooted in changes in the body, caused for example by an infection or cancer. There are objective changes. So when the sick pupil arrives, the question is whether the doctor will confirm the teacher's suspicion, and find some pathology or objective changes (pathognomonic signs). This is a critical moment in a budding illness career. Should the doctor decide that the diagnosis of ADHD is warranted – that the signs are present – she still needs to decide what processes are accounting for the disorder.

Attention difficulties are a general sign of simply 'being preoccupied with something else', such as distress, and so are not of themselves diagnostic – similarly with high activity levels. The doctor might find a disease which accounts for the behaviour being observed. I hesitate to call them symptoms because in our example the pupil is not conveying any personal discomfort. There is good evidence that some people who do not convey symptoms of personal discomfort still show other signs of being stressed – for example, high pulse rate and raised cortisol levels. Much more probably the doctor will end up with a group of signs that tend to be found together, without there being clear evidence of underlying pathology. When signs cluster in this way, in a regular pattern, we recognise *disorder*,[6] just as parents saw pattern in their child's crying and used that to interpret the cause. If Pamela tends not to want to go to school there is another pattern to her behaviour, which has to be taken into account when interpreting her current reluctance. With a familiar cluster of signs a biomedically focused doctor is usually expecting that in time underlying pathology will be found. A disorder can be thought of as like a disease, but without current clarity in the pathological processes. This means that one must be open to the possibility of a disorder not having a disease equivalent (a disorder can be seen as similar in kind to a phenotype, whereas a disease is conceptually more similar to a genotype).

Disorders reflect observed patterns of behaviour, which have become signs. The process whereby those experiencing 'disorders' become entitled to the same benefits in a society as those who are diseased is primarily a political process, dependent on faith in the appointed experts' abilities to distinguish meaningful patterns. Hyperactivity has been one of those conditions, like chronic fatigue syndrome, or repetitive strain injury, which as a disorder has been variously given the rights afforded those who have diseases, at different times in different cultures. Patients do not necessarily have disorders or diseases. Suffering and being ill is not synonymous with having a disease. The thinking behind the presumption that disorders will become diseases often reflects a pervasive mind/body dichotomy, whereby causes are attributed to either disease agents or psychological processes; but rarely is there a model for how they are intertwined (Taylor, 1979).

There is an uncanny resemblance to the primary processes occurring in families, in the medical dynamic of identifying a diagnosis, and confirming a disease or disorder. Parents are dependent on recognising pattern changes when their relationship with their child begins to deviate from their expected working model of how their child tends to respond. They can then decide whether their child can stay off school, be excused family chores, or other advantages which can befall the ill child – as opposed to when the pattern is not believed due to disease (Wilkinson, 1988). How the changes are recognised, labelled and responded to is central to the dynamic of dis-ease language development. As seen with the example of ADHD, there can be many experts: the child, the parents, the teacher and various health professionals; different forms of negotiation about the child's condition determine the child's understanding of his condition, and who is the powerful expert (often children miss out being expert on their own forms of discomfort).

Susan Sontag, the author who so lucidly explored the metaphorical meanings associated with diseases, says that with writing her books she wanted to reduce 'illness' to a scientific, biological fact, stripped of associated symbolic meanings (Sontag, 1978, 1989). It is as if she wished this 'illness/sickness/disease' distinction to be independent of the social meaning structure in which illness experiences have been placed. The layers of meaning, which arise in the process of interpretation of pattern, are also an inevitable part of the symbolic discourse[7] carried on in the corridors of the consultants'/parents' power.[8] It is not possible to control which meanings are attributed to which observations, but the process can be opened up to discussion.

Predicament

A tricky area for parents concerns children who are born with handicaps or other disorders. Their children are not ill. There is no *change* in their relation with their parents because of their condition. Their relationships have always been characterised by their handicap. People tend to get into a muddle when thinking that these children have disease/disorder, and therefore are ill. They can perhaps rightly be said to be sick, although this is debatable. They cannot fulfil normal social roles, although there is no change in their 'role' in relation to their parent. But they are definitely not ill. It is useful here to think that children struggle to live with their *predicaments* (Taylor, 1989), uncomfortable conditions that have to be lived with. This distinction becomes important when I return to how best to talk with them about their condition, as people would normally expect to engage an ill person through talking with them about *their* discomforts. For these people clinicians need to look with them at the predicaments to which they are exposed because of their disease/disorder. Further, it is not necessarily right to consider these people as patients in the sense I am using here, although the consequences of their predicament can have led to secondary effects of dis-ease. They can suffer from stigma and shame.

In summary *illness* is experienced, *disease/disorder* is observed, and *sickness* is attributed when social expectations are not being met and the reason is believed to be disease/disorder (Box 1.1). Our beliefs about causes, and ways of interpreting, bind together disease, illness and sickness models. Each of these is dependent on the other through how

---

Box 1.1 Dis-ease

Illness	'I feel ill'	*Experienced*	Symptoms
Sickness	'You are sick'	*Attributed*	Signals
Disease	'He has a disease'	*Observed*	Signs
Predicament	'A challenge to live with'	*Lived*	Stigma

---

people interpret behavioural patterns, and respond to them. This necessitates an understanding of how people come to regard discomforts as their own. The process originates with an attribution, which is the counterpoint to their own experiences. At first parental ways of interpreting their children's behaviour are decisive. The power balance is not just between doctors and patients, but first takes its character between children and their parents.

Illness behaviour and strategic symptoms

Mechanic defined 'illness behaviour' as the various ways in which individuals perceive, evaluate and act upon symptoms (Mechanic, Volkart, 1960). An understanding of the distinctions between illness, sickness and disease provides a framework for doing this. How do we recognise symptoms? How has the care we have received led to the development of a language of dis-ease? Attachment theory will enable a comprehensive description of why some discomforts fail to become symptoms, and why others can become exaggerated and misleading. Attachment theory is coherent with the formulation of Parsons that illness is 'socially constructed and biologically constrained' (Parsons, 1964).

The actual behaviour shown at any time depends on context. When other people are present, illness behaviour will be influenced by beliefs about those people – that is, their theory of the other person's mind. Illness behaviour needs to be seen as also being part of an interpersonal communication, and therefore susceptible to having strategic purposes. Appearance and reality are not the same. In some circumstances it appears to be so far outside the acceptable norms for illness behaviour that Pilowsky termed it 'abnormal illness behaviour' (Pilowsky, 1997).[9] He used it for the presentation of discomforts in bodily ways, without confirmed somatic disease or disorder, such as with hysteria (the term 'somatisation' – see Chapter 7, was not in general use at the time).

The concept of '*abnormal* illness behaviour' is not coherent with how I will be using illness behaviour, although I have no problems with Pilowsky's use of '*atypical* illness behaviour'. Focusing on the *function* of illness behaviour encourages an evolutionary perspective. The illness behaviour has been legitimate, in a communicative sense. It can be seen as an evolved way of coping with the 'complaint', the dis-ease. The form of the presentation is an indication of what sort of developmental processes have moulded the person's ways of presenting their discomforts, and their beliefs/experiences about choices for doing things differently. Pilowsky identified these processes in his classification of 'abnormal illness behaviour', where he describes the possibilities for 'abnormally denying or affirming' illness, and of illness focus being on either a somatic or psychological condition. My concern is with understanding the generative processes, and seeing the adaptive function of the behavioural strategies that evolve. When adopted in alternative settings to where they arose, difficulties can arise. Some of what the patient has experienced, and has given rise to the illness behaviour strategies they employ, will be available to them in what they remember. Other aspects are 'remembered' in procedural memory (the implicit memory for how things have been carried out which sits in bodily patterns of reaction – see Chapter 2). These are preconscious, rather than unconscious, and not open to discussion with their doctor, in contrast to their views about illness. It is Pilowsky's use of 'abnormal' to which I object. He introduced the term to avoid the negative connotations of hysteria. I believe the approach being presented here captures the spirit of his aim.

Attachment paradigm

As children mature, the influences on their language of dis-ease get more complex as more influences come into play. Their capacity to entertain several possible responses from those taking care of them increases, and they can transform information given to others – for example, they become able to deceive in a variety of ways. Biological constraints, such as genetic influences, brain anatomical organisation and physiology, affect their abilities in different ways as they mature. At the same time their breadth of interpersonal experiences also affect gene expression, and lead to brain changes during development (Deacon, 1997; Siegel, 1999).

Relationships, both within the family and with professionals, affect which symptoms are employed strategically, and how they are handled. I use attachment theory to bring some order to the interpersonal application of symptoms. This is not straightforward, as attachment theory is still undergoing development. There are various ways of identifying and interpreting the patterns of behaviour, and their strategic usage – their effective use to modify consequences which take into account theories of other people's minds. This can lead to disagreement about attachment classification. Attempts have been made to simplify measurement, either through simplifying the method or classificatory system, or both. Currently there is no consensus about which system is 'right', and I instead choose what I believe to be the most helpful. Pat Crittenden's 'dynamic-maturational model of attachment' (Crittenden, Claussen, 2000; Crittenden, 1999–2002) is currently the most comprehensive. She is concerned that we develop our attachment strategies in order to cope with danger and risk through maximising safety. These are central to the experience of illness, and so on pragmatic grounds I am adopting her classificatory system. Her approach is essentially an evolutionary approach, not seeing any attachment strategy as being inherently superior to the others, each strategy having evolved in its niche of adaptedness (Hinde, Stevenson-Hinde, 1990), and having costs when adopted in other settings. The strategies are initially properties of relationships (Hinde, 1982; Main, 1990). The niche consists of the family, embedded in its culture.[10] Attachment strategies change during people's lives as they respond to events and changed circumstances (Crittenden, Claussen, 2000). This occurs to a much greater extent than is found through doing research with largely well-off, middle-class families, where the lack of threat in their daily lives probably accounts for an undue degree of continuity in their attachment strategies.

Attachment theory is not right or wrong, but more or less helpful – both in accounting for research results and in helping to understand those who are ill. We need to retain a sense of scepticism for scientific theories – even quantum theory and the general theory of relativity are not yet compatible. We must expect those to which we currently adhere to be under constant revision and overtaken in the years to come. As quantum theory and the general theory of relativity emphasise, relationships need to be in focus, and outcomes can be unpredictable. Those who are looking for an answer to what people ought to do will not find it in this book. I hope that instead there will be greater understanding of how we come to be as we are, so that people can more easily find their own solutions – useful for their circumstances. Compassion grows through being able to view development from a variety of perspectives, and attachment theory helps integrate these perspectives. With a compassionate approach healing and hope are nurtured. This is a book for those who wish to facilitate the empowerment of others, rather than be more powerful themselves. It is easily coherent with the research into the non-specific factors that bring about change (Hubble, Miller, Duncan, 1999).

A psychosocial classification of disease

Different diseases present different challenges for parents and doctors when they are deciding whether someone is sick. The central process of discriminating between states of dis-ease is more or less emotionally charged, depending on the types of potential threat to the child's health. If Pamela had a rash that had to be distinguished from that found with meningitis, it would be a different worry compared to the rash of chickenpox – and only then if she did not have an immune deficiency disorder. If we classify illness and disease in relation to the types of threat, danger and risks involved, we have a classification that can be integrated with the attachment paradigm.

Diseases can helpfully be classified according to a psychosocial classification (Rolland, 1984, 1987) (Box 1.2). This system of classification is especially well adapted for showing the way different diseases affect identification of the state of dis-ease, and therefore the ease with which people can pick up on changes in another person's state. This again affects the ease with which illness experiences become integrated in children's growing language of dis-ease. Medical students are warned about this early in their training, because hormone changes, such as with thyro-toxicosis, can lead to such gradual changes that they are not at first

---

Box 1.2   Psychosocial classification of sickness

Beginning	Acute	Gradual
Course	Progressive – +/– resolution of sickness	Constant – +/– retaining vulnerability to relapse
Function	Reduced – (visibly cf. not visibly)	Retained
Prognosis	Deadly – (markedly cf. minimally reduced life span)	Not deadly

Source: Adapted from Rolland (1984)

seen to make a significant difference to how one is getting on with one's life. The more rapid the onset of a sickness, the clearer the change in functioning, the easier it is to discriminate the change and ascribe sickness. Such discrimination requires that there is enough pattern to the child's normal way of relating, so that 'disorder' can be discriminated. Altered attunement of parent and child modifies patterns of development, children's self-protective strategies, and, as a consequence, their neuro-biology (Kraemer, 1992). These again affect children's ability to discriminate forms of illness. When the functioning that is affected is particularly salient for the relationship it will be distinguished rapidly.

An example will illustrate what I am getting at. For three-year-old children colds come acutely, but they do not usually make any difference to parents and their children. They do not count as 'worthy illnesses'; no changes in daily routines result. Children with colds kiss their parents good night; they go to nursery. But for eight-year-olds colds are important illnesses. It is clear that they have a cold, there are visible signs, and there is no argument about whether they have a disease. They have found that colds can be used to renegotiate family duties, and for gaining treats. They can make a difference (see Herzlich [1973] for how illness can have a role as 'liberator' from adult duties). The difference is dependent on their greater understanding of the roles which illness plays in social negotiation, and being able to adopt the mind of the other person. The exception to the rule illustrates the dynamic. One three-year-old I met regarded colds as serious illnesses. His sister had a disorder of immunity so that colds were dangerous for her. It would be risky for him to be exposed to colds, so that if there were colds at his nursery he did not go. Colds had already made a significant difference to his life (Wilkinson, 1988: 183). There are both personal and cultural dimensions to developing understanding of the patient role and vulnerabilities to disease.

Different diseases have different courses, which affect the significance of having that disease. Children have the greatest chance of behavioural disturbances when they have a disease, if the course of the disease is characterised by relapses. For instance, the disease of epilepsy is associated with long periods of normal family relationships, but there remains a risk of epileptic fits even when children appear to be well. Children meet the gaze of parents, who regard them as at risk, even when they do not feel ill. Here it is the parents who are in a predicament. Their gaze may or may not convey their anxieties about the risk, and what might happen. Their strategies for coping with this kind of risk convey various ideals to children. Their body language may or may not 'give them away'. This is difficult, because however hard they try to hide their concern, the risk is there, and children may or may not be met with the same relaxed caring dance that could have been there before the diagnosis was made.

Cancer in children is usually curable today, but parental knowledge about cancer is seldom as up to date. One must expect them to be more concerned about the few per cent that do not recover. When children are in remission, the chance of a relapse is there, and this again alters the way children are attuned with their parents – even though they do not feel ill when in remission. The meaning of the disease for the parents defines the danger and threat, which is independent of the children's sense of discomfort, their subjective illness experience, which no longer guides their daily behaviour. They have become doubly 'patient', their own suffering meets the added burden of the transmitted anxiety from the parents, even when they do not feel like a patient (a sort of vicarious experience of the parents' fear). The term 'Damocles syndrome' is used to describe the hypervigilance and anxiety of parents who face the persistent threat of losing their child. This can lead to a pattern of over-controlled parenting and enmeshment of parent and child, as has been described between parent and their child with haemophilia (see Chapter 6 for a detailed description of enmeshment through illness preoccupation).

The degree, to which family members are on guard for the affective signals being conveyed varies considerably. Attachment theory will help us understand why some parent–child relationships will be more vulnerable in this situation than others.

If a disease affects children's functioning, so that it is clear that they are ill when they say they are ill, it is reasonably plain sailing. These diseases which affect children's general condition, such as influenza, are called systemic diseases. The children who get into the worst predicaments with their disorders are those who have conditions characterised by largely invisible problems (Ytterhus, Tøssebro, 1999). People are unable to make allowance for them, and instead can come to apply their criteria for deciding whether children are attempting to deceive them when they claim to be ill. This is especially a problem for clumsy children, who get into difficulties when they fail to meet expectations in the football team, or in sewing lessons. Children usually accommodate to children with a leg in plaster in the football team much more easily than to a clumsy child. They revise the rules to enable them to be included.

The real crunch for parents is whether the condition is or can be deadly. The prognosis defines one sort of risk, and the parents' strategies for coping with threat are mobilised. Their strategies mould their form of availability for their children, and will be described in detail in the rest of the book. In the climate of a threat to the security of their relationships, their attachment system of behaviour will be mobilised. Conditions are also characterised by anticipated risk, depending on parents' personal experiences. The information on risk provided by health professionals may or may not be relied upon. The emotional experiences that parents have had previously with similar illnesses determine how they make use of the information provided by the experts. If parents have had illnesses which caused them great distress, the least sign of a similar condition in their children can release an emotional response, which may prevent making use of rational information provided by the medical staff (see Chapter 6, sections Unresolved and Trauma). Prognosis is relevant both for the real degree of threat involved as well as for the believed threat.

Why, how and what?

This book uses the dynamic-maturational model of attachment to cover key questions for understanding illness behaviour:

- Why is the behaviour shown now?
- How did the person grow to respond this way?
- What is the function of the behaviour for people generally – its survival value?

But this book does not take up the final question necessary to understand the full nature of the behaviour:

- How has the behaviour evolved phylogenetically? (Tinbergen, 1951).

An application of attachment theory to understand how people discriminate and share discomforts throws up questions about the relation between somatic and psychiatric medicine, and of both of them to illness. Use of social networks affects both how people talk about illnesses, and their dispositions for certain illnesses and disease (Cohen *et al.* 1997; Felitti *et al.*, 1998). Understanding the dynamics of social networks for how they influence disease presentation is helpful for developing a research agenda about how to reduce morbidity for major killers of the Western world, such as heart disease, drug abuse and depression.

Communication between patients and their doctors is that area of medical practice which gives greatest cause for public concern, and which various government reports suggest needs most improvement. This book aims to provide a different way of looking at the issues involved, and to open the way for finding new solutions.

Gender has a major influence on mortality and morbidity, and the dynamic-maturational model of attachment can point to useful areas of enquiry. There has not been a battle to lay claim to the title of the 'weaker sex'. As males die more often in the first years of life, and die on average 5–10 years younger, they ought not to have a job on their hands to be given the title (Kraemer, 2000). But instead they still ripple their muscles, bulge their stomachs and shrug it off. I often ask medical students whether they would prefer to die first, or go more often to the doctor and live longer. Who is the weaker sex? Parents talk to their baby daughters more often about feeling states. The interesting questions revolve around how a sense of vulnerability, or invulnerability, can become transmitted through the gaze of the caring parent, and become associated with lifelong patterns of differing susceptibility to illness (note that we cannot at this stage say disease). The current view is that there is no evidence that women are simply more likely than men to report ill health, and in that way account for the gender differences in mortality and morbidity (Macintyre, Ford, Hunt, 1999). We also need to note that the higher mortality in the first years of life for boys is not found in China, Egypt or Bangladesh for example. Social processes necessarily interact with the biological.

In the process of attributing this dubious value of being the weaker sex to women in the UK[11] or Norway, for example, are they given an 'advantage', and facilitating an attitude to their health which makes it more likely for them to use others in order to overcome, or live with, their 'vulnerability'? Alternatively they take more to smoking in order to prove that they too are tough enough to cope with the onslaught of tar and cyanide in cigarette smoke (smoking amongst Norwegian teenagers is now more common amongst girls than boys). Are we encouraging the tough male stance, a 'no-tears-we're-girls' attitude – and how is this issue analysed in attachment terms?

Before returning to such issues I will cover the biological constraints affecting how we develop a language of dis-ease. The following chapter summarises their development and how this is relevant for understanding disease and the feeling of being ill. If your main interest is in the dynamic-maturational changes leading to our illness talk, then I suggest you return to this chapter when you have sufficient curiosity.

> Thinking about illness! – to calm the imagination of the invalid, so that at least he should not, as hitherto, have to suffer more from thinking about his illness than from the illness itself – that, I think, would be something.
>
> Nietzsche

Notes

1 I am using 'patient' to emphasise the individual's subjective discomfort. This state is present developmentally prior to it being labelled by another; the attribution of the state of patienthood, and with it an associated patient role, comes later. The link between the state of being a patient, one who suffers, and being recognised as suffering, is one of the prime concerns of this book and for the development of the language of dis-ease. The patient *role* is externally defined in a 'political' process. Where the socially determined role meets the subjective discomfort of the patient the language of dis-ease develops.

  The use of *patior* in relation to 'suffer, to have, meet with, be visited or afflicted with' became prominent after AD 430. Additional meanings are also found: submit to another's lust, to prostitute oneself, to pass a life of suffering or privation and to be passive. For my purpose it is reassuring that it has been used for 'being in a certain state of mind or temper' (Lewis, 1879: 1314–15). It could also convey being firm, stubborn and unyielding! It seems as if it also suits all who complain of the 'patient' role.

2 Changes in respiration patterns provide some of the most useful indices of arousal state. Darwin ([1872] 1998: 2) attributed his awareness of the connection between the movements of expression and those of respiration to the even earlier work of Sir Charles Bell. The subsequent differentiation and specialisation of sound–breath patterning has likely built upon this otherwise primitive index of arousal in producing primitive languages (Deacon, 1997: 234).

3 Hoffmeyer coined the term 'semetic interaction', from the Greek: *semeion* = sign, and *etos* = habit, for the structural coupling between habits and signs. Habits refer to regularities in behaviour, real or in the mind of the beholder, at the cellular or individual level, which trigger a response in the other; in other words, they have become a sign. The triggered behaviours become themselves 'habits', which trigger yet further responses in a recursive manner.

4 Those who follow the popular literature about why computers cannot develop a mind (Penrose, 1989, 1994) will note the crucial distinction here between digital processes, as inherent in the words of a language or nerve impulses, and the 'analogue' nature of suffering conveyed in the primary non-verbal signalling. The interpretation of the analogical state of suffering, and its transmission to others through the superficially clearer digital system of words, is of fundamental importance for understanding many of the misunderstandings that arise in communication about states of illness. It is essential to be able to take the chance of being misunderstood, and to be able to retrieve the situation afterwards.

5 I am here distinguishing preconscious from unconscious. The latter I reserve for an active process, which has meant that something normally available for consciousness has become unavailable. Preconscious processes are going on without us being aware of them all the time – for example, the reflex reactions that enable us to keep going on a bicycle.

6 *Symptoms* initially enable one to pick out the essence of a developing illness. Eventually they become everything designating the illness, a double quality

– both essence and totality. Symptoms are what one uses to make oneself understood as a patient. In contrast *signs* indicate the course of the illness. Interpretation of signs gives diagnostic qualities to symptoms. Symptoms are believed to be able to deceive, whereas signs are said to be 'definite'. Signs are linked to the disease, not illness. Signs, such as altered breath sounds, are revealed in technical ways, such as using a stethoscope, or a parent resorts to privileged folklore.

7 Deacon describes the hierarchical relationship between the three fundamental forms of reference – the iconic, indexical and symbolic, for how the symbolic is based in the other two (Deacon, 1997: 75).

8 I disagree with Morris that 'returning illness to science [will] not deprive [disease] of meaning but simply leaves it in the grip of a reductive, positivist, biomedical narrative that focuses solely on bodily processes' (Morris, 1998: 269–70). An elementary understanding of the interrelation of biology and emotion suggests that a comprehensive medical education has all the possibility to be a minded medicine. Doctors need to be mindful of how they talk about suffering.

9 A definition of abnormal illness behaviour:

> An inappropriate or maladaptive mode of experiencing, evaluating or acting in relation to one's own state of health, which persists, despite the fact that a doctor (or other recognized social agent) has offered accurate and reasonably lucid information concerning the person's health status and the appropriate course of management (if any), with provision of adequate opportunity for discussion, clarification and negotiation, based on a thorough examination of all parameters of functioning (physical, psychological and social) taking into account the individual's age, educational and sociocultural background.
>
> (Pilowsky, 1997: 25)

10 Think of a system of nested Russian dolls using Bronfenbrenner's terms: the cultural, or *macrosystem*, contains the family system where the child is intimately cared for, the child's *microsystem*. The school is another of the child's microsystems. Both of these are affected by outside influences, such as the parents' work situation or a reorganisation at school. These are referred to as *exosystem* influences on the child's microsystems. The way in which the various microsystems in which the child participates, here school and family, communicate is termed the *mesosystem* (Bronfenbrenner, 1979: 22–26). The child must again be seen as consisting of a further set of nested inner systems at biological levels – from body organs to the intracellular level.

11 'The description of women as "the weaker vessel" first appeared in Tyndale's 1526 English Bible, and Protestant manuals on the proper household regimen routinely repeated it together with the necessary subservience of women to men' (Schama, 2000: 341–342).

Chapter 2

Genes, brain and the internal milieu

Our limits and resources

The heart has its reasons that reason knows not of.

Pensées, Section IV Blaire Pascal

Pamela's parents had a special problem knowing whether she was ill, or not, because she spoke little, and had only in the last year begun to show signs of feeling secure after she was adopted from Sudan. They knew that she had had very little to eat for the first two years of her life, and that her biological mother had starved during the pregnancy. They expected that all the traumatic experiences she had had, including the death of her mother, would also have affected her – maybe even affecting her vulnerability to getting ill. They did not know how impoverished her early years in the refugee camp might have been, and whether that had affected her development. They did know that she had mainly been amongst children of her own age when they had first met her last year.

Pamela's parents do not know whether there are any biological consequences of her early development that might affect how she both experiences disease and communicates her discomforts. Illness behaviour evolves in the grey area between the appearance of suffering and coping with the discomfort. The language of dis-ease develops as part of illness behaviour. The limits and resources affecting how the language develops involve both the biology of the sufferer and how suffering is perceived by others. These dispose parents to know about their children in particular ways. What are the consequences if the parent is blind and cannot see changes of disease in their child, or a smoker with a poor sense of smell who does not notice the smell of a fevered child?

Understanding the origins of a language of dis-ease involves under-standing the principles governing the biology of how people experience discomforts, and discriminate between them. The discomfort, or dis-ease, of illness can be seen as due to the body being 'out of tune', losing the normal attunement of its various biological systems, which operate in harmony when all is well. How does Pamela know that feeling tired differs from feeling under the weather (as a tentative state of illness), and from feeling miserable? How is the stress of everyday demands distinguished from the stress of coping with illness? What is happening when some people tell of their dis-ease only when they have recovered from it, yet others seem to want to have told you about the dis-ease they hoped they had had yesterday? How do people learn the words to talk about illness, and how to use the words effectively? How do all the non-verbal ways in which we reveal whether we are unwell arise? These questions lead us to the biology of development.

Normal changes in body states, with which young babies and adults all have to cope – changing blood-sugar levels and feeling hungry, fluctuations in pulse and blood pressure, the level of carbon dioxide and oxygen in the blood, being tired – make demands on all of us to keep our body state reasonably stable. We call the narrow range within which our state fluctuates a state of homeostasis. We manage it without having to think about it.[1] We leave it to the body to get on with, or, more correctly, the somatic part of us, which I will refer to as 'organism' to emphasise its lack of mindfulness, leaves us to be mindful of other things. We can be more or less tuned in to these states (Bakal, 1999), and aware of what we are feeling. Emotions play an important role in the organism maintaining a steady enough state, so that our lives progress smoothly. In particular when extra demands are made on us we can feel stressed, although we need not register this consciously, in spite of our body's homeostasis being jeopardised. Both disease and stress alter the body's attunement, and make demands on, or strain, the system for maintaining homeostasis.

Genes

Parents of adopted children can come to wonder whether their children's different genetic make-up explains their differences from their other children, and can affect how they present their discomforts. Our genes affect us throughout our lives.[2] They enable the orchestration of brain growth, and the processes central to maintaining homeostasis and coping with stress. They affect processes influencing which environments we seek out. There are genetic effects on the likelihood of experiencing stressful life events, known to predispose to getting ill, which are mediated by heritable traits such as cognitive ability. But genes are the most inert components in cells. They are there to be read and transcribed.[3] The really interesting processes in cells are the ones that determine how the codebook is read.

Now, in the twenty-first century, we find tendencies to over-ascribe a central role for genes and the brain in *determining* behaviour, which for some includes both the form of language and also the evolution of different self-protective strategies – strategies to which we shall attribute much importance when describing nuances of the language of dis-ease. This is perhaps influenced by the current euphoria over elucidating the human genome. Steven Rose (1995, 2001) has termed this a vogue for neurogenetic determinism. Dominance of the brain over the body is mistakenly given similar precedence to that of genes as a 'causal agent' of human behaviour, although the brain is held as much in thrall by the information it receives from the body, as the other way round.

Only one particular language of dis-ease has been rather half-heartedly ascribed to genes – alexithymia, or lack of a psychological language for presenting discomforts (Taylor, Bagby, Parker, 1997: 93). Lack of a psychological language can alternatively be explained without primary recourse to genetics, but with a weighty familial contribution. Others have identified a genetic component to physical symptoms (Kendler *et al.*, 1995). There is no distribution of phenotypes in a population that cannot be made to conform to a genetic model (Rose, 2001).[4] It remains important to keep in mind a wide range of causal hypotheses about the origins of illness behaviour and symptom strategies. Attributing the cause to genes can lead to premature closure of the issues. Just as Norwegian runs in families, illness dialects can vary markedly between different families, and also within families when members have been 'abroad'. Starting school, for example, can be like entering a foreign world as regards which illness complaints are 'on'.

Genes facilitate the production of proteins,[5] but they do not of themselves cause behaviour. They enable trains of development, and they are sensitive to environmental conditions. For example phenylketonuria (PKU), is a genetically dependent disease, in which affected individuals cannot metabolise a particular amino acid, phenylalanine. The treatment consists in restricting the amino acid in the diet. It is only when the amino acid is present in more than minimal amounts that the absence of the gene leads to important consequences. Similar processes are important at the psychosocial level. Particular environments facilitate certain genes coming on-stream. Genes have their necessary environments in order to be expressed. Not all genes are equally active in all tissues of a person's body. The absence of genes only makes itself felt in certain contexts.

Particular genes are also associated with people searching out more of particular environments. When people are able to 'read' the significance of the recurring patterns found there, they are on the way to being 'structurally coupled' to that particular environment. Look at the ways in which birds' beaks are suited to eating particular seeds, which again means that the bird is structurally coupled to the environment where the seeds are available. It is as if they were active participants in a trans-actional process with the environment, where some fits lead to more exploratory activity than do others. Certain biological dispositions can facilitate characteristic experiences. For example, certain temperaments in children may facilitate characteristic parental responses, and they become mutually reinforcing due to the fit of the biological and psycho-social dimensions – a dual causality that makes such a pattern of interaction more resistant to change.[6] Genes affect children's environment, as children create their own environment through inducing particular responses from those around them, which again influence the children's behaviour recursively.

Genes alone do not provide the answer that determines how people come to share their discomforts as they do. They play a part in setting people onto particular developmental pathways, but then what they meet and hear along the way also reinforces the direction in which the genes have pointed.[7]

Family influences and brain growth

Tinbergen's second question was 'How did the person grow to respond this way?' There is a common assumption that the architecture of the brain sets limits on how people can experience discomfort. This would then affect the basis for a developing language to convey such discomforts to others. Genes do not determine the fine details of the brain's architecture. The brain achieves its adult form, with about 120 billion cells in the cortex, through a complicated dynamic involving its growth, dependent on genes initially, and interaction with what is happening around, the so-called epigenetic factors, or enviromes. As it matures a brain literally adapts to its body (Deacon, 1997: 194), which is itself fitting into its social niche,[8] another form of structural coupling.

Genes and the environment, particularly the social environment, affect brain growth. Largely before social processes exert their primary influence the brain grows through an *experience expectant mechanism* (Greenough *et al.*, 1987). This consists of massive overproduction of neurones prenatally. Additionally each neurone makes an excess of synaptic connections to other neurones. This reaches its maximum in the sensory cortex at about three months, and not until about 2–3 years in the frontal cortex. This is followed by an elimination of some of the excess, a process that begins prenatally and continues until about the second year. A radical pruning of those established connections that remain underused then follows this synaptical overproduction, so that by adulthood there is a reduction in trillions of synapses. This results in a sculpting of the evolving 'design'. Social processes and illness experience play their part. This is a protracted process (Chugani, 1999). Connectivity is specified *post hoc* through this adaptation of function (Deacon, 1997:197), and that is why it gets the name 'experience expectant mechanism'. How the neurones are used affects which connections survive: a classical sort of Darwinian evolutionary process – survival of the fittest at the cellular level. This further maintains the behavioural predisposition, which leads to just those connections being retained. It is as if patterns once established have tendencies to be self-perpetuating. This especially concerns patterns of behavioural predisposition, which facilitate self-protective strategies.

This should not be seen as a solely biological process, but the result of an evolutionary transactional dynamic, a structural coupling between social and biological processes. We would then expect certain forms of brain architecture to be associated with particular patterns of social interaction, without these being genetically determined, albeit with genetic contributions. Genes have determined that there is the initial *process* of overproduction, and then the following pruning process, but not the fine architecture that results. Note that neurones can also be lost through the effect of overwhelming stress in a process independent of what is described here, due to the neurotoxicity of high cortisol levels, a hormone produced continually in the body with especially high levels secondary to high levels of stress (high levels of cortisol are also produced when a foetus is undernourished, as might have been the case for Pamela).

Brain growth also occurs through the production of new synapses, called the *experience dependent mechanism*. It is believed that this mechanism enables the brain to store information unique to the individual, based on special experiences. When a mother looks after an infant, the relationship induces release of growth-promoting biogenic amines and neuro-hormones. During a critical period of resulting growth these enable connections between the subcortical and cortical regions that mediate the regulation and expression of emotion (Schore, 1994: 63). Emotions are important for developing self-protective strategies. They can increase neural plasticity, and in this way facilitate the creation of new synaptic connections (Siegel, 1999: 48).

These 'experience dependent' mechanisms contrast with the role of recurring patterns of usage, or lack of usage, which moulds the pruning described above. Recurring patterns of social interaction mould brain structure through the 'experience expectant' mechanisms, which give rise to particular forms of pruning. Whereas the emotions associated with particular events will encourage experience dependent extension of synapses.[9] One-off happenings are sufficient to modify brain structure, and some of them are important for developing self-protective strategies too. Recall of new facts is improved by particular degrees of emotion during the learning (McGaugh, 1990), and there are probably common mechanisms for these two processes.

Primary caregivers affect evolving brain circuitry through two routes. They establish repeating patterns in their interactions with their young charges, and provide unique experiences, and so facilitate the development of certain circuitry at the expense of other possibilities of brain structure. They also provide experiences that shape genetically determined potential by acting as psychobiological regulators (or dysregulators) of hormones that directly influence gene transcription, the process whereby genes are 'read'. This mechanism mediates a process by which psycho–neuro–endocrinological changes during critical periods can initiate permanent effects on the genome (Schore, 1997). For example, corticosteroids such as cortisol are produced and released into the blood as a response to stress. They permeate the blood–brain barrier, a structure that prevents larger molecules in the blood reaching the brain, and so have direct as well as indirect effects on the brain. They also directly influence gene function. Their circulating level is modified through parental attunement with their child, a psychosocial process. Caregiving becomes embodied and minded in the progeny.

Unpredictable modulation of the emotional response of patients when cared for in the health service must be expected to lead to similar consequences. People's emotional responses will facilitate conditioning to their circumstances, and may affect their being on guard, vigilant, with health professionals. Their genomes may even be affected through the cortisol response, the patient's age playing an as-yet-unspecified role.

Adult brain growth

Do not think that by the time you read this your brain has stopped growing, and decline has set in. The brain goes on growing and adapting in adulthood, dependent on the richness of the environment (Eriksson *et al.*, 1998; Gould, Beylin, Tanapat, Reeves, Shors, 1999; Garraghty, Churchill, Banks, 1998). It will also shrink again when particular uses are no longer maintained – just like muscle bulk reduces on bed rest. There is also evidence for a correlation between density of neurone branching, their dendrites, and hence number of synapses in the left temporal cortex and number of years of education (Jacobs, Schall, Scheibel, 1993). Brain growth need not be over by early teens, or for Pamela. There is no need to say that it is too late to teach an old patient new tricks, but it may be that the older patient needs to learn alternative tricks to those learnt previously (see the section on implicit memory in Chapter 3 and the possibilities for forgetting).

Foetal nutrition and maternal stress

Does Pamela's mother need to be concerned about effects of prenatal malnutrition and maternal stress on Pamela's social development and disposition to develop her illness behaviour in relation to particular diseases? The nutritional state of the newborn baby is associated with particular chronic diseases in adulthood, such as diabetes and hypertension. I cannot do justice to the literature on this point, but an introduction to the issues can be found in an editorial in the *British Medical Journal* – 'The relation between fetal malnutrition and chronic disease in later life: Good nutrition and lifestyle matter from womb to tomb' (Scrimshaw, 1997). For a more comprehensive exposition of the foetal origin hypothesis it is best to refer to the original author of the hypothesis (Barker, 1998). The newborn's status is dependent on the malnutrition and stress that her mother experienced during pregnancy. This influences how much nutrition the foetus gets, and results in changes in her structure and physiology – including brain growth (Teixeira, Fisk, Glover, 1999). Prenatal maternal stress in primates is associated with increased ACTH levels in response to stress in their offspring. This sensitising to stress can account for some of the vulnerability to disease, and possibly the changes in cognitive ability, found in the offspring of mothers who have been stressed. But of particular interest as regards the behaviour found with disease is that infants of stressed primates show less exploratory behaviour when their attachment system of behaviour is activated. They show marked clinging behaviour reminiscent of those with poorly developed self-protective strategies. They will make more demands on their parents for protection, at a time that their mother would be expected to be less available for them.

Perception

Parents' abilities to see signs of disease, and acknowledging children's illness, depend on their experience. Experience affects their attribution of significance to children's behaviour and appearance. The brain constructs an internal reality, as people interact with those around them, based on their past experiences and expectancies for the future. Experience shapes not only what information enters the mind, but also the way in which the mind develops the ability to process that information (Siegel, 1999: 16). Perceptions are predictive hypotheses, based on knowledge stored from the past. Perceptions may be up to 90 per cent memory (Gregory, 1998). How does that affect parental biases as they decide whether their children, or doctors their patients, are ill? The same biases operate as you read this book – and I write it. When we look at the influence of socialisation on children, parental experience will play a profound role in determining what they believe they have seen. This can lead to situations where parents are quite adamant that reality is different from that which their children 'rightly' remember. Appearance and reality have to be different. And people need to grow up to distinguish the two in order to maximise their safety. Children can cope with discrepancies without them being too troubling. They can also eventually recognise when what they have been told about the world does not coincide with their own experience. But it is not always easy.

It is not just previous experience that has this marked influence on what people notice, but also their degree of arousal and their state of emotion. The amygdala, a structure in the centre of the brain of importance for processing changes in 'arousal' (see pp. 28–31), has a greater influence on the cortex than the cortex has on the amygdala, allowing emotional arousal to dominate and control thinking (LeDoux, 1996: 303). What we think we are looking at – for example, what we think might be signs of disease – is profoundly influenced by what we have seen before and our emotions.

In spite of all these things happening with the brain, throughout its development the brain enables a feeling of continuous experience in much the same way as a film creates a continuous effect through the speed at which the frames are shown. Instead of being overwhelmed by a vast amount of sensory input, the brain arranges for limited access to awareness, depending on the importance of the information for survival. Information that may suggest the requirement for immediate action can lead to impulsive responses – such as jumping out of the way of a car, or withdrawing from the prick of the syringe, without the cortex having to think about it. New information gets through more easily than the unchanging background 'noise'. And it manages to create a sense of coherent and continuous existence in spite of irregularities in what reaches awareness. It is a different issue whether that sense is closely related to 'reality'.

Emotions and neurotransmitters: the foundations for feeling ill

Arousal and states of emotion are intimately related to understanding illness experiences, and developing adaptive self-protective responses to disease. They are devoted to personal survival (Damasio, 2000: 56). Emotions also influence people's decision-making, especially when they feel threatened or at risk (as with disease), and so will play an important role in the decision to consult about, and respond to, illness. How people feel their emotions affects their ways of relating to each other, and is determined through their biology.

I want to pay special attention to two dimensions. The first concerns how people handle their emotions, their ways of self-regulating them, and the subsequent potential for disguising emotional expression and achieving a degree of conscious control. This is important for developing a variety of self-protective strategies. The hypothesis being presented here is that these processes are intimately related to the languages of dis-ease that we develop, and to attachment strategies. People have the potential to hide their illness experiences, and cope with them in ways similar to those employed in relation to emotions. It is not to be expected that this is a conscious process.

The second concerns the identification of the processes involved in discriminating states of disease from emotional states. My hypothesis is that the basic processes for identifying emotions, also apply to disease/illness – and that the state of disease is a particular emotion to be distinguished from 'background emotions' (Damasio, 2000: 51), and subsequently known as the feeling of being ill.

Damasio describes a hypothetical sequence from having an emotion, to feeling, to knowing that one has that feeling as you perceive your emotional state that led to it (Damasio, 2000). It is only the last step that is consciously put into words. There is postulated a continually changing primary background state (Box 2.1), termed 'an emotion', from which we can recognise background feelings, such as being tired or 'under the weather' (Box 2.2).

In a similar way, conventional feelings of emotions, such as happiness, sadness, fear, anger, surprise and disgust are distinguished (Box 2.3).[10]

Box 2.1 Background emotions

An index of momentary parameters of inner state
- Smooth muscle status and striated muscle of heart and chest
- Chemical profile of neighbouring milieu
- Chemical profile signifying threat
    - to optimal homeostasis
    - to integrity of living tissues

Box 2.2 From background emotion to feeling the emotion: from disease to illness

Background emotion/systemic disease

Background feeling
also called 'vitality affect'

Discriminating and identifying the background feeling/illness
Fatigue, energy, some moods, or 'under the weather'

Facial displays of emotions have meanings in the social context where they appear, and they reflect not any 'true' self but one's motives within a specific context of interaction. The balance of signalling and vigilance, counter-signalling and counter-vigilance, produces a 'signalling ecology' with strategic emotional expression. A behavioural ecological under-standing can be applied to all feelings of the conventional emotions (Fridlund, Duchaine, 1996). Classically, the signalling of the socially refined feelings of the 'secondary' emotions such as shame, jealousy, embarrassment and guilt are seen as having their origins to a larger degree in the social system within which they have arisen. Signs of dis-ease need to be understood in a similar way, with expectation of finding an 'illness ecology', with strategic display of symptoms.

Box 2.3   Summary of emotions to feelings – disease to illness

Level 0	Status	Proto-self		
Level 1	Change in status	Background emotion		
Level 2	Pattern of change	Conventional emotion		Systemic disease state
Level 3	Awareness of pattern	Background feeling		
		Vitality affect		
Level 4	Identification of pattern	Feeling of anger, fear, desire for comfort	Feeling of fatigue, stress	Feeling ill

Although the feelings of conventional emotions play important roles in shaping behaviour – for example in a consultation with a doctor – they are not my main concern. The issue is how states of disease *become* distinguished, felt, and talked about – or not. The socially elaborated feelings of emotions enter into illness language to increasing degree as people grow older; the symbolic elements in 'talk' take precedence. The basis is 'If I am ill, how do I come to know it?' I am artificially splitting the biology from the social influences in this and the following chapter – focusing initially on the organism, the hypothetically mindless body. I focus on the biological constraints to the background emotions and how these become discriminated into categorical emotions[11] or states of disease. Identifying such emotion/disease distinctions is probably different from that involved in recognising other changes in the state of the body (Shields, Simon, 1991). Each change in level in Box 2.3 is an interpretative step involving identification of pattern. Habits have become signs. There is the potential for misattributing changes in background emotions as due to conventional emotion, disease or strain, as the same sort of interpretative step is involved in each transition (Box 2.2, 2.3). The first is a primarily organismic interpretation, the final cognitive. It is possible for us to believe we have an illness or stress, instead of a conventional emotion – or vice versa (the clinical implications of this are presented in Chapter 7, 'Ambiguous symptoms').

The major distinctions between conventional emotions and background emotions are shown in Boxes 2.3 and 2.4. Changes in the internal milieu as a *result* of conventional emotions can also be interpreted as if they were primary changes of background emotion, rather than secondary to an external factor. They can then be misinterpreted as being caused by a change in background emotions, such as with disease, if one is not open to the influence of the external factor and the role it plays in inducing conventional emotions.

I have adapted my analysis to the terminology and conceptualisations of Damasio, who has been particularly interested in emotions and feeling for understanding consciousness from his background in neurology. The representation of the state of the body across multiple parameters engenders a reference 'standard' of a 'proto-self' (Damasio, 2000: 22), a sort of template, the somatotopy (Aitken, Trevarthen, 1997), against which change, and indirectly stability, is recognised.[12]

The proto-self is an interconnected and temporarily coherent collection of neural patterns which represent the state of the physical structure of the organism in its many dimensions, at multiple levels of the brain. We are not conscious of proto-self.

(Damasio, 2000: an integration from pp. 154 and 174)

Box 2.4 The relation between background and conventional emotions

Background emotions	Conventional emotions
• Induced secondary to changes in internal milieu	• Induced secondary to external factors
• Focus of response – internal milieu	• Focus of response – musculoskeletal and visceral systems

The resulting change in the internal milieu to conventional emotions can function as interoceptive information and an inducer of background emotions.

Box 2.5 Brain structures required for proto-self

- Hypothalamus
- Basal forebrain
- Several brain stem nuclei
- Insular cortex, medial parietal cortices and cortices known as S2

Systemic disease and emotions are identified through changes from the reference state of the 'proto-self', which otherwise through automatic adjustments varies little. We say that the body maintains a state of homeostasis.[13] The infant's caregiver, through their attunement to the changing states, assists in maintaining the infant's state of homeostasis until they can take over this function themselves.

Pamela's parents will have noted her emotional behaviour, but Pamela's feelings about those emotions, the subjective dimension, are not visible. The basic mechanisms underlying emotions (in contrast to knowing the feeling of an emotion) do not need consciousness. People may be unaware of what induced their feeling of emotion, and they cannot totally control emotions wilfully (Damasio, 2000: 47). Emotions can thus appear to be unmotivated.

Damasio summarised central qualities of emotions (not referring here to the feelings of emotions):

- All emotions have some kind of regulatory role to play, they assist the organism in maintaining life – *and so have a self-protective function.*
- Emotions are complicated collections of chemical and neural responses, forming a pattern; they depend on innately set brain devices, with a long evolutionary history.
- The devices that produce emotions occupy a fairly restricted ensemble of subcortical regions, beginning at the level of the brain stem and moving up to the higher brain; the devices are part of a set of structures that both regulate and represent body states – *and regulation of the body state and its representation in disease is essential for self-protection.*
- All the devices can be engaged automatically, without conscious deliberation with a fundamental stereotypicity and regulatory purpose.

- Emotions affect the mode of operation of numerous brain circuits: the variety of the emotional responses is responsible for profound changes in both the body and the brain. The collection of these changes constitutes the substrate for the neural patterns which eventually become feelings of emotion.

    (Adapted from Damasio [2000: 51–52]; italics added)

The processes which lead to our conscious awareness of emotions, the feelings of emotions – and I hypothesise the experience of being 'ill' or feeling 'under the weather' – involve:

- The organism's attention (not necessarily a conscious process) being caught by an inducer of emotion – for instance, a particular object processed visually, such as the white coat of the researcher that induced reactions in children Sroufe was researching (Sroufe, 1995: 138). The conventional emotion that arose was reminiscent of those induced when they had earlier visited a doctor. The white coat may or may not be consciously identified as releasing their emotion.

Neither consciousness of the object nor recognition of the object is necessary for the following steps:

- Signals resulting from the processing of the image, such as the sight of blood or signs of emotions in facial expressions, activate neural sites, emotion-induction sites, that are preset to respond to the particular class of inducer to which the object belongs.
- The emotion-induction sites trigger a number of responses, both to the body and other brain sites, and unleash the full range of body and brain responses that constitute emotion.
- First-order neural maps in both subcortical and cortical regions represent changes in body state, regardless of whether they were achieved via 'body loops', or through recall of an emotionally charged event leading to an 'as if body loop', or combined mechanisms. Feelings emerge.
- The pattern of neural activity at the emotion-induction sites is mapped in second-order neural structures. The proto-self alters. The changes in proto-self are also mapped in second-order neural structures. The pattern of changing relationships between the activity at the emotion-induction sites and the proto-self, is organised in second-order structures.

    (Adapted from Damasio [2000: 283])

Emotions appear by courtesy of brain structures deep in the brain stem, under control of the cingulate region.[14] We can come to disguise some of the signs of emotions, but not initially to block the internal physiological changes[15] – the basic 'gut feelings' of emotions may not get to the level of being known feelings of conventional emotions, but the expression conveys some of the internal changes I am referring to. We are usually poor at remembering the content of emotions, remembering more accurately the situation where they arose, the external inducers of the conventional emotions.

Damasio points to the sequence in Box 2.2, background emotions → feelings → feelings of emotions, and he presents evidence from his own field of neurology for his hypothesis. Interpretations play roles in the transition from one 'level' to another, from interpreting pattern at the neural network level to parental interpretation of changed emotions in their children (for our purposes the background emotion is the one of most interest). Parents then feed back to their children recognition of that change, both with words as well as with a change in their affective attunement. In parallel to this, children feel their changed body states of the background emotions in their first-order neural maps in both subcortical and cortical regions. They discriminate that something is happening to them prior to them feeling *ill*. It is theoretically possible for parents to recognise disease in their children before the children feel ill – just about!

It is also possible for parents, when picking up changed background emotion showing in their children's 'motion', to make a mistake in misattributing the change to a conventional emotion or disease. Their children may be in discomfort because of one of the primary negative emotions (being sad, angry, or fearful). The organism of the children is responding to the pattern of body signals in the neural maps, and discriminating which of the emotions or disease corresponds to the change in proto-self. The belief that the cause of discomfort is due to a disease, and that you are ill and not sad, can be based on a misattribution in the coupling process between parents and children. Labelling by caregivers can either confirm or confuse children. This depends on the caregivers' attunement and ways of discriminating discrepant states. In children's formative years the adults' interpretations can be definitive – unquestioning, their labelling is taken on board. There is bound to be a sizeable chance that parents will get it wrong on a number of occasions.

The feelings that children get result from changes going on in the body. These will involve both feedback via nerves from body organs and changes in the substances reaching the brain in the blood, the humoral signals, and even changed cells of the immune system may be involved (Pert, Ruff, Weber, Herkenham, 1985).[16] The changes lead to the brain creating a picture of a changed state of affairs. The change may correspond to a pattern previously identified in the somato-sensory areas – and consciously recognised in the somato-sensory cortex. In response to the changed state the brain releases substances, such as neurotransmitters, that act on higher functions. These lead to further changes in brain function – for example, they can trigger crying. The neurotransmitters, involved in sending messages between areas of the brain, are also transmitters for the immune system. The immune system is intimately bound to the nervous system (Maier, Watkins, Fleshner, 1994; Dunn, 1989 in Toates, 1995). Just as brain patterns of response can be conditioned, so can the immune system. The immune system can also recognise changes in body states as change in 'proto-self'.

Neurotransmitter changes may play a role in enabling self-protective behaviour and release emotional attunement in a parent who then helps in the modulation of the emotion. There is some evidence that, when monkeys develop different attachment strategies, they have differing balances between the different neurotransmitters – substances such as dopamine, noradrenaline, and serotonin (Kraemer, 1992) (possibly familiar as being affected by the action of drugs for depression, hyperactivity and schizophrenia). This could be a consequence of the developmental changes in brain structure secondary to experience, the experience expectant and dependent mechanisms. In humans such changes would be expected to make attachment strategies more durable, and reasonably self-perpetuating. Those who approached others for help as part of their self-protective strategy – that is, who showed active attachment-seeking behaviour when in discomfort (see Chapter 4) – would continue to do so; those who had developed a defended self-contained strategy, where they did not actively approach others (see Chapter 5), may turn out to have a different balance between their neurotransmitters and so only with difficulty be more disinhibited in their attachment-seeking behaviour when in discomfort. On theoretical grounds, drugs, which change the balance between neurotransmitters, should be expected to alter people's self-protective strategies.

The chances of biologically founded strategies changing should be greatest at times when there is maximal biological change during development. This is during the first two years of life, and then to a slightly lesser degree in the next 2–3 years.[17] Another time for the evolution of new strategies can be during adrenarchy, 6–11 years, and is to be expected during puberty (Crittenden, 2000a).[18] It may be that pregnancy provides another window for change. The orbito-frontal cortex, where the vital integrative function of co-ordinating social communication occurs, retains its change potential throughout life (Schore, 1996). Neurobiological development may continue to some degree throughout life (Benes, 1998; Garraghty, Churchill, Banks, 1998).

Differing neurotransmitter ratios will bias interpretation of body signals in alternative ways, and modify the way people think about the feelings they get. They affect whether sensations are more often perceived as pleasant or unpleasant. Once the system for reading the organism is established, it becomes hard to change the narrative (not a narrative in words, but a sequential preconscious series of reading of the information coming in). It has been developed to maximise the chance of coping rapidly and effectively with the recurring demands on it, and will be biased to note the patterns as recurring *familiar* patterns even at times of beginning change.[19] Small deviations are not attributed meaning. This is a survival strategy, and it is generally useful that it happens automatically, so enabling the organism to focus on other processes requiring attention. Doing things differently to those well-tried and established patterns requires attention. During such a time a person can be in danger as there is reduced attention to potential cues of danger in the environment. The person will require a degree of cortical guidance to overrule established neural networks. That means conscious effort will be involved. A realistic aim with dis-ease needs to be control over our anxieties, but not to expect them to disappear. They become a predicament with which we need to live (Shalev, Rogel-Fuchs, Pitman, 1992).

Pain

The language of dis-ease is not synonymous with a pain language. Nevertheless pain is a potent inducer of negative emotions, and plays a major role in emotional response to injuries and diseases that give rise to pain. Pain plays a major role in setting off reflexive responses, such as the automatic withdrawal of your finger from a hotplate; but it is not these that primarily concern us here. The non-reflexive responses arise as part of the repertoire developed to cope with the negative emotions arising from pain, those felt emotions in consciousness which we do not like. People with pain suffer,[20] and so fulfil my criteria for being patients. Children develop various strategies to cope with states of discomfort, their self-protective strategies (Chapters 4–6), and these have varying biological correlates. One strategy, which evolves as part of a shaping of their behaviour, results in their minimising the show of the negative emotions associated with pain, but the changes in corticosteroids and other parameters of bodily stress remain largely unchanged. The private feeling state of discomfort may or may not be acknowledged. Other permutations also appear to be possible, such as showing more pain behaviour than expected.

Brain localisation and the somato-sensory areas

Specific areas of the brain are associated with verbal language. The language of dis-ease involves a variety of different brain phenomena. Background emotions are part of the response to threat essential for maximising survival. Illness is threatening and requires our self-protective strategies. These emotions, and the conventional emotions of fear, anger and desire for comfort, are culture independent, and this enables us to relieve suffering in different cultures and respond empathically to suffering people whatever their culture. Specific emotions are associated with whether we approach or withdraw, feel that what we do is rewarding or so negative that it feels like punishment. Their cultural universality leads us to expect to find common brain structures constraining their regulation and expression. Nevertheless, there appears to be no specific area in the brain that processes emotion, but discrete patterns of activation are associated with different emotions.

The presentation so far has looked at how the brain is 'embodied', moulded through genetic influences and experience, and the role of the emotions in this unfolding. In a complementary way the state of the body is represented in the brain. This is no linear relationship but a co-evolving structural coupling of brain and body. Lack of attunement of the body systems, as with systemic disease, is registered. And this sets the scene for restoring homeostasis, restoring the balance.[21] The development of a language for dis-ease requires an understanding of how such preconscious changes are made known, and communicated. It is not until the changes reach consciousness that we have the prerequisites for reflection on a shared language about such states. Nevertheless the background emotions will be visible to others, independently of whether people get a conscious feeling about the emotion/state of illness–disease (at this level they are tightly coupled, their distinction subsequently becoming more important as disease experiences become known as feelings of illness).

The body holds the brain in its thrall, as it signals its ever-changing state. The brain is continually receiving information from the body, the internal milieu, and, in a reciprocal two-step, that structural coupling mentioned previously, setting in action steps to modify the body's state. The brain also holds the body in its thrall. The information comes through various channels at the same time, signalling from many different subsystems about what is going on throughout the body. The brain cannot turn off these inputs, it is held captive by the body, but it can arrange filters to limit how far the information spreads. The input leads to the brain creating moment-by-moment maps of the internal milieu. Disease is identified as one sort of change in the pattern of proto-self.

Information reaches the brain from the viscera digitally, the on–off signalling of the nervous system such as conveyed through the C-fibres and A-δ fibres (the same nerve fibres that also convey pain signals) (Damasio, 2000: 149–153). Information from the musculoskeletal system also arrives digitally. Information reaches the brain in analogue form through the blood stream as varying concentrations of molecules such as blood gases, and glucose, as well as the effect of molecular concentrations on osmolality. Larger molecules are translated to neural information at the circumventricular organs in the brain stem, or the subfornical organs, as they cannot pass the blood–brain barrier.

This mixture of analogic and digital information is an example of code duality (Hoffmeyer, 1993, 1995a) whereby information is interpreted back and forward between digital and analogue states (see also notes 4 in Chapter 1 and 2 in Chapter 2). Kraemer refers to a similar transition as a 'transition boundary', and in his words 'what is *constructed* internally depends on the analytic system acting in relation to the stimulus' (Kraemer, 1992: 504). Together this dually coded information, also structurally coupled, enables establishment of the proto-self – a coherent collection of neural patterns which map, moment by moment, the state of the physical structure of the organism in its many dimensions (Damasio, 2000: 154).

The self at this level of proto-self is not something of which people have a sense. Perturbation of the proto-self associated with a change in background emotion during a systemic disease is registered without reaching consciousness. Feelings of these changes are eventually integrated largely in the right hemisphere, in what has come to be called the somatosensory cortex, which includes the insular cortex and the medial parietal cortices. People come to know that they have these feelings 500 milliseconds after the background emotion changed at the earliest; that is, change in the basic reference-state of proto-self. The changing pattern of signals from the internal milieu indicates that it is not a change in a primary emotion but a change in a background emotion, not coherent with the usual range of changes found. As it is 'observed' by the areas of the brain responsible for eliciting a meta-representation of the changing relationship between the proto-self and the diseased internal milieu, the individual comes to feel and then know that they are ill. And we come to know through symbolising in words that which our proto-self first identified.[22]

There is an interesting phenomenon associated with the time delay that occurs when things happen at a lower level in the brain than the cortex, which is where our sense of being aware of what is going on arises. It now appears that we 'make' a decision to act about 0.3 seconds prior to being conscious about having made such a decision. This leads to the counterfactual that volition follows intention. The effort associated with volition is a perception created by the brain due its computation of what will be required of it (Penrose, 1994: 385).

Primary emotions are likely to be experienced more immediately and intensely through the right side of the brain than the left. The right orbito-frontal region serves the vital integrative function of co-ordinating social communication, empathic attunement, emotional regulation, registration of bodily state, stimulus appraisal (the establishment of value and meaning of representations), and autonoetic consciousness (Wheeler, Stuss, Tulving, 1997; Tucker, Luu, Pribram, 1995). Autonoetic consciousness is the ability of the mind to have a sense of recollection of the self at a particular time in the past, awareness of the self in the present, and projections of the self into the imagined future. This kind of consciousness is said to enable 'mental time travel'. The relevance in this connection is that changes in the body state, as in disease, are co-ordinated in the same area that has to do with (a) empathic attunement with others and social communication – be that with parents, spouses or health professionals, and (b) the area that facilitates the ability to imagine what things will be like in the future.

The constructed representational world as created in the right hemisphere will also contain information derived from the emotional states of others (Ali, Cimino, 1997). A parent with a poorly developed right hemisphere function may be at a particular disadvantage in becoming attuned to the displays of affect and illness in their children. Siegel proposes that the right hemisphere requires emotional stimulation from the environment to develop normally (Siegel, 1999: 185). Here is a potential mechanism for intergenerational transmission of lack of attunement. However, appraisal and arousal circuits, the value centres of the brain, are located on both sides, whereas the right hemisphere is more capable than the left hemisphere of regulating states of bodily arousal (Schore, 1994). The right hemisphere is not just involved in regulating body states, but also preferentially enables the left side of the face, controlled by the right side of the brain, to express more emotion than the right side (Johnson, Hugdahl, 1991; Sergent, Ohta, MacDonald, 1992). We do not know if signs of disease are more visible on the left side, as sinister signs.

Negative primary emotions are stressful. Research has looked into the biological consequences of stress, but there has often been little clarity about links to the biological aspects of the emotions. Patients readily associate their illness and stress, but what is going on at the biological level?

Stress – tipping the balance

It is sometimes difficult to distinguish between feeling ill and stressed. The language of dis-ease covers both states of discomfort. One distinction depends on illness arising on a change in the internal milieu, while stress depends on an external strain.

There is little specificity about what is being referred to as stress in the literature, so that research into the consequences of 'stress' comes up with divergent findings. Stress encompasses repeated demands from the environment, major life events such as loss of a parent, and trauma and abuse. The meaning of the traumatic event is personally determined, and so a personal history is necessary in order to look at the importance of particular events for stress to an individual (Brown, Harris, 1989). Acute stress and chronic stress often lead to diametrically opposed outcomes. For example, acute stress can enhance the response of the immune system to infection, whereas chronic stress suppresses it.[23] High concentrations of the hormones that are released in response to stress lead to excessive death of neurones in crucial pathways responsible for emotional regulation (in the limbic system and neocortex) (Perry, 1997).

Acute stress can enhance learning, but chronic stress impairs memory. There are two different words – 'eustress' for the beneficial effects of stress, and 'distress' for the negative. Why is stress necessary for developing personal resilience (Rutter, 1985), and yet can be so destructive? How does it fit into the scheme of things as regards a language for conveying our discomforts? With stress I am not referring here to the secondary emotions that we come to feel when we are stressed (analogous to the secondary emotions which arise with pain), but the biology.

The other need for understanding the effects of stress is because people use their self-protective strategies to cope with the stress. They use their experience of stressful situations to identify when they need to be on the look out, when caring for others. Previous experience affects their current perception. How might such processes be embodied through the developmental processes so far described?

I return to Damasio's terminology, the background emotions, and fit stress into this framework. This enables comparisons to how feelings of illness and emotions compare to feelings of stress (Box 2.3). Stress is discriminated as a feeling arising from 'arousal' of background emotions, in the same way as feeling ill. Conceptually a situation arises characterised by moment-by-moment changes in background emotions. These can be *felt*, and subsequently *known*, as changes in our daily moods, or as changes in our state of health, or attributed to excessive demands of the environment – including personal relationships (in other words, stress). Stress is both associated with a change in the background emotion, as well as giving rise to a feeling of which we may become aware.

The criteria used by Toates point out where the boundary goes between something that can be felt as a strain, and the sort of stress that is being researched under the big S. He defines the main criterion for stress as '(a) a protracted failure of the [organism] to maintain alignment between its reference values and the actual state of the world, and (b) the absence of an assessment of near-future realignment' (Toates, 1995: 31). This is coherent with the framework I have been making use of, but does not actually help us distinguish stress from systemic disease. The reference values correspond to those of the proto-self in the terminology I have adopted. Additionally the 'organism' (the term is used instead of 'person' because the background emotions are not initially felt) reacts as if there is no anticipated possibility of returning to the balance of the proto-self.

Normally the hypothalamic–pituitary–adrenal axis, the HPA axis, is triggered by changes in the background emotions, and restores normality through adjusting levels of hormones. The HPA is part of the homeo-dynamic, alternatively called allostatic mechanism (McEwen, Stellar, 1993). Change in the HPA axis has been used as the basis of alternative definitions of stress. The behavioural response to stress involves action, usually said to be the choice between flight and fight, or freezing to the spot. The HPA system primes the organism for future action (again I use the term 'organism' instead of 'person' in order to emphasise that this is all happening preconsciously – personhood is not presumed, it is a mindless impulsive response). If subsequent events lead to such action having a successful outcome (i.e. return to a balanced proto-self), the HPA response is inhibited. Alternatively, if the person can *anticipate* that the demands of the situation can soon be met there might be such inhibition; in other words there is a possibility of a fast-forward play-through in autonoetic consciousness influencing the reactivity of the HPA system.[24]

If neither of the above options is available, and the challenge is interpreted as 'open-ended', potentially going on forever, the seeds of stress are sown (Toates, 1995: 31).

Stress phenomena have a certain time course. Over time there are increases in (1) hormonal levels, (2) frequency of stereotypies (special kinds of tic-like mannerisms such as absent-minded hair pulling), and (3) bodily indices of pathology (such as hypertension). But this time course varies for continuous, compared to repeated, stressful demands. The HPA axis is triggered by unexpected events, especially those involving some form of threat to the integrity of the organism/person. The threat can both be to the proto-self and an as-if threat in the mind. Fear and anxiety will be involved.[25] The axis habituates rapidly to repeated events, but with an exception – there remain high levels of adrenaline, associated with residual fear, high arousal level and accompanying physiological activation (Kirschbaum *et al.*, 1995). Symptom responses related to high pulse and blood pressure do not habituate, even though most of the HPA axis response has done so.

There is an important social constraint on the habituation of the HPA axis. When people are repeatedly stressed socially in small groups their HPA axes do not habituate as easily. They show greater anxiety and appear to be less self-confident. It may be that if a family is stressed there is a chance that their communal stress response will be delayed in habituating, and this must be expected to modify their children's experience of background emotions and discrimination of states of disease.

The same bodily changes, increased heart rate, sweating, and dilated pupils, arise when people recall past frightening events, in-mind as-if threats, the as-if body loop (Damasio, 2000: 281). The orbito-frontal cortex and the closely associated anterior cingulate, both primarily in the right hemisphere, monitor visceral responses. The body's response to what people have in mind lets them know how they feel. Somatic markers, actual or 'as-if', can be generated without consciousness, as part of the conditioning to the context where emotions arose. Through the representation of these bodily responses being kept isolated from working memory, impairment of functioning is avoided. This is achieved through a pattern of neural interactions in which somatic markers are not linked to the working memory processes of the lateral prefrontal cortex. Disease and stress are kept initially out of mind, and working memory continues to function optimally.

If people have organised self-protective strategies which can be regulated successfully, and they find themselves in situations with familiar demand characteristics, then activation of the HPA axis does not occur

(Toates, 1995: 122). This suggests that different effects of the hormones released as a result of activity in the HPA axis will be present when children or adults show organised, as opposed to disorganised, self-protective strategies. Disorganised attachment strategies will be associated with greater activation of the HPA axis. This hypothesis needs further testing, especially in the light of the refinements in classification of attachment behaviour introduced by Crittenden (Crittenden, Claussen, 2000; Crittenden, 1992–2001; Crittenden, 1999–2002) which has reduced the number who are classically classified as disorganised (Main, Solomon, 1986), or 'cannot classify' (Hesse, 1996).

Stress and disease

There are biological consequences of strain on the organism, because of disease, that directly affect illness behaviour. There is animal evidence that a substance produced during infections, the cytokine interleukin-1 (IL-1), reduces exploratory behaviour, feeding and sexual behaviour (Dunn, Antoon, Chapman, 1991). Exploratory behaviour depends on there being no need for closeness to another; as there is no need for self-protection, the attachment behaviour system is turned off. It could be that IL-1 turns on attachment behaviour. When injected it is said to lead to the same physiological responses in the body as when stressed. This is the substance that causes animals to sleep more when ill.

People who are under strain feel that they are suffering. Situations arise where their suffering can be attributed to sickness, and they achieve 'patienthood' – in contrast to being seen as stressed. It is not my primary purpose to look at how stress can predispose to illness or disease,[26] and so affect the frequency of illness behaviour, or alternatively how the causality of illness can be attributed to stress, which affords yet different role expectations. Cultures will differ in whether they afford to those who are suffering from stress the same rights as those who are seen as sick. I do not aim to cover the extensive literature on the relation between stress and actual altered vulnerability to illness (for a simple and concise starter see Stewart-Brown [1998]). This includes the literature on the links between the immune system and the nervous system (e.g. Maier, Watkins, Fleshner, 1994). My primary concern in this chapter is to understand the biological constraints that operate in patients who are presenting their discomforts, and the constraints in those who are interpreting the behaviour of the patient. In the way they talk together, with their bodies as well as with words, patients' states of illness are conveyed, and the patterns of interaction they repeat with each other become part of their illness-behaviour vocabulary and of their illness strategies for effective complaining and coping.

I believe that it is only because we do not have easily available instruments for measuring smell that we do not know more about the ways in which a person's smell changes with stress, and with illness. It may be that we will soon have knowledge about other substances that can release attachment behaviour (by choosing these terms I am implying an organism response from implicit memory – see Chapter 3). Smell has a particularly potent role in triggering memories, and an important role in a form of learning called conditioning, described in Chapter 3. For some people it has a central role in their view of the proto-self (Harré, 1998: 90).

Attachment and the developing brain

Close relationships provide important environmental influences that shape the development of the brains of infants and young children during their period of maximal growth. Thereby, caregivers are the architects of the way that experience influences the unfolding of genetically pre-programmed but experience-dependent brain development (see Kraemer [1992] and Schore [1994] for further details). The self-protective strategies which children develop to maximise their well-being in these relation-ships form the basis of their attachment strategies and associated brain development.

Attachment theory proposes that infants develop behaviour to maximise the protective qualities available to them from those looking after them. These become their primary attachment relationships. This attachment behaviour develops in relation to the recurring patterns of the relationship – that which is predictable and hence potentially controllable or escapable. The behaviour may involve approaching their caregiver at times of need. When the attachment behaviour system is not mobilised, the primary attachment relationship can function as a secure enough base from which to explore. By the time infants are about 18 months old they have a clearer awareness of their caregivers' 'theory of mind'. They modify what they do based on how they believe their behaviour will be perceived. Their attachment behaviour has become part of an attachment strategy guided by intention, and moulded by an understanding of other people's responses. For completeness I will therefore point out some brain areas that play a role in these central aspects of attachment behaviour.

Prefrontal brain areas have an important function in implementing *strategies* (Nelson, Carver, 1998). Poor development or damage in this area would make it unlikely that a person could develop and implement an effective interpersonal strategy. Lack of strategy would give their attachment behaviour a disorganised quality, associated with high levels of cortisol under stress, and long-term effects on health could result. It is also possible that the *development* of this area depends on attuned mothering.

The attachment behaviour system and the exploratory behaviour system cannot both be active at the same time. The left hemisphere predominantly mediates approach, and the right hemisphere withdrawal. Activation of the right frontal cortex leads to active withdrawal, fear and anxiety. In contrast low activity in the right frontal region leads to disinhibition of approach, with impulsivity and hyperactivity. Emotions associated with approach behaviours are experienced on the left side, and emotions associated with avoidance are usually processed on the right. Constitutional temperament and experienced attachment features may directly shape these patterns of frontal activation (Field, 1994; Dawson, 1994). If mothers are depressed there is a marked decrease in left frontal activation in both parents and children. If such depression lasts beyond the first year of life, infants may continue to show this pattern of decreased frontal activity (Dawson, 1994). In addition to these effects associated with the left and right frontal regions, bilateral damage to the amygdala leads to uninhibited approach and no fear, leaving subjects vulnerable (Adolphs, Tranel, Damasio, 1994).

Exploratory approaches open the way for structural coupling of infants with people who have more competent self-protective strategies. Adult ability to self-regulate their state 'infuses' the child with the same ability. This is mediated by a process of neural recruitment. Recruitment is the process whereby activation of some groups of neurones further activates other neural pathways. Recruitment in one individual induces neural networking of a supportive brain modulating form in another person, who because of their age and neural plasticity develops new neurobiological competence. Another capacity that grows in a similar way is the capacity to reflect on mental states, both of the self and of others. This emerges from within attachment relationships that foster such processes (Fonagy, Target, 1997). This is necessary for developing a theory of mind as a prerequisite for strategic use of attachment behaviour. Patterns of communication literally shape the structure of the child's developing brain. It is as if brain development takes place not in single brains but in communities of them (see also Maturana, Varela [1988: 181–184] for a description of third-order structural coupling and the embodiment of culture).

Infants both respond to the world of others, and play an active role in influencing how others respond. Thus when neuronal circuits become activated they create and reinforce their connections with each other. Once established, such a pattern in neuronal activation will tend to recruit similar patterns in the future. This is part of the preservation of pattern, multiply determined, referred to above. Schore concluded that mothers' skills in the proper affective attunement, or containment, of their infants have direct effects on the quantity and quality of their infants' brain development, particularly involving the orbito-frontal cortex (Schore 1994). The orbito-frontal cortex in the right hemisphere is a crucial area for integrating memory, attachment strategy, emotion, bodily representation and regulation, and social cognition (Siegel, 1999: 40).

Until the orbito-frontal system has become sufficiently differentiated on the basis of the infant's experience by about 18 months old, stressful socialisation becomes associated with hypoarousal (Schore, 1994: 66). The history of this development depends on the development of the autonomic nervous system. The sympathetic branch predominates initially, prior to the parasympathetic coming on line during the second year, at about 14–16 months.[27] This corresponds to the time that the child is beginning to move around more. The adrenergic system of the sympathetic branch of the autonomic nervous system drives more activity, and makes self-soothing more difficult, until the parasympathetic makes it easier to achieve a balance.

Conclusion

Pamela's development will carry shadows of her early experience, and yet she will have fitted into the niche provided in her new family. Her genetic endowment and early experiences are not deterministic, just as her current care is not alone deterministic of how she will come to form her own self-protective strategies when she handles stress. She will get a feel of her emotions through the way in which her adopted parents have been moved by her emotions. The essential interpretative steps have provided her with a way of presenting her basic discomforts, and coping with the help of the comfort available. Her dis-ease can be felt, labelled and responded to. Her biological endowment is not fixed, but can have predisposed her both to seek out particular situations which may be more or less healthy, as well as to be vulnerable to particular diseases – and hence colours her developing language of dis-ease.

Notes

1 Eating habits are at a different level of habit to those involved with adjusting breathing to levels of blood gases; people can nevertheless eat the relevant amount without having to plan the calories and vitamins.

2 Genetics can be responsible for change, rather than stability, throughout our lives. One example comes from work on intelligence. The heritability of psychometric intelligence (that measured by psychometric tests) rises as we get older and have more experience of the world (McClearn *et al.*, 1997).

3 The modern concept of the relationship between DNA sequences and the proteins they code for is of a fluid genome, with DNA strands being transcribed, excised, edited, shuffled, multiply translated, under the control of a myriad of transcription factors and control sequences called into play (Rose, 2001).

4 Connectionist modelling has clarified that networks operating with associative mechanisms can display properties typically associated with genetically predetermined and dedicated symbolic functions (Nobre, Plunkett, 1997).

5 The field is shifting from genetics to proteomics – the study of the production of proteins from the amino-acid sequences produced on genes.

6 Maturana and Varela describe structural drift as a property of all living systems. In this process structural change is occurring in the brain, not in the broad outlines of the circuitry/networks but in the final ramifications of the neurones and the efficiency of the synapses. These changes are 'congruent with the structural drift of the environment' (Maturana, Varela, 1988: 103). In this way the parental behaviour that triggers reactions in the child with a particular temperament disposition becomes structurally coupled with that of the child. They show a congruent drift of their behaviour in a reciprocal way, leading to structural changes in each of them; however, the age of the participants plays its independent role in the degree of structural change which results. Conceptually this is an example of a non-linear complex system showing emergent patterns with recursive characteristics.

7 Innate behaviour and learned behaviour are indistinguishable, the distinction only lies in the history of the structures that make them possible (Maturana, Varela, 1988: 170–171).

8 A distinction between the body as seen by someone observing the patient, and experience of being at one with that body, can be covered by adopting the Greek word 'soma'. The word was used for a living, self-sensing, internalised perception of oneself. In this distinction lies a similar distinction to that between my use of 'patient', who experiences suffering, and 'patienthood' for our observation of a person as patient.

9 Schore hypothesises that a critical period begins around the end of the first year:

> Maternal regulated high intensity socioaffective stimulation provided in the ontogenetic niche, specifically occurring in dyadic psycho-biologically attuned, arousal-amplifying, face-to-face reciprocal gaze transactions, generates and sustains positive affect in the dyad. These transactions induce particular neuroendocrine changes which facilitate the expansive innervation of deep sites in orbito-frontal areas, especially

in the early maturing visuospatial right hemisphere, of ascending subcortical axons of a neurochemical circuit of the limbic system–the sympathetic ventral tegmental limbic circuit. This imprinting experience initiates the maturation of a frontolimbic excitatory system that is responsible for the ontogenetic adaptations in the inceptive phase of the practising critical period–behavioral hyperactivity, high levels of positive affect and play behavior, and subsequently the establishment of the capacity to form an interactive representational model that underlies an early functional system of affect regulation.

(Schore, 1994: 65)

10 Disgust has now been suggested to have its own peculiar site of origin in the basal ganglia as a result of research into the prodromal state of those developing Huntington's disease, who appear to fail to distinguish the primary emotion of disgust.

11 The dynamic-maturational version of attachment theory is built on understanding the self-protective strategies, which make prime use of the feelings of emotion associated with the underlying predispositions for fight, flight or seeking of comfort when in danger or threatened. The categorical feelings of emotion can be seen as socially elaborated versions of these basic behavioural dispositions to action in response to the emotions. The primary distinctions being made when discriminating feelings of systemic disease from feelings of emotion are between feelings of anger, fear and disease.

12 In the words of Aitken and Trevarthen (1997):

Brains control actions and assess the affordances of the environment by motor and sensory systems that "map" the body in neural systems. This "somatotopy," which pervades sensory and motor fields and nuclei in all levels of the CNS and orders projections between them, is generated under the guidance of the regulator genes that also determine fundamental dimensions and complexity of the whole body. Activities and experiences are animated in sensory and motor regions from within the CNS by a unique system of motives that depends upon the coherence of the representation of the body-related behavior field in a consistent manner in all parts of the nerve net. Understanding the development of this essential organization representing an active body within a brain requires appreciation of different levels of description of the organism and its internal anatomy and function.

(Aitken, Trevarthen, 1997: 660)

13 'Allostasis' is an alternative expression introduced by Sterling and Eyer, and developed by McEwen (1998), to convey the important notion that stability is maintained through change. It is not static. He then uses this concept to describe continued strain as a burden to the allostatic system. The strain is then termed 'an allostatic load', to convey the continuing nature of the demands on the system. Through its responses the body adapts to the felt stress, and in the short term stress has several facilitative effects, such as facilitating new learning. When the system is overused, and maintained in high gear over time due to repeated strain, where there is lack of adaptation,

and eventually no longer any rise in cortisol or noradrenaline as part of the stress response, an allostatic load results, and the negative effects of stress occur. Yet another alternative expression for the dynamic process required to maintain a balance is 'homeodynamic'.

14 It is not my intention to describe accurately where different brain structures are to be found, and their anatomical connections. The areas are included occasionally for reference for those who wish to follow up details. For those interested in a detailed neurobiological description which is comprehensively integrated with a developmental perspective see Schore (1994), although all such presentations find it difficult to do justice to the brain as part of a complex adaptive system with the potential for change.

15 The situation gets very complicated to unravel because of its systemic non-linear nature. Ekman and colleagues have described how by taking on the facial expression of an emotion intentionally, this changes the physiology to be in tune with the emotion adopted – as if the background emotion has changed to be coherent with the displayed/felt emotion (Ekman, Levenson, Friesen, 1983). It may eventually be that those who manage to suppress part of their emotional display also modify the associated background emotion. This is no new idea. Darwin came to the same conclusion, and I quote him in full from his concluding chapter:

> He who gives way to violent gestures will increase his rage; he who does not control the signs of fear will experience fear in a greater degree; and he who remains passive when overwhelmed with grief loses his best chance of recovering elasticity of mind. These results follow partly from the intimate relation which exists between almost all the emotions and their outward manifestations; and partly from the direct influence of exertion on the heart, and consequently on the brain. Even the simulation of an emotion tends to arouse it in our minds.
>
> (Darwin, [1872] 1998: 365)

See also Damasio's discussion of 'as-if body loops' (Damasio, 2000: 281) leading to 'internal simulation'.

16 Greenfield describes the double role of peptides, both as transmitters and hormones. At higher frequency of stimulation nerves release peptides outside the synapse, and these then function to modulate nerve processes over a larger arena, functioning as hormones. Peptides are therefore associated with two different time courses of action (Greenfield, 1998).

17 It is only by the end of the third year that the corpus callosum allows for rapid transfer of information between the left and right hemispheres – it continues to mature for the first decade of life. The hippocampus becomes more myelinated during the second and third years.

18 In the Netherlands (Plooij, van de Rijt-Plooij, 1989) it has been found that hospital admissions of infants do not happen randomly in relation to their age. The age peaks, at intervals of weeks, seem to come at times when there are phases of new synapse adaptation in the brain. It is as if the times of biological change in the brain are associated with greater vulnerability to illness. The suggestion has been made that at these times the child ceases to have a coherent attachment strategy for a short period of time, becoming

temporarily disorganised, and that this strategy is associated with the greater illness vulnerability. Disorganised strategies are known to be associated with higher cortisol levels and changes in immune competence (Spangler, Grossman, 1993; Hertsgaard, Gunnar, Erickson, Nachmias, 1995).

19   I believe that Darwin was concluding something similar:

> Our third principle is the direct action of the excited nervous system on the body, independently of the will and independently, in large part, of habit. Experience shows that nerve-force is generated and set free whenever the cerebro-spinal system is excited. The direction which this nerve-force follows is necessarily determined by the lines of connection between the nerve-cells, with each other and with various parts of the body. But the direction is likewise much influenced by habit; inasmuch as nerve-force passes readily along accustomed channels . . . Whenever these emotions of sensations are even slightly felt by us, though they may not at the time lead to any exertion, our whole system is nevertheless disturbed through the force of habit and association.
>
> (Darwin, [1872] 1998: 347–348)

20   It is possible to operate on those with intractable pain so that they cease to suffer, but remain aware that they have pain. It involves operating on the frontal lobes. After the operation they no longer show pain behaviour. The emotion induced by the pain is modified by the operation, but not the experience of being in pain. The same effect can be obtained by the use of self-hypnosis so that people cease to be bothered by the pain.

21   The circadian rhythm of the body, the way in which amongst others cortisol, body temperature and melatonin fluctuate in a regular pattern depending on the time of day, can also be lost during illness.

22   Damasio describes what happens in the condition of anosognosia. With damage to the somatosensory cortex in the right hemisphere in particular areas, for example after a stroke that would leave them paralysed down the left side, patients are unable to acknowledge that their body is not functioning normally (Damasio, 2000: 211). This disorder shows the prime localisation of the somatosensory information in the right hemisphere, as the condition is not found with corresponding lesions in the left hemisphere. The right hemisphere integrates information from both the right and left sides of the body. It is not clear how old people have to be before the degree of lateralisation is sufficient to produce this effect.

23   The release of cortisol and noradrenaline, which may act synergistically, leads to a reversible decrease in immune cells in the blood as they move to line the blood vessel walls, i.e. places where they may be needed (Dhabhar, McEwen, 1999). The effect lasts about six days. This protective effect found with acute stress can be suppressed by dexamethasone, a steroid. It does not occur if the organism has been subjected to chronic stress. In the face of chronic stress the suppression of this response lasts about 35 days in a rat. The equivalent detail for humans is not known.

24   See note 15 reference to the 'as-if body loop' hypothesis of Damasio.

25   The most consistently shown biological abnormality in major depression is increased activation of the hypothalamic–pituitary–adrenal axis (Dinan,

1999). At the moment we do not know why the axis does not habituate in depression, in contrast to under stress, but it may involve reduction in a special form of messenger RNA (McQuade, Young, 2000), potentially an effect of sustained cortisol levels on gene transcription. Stress and anti-depressants have reciprocal actions on neuronal growth and vulnerability (mediated by the expression of neurotrophins) and synaptic plasticity (mediated by excitatory amino acid neurotransmission) in the hippocampus and other brain structures. Stressors have the capacity progressively to disrupt both the activities of individual cells and the operating characteristics of networks of neurons throughout the life cycle, while antidepressant treatments act to reverse such injurious effects (Reid, Stewart, 2001).

26 Stress correlates positively with children's poor health (Meade, Lumley, Casey, 2001).

27 The biology of this period of development leads us to anticipate an issue in the following chapter. The 'strange situation' is a method used to elicit the attachment behaviour which 12-month-old infants use to handle their changing emotions with other people. In order to do this they are separated from one of their parents. The biology suggests that, as advised when using the method, one keeps to the age range, and does not employ it for children over 14 months. The attachment *behaviour* found at 1 year is to be expected to have changed by the time the child is 20 months old. Other classificatory systems which explore the *strategic use* of the behaviour in the child's repertoire, such as the Preschool Assessment of Attachment (Crittenden, 1992–2001), will be needed for the older children.

Chapter 3

Learning and memory
A basis for understanding development and change in the face of threat and danger

> By nature, men are nearly alike; by practice, they get to be wide apart.
> Confucius

When Pamela's parents were anticipating her arrival, they read the latest books on child development, got advice from their supportive adoption agency, and talked to other adoptive parents. They hoped they were as prepared as possible. When things started to get difficult when bringing up their first child they had thought that it was because they were not good enough as parents. It took a second child to teach them that children are born different too. Now they have to try and make sense of Pamela, and are swinging wildly between thinking that it is so hard to read her because she was born that way, has experienced so much in her short life, or they are just not up to it. The more they try and get it right the more exasperated they become.

What is learnable by infants and children, and is functional culturally, shapes their language of dis-ease. The primary cultural context for most infants is their family, but by school age their culture is much more complex (Bronfenbrenner, 1979). Development is the process whereby people come to understand reality in its full complexity, and their place in it. People become structurally coupled to their environment of development. In this chapter I present a current understanding of memory systems and their roles in helping people learn from experience and appreciate reality. When taken together with knowledge about how the brain develops, and registers emotions and states of disease, we then have a basis for what is learnable about disease and a foundation for understanding the language of dis-ease, the communicative system of symptoms. This entails knowledge of the world, of words and social processes.

Memory

Memory is what enables the past to affect the future, and in that way people protect themselves from danger, such as disease, and cope with threat, such as an epidemic. Experiences become part of a repertoire, which enables people to relate competently, in order to protect themselves with the assistance of others when troubled by disease. In order to understand the way people learn their language of dis-ease, their ways of coping and complaining, we need to know how people remember.

The brain develops its structure so that its function best fits the recurring demands on it. We have seen that it 'learns' through pruning out synapses, those connections to neurones that have not been needed during the first few years. There is a complementary form of learning whereby repeated activation of a group of neurones leads to that circuit being easier to activate, a lower threshold to setting off firing of neurones throughout the whole sequence, next time a similar signal pattern comes along. This change in synaptic strengths, as a result of repeated firing, is simple learning (Milner, Squire, Kandel, 1998). It is how experience initially affects memory systems through repeat stimulation – whereas pruning is secondary to lack of stimulation. Memory storage is the change in probability of activation of a particular neural network pattern in the future. 'Neurones that fire together, wire together' – a saying usually attributed to Hebb (1949: 70), but proposed in principle earlier by Darwin ([1872] 1998: 347).

Experience also affects the way our genes function, and epigenetic factors shape our developing brains. As Milner, Squire, and Kandel have reported, 'recent work on plasticity in the sensory cortices has introduced the idea that the structure of the brain, even in the sensory cortices, is unique to each individual and dependent on each individual's experiential history' (Milner, Squire, Kandel, 1998: 463).

Memory is not a static thing, but an active set of processes. 'Remembering is not merely the reactivation of an old engram,[1] it is the construction of a new neural net profile with features of the old engram and elements of memory from other experiences, as well as influences from the present state of mind' (Siegel, 1999: 28). Perception is largely memory. A simple example illustrates this. In the media faces are disguised by presenting them as a composite of large blocks of print. If you screw up your eyes tightly so that you only just see the picture, it will look much more like the face that you are not supposed to see. There has not been any increase in the information reaching the brain, but the brain is tuned to make allowances for the distorted perceptions arising when the eyes are screwed up, and so 'sees more'.

Brains actively create an impression of continuity of experience through making use of these qualities of memory. They construct a view of the past, the present and what they anticipate the future to bring. This is an active process making use of all the memory at their disposal. Memory appears to be organised in several systems which are reasonably coherent, but not necessarily so. People cannot always make use of all their memory, especially when affected by major trauma. Memories are not fixed. Instead each time elements are brought into working memory to be integrated in relation to the task at hand, the demands of the present affect how they are reconstructed (Edelman, 1989).

Taking a history is an integral part both of research strategies exploring the meaning of a person's illness, as well as of doctors' attempts to get to know their patients. Understanding memory systems enables better interpretation of the information provided. The biological constraints on memory affect what people know about themselves, and what others might come to know about them, which they do not necessarily know about themselves.

When people bring something to mind, their representations come in many forms, including perceptual ones (like visualising a doctor's surgery), semantic ones (like hearing the words 'blood pressure', and knowing their meaning), and somatic ones (such as having a feeling of 'collywobbles' because when you were last at the surgery you had an injection, and you had a string of feelings about that). Binding together these various neuronal activation patterns constructs our memories. These are termed 'associational linkages' between different parts of the memory system. Memory forms the foundation for both experiences of reality (behavioural responses, emotional reactions, perceptual categorisations, schemata of the self and others in the world, and possibly bodily memories) and explicit recollections of facts and of the self through time.

Implicit memory

Infants' first memories are in implicit memory. Implicit memory provides people with information about the motor patterns required for adapting to particular situations. It is particularly suited to enable quick self-protective action. The motor patterns arise preconsciously. People do not have to think about them. These preconscious memories and the motor learning for how to carry out complicated movement patterns are stored in a subsystem of implicit memory called *procedural memory*. As preconscious memories they are stored at levels analogous to those for background emotions, i.e. prior to knowing about feelings of emotions, or of these motor habits.

Riding a bicycle is something that, once mastered, is never forgotten. The learning sits in us, and is not easy to get hold of through thinking about it. Another example of learning that sits deep is related to the body habits that we develop. These include how people cuddle up to others, touch people and basic non-verbal communication. Most people in England nod their heads up and down when they agree with something. It's a way of saying yes. Alternatively moving the head from side to side conveys 'no'.[2] What do you believe when you see a party political broadcast where the politician says he agrees, but moves his head from side to side? Try this for yourself now. You will probably find it quite difficult, and odd in a puzzling way. I am not sure that the English politician, the late Roy Jenkins, would have been aware that he had tried to sell his audience a double message. Like children who are trying to understand communication, people usually resolve such mix-ups by relying implicitly on the head movements, rather than the words used.

As implicit memories are the first memories laid down in infancy, children have 'organism', or body memories, from before the time when they can 'remember'. This is a result of the way in which the brain develops after birth; levels in the cortex connect up to each other, regions of the brain connect up to each other and myelination spreads throughout the brain. Myelination is the process whereby sheaths of myelin, a fatty substance, form around the nerve axons, with the result that the neurones transmit signals much more effectively, with less electrical interference of transmission in neighbouring axons.[3] Implicit memory relies on brain structures that are intact at birth and remain available to us throughout life. Such memories are not forgotten, but their application in reflexive motor responses can come in competition with other memories.

What is so special about this very early memory is that it is preverbal, and it does not require conscious processing during encoding of information or retrieval (Squire, Knowlton, Musen, 1993). The organism knows more than a person's minded body in this domain. In other words, a nurse can get clues about early experiences of a sick child, or adult, about which the patient may not be aware. It will not be possible to confirm or refute any theories that the nurse may have about the experiences other than through third-party informants. This is no hocus-pocus, but a consequence of brain growth and the way implicit memory arises.

Implicit memory includes both motor patterns and responses, and also *imaged memory*. The proto-self receives implicit information from the body continually. The information, giving rise to changes in the proto-self, leads to the existence of background emotions, from which we come to get feelings, and in the end know the feeling of, for example, illness, tiredness, or stress. These background emotions are there before people can know about them. These patterns of affective changes can be associated with particular happenings through the synchronous firing of neurones, and the resulting affective memory, arising preconsciously, is an imaged memory. When these firings of neurones arise on the basis of signals from the internal milieu they give rise to somatic images in imaged memory. With recurrence of the external events the imaged memory can also be triggered preconsciously. Should Pamela have been taken to the surgery, and had a traumatic time – even as a two-year-old, she could react to the surgery again with emotional changes triggered by being in the same place. It is possible to be familiar with something emotionally with our organism, without knowing the feeling involved. Imaged memory is also operative in infancy. Newborn infants are learning a lot about the world they live in – and the learning is preconscious. It affects the way they come to do things and feel things throughout life.

An infant cannot plan for the future; this requires much more experience and cortical control. Nevertheless it will be advantageous if an infant can anticipate what is likely to happen. Implicit memory systems enable this. Learning follows classical behavioural learning principles of conditioning. The responses are controlled by their antecedents, not their consequences (they are respondents rather than operants) (LeDoux, 1995). The occurrence of one relationship pattern is associated with a sequence of interaction and specific emotional reactions. Cell assemblies that have fired together tend to signal together when triggered in the future. When some of the pattern or context changes, the functional connections remain and so there is a good chance that because of the reduced threshold for firing the whole sequence will still be mobilised. Through conscious effort such output can be brought under control. All is otherwise happening preconsciously.

People therefore function as 'anticipation machines', constantly scanning the environment and determining what will come next on a probabilistic basis. The brain is able to make 'summations', or generalised representations from repeated experiences, and these form the basis of the working models of relationships as dispositional representations, crucial to the arguments being presented in the rest of this book. Anticipating the future may be a fundamental component of implicit memory – answering the question *where* one might be in danger, distinct from the capacity to plan for the future (Siegel, 1999: 31) – answering the question *when* one might be in danger. Our organism knows more about what the future is likely to hold than we do through learning these recurring sequences. It can also reveal what people might otherwise hope to have kept to themselves, as their responses to anticipation of what might happen are also released preconsciously. The more complex and deliberate aspects of planning depend upon explicit memory (see pp. 58–62).

Priming is an aspect of this 'anticipation machine', a part of the implicit memory system. People are primed to identify recurring patterns. This can be seen with 'getting one's eye in', whether this is batting at cricket, looking for golf balls in the rough, or recognising rashes through seeing them repeatedly. Once one has got one's eye in, the benefit remains even after a delay of a few weeks.

Just as people do not forget how to ride a bicycle, there is no wiping out of implicit memory with time. The dispositional representations of working models of relationships are durable in the same sort of way. Motor patterns – such as the backing away at the sight of the needle – sit there, but it is possible to bring them under mental control so that we actually do something else. The emotional memories do not go away, but people can learn to control the emotionally charged behaviour and develop a strategic way of coping. People can develop alternative ways of living with them. One way of treating negative emotions of this kind is through a programme of extinction, where one stays with the anxiety-provoking needle until the anxiety level drops. Knowing that the anxiety level will drop if you hold out is essential. Emotions 'extinguished' in this way tend to recur with time, and the process often needs repeating. The underlying implicit representational patterns have not been eliminated. The emotions can also recur under stress (LeDoux, 1995). In addition what was learnt under stress comes up again when stressed. Previous imaged memory of an early hospitalisation will recur when re-hospitalised. Procedural memory shows itself when people engage in situations that repeat the motor demands made of them previously (skills for example) (Fonagy, Target, 1997). Implicit memories are as hard as nails.[4] Although you do not forget how to cycle, you can choose to swim instead. Although you might have been terrified by the old-fashioned dentist's drill, the terror can be overcome even though it is based in the past and turns up uninvited in the changed circumstances of current dental practice.

As people get older they can pay attention to what is happening, remember the details and explicitly recount them to others. Without focal attention, though, items are not encoded explicitly. Implicit memory will still be intact, but explicit memory is impaired for that event. Lives become shaped by reactivation of implicit memory, but this sort of remembering is associated with lack of a sense that something *is* being recalled, as this is all happening implicitly below the level of the cortex (Wheeler, Stuss, Tulving, 1997). When implicit memory is reactivated in the future it does not have a sense of self, time, or of something being recalled. It merely creates the mental 'experience' of behaviour, emotion, or perception.

Explicit memory

In contrast to implicit memory, activation of explicit memory gives us the feeling that we remember something. People remember the times they were ill in episodic explicit memory. It is what we usually think of as memory. By around the second birthday maturation of the brain's medial temporal lobe, including the hippocampus and the orbito-frontal cortex, enables us first to use other types of memory than the implicit, and to plan for the future as well as anticipating it. People can know what it was like to have influenza when they were four years old, but not when they were one-year-olds. Infantile amnesia is present for at least the first 18 months of life. By the time children are four years old, they can plan how to avoid getting taken to the doctor's. Episodic memory enables a picture of them-selves over time. They have a sense of time. They can talk to others about themselves and how they are.

The prefrontal regions of the brain are thought to carry out the process of creating an episodic 'retrieval state', in which a match between retrieval cue and stored representation can occur (Wheeler, Stuss, Tulving, 1997). When there is a match between retrieval cue and memory representation, the process is referred to as 'ecphory'.[5] Ecphory depends upon features of the eliciting stimulus, and the form in which representation has been stored in memory. This effect of context on the retrieval of explicit memory reveals how retrieval is enhanced when conditions have similarities in the physical world, or in one's state of mind (emotions, mental models, states of general arousal), to those that were present at the time of the initial encoding. Explicit memory is said to be 'context dependent'.

The process of retrieval has been suggested to function as a 'memory modifier'. The act of reactivating a representation can allow it to be stored again in a modified form (Siegel, 1999: 42). This is why narrative therapy, amongst others, can play a part in modifying earlier patterns of memories retrieved during the process of creating new stories to account for what had happened. This enables people to live with their past in different ways.

People sense, perceive, or filter explicit memory through the mental processes of implicit memory. They can scan for the shadows that such implicit recollections cast on the stories they tell, as well as on non-verbal aspects of behaviour and communication. Where there is a match between retrieval situation and memory representation, the process gives rise to an ecphoric sensation.

> Many things could have caused Pamela's lack of energy that morning. She nevertheless had some previous overwhelming experiences of lacking energy due to famine that coloured the whole picture, so that the nuances of her current febrile illness became lost in this over-whelming black shadow from her past. As she put it so poetically, she felt that she had no bones in her.

Memories are created. People can have a definite sense that something happened, that they have retrieved a memory, when the supposed happening did not occur. This has led to problems with false accusations of people having abused their children when they were younger, and 'the false memory syndrome' (Brandon, Boakes, Glaser, Green, 1998). Talking about memories does lead to their modification.

If events are gone through with acknowledgement of the emotions experienced (in contrast to those that were interpreted as being present, independent of what they were feeling), children are able to recall more details about their lives later on. 'Memory talk' (the talk in which children and parents engage prior to, during, and/or after an event) works to organise, to integrate, and thereby facilitate, children's memory for it. With non-intrusive carers it appears to have a direct effect on the development of explicit memory (Bauer, Wewerka, 1995).

One research method used to investigate attachment strategies in people over the age of 16 is the Adult Attachment Interview (AAI). AAI attempts to identify these shadows of implicit memory when interviewees recount their history, an explicit memory, in order to find out more about how implicit memory has been affected by early upbringing. It does this through analysing the prosodic elements in the discourse – the dysfluencies, their form, such as stutterings and pauses, and what triggers them.[6] How did situations which were threatening for them as children affect implicit memory, and are these coherent with the way in which adults talk about these events? The AAI has questions that attempt to address particular memory systems in order to see how coherent they are, as well as questions that demand integration across memory systems. Situations covered include when they were ill, injured or in need of support. We will now look at some of the explicit memory systems, the semantic, episodic, and working memories, which the AAI explores.

Semantic memory

Knowledge about what goes to make up a healthy diet is typically stored in semantic memory – similarly the words people have learnt about illnesses, and the facts they have learnt by rote at school. Naming of children's emotions gives them labels for their feelings, which are retrieved from semantic memory. What others have told them about what happened to them, before their explicit memory provided them with durable memories, is also stored in semantic memory. Semantic memory is for the kind of facts which positivistic scientific methods are adept at finding – 'Is this proposition true or false?' Semantic information can be true or false, right or wrong. Wheeler, Stuss and Tulving have summarised recent neuro-imaging studies which suggest that memory for facts, including events, is functionally quite distinct from memory of the self across time, autobiographical or episodic memory (Wheeler, Stuss, Tulving, 1997). Recall from semantic memory appears to involve a dominance of left over right hippocampal activation, whereas autobio-graphical recall, in contrast, involves more of the right hippocampus and right orbito-frontal cortex. Semantic memory is conveyed in words. In this book I am using the language of dis-ease to convey more than the verbal items. I include the way in which people talk about their discomforts, the implicit shadows appearing in their behaviour and the prosody of how they talk about illness, as well as the implicit affective tone from imaged memory.

Autobiographical or episodic memory

Personal illness experience is explored with the help of specific questions in the AAI. For example, one asks for five adjectives to describe a person's relation with one of their parents as far back in childhood as he can remember. The person is likely to come up with words from semantic memory, which may be more or less idealising. The same could be tried in relation to an illness. If one then follows up the question by asking for examples that can illustrate why those words were chosen, the interviewer begins to make demands on the person's episodic memory for what happened. Having laid the premises for potential responses to the second question in the choices made for the first, respondents end up with varying quandaries. Sometimes they find they cannot provide examples that fulfil Grice's maxims for adequacy of response – the quantity of information, its quality, relevance and manner of telling are appropriate to what was being asked for (Grice, 1975), and reveal their dilemma indirectly through the shadows of their implicit memory in the dysfluencies apparent in their answer – stuttering, long pauses, etc.

> Pamela could perhaps tell the doctor that she felt quite fine really when she was last sick, but the terror she had experienced at reliving the refugee camp feelings might be revealed when she stuttered over her answer to his request for examples about ways in which things had been fine. What is more usual is that she would try to avoid having to reply with anything concrete by saying, 'I don't know.'

The hippocampus and prefrontal (including orbito-frontal) regions of the brain, especially in the right hemisphere, mediate explicit autobiographical memory. These same areas are involved in spatial and temporal mapping, and assist episodic memory, providing people with pictures of themselves over time. Many individuals look to the left during autobiographical recall, activating right prefrontal regions. These regions undergo rapid experience-dependent development during the first few years of life (continuing possibly into adulthood) and are postulated to mediate autonoetic consciousness, that sense of being able to project yourself forward in time to new scenarios, a form of personal 'mental time travel'. This is what enables planning for that future admission to hospital, whereas at an earlier age with solely implicit memory to guide, infants can anticipate the associated emotions to be encountered based on previous experience but cannot plan how to do anything about them. By the middle of the third year of life, children can co-construct narratives about external events and the internal, subjective experiences of the characters (Miller, Potts, Fung, Hoogstra, Mintz, 1990). Children know that it is their own episodic memory, that it is autobiographical, because they can attach to the memory information from all their senses (verbal semantic memory lacks this quality).

> When going through an accident with a young boy who had been run over by a car, it was important to enable him to refer to how each of his senses was involved in his memory. There was the smell of burning rubber, the warm sticky feeling of his blood, the noise, as well as everything that was said.

A danger with debriefing after a crash is that the focus is on what people have been told, their semantic information, rather than helping them focus on their episodic memory. Their episodic memory is unique, and reflects sensory information and associated primary emotion in a temporal sequence. Their memory will be created in relation to their previous experience. It is impossible for others to know what they are actually feeling.

With the different storage systems for episodic and semantic memory, people can get into difficulties if what they have been told was the matter does not coincide with what they experienced as being the problem. Memories are created anew on retrieval, and need to be so taking account of dissonant information. For example, a child can have found an episode of illness very scary, but her parents may not have been aware of how scary it was, and repeatedly minimised the episode, saying it was nothing to worry about and that she hadn't minded it at all. The opposite can also occur, with parents telling children that they were exceedingly worried when they were not. The child will retrieve the parental view of things from semantic memory, whilst her own experience comes from her episodic memory. These memories come predominantly from opposite sides of the brain, and will depend on good function of the corpus callosum (that part of the brain conveying information from one side to the other) for integration. This is not functioning well until children are about three years old, and it continues to mature for the first ten years of life. There are therefore biological constraints on making equally good use of both memory systems at the same time. It may turn out that marked divergence between what children have been told they have been feeling, compared to their own experience, actually affects the development of lateralisation of the brain, and the resultant function of the corpus callosum.

Whose reality will prevail when children recount their illnesses in years to come? The stories they tell will depend on the potential for disagreeing with powerful adult views, and the attachment strategies they have developed – additionally, the context where they tell the story about what 'really' happened will also influence what they say. This means that when a school teacher is trying to find out what happened to account for the pupil not coming to school, it is not a simple question of retrieving an engram. The pupil recreates a representation from the information available in various memory systems, depending partially on the teacher's current reasons for 'grilling' the pupil. Recounting an illness history is also a moral issue.

Working memory

The encoding process for both forms of explicit memory (semantic and episodic) appears to require focal, conscious, directed attention that activates the hippocampus. Mimicking is also very effective. Information is temporally stored in a sensory 'buffer' zone, from which selected items from this huge immediate sensory load are then placed in 'working memory'.[7] The sensory signals can then remain in working memory for up to about half a minute. Working memory is thought to be independent of gene-activated protein synthesis. It involves functional (not structural) alterations in synaptic strengths (Nelson, 1993). The lateral prefrontal cortex is thought to be a primary mediator of working memory (D'Esposito, Detre, Alsop, Shin, Atlas, Grossman, 1995).

Cortical consolidation and long-term memory

Information can be held in working memory for only a short period. In order to become a part of permanent explicit memory, a process called 'cortical consolidation' is thought to occur. Consolidation may make new associational linkages, condense elements of memory into new clusters of representations, and incorporate previously unintegrated elements into a functional whole. In cortical consolidation, information is finally free of the need for the hippocampus for retrieval. This consolidation process appears to depend on the rapid-eye-movement (REM) stage of sleep (Winson, 1993).

It is also important to be able to forget (Trivers, 2000). In contrast to the durability of implicit memories we are familiar with the problem in remembering everything we have tried to learn or experienced. Revising for an exam taxes semantic memory, and people cannot always recall what has happened to them some time later. I will not go into how we come to forget; the importance lies in the contrast between implicit and explicit memory, with the potential for forgetting from explicit memory.

Dissociation

Memory is as accurate as possible when people make use of information from their complete memory system. But things do not always go smoothly. Some research has focused on the effects of life-threatening and serious trauma, such as childhood abuse, and traumatic accidents; dramatic treatments and diseases must be expected to give the same results. Trauma can lead to dissociation within the memory system. This concerns both the storage of information and its retrieval. It can happen that overwhelming stress leads only to implicit memory for the event, as autobiographical memory, requiring focused attention, is impaired. The intact implicit memory for the event can include intrusive elements such as behavioural impulses to fight, flee, or freeze (for example 'play possum'), as well as other emotional reactions, and bodily sensations, somatic imaged memories, and intrusive images related to the trauma (Siegel, 1999: 51).

Experience of the event shows in how people carry themselves, and which bits of imaged memory colour the basic emotions of the moment. People do not necessarily know that they are remembering anything at that moment from implicit memory, but it is clear to those nearby that something is happening. Their behaviour lacks coherence, without them knowing about it. Due to the powerful conditioning effects of emotions, the overriding importance of the changed background emotions will cast shadows on whatever is happening at the time. This can lead to some very confusing conversations with those who are close, and it does little to help them to assert that you know more about what is happening to them than they do themselves. In such a situation their whole body can begin to react with a repeat of the original reactions. Their heart can be hammering away, they sweat profusely, and over-breathe. Their hyperventilation can lead to feelings of shortness of breath and dizziness. There may also be a feeling of depersonalisation. The biological consequences of such severe stress include vasoconstriction of the cerebral vasculature, so that circulation to the brain is impeded.

Early child maltreatment is known to lead to damage of the hippocampus, which has important roles in memory formation and retrieval – especially for episodic memory. It may directly affect circuits that link bodily response to brain function such as the autonomic nervous system, the HPA axis, and the linkages between the nervous system and the immune system (van der Kolk, 1996). I referred above to the neuro-toxic effects of high cortisol levels. These changes directly affect the development of regulatory brain structures that are responsive to basic brain–body processes. They may explain the markedly increased risk for medical illness in adults with histories of childhood abuse and dysfunctional home environments (Felitti et al., 1998).

In other words, people who have had traumatic experiences, and who dissociate, can come to experience a variety of symptoms and have fewer ways of retrieving a state of homeostasis. They will not know why this is happening, as it is happening implicitly. There can be real problems trying to make sense of their symptoms. The symptoms are typical for stress, but can easily also be seen to be signs of a variety of diseases. Depending on their experience with these symptoms, and the symbolic value of their discomforts, a vicious circle can be started in which they then believe themselves to be seriously ill. Repeat health consultations can follow in which patients' discomforts, founded in their implicit memories, are not coherent with any disease model with which health professionals tend to operate – and the patients cannot provide the relevant information about previous traumatic experiences to help solve the difficulties. As their perception is about 90 per cent based on memory of what to expect, substantial biases in perception will predispose to recurring dissociation and repeat bouts of unexplainable symptoms.

I return to the role that memory dissociation can play in disorganised attachment patterns, and the role these patterns can play in misattribution of sickness, in Chapter 6.

There is also scope for another kind of dissociation between a person's behaviour and their neurobiology. There is the potential for a lack of coherence between a person's apparent drive for attachment, their seeking out of others when in need of sustenance, including need for assistance with bio-regulation, and their actual physiological state (Kraemer, 1992). There can be biological signs of stress, such as high cortisol levels, pulse and blood pressure, without signs of seeking another and so making use of that contact to achieve a new homeostasis in the face of stress. The words to convey stress need not correspond to the other markers of stress.

Box 3.1 illustrates components to the stress response. In order to understand why research on stress provides confusing results, it should now be clear on the basis of some understanding of memory systems, dissociation and proto-self and background emotions that there is absolutely no reason to presuppose a simple stress response in which all these dimensions are coherent. Exactly the same situation is bound to apply to disease and illness, given the way in which the brain and organism necessarily function.

Box 3.1 Stress components

- Physiology
- Behaviour
- Subjective experience
- Words available to convey the feeling
- That which is conveyed about the feeling

A summary of memory, emotion and feeling ill

Box 3.2 summarises aspects of memory systems and places them in relation to the illness and disease concepts presented in Chapter 1.

Box 3.2 Words, behaviour, physiology and feelings

Words used	Semantic memory	**Sickness**	Attributed
Behaviour	Implicit memory	**Illness behaviour**	Observed
		Signs	
Physiology	Background emotion	**Disease**	Observed
	Implicit memory		
Felt emotion	Emotional memory	**Illness**	Experienced
	Imaged memory	**Symptoms**	

There is no obligatory one-to-one correlation between the above.

An illness episode is remembered in *autobiographical memory*, although the subjective discomfort may also be remembered in an *implicit somatic imaged memory*. Sickness attributions are remembered in *semantic memory*. Systemic diseases and disorders lead to lack of attunement of body systems and a *change in the proto-self, basic emotions*, which may be subsequently felt and known as an illness. Localised diseases, for example a breast tumour, would not be expected to lead to sufficient change in proto-self to lead to a feeling of being ill. A predicament with which one is born will *not be distinguishable from the proto-self*, and will lead to no specific memories. Instead, how others react to the person in their predicament gives them information in semantic memory about their state, and the other's emotional response induces an emotional response secondary to their potentially distorted affective attunement. The illness behaviour of infants is remembered in *implicit procedural memory*, and will be incorporated into their later strategic displays of illness, along with words from semantic memory and emotions from imaged memory, producing a language of dis-ease.

Understanding the ways in which memory systems operate affects how information is interpreted. It entails a critical stance to research results based primarily on results from one or other memory system. This can be semantic information, such as from questionnaires, in contrast to information from episodic memory as available from some qualitative studies, or from video and audiotape sources, which might be interpreted according to an understanding of implicit memory. A person's biological make-up is the result of a fine attunement between their genetic endowment and how this has enabled them to be structurally coupled to their environment – especially the environment in which they grew up. The balance is disturbed when people are ill.

Information presentation to memory

> Behaviour is not caused by biological errors. The errors create the possibility for losing out on learning, or for deviant learning.
>
> Bill Fraser, Professor of Learning Difficulties

Temperament, genetics and danger

Learning depends on which sensations get through to be stored in the different memory systems. Theories about temperament are varied. Some propose that temperament is based on a collection of genetic influences, which affect two to three processes of key importance for controlling information access to the brain (for a criticism of temperament as a primarily genetic construct see Kraemer [1997]). One 'factor' affects the ease with which the brain registers incoming signals, the ease with which it is aroused. This depends on the level of change necessary to be regarded as a difference sufficient to *initiate* a signal. For example, in the retina of the eye cells are capable of responding to single photons, but the system would be too prone to register noise, insignificant stimulation, unless there was a degree of inbuilt redundancy; for 'safety' the cells usually respond first when the light intensity corresponds to about eight photons. Theories of temperament suggest that similar processes are going on in all sensory systems, but the level of stimulation required will vary. The second factor concerns the *intensity* of response that arises for a particular level of stimulation. This can be imagined to correspond to the rate of neuronal firing once the threshold to achieve stimulation has been passed. A potentially independent third factor assumes a similar role for interoceptive information, such as from the internal milieu giving visceral feedback (tension in the wall of the intestines for example), which can influence the intensity of a conscious fear response and may prove to be of importance for registering systemic disease (Kagan, 1994: 101).

Regardless of people's sensitivity and arousal to sensory stimulation, they nevertheless have to learn strategies to manage their own tension/arousal. Temperament factors can mean that the initial challenges for some parents to help their children settle are greater than for other parents.

Just as poverty makes good parenting more difficult, the theory goes that some children's temperaments can also make good parenting more difficult.

Children's temperament is largely independent of the attachment strategy that they develop (Seifer, Schiller, Sameroff, Resnick, Riordan, 1996).[8] It is probably unhelpful to try and distinguish the relative roles of temperament and attachment too rigorously, because inherited temperament characteristics coupled with children's experiences mould their future reactivity and arousability. In parallel processes the social experiences of children mould their developing brain and biologically rooted tendencies. Attachment strategies form in this developmental hothouse; the strategies are social expressions of biological predispositions formed in the intense creative pressure of the infant's early environment. The working models of relationships are biologically founded, characterised by particular organisation, co-ordination and integration of perception, emotion and behaviours. The different strategies that evolve provide children with a flexibility of response, adaptive to the various demands of early environments (Sroufe, 1995:147).

A similar three-factor construct to the three-factor model for temperament has been developed to explain responsiveness to stress, and by extension may be applicable to the discomforts of illness. *Threshold* represents the amount of stressful stimulation needed to produce a stress response (or feeling ill/stressed). *Dampening* refers to the ability to stop responding to a particular stimulus once the threshold has been reached or passed (or ability to live with dis-ease). *Reactivation* refers to the ability to become aroused again after prior arousal and subsequent dampening have occurred (or be sensitised to recurrence of illness symptoms) (Lewis, 1992).

Transformations of information

There are two primary sources of information available to people as they build up their self-protective strategies and their working models of relationships. People can register information that something has changed, either round them in their environment or inside them in their internal milieu, and the intensity of that change. When something changes, people register that one thing follows another. They register a temporal sequence. Implicitly they also attribute causality to the events, believing that one thing leads to another. This may be correct or incorrect, as the sequence might have been coincidental. This gives us either 'true' or 'erroneous' temporo-causal information. Crittenden employs the term 'cognitive' to specify this type of information in her dynamic-maturational model of attachment (Crittenden, 1999–2002). The information available in the identification that a sequence of events has occurred previously enables people to know when they might be in danger. The learning follows the principles of behavioural learning theory.

Danger is more likely when the degree of change in incoming information is extreme. Registering information about intensity of change is evolutionarily adaptive, as this is connected to learning about places where one might be in danger. The intensity leads to non-specific arousal; for example, suddenly going into the dark or being left on your own as a small child. The diffuse tension experienced becomes associated with the feelings associated with fight, flight or freeze – anger, fear and desire for comfort. Crittenden terms this sort of information 'affective' (Crittenden, 1999–2002). The situations may be truly dangerous, or they may be deduced as such in error. Associative learning leads to the learning about where one might be in danger being generalised to similar places.

The consequences of behaviour determine the likelihood of the behaviour being repeated, and the meaning attributed to the behaviour. An unpleasant response reduces the chance of repetition. If a particular behaviour is associated with an expected 'dangerous' event not recurring, then there is likely to be a compulsion to repeat the behaviour – even though the expectation of occurrence might have resulted from erroneous learning of a previous coincidence. The more dangerous the happening which was 'prevented', the greater is the likelihood that the 'preventive' behaviour will be repeated. Here lies also the greatest chance for erroneous learning that is hard to work out.

Affective information provides information about dangerous and safe places. Danger increases the chance for erroneous learning about places, in a similar way to the erroneous learning about causal logic of one thing leading to another. This can lead to withdrawal in fear from places that are not actually dangerous, or aggressively approaching people identified as potentially dangerous when they are in fact non-threatening. Similar errors can lead to people approaching strangers for comfort, when they have erroneously identified them as safe enough. One source of the affective information available comes from mobilisation of the autonomic nervous system, which provides information through an altered body state. The autonomic nervous system is what causes our heart to miss a beat, pulse to race, etc. When these changes are marked, they may specifically lead to somatic imaged memory in implicit memory.

Conditioning

Emotions are very easy to condition. Places associated with negative emotions induced by pain can induce the same negative emotions, and potentially *feelings* of those emotions, even though next time you were not in pain. The person has been conditioned so that the context induces the same emotional response. The same happens in hospital in connection with operations, although the drugs given as pre-medication are partially chosen for their effect in reducing the likelihood of such a negative conditioning. Conditioning also occurs with chemotherapy, which makes patients feel sick and often vomit, when being treated for cancer, so that they vomit at the sight of the nurse coming to give the chemotherapy. The cells firing together are subsequently triggered together at a lower threshold. The associated emotional reaction increases neural plasticity, and the cells rapidly become a functional unit firing in unison. When the circumstances change the functional unit remains easily triggered, such as by elements in the context that are sufficiently like those present when the initial response became established. Such context effects on conditioning of emotions extend to fundamental emotional indicators in other people – their voice, body signals, and facial reactions, such as gaze and facial expression. These can colour the circumstances so that they alone are sufficient to trigger a person's emotions. This sort of learning is going on preconsciously, and so may have a direct impact on a person's own emotional state *before* the involvement of a linguistically informed consciousness, or a rational analysis of an ongoing experience. It can nevertheless be connected up to consciousness, so that it is possible to avoid being controlled by all that happens preconsciously (see 'Memory' section, and Bechara, Damasio, Tranel, Damasio [1997]; Adolphs, Damasio, Tranel, Damasio [1996]).

A particular area of the brain, the prefrontal area, is required in order to overcome the emotional immediacy of powerful reinforcers that maintain the conditioned response (nice things happening lead to people doing more of the same thing). If people are going to alter the habitual responses that they have learnt and 'remembered' in implicit procedural memory, then this area is necessary – the more powerful the past conditioning and the more important the competing alternatives, the more difficult the shift and the greater the need for prefrontal influence. The prefrontal cortex is important for both emotional and cognitive aspects of learning, and its development is dependent on fine enough attunement of mother and child early in life.

Shaping: distortion, omission and falsification

Infants' behaviour alters through the ways in which parents respond to them. Behavioural learning principles apply to the procedural learning in implicit memory for their motor patterns of responding to what they have learnt about danger, both the when and where of danger, and its probability. This information is first available preconsciously, and then for conscious appraisal.

Parental behaviour emphasises for children that they attend to particular sequences of events, and pay less attention to other things happening at the same time. The gaze and response of the parents brings particular sequences to mind, preferentially to other sequences. Parents have a special role as they are assisting their children to modulate the arousal experienced whilst these streams of events are passing. Through their particular responsiveness they build up familiar patterns that shape the children's behaviour in particular directions, some tensions become easily modifiable, some not. This shaping of the children's behaviour according to behavioural learning principles can lead to transformations of the information available to children, as some information becomes distorted, other information becomes omitted, and yet other information can be falsified.

Information may be *distorted* through one aspect of the information being overly emphasised, at the cost of giving a distorted picture. This is especially likely when the information is complex, so that causality is simplistically attributed to one aspect of what occurred, to the exclusion of other information. Alternatively, complex feelings involving feelings of anger, fear and desire for comfort become simplified to being just fearful, or just angry. This shaping of models of causality and affect to become only partially accurate through behavioural learning principles gives people a distorted view of both cognitive and affective information. The forms of distortion are explained in the subsequent chapters, and summarised here. People using dismissing type A attachment strategies tend to idealise those who have cared for them, or exonerate them from personal responsibility for their difficulties, at the same time as these people may take too much personal responsibility for what happens to them. People using preoccupied type C strategies tend towards simplistic models of blaming and rationalisation.

When information in terms of stimuli from either their internal or external milieu proves not to be predictive of discomfort and danger, then there is a chance that it will be *omitted* from processing. For completeness I summarise them here, but the explanations for why they are like this come later. The dismissing type A strategies are associated with people placing little reliance on information from their affect, their feelings of anger, fear and desire for comfort. The significance of these signals is omitted. The preoccupied type C strategies discard information about causal relations.

Appearances are not the same as reality, and children learn about *false information*. One step in this learning involves parents attributing the wrong affective state to their children – for example, infants showing fear smiles, which are mistakenly responded to as if they had been friendly smiles. This can result in defusing threatening parental behaviour (Hinde, 1982: 213–215), which suits infants so that their fear smiles take on new functions to appease others. The negative affect associated with their fear smiles can become false positive affect in preschool children. This is typical for the dismissing type A strategy. In contrast the preoccupied type Cs have developed simplistic models of blaming and discarded some information about causal relations. They can come to false information about their own role in events, claiming innocence or false victimisation.

The transformations of information are dependent on children having more complex abilities to process information, and take into account the way their own behaviour will appear to others. This is associated with them going over to strategic use of attachment behaviour in order to maximise their chances of being cared for, their self-protective strategies. They learn that it is not just a situation that has the same characteristics as the previous time they were in discomfort, but their evaluation of it becomes more sophisticated. Their response is not just preconscious conditioned behaviour, but includes cognitive evaluation of their implicit learning. They learn to integrate information from various memory systems. They have developed a theory of mind in other people, and can see how they appear from someone else's perspective.

Box 3.3 summarises how the cognitive and affective dimensions to information are further processed in memory, and finally come together to influence memory for events and working memory. Connotative memory is deduced theoretically by Crittenden (1992–2002) and further described by her. It may appear confusing to include this here without further elaboration, but it is mentioned for completeness. It may turn out to correspond to what others have termed 'hot cognitions' (see for example Goodyer, 2002).

Social development

Social development depends on infants' experience, and their genetic endowment. Transformations of information bias infants' interpretation

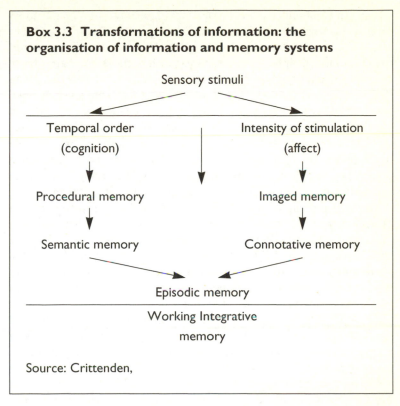

Box 3.3 **Transformations of information: the organisation of information and memory systems**

Sensory stimuli

Temporal order (cognition) — Intensity of stimulation (affect)

Procedural memory — Imaged memory

Semantic memory — Connotative memory

Episodic memory

Working Integrative memory

Source: Crittenden,

of their experience. With recurring perceptual and response biases, their development follows a kind of developmental pathway. Some environments will be perceived as more in harmony with these biases than others. Within their familiar milieu infants learn to regulate their own further development. They also learn to modulate the tensions that arise when they are under threat. Initially this is through others taking care of them, but subsequently they become self-regulating. This section describes some of the interpersonal processes associated with social development, and incorporated into an understanding of the development of attachment, beyond the implicit learning and transformations of information described above.

Before birth babies have learnt a lot about the world they are to land in. Their development has not just been a genetically determined biological process. Parents' expectations about their babies' personalities affect how they will be met, and can predict how they will be coping with their parents one year later (Benoit, Parker, Zeanah, 1997). Their mothers' varying internal milieu – including smoking and use of alcohol, stress responses and response to illness – will already have influenced their start to a life outside the womb. Nevertheless I follow tradition and start my description of infants' development with what happens after birth. In order to understand how children develop effective ways of sharing their discomforts with others, and so survive, I focus on developmental *processes*. This gives a picture of what resources children have at different ages regardless of what cultural context they grow up in. These processes will be coherent with the biological constraints and resources which guide development, amongst others the temperament factors and understanding of the when and where of danger. Infants become increasingly structurally coupled to their environment, including those who care for them.

In the beginning infants are largely dependent on someone else to protect them. They cannot move away, but can turn their head to avoid looking at someone. They display the ups and downs of their changing state through the probably universal expressive facial displays of the background and primary emotions (Ekman, 1992). Their parents are working out how much they can cope with on their own, and when they need to intervene. When is crying a sign that the baby needs to be picked up; when is it best to let them get on with adjusting the balance themselves? Gergely and Watson have brought together elements of learning theory in a novel way that is sufficient to bridge gaps in our knowledge to explain emotional development.[9] They propose that 'parent affect-mirroring provides a kind of *natural social biofeedback training* for the infant . . . based on *contingency detection and contingency maximising*' (Gergely, Watson, 1996: 1190). They have developed a detailed theory based on learning the relationship between the effects of what infants do and what that leads to. When infants are face to face with their parents, they are usually getting millisecond-by-millisecond confirmation that they are in tune with another. Frame-by-frame analysis of video recording shows that attuned parents are responding contingently to the small facial movements made by their infants. They keep the beat. Attention is held and develops through tight contingency (Posner, Rothbart, 2000). This happens so fast that it must be happening pre-consciously, although conscious awareness comes later and gives an impression that the parents chose to do all that cooing and making funny faces voluntarily.[10] Subsequently, exact attention is no longer required when the nervous system has been primed through recurrent experiences of seconds to minutes duration.

Infants appear to be able to work out the likelihood that something that is about to happen is the result of something they have done (termed the 'sufficiency index'), and the likelihood that something which did happen was preceded by something they had done (termed the 'necessity index'). These are parts of the procedural learning about the connections between events, the ways in which children are structurally coupled to those taking care of them. These 'indices' also provide information about the degree to which parents are predictable responders to what the children do. Children learn about their effectiveness, their sense of 'agency', which in terms of neural change represents contingent change in the parent sensory image subsequent to activation of a neural circuit in the child. Children appear to work at finding out how predictable parents are through a contingency-maximising strategy, which works by varying their own responses, and seeing whether the sufficiency index changes in relation to the necessity index. Remember that we are here talking about preconscious learning. The patterns of neural firing associated with children's responses are related to the sensory signals within a particular time-frame, and deviation from the expected patterns is registered.

Gergely and Watson propose that

> repetitive presentation of an external reflection of the infant's affect-
> expressive displays serves a vital 'teaching' function that results in
> gradual sensitisation to the internal state cues as well as to the
> identification of the correct set of internal stimuli that correspond to
> the distinctive emotion category that the baby is in.
>
> (Gergely, Watson, 1996: 1190)

When parents mimic their children's expressions, this is usually done somewhat theatrically with a deliberate emphasis that distinguishes it from the real affect. This is similar to when parents talk to infants in 'motherese', the special singsong prosody of baby talk, in order to facilitate their language learning.[11] Gergely and Watson propose that infants build up an association between what they see and their inner state preceding the parental display. Through the correspondence between the parental display and that of their infants, the infants learn by association about their background and primary emotions. The contingency of the parents' behaviour on the children's display facilitates the children's communicative competence through emotional display. The closer the connection in time, the clearer becomes the children's sense of agency, their sense that they are effective in bringing about change in another.

Through parental emotional attunement with their children, children come to identify meaningful changes in their internal milieu. Parental responses, such as cuddling them, lead to other changes, which potentially lead to restoring emotional balance in the children. This description is at the level of preconscious processes, but in this way parents create the basis from which infants can come to feel, and know about their feelings. The consequences involve not just procedural learning about their body state, but also how changes in that state, when picked up by another, can set in motion other reactions so that they feel better – the crying stops when they have been held, rocked or stroked. Children learn that a particular aspect of their being is being attended to, and in the process of engaging in a dialogue of turn-taking, learn how to maintain attention to get the soothing they require. Children's brains develop in line with their parents' ability to be in tune with them. Children's initial regulation of their internal state depends on the parents' ability to recognise that something is up, and find an appropriate response. Parents first turn to their distressed infants; later children learn to turn to them for help when they fail to get on top of things. Non-verbal communication is the medium in which states are aligned.

Children learn about causal sequences through the timing of parental responses. More correctly, one event following another should be termed an association between events. These associations are experienced as if they were causal. Contingent parental responsiveness is associated with children's experience of being socially effective in later years. One thing leads to another. Children learn more about their in-tune structural coupling with their parents through adjusting their own procedural display and finding out whether it elicits the same response. They try their hand at 'jazz'. Through biofeedback from their parent they eventually land on an evolved style of presenting their discomforts, which is sufficient to elicit the soothing they benefit from. They become physiologically attuned with their parent too.

This attunement with infants is a body attunement.[12] When people go to sleep with a spouse or partner they will notice that their pattern of breathing gets to be in time with that of their spouse – not always, but often (Lyon, 1999). When babies sleep in the same bed as a parent, they awake in synchrony throughout the night – and not just because the baby cries (McKenna, Mosko, Dungy, McAninch, 1990). Laughter is infectious, and crying is also infectious. Newborn babies in the nursery respond with crying to the crying of their room-mates. Theoretically I expect depression to be similarly 'infectious'.[13]

An alternative parental strategy when infants are ill at ease is to distract them. This leads to a different infant procedural memory of their capability for self-regulation. The discomfort gets controlled through their attention being directed to something else, away from their emotions, but they do not learn that what they did, co-operatively with another, had anything to do with achieving this. Instead they learn that another person takes over when things have gone too far, and the strategy to adopt is to seek out another who should take over. They become passive receivers of help, rather than active participants in tune with others and in tune with themselves.

From behaviour to strategy: intersubjectivity and mirroring

One-year-old infants can intend and attribute intention to others. They appear to have a capacity to apprehend the interpersonal significance of other people's emotions and behaviour and regulate their own responses accordingly. They have learnt that other people identify and respond to their emotions. These are communal feelings, which are partially shared. Emotional displays are particularly effective for communication, and facilitate children learning about interpersonal intention. They gain their sense of own effectiveness, and sense of agency. By two years they can refer to a range of feeling states in self and others. We say that children have become intersubjective when they have the capacity to have in mind the mind of someone else. Understanding this changeover is necessary in order to understand the changeover from self-protective behaviour, to the strategies used by two-year-olds (and believed to be first discernible from about 14–15 months old when the parasympathetic nervous system first enables infants to calm themselves to an appreciable degree).

A group of crying infants in a nursery experience communal distress. Their distress behaviour is reflexive to another's distress. In order to maximise their self-protective abilities they need to distinguish when this communal distress is primarily arising in themselves, from when they have 'caught' it from others. This requires being aware of these contagious effects of affect, and being able to attribute their own secondary distress to the primary distress of another. It appears as if this develops in relation to parents, through their near parodying of the infants' emotional displays, as described above.

An example from the everyday work of nurses illustrates this. Fonagy and colleagues found that mothers who soothe their distressed eight-month-olds most effectively following an injection, rapidly reflect their infants' emotion, but this mirroring is mixed with other affects (smiling, questioning, mocking display, and the like). They ensure that the infants recognise their emotions as analogous to, but not isomorphic with, their experiences (Fonagy, Target, 1997).

Mirroring of infants' dis-ease would be expected to fail if it is either too close to the infants' experience or too remote from it (see also discussion of 'pretend illness' for the same sort of process occurring for older children in Wilkinson [1986]). If maternal mirroring is too contaminated with the mothers' own preoccupations, then infants' experiences of intersubjectivity will be confused, and their potential to discriminate their own dis-ease from that of another will be jeopardised. In the feedback hum vignette the girl's symptoms of anxiety signified a potential catastrophe (e.g., heart attack, imminent death, etc.) for her father. His original response exaggerated her emotions, rather than enabling her self-modulation of her own dis-ease, with an ability to discriminate between what was her father's and what was her own.

The prime skills, which the infant's parent has to provide in order to help the infant get control of their own dis-ease, are summarised in Box 3.4. The skill involving a 'parody' of the infant's emotion is referred to as referential decoupling. The infant's relationship with her parent or other primary caregiver is the critical element in the infant's milieu. It enables infants to know about what is happening around them, their reactions to this, and ways of coping with the emotions that arise. They learn to use relationships as starting points to modulate their own tensions, and to retrieve a degree of relaxation.[14] Relationships hold the key to successful coping and complaining.

Box 3.4 Relaxation and tension control

Caregiver shows

- Accessibility
- Sensitivity
- Acceptance
- Co-operation
- Referential decoupling

Impeded by ignoring, insensitivity, rejection, interference and lack of discrimination between own and others' feelings.

Phases in development of attachment: a summary

Young children's ability to control their own internal milieu has depended on their history of affective attunement with their parents. Their skills build on the preceding steps of experience-dependent and experience-expectant mechanisms of brain growth. They enter onto a developmental pathway which can appear to be organised as if in phases, as the brain's development is not a smooth process, becoming a more complex organ as increasing levels of cells in the cortex become connected up. These apparent phases are associated with developments in infants' and children's 'sense of personhood' which are listed in Box 3.5.

Children's attachment appears to develop in phases, with increasing competence and developing differentiation of their personhood. Each phase is necessary for subsequent development. These phases are summarised in Box 3.6. Attachment behaviour patterns appear before children's strategic use of attachment and their ability to plan forward in time.

Box 3.5 Development of personhood through growth and maturation of memory systems

- *0–2 months* Experience increasing co-ordination of sensory information and early imaged implicit memory, especially in relationships with VIPs.

- *2–5 months* Movement, co-ordinated with integrated perceptual awareness, extends personal awareness. Beginning of identity as effective agent who can achieve things, and first dispositional representations in implicit memory.

- *6–14 months* Intersubjective communication, through experience of mirrored affective attunement, leading to awareness of emotions and feelings, including those that can be shared and those that are taboo.

- *15–18 months* Language and semantic memory introduce possibilities for meta-cognitive processes, reflection and symbolic thinking. Development of parasympathetic nervous system enables self-modulation of affect.

- *30+ months* Autobiographical memory enables a narrative view of own history, as well as the possibilities in the years to come for self-deception in own view of self.

The self is continually being reconstructed as contributions from memory systems make themselves variously available in working memory, from which they subsequently reinvest their own past in a modified way in a recursive process.

Box 3.6   Phases in development of attachment: first 2–3 years

- *0–2 months*   Pre-attachment: prior to reliable co-ordinated access to implicit memory.

- *2–6 months*   Discriminating social responsiveness: follows from the 2–5 month changes in Box 3.5.

- *9–14 months*   Attachment behaviour: without taking into account their awareness of the other's sense of attunement with them and the effects of the other's intentions.

- *15+ months*   Attachment strategies: dependent on self-soothing abilities following on from development of the parasympathetic nervous system and meta-cognitive abilities.

- *30+ months*   Goal-corrected partnerships: depending on autonoetic consciousness and involving more advanced intersubjective experiences.

These behavioural, and subsequently strategic, responses that enable children's self-protection build on the information that children have in their implicit memory, leading them to be disposed to respond in ways formed through the responsiveness that they have experienced. These dispositions have several elements and are summarised in Box 3.7.

These working models of relationships are initially behavioural responses, and in the phase '9–14 months' it appears as if infants can entertain up to three or four different response patterns. There is only a

---

Box 3.7   Dispositional representations – working models of relationships

Preconscious expectations at the level of implicit memory:

- Own and other's behaviour in given contexts
- Acceptability of the self to the other
- Emotional availability of others
- Ability of others to help modulate own tension
  - Provide protection

---

marginally significant association between the attachment classification with mother and father. However, each is powerfully predicted by the attachment classification of the respective parent on the AAI. Each parent creates a particular developmental niche for their infant, which is characterised by their own current working models of relationships (Fonagy, Target, 1997).

Nevertheless, by the time that children have developed strategies they appear to land on one dominant strategy. This tends to be that which they have developed in relation to their mother, regardless of the respective qualities of their relationships with their mothers and fathers. Exactly why this should be so is uncertain. Their motor patterns of behaviour which have characterised their infancy become characterised by psychological strategies taking into account their models of interpersonal psychology. For example, infants can inhibit their motor patterns of behaviour, whereas children can inhibit their displays of affect. The strategies employed by children as early as 24 months, which depend on their intersubjective skills and attribution of intention to others, are of much greater predictive value for knowing the strategies to be employed in their future than the attachment behaviours of infancy (Vondra, Shaw, Swearingen, Cohen, Owens, 2001).

Language

The language of dis-ease, which people develop, will have been shaped through what is learnable by infants and children, and what has been functional as they have been growing up – both within their family and culture. It will change in relation to the different phases associated with their development (Box 3.6). Their language of dis-ease is distinct from their thoughts about dis-ease. Language begins in social interaction, whereas thought is a product of the nervous system. Language is what triggers co-ordinated behaviour within the social group. It therefore has a key place in the development of culture extending beyond the infant's primary niche of development. In relation to dis-ease it enables the development of self-protective strategies. Language is strategic.[15]

The strategic quality reflects the speaker attempting to take into account their view of the listener's perspective. Nevertheless it is only the receiver of the message who knows what they 'received'. Their understanding of what has been communicated will again depend on their theory of mind about the person who sent the 'message'. Language is a continual process of best guess 'languaging' (Maturana, Varela, 1988: 210), dependent on approximate views of each other's views of each other, their continual readjustments, and the dispositional representations that meet in this process (Box 3.7).[16] We work out our lives in a mutual linguistic coupling, a linguistic co-ordination of actions. We are constituted in language in a continuous 'becoming' that we bring forth with others (Maturana, Varela, 1988: 235).

Developmentally the important processes as regards the use of words to communicate dis-ease concern:

1   Parents *expanding* their children's utterances into well-formed equivalents. Parents supply the missing grammatical and semantic elements.
2   Parents *commenting* on children's actions and focus of attention rather than questioning.
3   Parents *following the child's lead* (Hampson, Nelson, 1993).

These processes are disturbed when children grow up with depressed and neglectful parents, who are less effective conversational partners. They provide less expansion of their children's verbal language, which may instead be primarily supported by their siblings' or peers' responsiveness (this tends to be much below the level provided by average parents) (Hart, Risley, 1995).[17] Hoff-Ginsberg more recently demonstrated large differences in amount of input associated with socioeconomic class differences in mothers (Hoff-Ginsberg, 1991).

How parents talk with their children is also believed to play a crucial role in how they develop their autobiographical memory (Fivush, 1994). The earliest communication is about infants' emotions (Trevarthen, 2001) – and therefore also their states of dis-ease. We must expect that parents' responsiveness to, and extension of, their children's dis-ease signals play a crucial role in the development of autobiographical memory, and also their imaged memory. This will develop into their connotative memory and provide the affective dimension to their learning about their states of dis-ease. How parents respond to and extend their children's contributions will shape their language with the potential for the transformations presented above. The way in which parents enable their children to place their experiences within a cultural narrative enables the children to cope with the cultural expectations and become structurally coupled – not just to their family norms but also to those of their culture.

Symptom talk

Symptom talk is a special variant of 'languaging' and evolves on the basis of the way in which parents respond and extend their children's presentations of their emotions. By the time children are 3–4 years of age they usually have become much more facile at using words to describe their inner states and intentions (see Wilkinson [1988] for a description of states of illness provided by three- to four-year-olds).

Symptoms come in episodes, and therefore are spatially–temporally structured. Children learn preconsciously the contingencies about where and when symptoms have arisen. The way in which parents talk to them about their symptoms culturally embeds these experiences in the social norms. Words are provided which fit with the parents' observations. Semantic memory develops, and the words learnt more or less fit the emotional experiences of the children.

Children learn to attribute cold symptoms to being outside and getting cold. Because a runny nose arises secondary to a mucosal reactivity to cold, the same sign can arise on both the basis of being cold, and of getting a cold. In this way culturally acceptable attributions have a coincidental origin, and maintain erroneous information in a socially acceptable way. There is also a moral prerogative to carry out the health-bringing behaviour of dressing adequately to keep out the cold in that society, which is maintained through such erroneous coincidental learning.

Symptoms arise on the basis of initially vague tensions,[18] which can be resolved into something positive or negative. The concept of 'negative affectivity' describes the tendency to experience and report negative self-states, such as physical symptoms and uncomfortable emotions – states of dis-ease. Here the vague tensions are attributed to something negative. This is found to occur more often in families where there are several negative happenings. For example, the number of physical complaints amongst children at a gastroenterological clinic correlated with the number of negative events in their families. Also the more frequent the negative events in their families the more often they were ill (Meade, Lumley, Casey, 2001).[19]

Children's growing preoccupation with their internal states shows up in their shift in understanding of causes of their symptoms. Between the ages of 33 and 40 months they change over from predominantly being concerned with what they or others have done, to predominantly talking about their internal state and how that relates to their actions. Their psychological understanding has taken over. At the same time they talk more about social rules. Those children, who early on include causal thinking in disputes with either their mothers or siblings, are those who become more successful in their assessments of the role of inner states by the time they are 40 months old (Dunn, 1994).

Preschool children understand that the emotional impact of a situation depends on the beliefs and desires of those involved. In the early school years they recognise that a person's past behaviour and past experience offer clues to their appraisal of a current situation (Harris, Johnson, Hutton, Andrews, Cooke, 1989). Six-year-olds are sensitive to the mental antecedents and to the mental consequences of emotions. Their concept of feelings extends forward and backward in time. In that respect, their conceptualisation of feelings is similar to that of a script. It involves knowledge of a temporally and causally organised sequence of events (Harris, Saarni, 1989).

As children get into the school years they handle 'tensions' in more complex ways. They appreciate that more than one emotion can be experienced at the same time. They have increased capacity for simultaneously keeping in mind more than one scenario; their autonoetic consciousness includes the possibility for several future alternatives. They also explore more fully the events that were associated with particular tensions, and to which they attributed causality. Their analysis of situations enables them to come to more detailed conclusions. They also become aware that their personal histories affect how they perceive and respond to their feelings.

This growing self-reflection probably depends upon the form of 'memory-talk' engaged in with those close to them. In the relative absence of such self-reflection there will be a developmental lag between the expression of emotion and experience of feelings, and also knowledge about emotions. Memory talk facilitates socialisation and helps children know what sorts of emotions arise in particular social settings, as well as which ones are acceptable to display in particular settings. Understanding social context provides children with information about what to feel in response to otherwise unclear 'tensions'. The details of these processes are covered in the next three chapters. The 'emotional scripts', which arise on the basis of symptom-talk, are hypothesised to be part of connotative memory. Such scripts will differ markedly for different ages and in different cultures for particular situations.

Asthma symptoms

In view of Pamela's hypothesised trouble with asthma I include a section whereby research into the symptoms of asthma illustrates some further important details concerning the origins of symptoms.

Children with asthma, who have developed negative affectivity, have more symptoms of asthma, but without physiological measures of broncho-constriction, which is the narrowing of airways characteristic of asthma and believed to be responsible for the symptoms of asthma (Put *et al.*, in Van den Bergh [2001]).

The symptoms of asthma also illustrate how a learnt component is playing an important role prior to a patient having a conscious awareness of what is happening. Patients who have involuntarily been conditioned to have symptoms of asthma will not immediately be able to engage in the learning talk with their parents, which could have aided the development of self-reflective function, and so facilitate their coping and finding personal solutions. They will appear to have learnt to have symptoms without knowing why. Van den Bergh and colleagues manipulated smells, so that people became conditioned to environmental factors of which they were unaware, and which subsequently triggered asthma attacks. Such conditioned learning occurs preconsciously, and the subjects were not aware of which environmental factors triggered their attacks. They discovered that a crucial factor involved what the people thought and felt about the smells to which they were exposed. Through a combination of conditioned learning, and manipulating what the patients thought through images and text, the subjects got symptoms provoked by increasingly lower percentages of CO_2 in the air they breathed. Frightening words were particularly effective in facilitating the learning of symptoms. Once subjects had been conditioned to one smell, they more rapidly learnt symptoms with new smells – a process of generalisation. In other words, both internal cues (their fear on hearing the text) and external cues (their conditioned response to smells) could become new triggers for symptoms (Van den Bergh, 2001).

Conclusion

Retrieving information from memory is a bit like entering a hall of mirrors. The mirrors can be curved, so that one's affect and understanding of causal relations become distorted, diminished, denied or exaggerated. It is important to know that they are mirrors otherwise one loses touch with a sense of self. Some parents reflect their children with real terror at the sight of the emotions they meet in their children. We will look in greater detail at the distortions that can occur in mirroring in subsequent chapters – both lack of attunement and parents who become emotionally overwhelmed or dissociate when faced with particular emotions in their children.

Children protect themselves when they have identified connections between what is going on around them, their feelings about the emotions that have arisen, and what it all means. They then need to be able to do whatever is necessary to cope with the discomfort. If they are frightened because of some danger they have identified, they will need to decide what action to take, as well as how they can regain equanimity. This all sounds terribly logical, but we have seen that people do not operate logically. The organism, the mindless body, can know about danger before people have a chance to think through a logical plan. Only later will they wonder why they turned tail and ran away, or played possum and froze. In some situations people have to take action and think later to save themselves.

Children's symptoms become refined through how parents talk with them about their dis-ease. Their language develops through learning a vocabulary of significant complaints, and how such a vocabulary can be employed to maximise their self-protection and ability to calm their dis-ease. Through illness they become socialised into the ways of disease. Their coping and complaining become structurally coupled and culturally coherent.

Notes

1   Richard Semon published a monograph in 1904, 'Die Mneme', where he first introduced the terms 'engraphy' for the coding of information into memory, 'engram' for the enduring change in the nervous system, the memory trace, and 'ecphory' for the process of activating or retrieving a memory (Schacter, 1996: 57).

2   As Darwin pointed out:

> The evidence with respect to the inheritance of nodding and shaking the head, as signs of affirmation and negation, is doubtful, for they are not universal, yet seem too general to have been independently acquired by all the individuals of so many races.
>
> (Darwin, [1872] 1998: 352)

3   This development enables neurones to function on/off (i.e. digitally like a computer), whereas the spreading effect leads to diffuse influences affecting how the more specific neuronal signals are interpreted (i.e. an analogic effect).

4   Darwin had the same impression:

> Actions, (*associated with the expression of the emotions*) which were at first voluntary soon became habitual, . . . and may then be performed even in opposition to the will.
>
> (Darwin, [1872] 1998: 356)

5   See note 1.

6 Dysfluencies are analysed differently in the dynamic-maturational model compared to the classificatory process developed by Main and colleagues for their version of the AAI (Main, under contract). It is not my purpose to present these details, but rather to make interested readers aware of the need to read the literature critically.

7 Working memory was previously referred to as short-term memory.

8 Crockenberg found an association between neonatal irritability and insecure attachment at 12 months – but only for those whose mothers showed reduced sensitivity to their infant and who additionally had little social support (Crockenberg, 1981).

9 Gopnik and colleagues have popularised an alternative view of this process. They hypothesise that infants have innate mechanisms, active from birth, which allow them to attribute emotional states to others. They suggest that when infants mimic adults' facial emotion expression, an inborn circuit in the infant leads to the same emotion arising in the infant (Gopnik, Meltzoff, Kuhl, 1999). Later, infants could then come to know the feeling of that emotion.

10 One dilemma facing parents who try to rectify relative neglect from their own parents by reading books and going on courses is that they participate in an intellectually guided dance with their infants. Their responding is of necessity a few more milliseconds delayed, compared to that which others engage in spontaneously using their preconscious abilities. Intellectually guided caregiving is not quite as good for helping infants learn their parents' accessibility.

11 If infants are deaf then mothers exaggerate the visual features of their facial communicative expressions (Fernald, 1992). If the emotional state was not distinguished from real parental emotion then the infants' states would remain in high gear. The infant would be in a state of emotional distress through reacting negatively to the parental state. The essential distinction between real and 'pretend' is referred to as 'referential decoupling' (Gergely, Watson, 1996).

12 In China the expression '*ti hui*' means to empathise and is often expressed as the ability to understand with the body alone, without words. The expression '*ti yan*' means that to truly understand you must experience with your own body. The highest Chinese virtue, '*ren*', views the body-self as part of other human beings and nature (Tung [1994], in Bakal [1999: 81]).

13 A highly respected research paradigm for exploring the genetic contribution to depression looks at the occurrence of depression in mono- and di-zygotic twins. Interpretation of these results should be more complicated than it is made out to be, because of the greater chance for structural coupling between mono-zygotic twins, and for the varying degrees of infectious attunement to be expected between mono- and di-zygotic twins depending on a variety of context factors which are not usually recorded. Age of adoption is particularly critical for understanding research on adopted twins, given the experience-expectant and experience-dependent processes of brain development.

14 Relaxation is achieved in a variety of ways in adults. It may be that substance abuse as a way of coping can have its origins in a history of disruption of the effective use of social contact for developing self-modulation of disruptive affect. Infant mammals appear to depend upon social contact to maintain

endorphin levels. The amount of time they spend close to other people is decreased by morphine and increased by naloxone. This suggests that the opioid agonist morphine can serve as a partial substitute for the caregiver (Herman, Panksepp, 1978). Separation distress may reflect a state of endogenous 'endorphin withdrawal'.

15 See Maturana, Varela (1988), Deacon (1997) and Hoffmeyer (2000) for fuller descriptions of understandings of language pertaining to that used here.

16 This comes about through the co-ontogenic co-ordination of their actions. Essential to a linguistic domain is the co-ontogenic structural drift that occurs as the members of a social system live together. To an observer of the social system, from the outside, it will appear as a remarkable congruence of a dance of co-ordinations (Maturana, Varela, 1988: 209).

17 In a year, the difference in exposures would cumulatively result in 250,000 utterances versus 4,000,000 utterances. This is predictive of verbal language development at both 3 and 9 years old.

18 Sroufe advocates the use of 'tension' instead of arousal. Tension is seen as a natural by-product of engaging the environment, and people are seen as seeking out a degree of tension (Sroufe, 1995:140–141).

19 Children' s skill in identifying and communicating their feelings is related to children's health status, but the direction of the relationship is a function of who reports the children's health. Greater emotional skill of the child is related to better health when reported by the child, but to worse child health when reported by the parent. The health reports of children and parents are quite different, and parents' views may be affected by children's skill in communicating their internal states. The frequency of visiting the physician, rather than the parents' reports of children's symptoms, tended to have the strongest relationship with children's skill in identifying and describing feelings (Meade, Lumley, Casey, 2001).

Chapter 4

The ideal patient

The 'balanced' type B attachment strategies

> Happiness is when what you think, what you say, and what you do are in harmony.
>
> Mahatma Gandhi

When Pamela began with frequent bouts of tummy ache, at about ten years old, her mother struggled to work out what was going on for her. Pamela said little about her concerns, but was clearly upset by her stomach pains. Her way of doing things contrasted with that of Pamela's mother and her older siblings, Ben and Prue, who were used to telling others about their troubles when they arose. If they were ill, it was clear to those close to them. Her mother could keep her discomfort reasonably hidden if needs be, or if she had to make certain that others understood that more action was needed she could perhaps lay it on a bit thick. If her stomach felt churned up, she knew if it was because she was worried or had an illness coming on. She did not hold back from sharing things with others, and trusted that they would do things to help her. This made it all very easy for her husband to feel that he was useful and a competent husband when his wife needed him. She made an ideal patient.

Newly trained nurses and doctors feel competent when their patients trust them with their complaints. They can find out what a patient like Pamela's mother would prefer, and respond rapidly. Everyone is satisfied. The professional feels competent, and the patient feels taken care of. Similarly if children tell their parents about what is up, the parents are helped to be competent in their care taking. In this chapter we will look at what sort of developmental processes facilitate this open and honest presentation of discomforts. We usually assume that all patients are ready to present their discomforts, if only doctors had more time for consultations, were better listeners or there were a better staffing level of nurses on the ward. In the next two chapters we will see why this analysis of the communication dilemmas for health professionals, and for parents and children, is an oversimplification. I return to understanding Pamela's illness behaviour in the subsequent chapters. In the meantime this chapter explores the necessary prerequisites for trusting intimate partnerships, in which no part expects to be made use of unnecessarily, founded on the key elements from the preceding chapters. This is associated with self-protective strategies with the characteristics of balanced type B attachment strategies when their attachment behaviour systems are mobilised.

In this chapter I will describe processes that hypothetically have been going on between Pamela's mother and her other children, Ben and Prue, during their early years; and hypothesise how their illness behaviour has arisen. Dynamic developmental processes have enabled them to refine strategies for intimacy, which have traditionally been classified as secure attachment patterns. I will describe the classification of their attachment behaviour as being 'balanced'. They have an ability to make balanced and flexible use of affective and cognitive information in order to ensure their safety.[1] It is necessary to use a system of labelling which is neutral, instead of implying that one kind of attachment strategy is better or worse than another. 'Secure' attachment, the term usually chosen, has been seen as the desirable norm. Nevertheless, forms of attachment behaviour and their strategic use have arisen as adaptations to the particular dangers to which people have been exposed, and how those caring for them have met their needs when their infants were vulnerable. All patterns of attachment are adaptive under some set of conditions and maladaptive under another set. It would not have high survival value to trust everyone openly in Sarajevo at the height of the conflict, as a naïve 'securely' attached person might have been disposed to do.

I will be using the same classification system regardless of the age of the person involved, using the same letters of the alphabet for the categories as found in both children and adults. This is in line with the research findings of relative durability of *strategy* across different maturational phases, although it does not imply necessary continuity of either strategy or behaviour. Findings from the more detailed dynamic-maturational system of classification suggest that there is more chance for change during the lifespan than previously envisaged (Crittenden, 2000a, 2000b). Seeing attachment behaviour as being strategically organised implies that the strategy can remain constant, although the behaviour used to maintain the strategy, the phenomenology, may change as children's competencies develop. The behaviour used becomes more complex as their understanding of human relationships becomes more complex. Experience can make us better liars, as well as more socially sophisticated.

If it is necessary to use deception in order to minimise the danger to which you are exposed, you get much better at it with time. Your life may depend on it. On the other hand the same behaviour can be found in those using different attachment strategies. One needs to know the person's motivation, and the anticipated function of the behaviour, to tell the difference. Such causal deductions depend on identifying the behavioural contingencies, the antecedents and consequences. Chance can lead to some contingencies arising; the brain can fail to distinguish true from erroneous causal deductions. It is essential that we elaborate attachment theory, in ways that are compatible with knowledge of biological maturation and learning, and ecological complexity, to reflect the complexity and variation of adult behaviour (Crittenden, 2000a: 347).

Attachment theory is coherent with the bio-psychosocial research presented in the preceding chapters.[2] A theory is a way of making sense of observations; it tries to account for the observations in the most parsimonious way. It requires other forms of inquiry to see if accounting for what is met in practice is warranted. This concerns ways of relating, as well as some associations with biological variables such as cortisol, and measures of immune function (see, for example, Reite, Harbeck, Hoffman [1981]). Research has not advanced so far that the applications of attachment theory in relation to understanding the language of dis-ease have been confirmed. The current stage of knowledge is that the theory is more or less useful, both for people trying to make sense of what happens when people in distress meet and for researchers trying to conceptualise the issues involved and design the follow-up projects. The truthfulness of the presentation needs to be judged against criteria of coherence. Those who are familiar with literature, to which I have not referred, can use the criteria of coherence to see whether the presentation here can account for other observations. Attempting to test whether the analysis is correct through introspection will meet difficulties that are secondary to varying degrees of integration of 'knowledge' from different memory systems. Much learning is preconscious and visible to others before it is intellectually accessible to subjects. People cannot always make use of their memories for what has happened, when they are in conflict with what others have told them has happened.

Attachment and the danger of disease

John Bowlby defined attachment as the 'disposition of the child to seek proximity to and contact with a specific figure and to do so in certain situations, notably when he is frightened, tired or ill' (Bowlby, [1969] 1982: 371). Attachment theory, which has been built up to account for the form of such attachment behaviour, has proved to be very fruitful for understanding how people of all ages evaluate danger, and handle threat and discomforts. What one needs to know about danger in order to be safe is when and where it may occur, and how likely it is. When this information is lacking, such as with the outbreak of BSE (bovine spongiform encephalopathy) in England and the risk of vCJD (variant Creutzfeld-Jakob disease), governments and parents convey to their children a wide variety of possible risk scenarios. Children and adults are continuously being exposed to various kinds of danger. Disease is one sort that concerns us here.

Danger

Some dangerous situations require that we defend ourselves, others that we run from the danger, and yet others that we seek help. These three forms of action have their corresponding basic affective states of anger, fear and desire for comfort. When people feel ill it is not a self-protective option to become angry, or 'run away' from the illness, although getting angry when one is handicapped by an illness, or symbolically running away from the threat are seen often enough in practice. The child's desire for comfort is paramount. Should the desire for comfort not be met, then there may be a second-best protective strategy involving getting angry in order to ensure catching the attention of someone.

During development children learn how best to handle danger. If dangerous situations are predictable because they happen at predictable times or seasons of the year, these are tackled in different ways to dangers that are predictable because they happen in the same place, or with the same people. The danger to a child of having an epileptic attack is largely unpredictable, but parents and children usually try to identify their vulnerable times. This is somewhat easier for other diseases associated with relapses, such as asthma attacks or hypoglycaemic attacks for those with diabetes. How that specific child from that specific family sees the danger in that context with his history of 'attacks', determines how the attachment behaviour system will be mobilised. Children's socio-emotional development will shape the attachment form, which will be constrained through the biological influences on behaviour, as well as these providing the potential for flexible responding and new learning. The psychosocial classification of the disease can help predict which sort of demands will be made of the attachment behaviour system.

Attachment behaviour and health rituals

The attachment behaviour system, mobilised under threat, contrasts with an exploratory system. When the desire for comfort is not present the child is prepared to explore. If the danger of an asthma or epileptic 'attack' is ever present, and the attachment system mobilised, then the likelihood of the child becoming relatively autonomous will be jeopardised. Although children growing up are referred to as becoming autonomous, I prefer the expression that they grow up to have a balance between independence and dependence on others. This will vary according to circumstances. An attachment behaviour system is recurrently mobilised. People learn to live with their response biases in different ways in order to cope with different circumstances. It is human to acknowledge need for comfort from others, a need to depend on their closeness, and live with it rather than becoming 'autonomous'. The sense of safety people can get from being with others is additional to the habits and rituals they have developed, which also assist them to feel safe. They learn whom to trust with their vulnerabilities.

Various 'healthy habits' are learnt, and more or less available to introspection. They are variously stored in procedural memory, talked about with help of semantic memory, and rarely the origins are remembered from episodic memory. Asking people why they have some of their 'healthy habits' is usually the entrance ticket to a voyage of exploration into their life and cultural history. Some things they have learnt as a habit very early and stored in implicit memory, such as having windows open at night, or learnt when older because they have been told to do it (rationalised as being to let in fresh air – semantic memory), or learnt from experience that it helps (for example, bedroom temperature affects the quality of your sleep – episodic memory). Disease is inherently unpredictable, but creating ways of understanding what can precipitate disease can lead to it appearing to be more predictable, and so apparently more easily coped with – such as the parental injunction 'If you do not put your woolly hat on before you go out, you are going to catch a cold.' The superficial similarity between catching a cold, and being cold, makes this culturally linguistically embedded understanding especially durable and 'logical' to a child. In Norway it is a general phenomenon that children wear their woolly hats each winter until they reach adolescence, when the majority abruptly end the habit. Wearing of woolly hats was not something they were doing based on their own experience, but in compliance to powerful others.

Children learn about the dangers of going outside without enough clothes on when it is cold, and the importance of hygiene for preventing diseases (see Douglas, 1966; Wilkinson, 1988). Knowledge about the many potential dangers at home is transmitted from generation to generation in subtle ways. For example, a family is encouraged to employ protective rituals, such as having the window open at night to let in 'fresh air'. Fresh air has organised household rituals for several hundred years, since before theories of miasma were dominant. It has come to mean different things for each generation. The children I have talked to recently in Norway are unclear whether it is to let out radon gas (healthy), or slip in car exhaust (unhealthy), rationales that their grandparents did not have available. They would nevertheless sympathise with Florence Nightingale, who insisted that fresh air was not cold air. The 'lady of the lamp' may be surprised, just like the children, that this important health-giving practice is not rigorously enforced when they come to hospital today. How do children understand that? Parents use the notion of fresh air in the United Kingdom and Scandinavia to explain a routine that they find necessary, but which when pushed they find difficult to integrate with their twenty-first century system of explanation. Such rituals are encoded early in implicit memory systems, prior to people reflecting on their origins. The habit of sleeping with the window open is embedded and upheld in cultural and family norms.

Children's bedroom windows are opened at night, but, puzzlingly to them, not always during the day. They learn early that night-time is a time of potential danger to their health (Wilkinson, 1988: 154–155). If they can wake up in the morning feeling ill, when they did not feel ill when they went to bed, then it is natural to think of night-time as being potentially dangerous.

In order to understand the potential dangers of a particular setting, be it a cold day playing in the snow or the sun streaming down onto a playground in Australia, it is necessary to put oneself in the position of the 'protagonists', with an understanding of their personal history. A particularly poignant example comes from understanding why immigrant Turkish women in Stockholm do not like letting fair-haired Swedish nurses examine their children at the health clinic. It turns out that they were protecting them from the dangers inherent in meeting foreigners. Foreigners are understandably seen as potential sources of infection, with those who have travelled furthest being those who can expose your child to the illnesses to which they have least resistance. Fair-haired people were those who were least often seen in their original communities in central Turkey. They would probably have travelled furthest, risking carrying with them unfamiliar strains of disease. The mother's protective 'health behaviour' on behalf of their children was seen as an unhealthy strategy in their new homeland (Sachs, 1983). The mothers overgeneralised the danger of fair-haired foreigners to their new homeland where they were the foreigners. Being foreign is a question of difference, not an absolute. Their behaviour was guided by their implicit memory, and not immediately open to reflection.

Temperament, genetics and danger

Children respond with anger and fear when threatened as part of their way of organising their behaviour. Activation of a fear behaviour system can lead to activation of an attachment behaviour system as part of the child's attachment strategy for coping with distress and discomfort (Stevenson-Hinde, 1991). Both the temperament and attachment literatures describe behavioural systems for handling fear and anger. The attachment system distinguishes itself as it looks at how one learns the contingencies that shape the response systems. It has an additional focus on the desire for comfort.

Some danger signals are 'pre-programmed' to be recognisable by all children, such as the noise of a scream, and at a particular age the warning sounds of animals such as the barking of dogs. Primarily, though, 'pre-mobile' newborn are protected from danger by their parents, who identify what threats are present. With children's increased mobility parents need to identify what dangers their children can come to. Their understanding of what is threatening is transmitted to them before they can think about it; it becomes embodied in them and shows up via their procedural memory affecting their motor patterns of behaviour. Children are different, and so a parent needs to know what particular dangers they can come to. Children have different temperaments. Parents who felt responsible for all that went 'wrong' in relation to the upbringing of their first child, soon learn with the second child that the child's genes contribute to children responding differently. With the first child it's all the parents' fault, with the second it is the child's! Parental experience of local dangers with their first child leads to a different understanding for the second child.

Attachment and caregiving

Infants' caregivers determine their security through their care. The way in which they do it is a crucial experience-dependent influence on brain growth, which is decisive for the durability of the attachment strategies that people develop. They try both to ensure a safe physical environment and to modulate the uncomfortable feelings associated with being in danger. They have a dramatic influence on children's points of tolerable tension. Infants can find that in the caregiver's presence high tension need not be disquieting, and the situation can turn out all right. When they are comforted their physiological disequilibrium is calmed (see Fonagy, Target [1997] for further discussion). Environments that provide safety, opportunities for social integration, and the ability to predict and/or control what is happening are those most likely to contribute to health (Bakal, 1999: 46). Resilience results from successful coping with stress.

Attachment theory proposes that the way in which people adapted to how their parents were available for them when they needed them provides them with strategies that they then employ when they encounter other people. People develop working models of relationships – their predispositions – based on experience, to relate with particular biases. They are also predisposed to perceive relationships through the eyes of their experience. These evolved strategies of perception and action reflect their structural coupling to those on whom they originally depended, which then determine their expectations of others. As people expect strangers to react in similar ways to those they have grown up with, they anticipate their responses and feel relatively at ease when they conform to their stereotypes. At times they push this to the limit, provoking behaviour in such a way that it has a greater chance of conforming to their expectations – and thereby can feel more 'at ease', even if the familiar behaviour is abusive. The situation becomes predictable. Genetic influences also affect which environments people seek out.

Development is like a growing tree being blown into shape by strong prevailing winds. It adapts and develops roots that make it as secure as possible, whilst above ground it can appear to defy gravity. Should autumnal gales come from unexpected quarters it will be particularly vulnerable, but given small changes it adapts. The tree 'anticipates' particular challenges and it is well equipped to meet them. It is structurally adapted to the place where it has grown up. Its developmental trajectory can change, though, in two different ways. Each year the new seasonal growth is partially a response to what has happened the preceding year, and partially further maturation of the tree. Children's experience leads them to anticipate particular dangers, and ways in which people will help them through the challenges. Throughout their maturation the developmental pathway they are on, formed by the regular use of particular ways of relating, can change direction, a bit like seasonal influences on the tree growth. Preschool and adolescence are important maturational phases where new strategies might arise and propel the child onto alternative developmental paths. If children are exposed to particular traumatic events during these periods, their models of relationships and how they view the security of their situation may change. They may suddenly see themselves as vulnerable, and modify their attachment strategies in order more effectively to make use of those close to them, or to avoid being misused.

There is a danger in the language I have used, that one may think of attachment strategies as being carefully thought out, employed in a consciously planned manner. Behaviour appears functional and consciously guided. Instead we see from the preceding chapters that biological predispositions, established early in life, set the tune. The structural coupling between child and mother helped form the child, and is what the child takes on to their encounter with someone else. Brain growth depends on both genetic endowment and experience. The child's repertoire of responses is being shaped through the combined influences of biology and social interaction. It is not just what the child remembers, but what has become part of the child – this latter not necessarily being available to consciousness. Some ways of responding get easier, whereas others become more difficult as time goes on. Those nerves that have fired together have become wired together, with a lower threshold for response. Choice becomes biased towards those repeated patterns that have most often been rewarded. The reward is feeling more at ease; dis-ease has been minimised. As the child's capacity for reflection increases, their ability to make choices changes. Nevertheless, some of their options are going to be much more difficult than others. As LeDoux puts it 'emotional memory may be forever' (as in implicit imaged memory) (Shalev, Rogel-Fuchs, Pitman, 1992). Superimposing cortical inhibition on the behavioural expression of our patterns of relating and our emotionally charged memories may be the only way to change direction. Changing automated habits is difficult, and they are likely to crop up again under stress or the influence of alcohol or disinhibiting drugs, when ability to control them by using reason can be jeopardised.

Responses to signs of danger are set to arise at the preconscious level. This is a necessary prerequisite for survival, as responses which do not need processing at higher levels of brain functioning are quicker, and can lead to a greater chance of surviving danger – provided the response is appropriate. Learning in procedural memory at this preconscious level follows learning theory principles, such as operant and instrumental conditioning.[3] Our behaviour becomes 'shaped', and to an observer usually appears to be functional. It is only when the behaviour, which was functional in one environment, appears in another situation where it is released by some of the similar contextual signals, that it may appear dysfunctional. With illness behaviour and symptom strategies one needs to enquire of the context where they arose in order to understand the adaptive value they had originally. Yet the patient cannot be expected to have immediate insight into such preconscious processes, although higher brain processes will eventually be necessary to change the direction of the illness behaviour or application of the symptom strategies.

Adulthood and the balanced (secure) type B classification

The form and strategic use of the child's attachment behaviour, and so its classification, is dependent on the history of the relationship between mother and child (Dunn, 1993: 114); it does not just depend on what the mother brings to the relationship.[4] Understanding mothers' contributions will help us understand how the resources which Pamela's mother brings to her attempts to console her children affect how they share their disease with her and subsequently with others. Pamela's mother's strategies depend most on what she has learnt through her own upbringing. This includes the motor patterns associated with being together, which sit in her preconscious memory from her early time with those who looked after her. She has also gathered experience along the way with Ben and Prue, and what worked for them is more likely to be repeated with Pamela. What she has learned about keeping herself safe, she applies to bringing up her children. She conveys what she has learned about potential dangers, whether she plans to or not, as shown in her affective expression. Some symptoms, with which she is familiar, will give rise to greater concern than others, depending on her view of the dangers that can follow.[5] In addition, what parents read about bringing up children (semantic memory) can help them to reflect on what happens (episodic memory), but it is more difficult to integrate this with their procedural memory of previous experience in relationships.

Pamela's mother protects her, and ensures that she can be as comfortable as possible through any episodes of disease. She conveys the knowledge she has about illness experience and disease, and especially what makes one vulnerable to being ill – just as she did with Ben and

Prue. She maintains family hygiene standards. To understand the language of dis-ease we need to know more about how she relates to her children when she is doing this. When her first two children were infants there would have been several important small details concerning how they were together which are important for them developing a form of relating to her, which is called 'balanced' – the type B classification of attachment. I will hypothesise that she has shown an ability to make use of both cognitive and affective information in how she met the needs of her children. She could both reason clearly and recognise what sorts of danger might be present when and where, and respond appropriately. She could use her emotional reactions constructively. This is not quite as straightforward as one might hope, but is typical for an adult who herself has a balanced form of attachment.

What she will have been able to do is communicate with her children in such a way that whatever she says is also in tune with how she says it. Children primarily read the non-verbal messages, as these have precedence given their priority in the development of speech. In order to get the feel of what this distinction is about, try saying something that is different from what you convey with your body language. In Chapter 2 we saw how implicit procedural memory could be in conflict with explicit semantic memory when I invited you to nod your heads up and down, as if in agreement, whilst you said 'no'. Children have a well-developed ability to identify when their parents are misleading themselves. They know when they are saying something they do not really mean. Most parents have examples of when they have been found out – although they may not have intended the deception. Their children's ability on this front is usually better than that of their spouses. Children are more integrally structurally coupled with their parents than couples are with each other, due their development having co-evolved with the establishment of the relationship to a greater extent than the adults' structural adaptation to each other.

Pamela's mother will have taken responsibility for helping her small children regulate their relationship with her. If things begin to get out of hand, she helps get things back on an even keel. She does not blame them for things getting difficult between them, recognising that they do not have the social skills for repairing relationships that she has. She has the ability to take their perspective, and see herself from their point of view. When they are distressed she can empathise with them.

Pamela's mother has expectations about how children are; she responds as a good dancing partner, who knows what steps to expect. She guides, and repairs when her 'partner' treads on her toes by mistake. She knows

---

Box 4.1 Balanced attachment figures

- Communicate effectively using reciprocal patterns of non-verbal signals, coherent with what they say. They are in synchrony with other people.
- Can de-centre attention, which enables taking the perspective of others.
- Identify with their children, which entails accepting responsibility for regulating relationships.
- Empathise with others, including being able to put their children first, even when they themselves are distressed.

These skills reflect integrated cognitive and emotional mental processes.

---

that Ben and Prue are not yet conversant with the latest dancing steps. These responses are happening moment by moment, delicately dovetailed to retain synchrony. The speed of response is so fast that when taken up on video and reviewed frame by frame one realises that effective 'repair' has to be happening preconsciously. There has not been time for a cerebral analysis of what has happened. The response has been 'impulsive', springing from her procedural memory of 'dancing'. Just as riding a bicycle requires rapid adjustments, learnt and retained in implicit memory, so does dancing 'tango' with her young child.

Pamela's mother has a working model of parent–child transactions at the level of implicit memory. That means that she does not *know* about it in the usual sense of conscious awareness, and yet it is so inherently a part of her that she can respond using it especially quickly. The model will potentially be flexible enough to accommodate the various constitutional factors that might characterise her children, such as different temperament factors, or any hereditary disorder, which could lead to her child responding out of the normal frame of reference for her model – Down's syndrome perhaps. Parents' working models appear to be influenced by their own attachment histories, and they are revealed in the present in what Main has termed their state of mind with respect to attachment (Main, 1991). When a parent has a balanced attachment strategy, this shows in their narrative about their own attachment history. They can make use of all their different memories for their childhood experiences to produce an integrated coherent story – a balanced picture emerges. For example, their semantic and autobiographical episodic memories are both accessible and understandable in the light of their imaged memory for emotionally charged events, and the procedural form to their interaction with the interviewer. Their history is both emotionally alive and logically coherent in a way that is understandable to a stranger.[6] When they relate to a doctor or nurse, there is the same quality of meeting someone in an open and honest dialogue, where it is possible to explore concrete details about what happened when and where, as well as the emotional aspects to the illness.

Fonagy and colleagues have shown prospectively that maternal representations of attachment noted during pregnancy predict subsequent infant–mother attachment patterns (Fonagy, Steele, Steele, 1991). The work of Zeanah and his team showed how parental attitudes to their unborn child predicted the child's subsequent personality (Benoit, Parker, Zeanah, 1997). As yet the connections between personality development and attachment patterns are not clarified, but it is possible to account for most personality variants by judicially mixing constitutional ingredients and attachment strategies reflecting socio-emotional developmental processes.[7]

When early socio-emotional development leads to a balanced use of cognitive and affective information about threats and danger, and comprehensive coping strategies, we know that the parents have been in affective attunement (Stern, Hofer, Haft, Dore, 1985) with their children. Affective attunement is the way in which internal emotional states are brought into external communication within infant–caregiver interactions. This needs a bit of explanation. First Pamela's mother is able to 'align' her state to be *approximately* like that of her children, the referential decoupling described in Chapter 3. The children need to identify that there is some similarity, but also a difference. In affective attunement between older people both partners contribute to the alignment, and, surprisingly, young children align their state to those they are attuned with. There is an experience of matching of emotions, and some anticipation of what the other's state may contribute to the situation. It will not always be helpful for a mother's children that she is closely aligned with their state, as at times she will need to be attuned to their state without being aligned to it. In this way she can contain their distress, and so make it manageable (Fonagy, Target, 1997; Trevarthen, Aitken, 2001).

At times the infectiousness of crying and laughter leads inevitably to an initial alignment, but a subsequent extrication to a state of being attuned in a more limited way can be necessary for the mother to be able to help her crying child. At other times the distressed crying leads to an emotional resonance, a sort of emotional contagion, which affects the mother comprehensively and is difficult to modulate. The resonating state can then continue in the other person long after the child's primary distress has abated. Avoiding this requires that a mother has moderate skills of self-regulation of her emotional state in order to be available for her children with a balanced degree of maternal affective attunement. This again is necessary for her children eventually to manage self-regulation of their distress. Those mothers who can soothe their children effectively manage to combine a mirroring of their children's distress with other aspects of display which are incompatible with having *exactly* the same affect as the child, such as smiling, gentle mocking, etc. (Fonagy, Steele, Steele, Leigh, Kennedy, Mattoon, Target, 1995). The infant recognises their mother's resonating emotion as analogous to, but not isomorphic with, their experience. If their mother continues to resonate in the way described above they cannot manage effective soothing.

Fonagy and Target identify the role played by an adult's 'reflective function', their preconscious ability to tune in to their infants' emotional state of mind, their capacity for affect attunement communicated with facial expression, vocalisations, body gestures, and eye contact.[8] Each individual becomes involved in a mutual co-regulation of partially resonating states (Fonagy, Target, 1997). The matter of the mind matters for secure attachments. Schore describes how such processes also mould the connections of the developing brain, and are essential for development of the frontal lobes (Schore, 1994). The right orbito-frontal region of the brain brings together many of these central functions (Box 4.2).

Sensitive mothering[9] involves the ability to enter into an affective attunement with children. It is not just the ability to react speedily, for example to their crying. It is as important that the response to the crying be sensitively handled too (van IJzendoorn, Hubbard, 2000). Sensitive

---

Box 4.2 Right orbito-frontal region

- Registration of body state
- Stimulus appraisal – value and meaning
- Emotional regulation
- Empathic attunement
- Co-ordinating social communication
- Autonoetic consciousness
    - Sense of self in past, present and imagined future
    - Mental time travel

mothering is believed to be the key determinant of the different qualities of attachment. Several areas of maternal competence are related to the concept of sensitive mothering. These include mutuality, synchrony, and an ability to provide emotional support (De Wolff, van IJzendoorn, 1997) – and I anticipate that the more comprehensive concept of affective attunement can come to have elements of these ingredients subsumed under it. Sensitive mothers also facilitate their children's cognitive growth through scaffolding their intellectual experiences, such as with memory talk; and motivate their children through their appreciation of their accomplishments.

Sensitivity to the child is not enough on its own to account for a child's pattern of attachment behaviour. In their recent meta-analysis, De Wolff and van IJzendoorn (1997) found an effect size of only r = 0.24 for the association between sensitivity and infant pattern of attachment. As well as sensitive parents' abilities to decode their children's signals, they need to respond helpfully. This extends the role of parental understanding of their children. They need to adapt their understanding to how their children need different things of them in different situations. Sensitivity needs to be considered together with responsivity, and therefore some workers emphasise the need for synchrony of mother and child (Isabella, Belsky, von Eye, 1989). The critical issue for attachment theory is how children's handling of relationships enables them to cope with danger. The key issue for sensitivity may turn out to be the ability to determine when protection and comfort are *needed*, and not just *desired* by the child. Mothers of children who come to be classified as balanced, often react somewhat slower to crying than mothers whose children develop type A patterns of attachment, one of the traditionally termed 'insecure' patterns presented in the next chapter. It may be that they are discriminating situations where they have to respond, from those where the child would like them to respond. By delaying a fraction they are responding in such a way that they give the child room to scaffold their own tentative first responses to self-regulating their distress (van IJzendoorn, Hubbard, 2000). These children subsequently cry less than those whose mothers respond immediately.[10]

In the long term, children need to develop skills for self-regulation of distress and to lay the foundations for their relative independence in the future. These may be fostered more effectively when parents create such opportunities for the development of self-soothing skills.

Children may desire protection in situations when they do not need it, or need protection when they do not desire it. A critical issue becomes the parents' ability to determine whether the situation is dangerous or safe.

If there is danger, parents must decide whether it is best to protect their children or to promote their children's ability to protect themselves. If children are safe, parents must determine whether their children need information about the safety of the situation or need comfort (Claussen, Crittenden, 2000). The protective behaviour adopted by parents needs to be flexible in order to safeguard the children, as danger is context-dependent, as well as varying from one developmental period to another – from one medical setting to another, from one phase of an illness to another. This style contrasts with controlling-intrusive and unresponsive parenting which I present in the next chapter.

Parents who have a balanced access to cognitive and emotional information about potential danger may or may not know enough to protect their children, or be able to decide whether they can use the opportunity to facilitate their children's own abilities to protect themselves. Adults who have grown up in a protected milieu, with material resources and stability and continuity in their family – for example a middle-class family in an affluent neighbourhood – are more likely to have a stable attachment strategy, with a greater chance of type B attachment strategy. But a balanced type B attachment strategy, when people have such a background,[11] does not mean that they can evaluate potentially dangerous situations as comprehensively as someone who has what has come to be termed an 'earned B' classification of their attachment (alternatively 'mature' in the dynamic-maturational model). An earned B classification is used in scoring the Adult Attachment Interview (AAI). It reflects adults' balanced access to cognitive and affective information, and at the same time acknowledges that the information about their childhoods shows that they would previously have been classified as one of the popularly termed 'insecure' categories (A, C, A/C or Dx). The insecure categories will be described in Chapters 5 and 6. If Pamela's mother had an earned B classification we would expect her to have greater knowledge about the sorts of strategies that people develop to cope with danger. She would also be aware of the potential dangers children can encounter in a different way. This would mean she was better prepared to meet the demands of caring for Pamela.

For Ben and Prue, their mother's experience with dangerous situations could be turned to their advantage. If they were growing up in a sheltered environment it may be helpful to teach them about when it is appropriate to be fearful, and not trust someone. This can mean inhibiting their natural inclination gradually to approach and trust relative strangers. The Turkish immigrant mothers from near Stockholm can be seen as doing this with their children. The children may also need to know when to do exactly as someone says, in spite of their tendencies otherwise to discuss and enter into an open dialogue – for instance in an emergency at the accident and emergency department. If she did not teach them these things they would be the ideal victims of predatory adults, and she would not have been protective enough. The more stable the secure environment, the greater the children's need to learn to be flexible in relation to dangers which exist but with which they are unfamiliar – the dangers of diseases in the tropics for those who have grown up in an equatorial climate, for example. I do not wish to imply that she should teach them about the hidden dangers straight away, but, once they have established their balanced attachment, doing so in such a way that the dangers are seen as manageable, given the strategies that she introduces them to. Mothers of children who are described as secure and balanced teach them coping strategies throughout their childhood. They help them make use of facts, semantic information, and their feeling about what is up, affective information available through their attunement.

Parents classified as balanced make full use of integrated information from all their different memory systems. This enables them to evaluate situations across all dimensions, both consciously and preconsciously, and respond in synchrony with their children, making full use of their reflective function. They can still do this when the situation becomes very demanding and stress is high, and will still tend to look on the bright side of things.

When the demands of a situation increase, there will be a tendency for the parent to reveal their own attachment strategies to an increasing degree. For some parents, who appear to make full use of all the information available to them, when exposed to particularly stressful events we find that they dissociate (see Chapter 3). If they feel threatened, implicit imaged memory, with records from where they have experienced danger, can lead to distortions in how they respond to the situation. They fail to integrate that information with what they otherwise have available from their explicit episodic memory for events and semantic memory for facts, and even other implicit memory (e.g. the procedural). They can then cease to meet the requirements for functioning as a sensitive secure attachment figure (Box 4.1). They can overgeneralise the danger potentially inherent in a situation, but can also deny potential dangers. They cease to provide a secure base. This pattern is only clear if they are seen when under threat, although with experience small subtle distortions in their daily behaviour can sometimes be picked up. The behaviour of these parents is misleading, as it is easily confused with that found in secure parents. This difficulty is found clinically, and in the research literature, where early in the development of analysis of attachment behaviour there were surprising allocations of abusing and neglectful parents to the 'secure' type B attachment classification. On a ward one sometimes sees the behaviour of parents change dramatically when a disease progresses to being critical, and the threat inherent in the disease becomes tangible. Sometimes it is because of previous parental illness experience. At other times it is because they are unable to contain the threat of loss of their child, as such a threat was present in their own upbringing, used either as a control tactic or through being exposed to life-threatening violence. If such information is available through history-taking, the psychosocial classification of disease can be used to anticipate when in the course of a disease such crises might arise. I hypothesise here that Pamela's mother retains her capacity for reflective function under threat, and has provided a secure enough base for Ben and Prue, and is attempting to engage Pamela in a similar way.

A perspective from the Adult Attachment Interview

The Adult Attachment Interview (AAI) is used to identify the strategies that the adult has developed to handle danger and threat.[12] The questions in the AAI attempt to find out what knowledge the person has available from different memory systems about central issues in their lives. The issues are of importance for what we are interested in here, as they cover how the parents of the adults were available for them as children when they needed comfort – including when they were ill or injured themselves. The questions provide information about *how* the informant is able to tell us about *what* happened to them. How the questions are answered gives us a picture of whether the informant is able to make use of information from several memory systems. For example, if you try to describe your relationship with your own parents as far back as you can remember, you may find that when asked to give details which can illustrate why you described the relationship in that way, you get stuck. Using knowledge of the semantic and autobiographical episodic memory systems we believe that this reflects a problem with making use of our own experience, when reflecting on what others have told us about how things were. If a clinician should use this information when taking a case history with a sick patient, it highlights the need to address questions directly to different memory systems. If a young patient says that her relationship to her parents is good (answering from semantic memory), it is necessary to follow up with a question directed to episodic memory ('Give me an example which shows why you chose this word'). For Ghandi's view of happiness, that in order to feel all right, what you think, say and do need to be in harmony with each other, it is a requirement that you have harmonious access to your different memory systems.

It appears as if the AAI is particularly useful for eliciting important data that can give more reliable information than direct observation of parenting behaviour. It predicts the attachment behaviour that children show in the Strange Situation (a research situation for identifying young children's attachment strategies), more reliably than direct observations of parenting behaviour (van IJzendoorn, 1995). For example, Pamela's mother is here hypothetically assigned a type B balanced classification, and this would correspond to the quality of her infant's attachment to her in 65–85 per cent of cases. I have described her reflective abilities and use of integrated information from all memory systems, both cognitive and affective. These will enable her to provide a coherent narrative when describing her own experiences and childhood history, and also when providing a history for her children's illnesses. She will be able to put herself both in the shoes of her parents as well as those of her children. I expect her to be able to see things from the doctors' and nurses' positions should her children need to be admitted to hospital, at the same time as she would not lose sight of her own position. Growing up with a mother who manages this complexity helps children organise themselves – both at the level of their brain growth and socio-emotionally. Their children will eventually be able to regulate their everyday states of discomfort without recourse to assistance from others, unless they should wish to do so. Biological parameters of stress such as cortisol level, high pulse and blood pressure will be as expected. If the children appear to be managing stress these parameters are likely to confirm this to be so. They will also find it easy to get help from someone else, should their distress be marked. Health professionals will find it easy to build a therapeutic alliance with parents like these. These parents will be able to modulate their own stress, and so facilitate their children being in a good physio-logical state, for example after an operation (Skipper, Leonard, 1968). They will be able to describe their own feelings. This constellation is associated with experiencing fewer somatic symptoms (Lumley, Stettner, Wehmer, 1996). They recognise somatic aspects to emotions. Putting words on eventual emotional distress reduces autonomic arousal, and also appears to protect against somatic symptom formation (Taylor, Bagby, Parker, 1997: 120).

Childhood and the balanced (secure) type B classification[13]

Infants' attachment patterns of behaviour when relating to each of their parents are largely independent of each other (Grossmann, Grossmann, 1981; Steele, Steele, Fonagy, 1996). Parents have different mental models, different representations of what it means to be a parent, as well as infants responding differently to the overtures of their mothers and fathers. With one parent they can enjoy a waltz, with the other a tango, and yet their parents may prefer to polka. Children's differential responsiveness to their parenting is clear. Yet children also have limited repertoires to call upon, and these will bring forth different aspects of their parent's parenting skills. Infants' attachment behaviour patterns are acquired in relation to specific caregivers. The skills that infants develop to handle their relationships become embodied through brain and body growth, so that they are increasingly likely to be employed and generalised to other relationships. Ben and Prue could have developed different patterns of attachment behaviour in relation to their parents. It is currently unclear how many specific strategies an infant can employ, but it appears to be between three and four – for example mother, father and day carer or older sibling. These are whittled down with further experience so that eventually children in Europe and the USA adopt one predominant attachment strategy for use with strangers, usually that which they developed in relation to their mother, independently of whether the father has the more balanced strategy. The predominant strategy is not a description of how they relate under normal conditions at ease with each other, but when under threat – when ill and 'dis-eased' attachment behaviour systems, strategically organised after infancy to be functionally effective, are mobilised.

Securely attached infants can use communication with their mothers, and after a while their ability to regulate their own discomfort, to retain a moderately stable proto-self. Through her mother's affective attunement Prue could be enabled to make use of information available from her emotions and her feelings about her emotions. She will have recognised her emotions, and through her mother's discrimination between her various emotions, and her states of illness, have the beginnings of a dis-ease vocabulary. She will also have learnt to identify when and which situations might be dangerous, as well as which situations can threaten her health. These can give rise to uncomfortable emotions, potentially eliciting feelings of anger, fear and desire for comfort. It takes a longer time to learn what the relative risk is. It is evolutionarily adaptive to react in most situations, once one has identified them as potentially dangerous, rather than taking the time required to take the degree of risk into account. For smooth social functioning it is nevertheless essential to avoid over-generalising – and to use the example from the inborn fear of dogs which tends to arise at about 3–4 years old, this passes when one realises that one does not need to be afraid of most dogs. In the caregiver's presence high tension need not lead to aversive experience of dogs or behavioural disorganisation, but rather can give rise to the feeling of coping with dogs – a step towards a feeling of resilience and an internal locus of control.

House cleaning rituals have an element of warding off the dangers of dirt and pollution, and depending on the culture, evil spirits. Cultures regard 'foreign' dirt as more dangerous, and each land believes that its routines are the best. This includes their health services and hygiene practices – such as hand-washing routines and use of facemasks when operating. It has proved impossible to check out many hygiene rituals in controlled studies. If the routine has been ritualised and culturally bound, advice that the routine was not necessary cannot be believed. Within a tradition of upholding family and cultural values, children are introduced to how the adults become emotionally involved with the task. How do Muslim parents react in Norway when their adolescents let slip that they have eaten a frankfurter? How does the adult react when the hygiene rules of the house are broken, such as putting dirty Wellington boots on the kitchen table? It is good manners, rather than real danger of disease, which prevents people eating off most floors. TV advertisements, such as a Domestos campaign for a bleach sold in both the UK and Norway, play on concerns about being unclean, and encourage a moral virtue through exaggerating the need for killing germs or cleaning the floor, so that more of their product will be bought. A current hypothesis that the increased tendency to asthma is secondary to a more sterile environment (Johnston, Openshaw, 2001) has still to be tested against the alternative explanation that it is how the parents transmit their hygiene standards and the resulting emotional reaction in the children, which facilitates the necessary biological priming.

What children take to the challenges that arise are a set of expectations – both conscious and preconscious, about how people react, how they tend to react to them, and how they tend to relate to other people in such situations. These expectations derive from their experience with those who have been looking after them, with the earlier influences being relatively more embodied and structurally more enduring. These expectations do not determine how they will react, but make some responses more likely. Those who have a balanced attachment will have more responses to choose from, a greater flexibility of response to the varying demands of situations because of their access to both cognitive and affective information. This greater flexibility of response does not lead to such children fitting in with the adults at all costs, as children who are more in synchrony with their parents show less passivity. As infants they can, when needs be, show a greater willingness to follow their sensitive mother's guiding commands or prohibitions (Ainsworth, Bell, Stayton, 1974). There appears to be a greater degree of reciprocity and mutual pleasure in their relationships, so that they enter into virtuous circles that are mutually rewarding. In these circumstances mothers and children can be expected to be more open to their environment; their exploratory systems of behaviour will predominate rather than their attachment behaviour systems. They can make happy new discoveries as well as inadvertently risk exposure to danger. I hypothesise that they develop predominantly internal rather than external loci of control – a belief that they are effective agents to bring about change, rather than passive victims of external forces or chance occurrences. Their parents will have responded to them as if they expected them to be effective. They will depend less on superstition to ward off evil influences.

What happens is that the sense of feeling safe, once children have repeatedly been in comforting situations, gradually becomes internalised as part of their feelings about themselves. A psychological function, which is externally regulated in one phase of infancy, is internalised and auto-regulated in the succeeding phase (Schore, 1994). It is hypothesised that children can bring back the same feelings through a form of remembering, called their evocative memory, which can retrieve an image of their attachment figure and indirectly be used for comfort. Children also put varying faith in their cuddly toys as sufficient substitutes for evoking comfort. But not all attachment figures are comforting.

Not all infants are easy to soothe. Some researchers describe the difficult-to-soothe infant as having a difficult temperament. Other constitutional factors, such as genetic influences, and biological consequences of influences on foetal growth (see also Crockenberg [1981]), also effect how easily parent and child establish synchrony. But to repeat, temperament is not the major factor in determining attachment behaviour and the development of subsequent attachment strategies.

Biological factors both influence and are influenced by the different forms of attachment. Gunnar reasons that the HPA axis is primarily buffered against stressful demands through the modulating influence of secure caregiving (Gunnar, 1998). With colleagues she introduced 18-month-old children (type B attachment pattern) to a stranger clown, when with their mothers. Although they approached the clown fearfully there was no increase in their cortisol – regardless of whether they were regarded as inhibited temperamentally in new social situations – whereas inhibited and 'insecurely' attached children (type A, C, A/C or Dx attachment patterns) showed increased cortisol levels. The more these mothers pressed their children, often intrusively and insensitively, towards the clown, the higher their children's cortisol (Nachmias, Gunnar, Mangelsdorf, Parritz, Buss, 1996). Before a doctor takes a blood or saliva sample for cortisol it is necessary to think how the child was helped to participate, and whether this will affect the result – similarly when one measures pulse and blood pressure.

We do not know if the clown was seen as dangerous because of his strangeness. Familiar contexts increase our tolerance for arousal. When infants experience parents as predictable in their responsiveness, infants react benignly to new situations provided their caregivers are accessible. Infants can manage this sort of evaluation by late in their first year. But their particular recent history can overturn the expected pattern, as Sroufe and colleagues inadvertently found when they wore white lab coats and infants, aged 10–12 months, came to them having recently visited a doctor for an injection (Sroufe, 1995: 138). Changes in response also occur when there have been major changes in life circumstances, and/or when the behaviour of attachment figures changes. Some parents change their behaviour markedly when old memories are aroused after grave prognostic information concerning their children's disease. In these circumstances the sudden disruption to parent–child relationships, secondary to change in the parents' emotional availability, can be quite traumatic.

When one of my medical students was taking up his training interview with a nine-year-old boy with newly diagnosed diabetes, the patient hit him. The purpose of the tape recording was to learn communication skills with child patients. Analysing the sequences in the dialogue we saw that the patient was provoked by the student denying the boy's view that the doctor had given him diabetes, something the patient repeatedly asserted, and just as steadfastly the student denied, until he was hit. The underlying experience from the patient's point of view appeared to be that when he came to the doctor he only felt mildly unwell, but after his mother was told the problem he became seriously ill, and she did not manage to contain his stress. The doctor was then rightly given the blame for him being put in a tight corner, where he not only had a more serious illness than he had bargained for, but also had to manage more on his own. He felt abandoned, and the doctor was to blame.

Children's understanding of contexts, based on their previous experience, is what determines how they respond. They respond knowing about the likely sorts of danger, and how best to protect themselves. They have learnt about the different sorts of danger associated with different signs of disease, and learnt about the potential dangers of different symptoms. Environments that provide safety and opportunities for social integration, and facilitate the experience of being effective through being able to be in control (related to internal locus of control) or being able to predict what might happen, are those which are most likely to contribute to health (Taylor, Repetti, Seeman, 1997). Their relationships, an important characteristic of their milieu, are part of this environmental effect. Health is part of children's general resilience to adversity. Cicchetti and Rogosch have noted that resilience depends on a continuing balanced dependence on others (Cicchetti, Rogosch, 1997); resilience emerges out of the ability to self-regulate and organise, which again occurs within affectively attuned interpersonal experiences. These children will be emotionally intelligent (Salovey, Mayer, 1990).

From one-year-old to starting school: a perspective from use of the Strange Situation and the Preschool Assessment of Attachment

Pamela's early experience is beyond what a normal secure middle-class mother can understand, except in her wildest fantasies. I return to Pamela's attachment strategies in the next two chapters. In the meantime we will look at what has happened with her two older siblings, Ben and Prue. Developmental changes in childhood lead to the need for different ways of looking at their attachment from infancy to school age.

For infants of 10–14 months, attachment classifications are ascribed on the basis of observed patterns of behaviour seen in the Strange Situation (SSn) (Ainsworth, Blehar, Waters, Wall, 1978). After this age children are beginning to adapt a wider range of behaviour to their social interactions; they begin to employ a theory of mind which leads to them employing behaviour strategically. Those who have balanced type B attachment have initially the greatest range of behaviour to choose from, and can do so most flexibly. With their greater linguistic and communication skills, they can maintain contact with their parents from a greater distance. They become more socially sophisticated, understanding other people's intentions, and make use of their theory of mind. Through discussing joint goals with their parents, they can manage longer periods of separation, and a wider range of shared behaviour. They organise their behaviour in relation to their attachment figures. Their behaviour needs to be understood for its function in the dyad. What went before, and what follows the behaviour, highlights the function of the behaviour and the strategy of which the behaviour is a part (see scoring of the Preschool Assessment of Attachment [PAA] in Crittenden [1992–2001]). Physical intimacy becomes less important, whilst psychological proximity and intimacy increases.

Once children are into the preschool age range their illness behaviour needs to be seen strategically. It is not sufficient to describe the behaviour. The same behaviour will be found associated with various attachment strategies as a kind of equifinality. The PAA scoring system notes the behaviour that preceded and followed the attachment behaviour, identifies recurring patterns, and notes how many memory systems are involved (there need to be at least three memory systems coherently involved with the attachment strategy for valid classification). Illness behaviour is a response to the dis-ease, and will vary depending on which behaviours are in the child's repertoire, their previous experience of what worked when they last felt like this, and other aspects of their evaluation of the context. With parents present their behaviour and physiology will show varying signs of distress, depending on how they experience the helpfulness of the relationship. Their behaviour needs to be interpreted as a function of the dyad – the parent and the ill child. The child's attachment strategy in the preschool period is of greater predictive value than the pattern found in infancy for what sort of behaviour the child will show in the years to come (Vondra, Shaw, Swearingen, Cohen, Owens, 2001).

The ideal illness language

By 'ideal' I am referring to the patient who tells you openly about how they are feeling at the time – patients who make you feel the ideal caregiver. Their verbal and non-verbal communication gives the same message, negotiation with them is open and direct, and they expect to be supported by their parents, friends and health service staff. Given a chance they will trust you. These patients are emotionally literate. Because they are open and direct they are not disappointed either! These are the resilient patients – but the naïve Bs are also potentially the psychopath's easy victims. These are the patients who take on partial responsibility for getting themselves well (age-appropriate participation); that is, the classical description of the sick role where ill people participate in getting themselves well again – what Herzlich termed 'illness as an occupation' (Herzlich, 1973). They are the ideal patients for newly trained nurses,[14] even though they will not hold back from asking the awkward questions. Newly trained clinicians can acquire feelings of competence with these patients, before meeting the more challenging styles to be described in the next chapters.

All these attributes follow from the set of expectations that are built up through the sort of experiences described above. If your needs have been met, you do not worry about telling other people about what you need. You expect a helpful response based on previous experience. You will also be aware that it's not always possible to convey what you are needing clearly, but that is no problem because you have found out many times before that it will be possible for those looking after you to help you formulate what you need without imposing their own views. You persist until you succeed. You will also feel safe enough to try out new treatments, and will be an active participant in planning for the trial, asking the appropriate questions and being prepared to fight a bit for what you require if needs be. You will tend to collaborate, rather than comply with the staff. You have previous experience of 'goal-corrected partner-ships' (a phrase used in the attachment literature to emphasise that adults and children with type B attachment are used to being heard and jointly negotiating about what they will do), and expect to collaborate with any project to do with your health.

The basic affects of anger, fear and desire for comfort can all be brought into service when necessary. Being an ideal patient does not mean that you do not come into conflict with others, but I would expect such conflicts to be resolved. You have not found it unhelpful to be honest. Just as parents of children classified as type B have taught them ways of coping using both cognitive and affective strategies, so they will use these when ill. They make good use of information, and can rely on their gut feelings to follow the treatment process.

This is where they start. They can meet a nurse who can dance the same dance, and then it is all hunky-dory. Many hospitals are being acutely squeezed in the political belief that it is possible to save more money without this jeopardising patient care. Some hospitals solve the problem by reducing staffing, which can mean that the initially 'secure' patient begins to feel insecure when they no longer are heard by the pressed staff. Staff may be dysfunctional in their communication with their patients. Staff supports no longer function, and they resort to basic insecure communication strategies, which do not tango with such a balanced attachment type of strategy. Those who have 'earned' their ideal illness behaviour the hard way, like the earned B type attachment, would, I expect, be able to make allowances for this, and even have room for supportive comments in the light of how they can put themselves in their shoes. For some patients, especially in childhood, hospital experiences can be sufficient to alter the whole trajectory of their developmental pathway. At a time of greatest dependency on others for basic care (feeding, washing and going to the toilet), they may be let down. The 'ideal' type is no longer the best, but still idealised. The resilient type B strategy gives way to those that I will now describe in the next two chapters. People can either aim for self-sufficiency or begin to make a scene and fight 'for their rights', alternatively playing helpless and exaggerating their neediness.

It may turn out that the good prognosis found for those who have close relations with others rests on them having type B attachment strategies. Feelings of psychological closeness with parents predicted health and illness experiences up to 35 years later (Russek, Schwartz, 1997). Social support buffers the effects of stress on infectious illnesses in children (Cobb, Steptoe, 1998), and the outcome of trauma is best predicted by the person's capacity to derive comfort from the presence of another human being, rather than details of the history of the kind of trauma (van der Kolk 1996).

> The soul is a form of music which plays behind the curtain of the flesh, one cannot paint it, but one can try to make it heard.
>
> Henri Fantin-Latour, 1869

Notes

1 Someone who has not been exposed to serious threat during their development, perhaps growing up in a well-endowed, upper-middle-class family from a stable suburb and with sufficient emotional support, will not necessarily have developed antennae for picking up subtle cues about social dangers such as are necessary to handle those of, for example, a psychopathic disposition. Those who develop the attachment pattern classified as type B will not necessarily be secure. They nevertheless will have access to both cognitive and affective coping strategies in a way that can be described as 'balanced'. This is a central formulation of Crittenden's dynamic-maturational model of attachment theory.

2 It is not my aim to review the development of attachment theory and place it in its historical context. Here it is sufficient to mention a few of those who have played and are playing central roles in the field so that interested readers can search for their papers: John Bowlby, Mary Ainsworth, Inge Bretherton, Jude Cassidy, Pat Crittenden, Peter Fonagy, Karin and Klaus Grossman, Marinus van IJzendoorn, Mary Main, and Alan Sroufe. I will not go into details of why I find it necessary to modify some of the conceptualisations

that have otherwise characterised attachment theory. This can mean that some readers will feel that I do not do justice to the enormous amount of research being carried out in slightly differing traditions, and to the debate going on within the field. My aim is to make full use of a theory to explore the language of dis-ease, where the theory informs rather than guides. I owe a large debt to those who have gone before, and in particular to an inspiring meeting with John Bowlby and long-standing discussion with Pat Crittenden.

3 Mental models bias cognition to facilitate a more rapid analysis of a current perception, and to help the mind anticipate which events are likely to happen next.

4 Attachment is here viewed as one level in a hierarchy of systemic processes that extend from intra-individual systems (genetic, biochemical, physio-logical) to dyadic systems (communication, attachment relationships, such as mother and child) to multiperson, macro-systems (family systems, social ecological systems). Attachment theory addresses the protective function of certain dyadic relationships.

5 Box 7.2 shows levels of medical care. This box is adapted from Crittenden's figure for levels of parental care, and can be applied to the discussion here.

6 Their narrative meets the criteria of Grice's maxims (Grice, 1975).

7 Schizoid personality does not fit into this dynamic so easily, and it is the personality pattern that has greatest genetic loading and can be validly diagnosed at the earliest age in childhood.

8 The concept of reflective function is complicated and it may help to include some quotations from their paper. They . . .

consider reflective function to be the mental function which organizes the experience of one's own and others' behavior in terms of mental state constructs. Reflective function concerns knowledge of the nature of experiences which give rise to certain beliefs and emotions, of likely behaviors given knowledge of beliefs and desires, of the expectable transactional relationships between beliefs and emotions, and of feelings and beliefs characteristic of particular developmental phases or relationships. Its essence is not that the individual should be able to articulate this theoretically . . .

Individuals differ in the extent to which they go beyond observable phenomena to explain their own or others' actions in terms of beliefs, desires, plans, and so on. This undoubtedly high level cognitive capacity is, we believe, an important determinant of individual differences in self-organization, intimately involved with many defining features of selfhood such as self-consciousness, autonomy, freedom, and responsi-bility . . . Introspection or self-reflection is quite different from reflective function as the latter is an automatic procedure, unconsciously invoked in interpreting human action. We see it as an overlearned skill, which may be systematically misleading in ways much more difficult to detect and correct than mistakes in conscious attributions would be. Reflective function similarly lends a shape and coherence to self-organization which is outside awareness, in contrast to introspection, which has a clear impact on experience of oneself.

(Fonagy, Target, 1997: 680–681)

9 Research money has seldom supported research on both mother and father. Predominantly mothers' skills have been investigated.

10 Older infants can be reassured by the presence of their caregivers or their caregivers' response to their vocalisations. They need not use the less differentiated signal of crying.

11 Some refer to this as a naïve type B attachment.

12 AAI classifications are independent of verbal and performance intelligence, and social desirability (Ammaniti, van IJzendoorn, Speranza, Tambelli, 2000). One problem with the AAI arises because it continues to be developed by different researchers. Crittenden's version will be available through a website devoted to her work accessible through Southampton University, England (www.soton.ac.uk/?fri), and is currently the form which I anticipate being most easily available. Different scoring systems are used for differing versions, and this makes unravelling the findings in the literature complicated.

13 Within the type B range of attachment strategies the dynamic-maturational model distinguishes up to five different subtypes, each given a code – B1–5. The archetypal 'secure' pattern (infant)/strategy (preschool and older) is coded B3, and is termed the 'comfortable' B type attachment in the dynamic-maturational model. B1–2 ('distanced from past' and 'positive reframing of past') are more 'reserved', whereas the B4–5 ('optimism for future' and 'complaining acceptance') are more 'reactive'. All share a balanced use of cognitive and affective strategies, but they vary, amongst other things, as regards display of affect. In order to cover all possibilities BO ('balanced other') can also be used, and may be related to the relatively fragile balance of the 'earned' B (Crittenden, 1992–2001; 1999–2002).

14 It is not always easy for hospital staff to set up referrals to a liaison psychiatrist or psychologist, but these emotionally sophisticated patients tend to find this understandable and not a threat. With the current trend in Norway for debriefings after accidents, they tend to ask for such a meeting with the liaison staff. In contrast those who are severely lacking in any emotional vocabulary, and have a limited social network with little sign of intimacy, tend to refuse such a suggestion. The 'ideal patients', though, have usually done all the ingredients of a defusing immediately after the accident with those to whom they are close, and continue to make good use of their social network. They usually do not need special clinical attention, whereas those who do not accept the offer appear to be potentially more vulnerable.

Chapter 5

'I'm OK; don't worry about me'

The 'dismissing' type A attachment strategies

Nothing is so difficult as not to deceive oneself.

Ludwig Wittgenstein

Pamela is at a loss for words. She still gets her regular tummy aches when the going gets tough, and seems unable to tell her mother and father what it is that worries her. Sometimes she tells them about things that have happened at school the preceding week, but seldom do they hear of things soon enough to be able to help. She has begun to be troubled with asthma, and is very conscientious in her use of inhalers. She makes good use of all the information she gets, and manages well on her own. Her parents, though, find it difficult to rely on being warned early enough, if her wheezing gets out of control. She remains placid, self-contained, rarely getting into conflict with her parents, whom she idolises.

I will describe in this chapter the experiences that can lead people to being unable to adjust their level of distress, or make use of others to help them. These experiences affect how they respond to offers of assistance and consult with health problems. Nurses and doctors meet many patients who maintain an outward appearance of stoic calm when faced with a grave prognosis. Many will not want to talk about their condition. Clinicians only get worried about some of them. Dismissing type A patients are some of those who puzzle them. Clinicians do not always know what they have noticed. It can be a sense that the patients' apparent calm is not quite coherent with other signals that they are discomforted. There may even be an ambiguous message creeping through at times of crisis, conveying 'Don't ask me how I am, keep your distance, *and* please come and take care of me.' What happens when clinicians feel driven to ask for help to such patients?

The clinician's dilemma is compounded because often the self-sufficient quality to such patients' early coping in the course of their disease had been highly valued, and encouraged, by the staff. Denying cancer is effective, and children who do so live longer (van Dongen-Melman, Sanders-Woustra, 1986).

An attachment perspective, together with a biological understanding of development, helps in understanding how children and parents cling to well-tried ways of being together, such as the dismissing strategies to be described here – whatever their costs, when the demands being made on them for supporting each other are at their greatest. 'Working models of relationships' are not easily modifiable. They are embodied. Those who have been with struggling parents and children throughout a long course of a threatening disease will have experienced the consequences of their attachment strategies. In a way they will also have become structurally coupled to the family. This chapter will show how Pamela's complaints and coping through self-protective attachment strategies can have developed, and what sorts of vulnerabilities she is likely to have. I will come back to ambiguous symptoms, such as pains of unclear origin, in Chapter 7.

Staff on wards where children have been patients for longer periods have often found that after a reasonable honeymoon period in the first couple of weeks these patients have become particularly angry with those nurses to whom they have been closest. The same change, from avoidance of conflict to heated engagement, can also characterise some adopted children after an initial settling-in period. These responses can also be understood within the dismissing attachment framework being offered in this chapter.

Pamela's difficulty in telling her parents about her discomforts when she has them is a predicament. It jeopardises her chance of getting help. Such self-sufficiency may also be idealised:

> Separation from all society is regarded as sublime . . . To be sufficient for oneself, and consequently to have no need of society, without at the same time being unsociable, is something bordering on the sublime.
>
> Kant

Adulthood, parenting and the dismissing type A classification

In many families children develop the same attachment strategies as those used by their parents. The range of dismissing type A strategies as used by adults can set the form of attunement with their child, such that the child can set out on a 'dismissing' developmental pathway. About 74 per cent of young children seem to retain the same attachment strategy throughout their childhood and adolescence (Ammaniti, van IJzendoorn, Speranza, Tambelli, 2000), although this result may be biased in favour of continuity because the authors primarily refer to research in which behaviour, rather than strategy, was classified. This research was done using less differentiated classificatory systems than the dynamic-maturational model of attachment. We should expect more change during the life cycle, in accordance with maturation-based increase in the sophistication of the strategies that can be employed. Other classificatory systems have noted that the percentage with 'cannot classify' and 'disorganised' increases with age; the majority of these classifications are accommodated within the dynamic-maturational model, leaving only a few with no current effective strategic use of attachment still to be scored disorganised (presented more fully in the next chapter).

The exact way in which adults' self-protective strategies for coping with threat and danger can become those that their children use is not yet clear. There are hypotheses about how such transmission may occur. These depend on how social processes between parent and child set the scene for how children develop their ways of tackling the demands made of them to cope with the world they live in (see Chapter 3). The same social processes also lead to biological changes. I listed some of the central social processes in Box 4.1. In this chapter I present deviations from these, and summarise the variations associated with the dismissing strategies in Box 5.1. These need to be gone through in detail to understand what follows. Some, but not all, children would be expected to develop dismissing strategies through being taken care of in this way.

These developmental processes influence how information presented and available to children can become transformed. The negative affect is initially omitted, but subsequently through shaping of parental responses to infants' smiles they have available the potential display of false positive affect by the time they are 2–3 years old. Although their learning about temporal contingencies for events is more accurate than their transformed information about affect, they nevertheless are exposed to parents who come with misleading information about the antecedents and consequences of events they have experienced. These experiences in infancy become more pronounced when children become mobile, and parents have to set more limits on their children in order to keep them safe. Children exposed to misleading presentation of temporal–causal sequences learn to distort temporal information themselves. The characteristic transformations of information used by infants and children with dismissing

Box 5.1 Dismissing type A attachment figures

- *Communicate non-reciprocally* in restrained or agitated 'over-bright' manner; there is a lack of attunement and synchrony with their children. Non-verbal signals, such as smiling,* may not be coherent with what they say or with their children's state. Alternatively, lack of attunement is a result of either psychological withdrawal or intrusion, stimulating children to perform from their own perspective. Negative feelings are avoided, denied or falsified.
- Find it a *challenge to take the perspective of others*; instead they continue to take the perspective of former authority figures. Expect children to match them. Are poor at negotiating differences in needs, and acknowledging other perspectives, and strategies.
- *Identify with how things ought to be*, which includes a relative idealisation of how their parents brought them up, with shortcomings being seen as because they themselves were not good enough. When accounting for behaviour in others, employ those rules learnt in their families.
- *Under stress they primarily employ self-reliant protective strategies*, and expect their children to do the same (rather than being available for their children). Empathise with others, primarily when not distressed. Children are expected to take responsibility for regulating their relationships with their attachment figures, and most do.

The predictability of these responses facilitates *children* developing reliable cognitive mental processes that facilitate their coping, relying on the predictability of causal temporal relations in interpersonal relationships. People do what children have come to expect that they will do. The emotional dimension to relationships is less salient, and often is expected to be misleading. Like their parents they often 'dance solo', acutely aware of the power dimension to relationships.

Produced with assistance of Pat Crittenden.

---

* Ethologists identify both fear smiles and smiling associated with positive affect. The first is associated with a wider opened mouth, more show of teeth and lack of smiling round the eyes. Attribution of positive affect to a child showing a fear smile is an example of the sort of simple misattribution associated with the dismissing strategy.

type A attachment strategies are summarised in Box 5.2. These reflect transformations to which they have been exposed at earlier phases of development.

If someone looks after children in the way described in Box 5.1 there will be several important consequences for their recognition of emotions – including their embodied states of dis-ease, their ability to regulate their own affect or make use of others to help them regulate it. The qualities in the relationship become internalised as part of their working models of relationships, which are also employed when meeting strangers. Instead of their discomfort being responded to by parents, so that their needs are in focus, and distress contained (the 'B' experience), they find themselves caught up in their parents' ways of coping. Caregivers' attitudes and definitions of their children's needs dominate without these being in synchrony with the children; children's semantic memory, containing

---

Box 5.2 Transformations of information: characteristics of the dismissing type A

Age	Affect	Cognition
	Type A	Type A
Infant	Omit negative affect	
Preschool with theory of mind	Falsify positive affect	
School age with theory of mind		Distort temporal information in favour of greater than real predictability

In addition it is possible to come to *erroneous* conclusions due to coincidence, and to *truly* predictive cognitive or affective information.*

---

* When a preschool child uses false positive affect, it follows on from the false attribution of positive affect in infancy. Infants have been exposed to distorted negative affect before they are able to use it in the preschool period. It is more complicated to discern distorted temporal information, where the ordering of events was not as one was told, and falsified information provided first during the preschool period is too complicated for children to use until they are at school age.

information transmitted by their parents, will not be coherent and integrated with the children's episodic memory information based on their own experiences. The children's developing self is sacrificed to parental needs and they begin to have problems making use of all the information potentially at their disposal in their memory systems. If they did so they would be confronted with a major discrepancy between transmitted reality and experienced reality. Children do not have the ability to handle this in their early years, and powerful adults' views of the world predominate. This compromises children's developing reflective function. Parents' definitions of their children's dis-ease, their attribution of sickness, need not correspond to their children's illness, which may in fact be ignored.

Parents can react to children's illnesses with responses like, 'Don't fuss; there is nothing to worry about', or irritation and impatience. They may withdraw and become even more unavailable when demands are made of them to care for their children. The golden rule of these children becomes, 'Do not show your dependence', because otherwise the chance of being rejected by your parents increases. When children's affective distress is poorly modulated, their attachment behaviour system will still be mobilised. Nevertheless, they have also learnt that they are not responded to if they make demands of their own.

The varying degrees of the interactive processes are associated with various strategies, which have been labelled as shown in Box 5.3. The box is based on the dynamic-maturational model and developed with assistance from Pat Crittenden, although the responsibility for any misunderstandings is mine alone. People cope with parental rejection of their attachment approaches through either denying the rejection and idealising the adult, or seeing themselves as unworthy and so deserving of the rejection.

Children come to realise that it helps to make certain that their care-givers do not feel that they are not good enough. They make compromises in order to maximise their chances of closeness to their attachment figures. The first 'rule' is to disguise attempts at closeness, because if they are identified they will be more likely to be rebuffed, and rejection is felt as a punishment. Small children become adept at keeping their parents under surveillance, without them knowing it. They do not cling to their parents, and so were initially seen as some of the more secure children by Ainsworth. They also show little in the way of signals to their parents that they appreciate and require closeness – they cry little for example, but this does not mean that their physiology is not under stress. They deny the need to talk about usual care issues with their parents – and also with health professionals. Through experiencing parents who failed to

Box 5.3 Dismissing type A strategies

See the parent/other as 'good'	See the self as 'bad'
A1 _Socially facile_ Idealise, exaggerating the good qualities and minimising the negative of others, so as to avoid conflict, elicit good will and maximise chance of protection.	**A2 _Inhibited_** Exaggerate own negative qualities when accounting for their distress, thus, minimising the need to face conflict with others over their limitations.
A3 _Compulsive caregiving_ Take others' perspective and meet their needs, in order to increase the probability that they will be psychologically available and thus able to protect them or at least not jeopardise their chances of safety. Exonerate their attachment figures.	**A4 _Compulsive compliant_** See self as responsible to follow others' rules and meet their expectations; in conflict, the self is wrong. Compliance protects the self from hostility and so increases chance of safety.
A5* _Compulsively promiscuous_ Idealise the potential of unknown strangers to love and protect them. Use of sexuality or social bravura (false affect) in the service of false intimacy.	**A6 _Compulsively self-reliant_** Unable to meet the needs and standards of others; opt to function without depending on others (false affect). Dismissing of desire for comfort.
A7† _Delusional idealisation_ Resort to delusional processes to enable idealisation of others who will serve a protective function.	**A8 _Externally assembled self_** Have found themselves so unacceptable to others that they lack a personal sense of self, and use others' responses to define themselves in adulthood.

Produced with assistance of Pat Crittenden.

---

* Before the dichotomy into 'idealising the other' compared to 'denigrating the self' was identified by Crittenden in 2000, the subcategories had already been named in reverse.

negotiate with them, they themselves will tend not to negotiate issues with others – for example, when they have to have a blood test in hospital they will blankly refuse or meekly submit, rather than negotiating about which finger the blood should be taken from, or the need to wait until they have a comfortable position on mother's lap. They attempt either to be omnipotent, or refuse active participation or effective collaboration. The family dance has been determined by the dance that mother prefers, and the dancing partner has then been clumsily directed to follow the steps which mother has decided the child should follow. On meeting health professionals, such children – and subsequently adolescents and adults – will expect 'paternalistic' communicative strategies from their doctors (as a stylised way of describing a one-way communicative style), and will either submit to powerful figures and comply with their commands,[1] or surreptitiously appear to comply before going their own way.

Other children find that they can maximise closeness to their parents through looking after their parents' interests, and even soothing and stroking them. At times this can remind one of the grooming behaviour which submissive animals perform for the dominant members of the group. Through psychologically caring for their parents, such as petting them, they achieve closeness, but it is at the cost of not having their own needs met. The adults feel better, and so indirectly the children's emotional discomforts will also be reduced. This strategy seems to arise most often with depressed withdrawn parents. It can lead to children using the compulsive caregiving A3 strategy, the same strategy that I expect to occur more often amongst those providing care in health services and nursing homes. This is not the same process as occurs when children provide physical care for handicapped parents; provided the parents retain the adult role psychologically there is no role reversal.

Yet other children find that they can distract themselves effectively from their unrequited needs through redirecting their attachment behaviour, as if it was a form of exploratory behaviour. Some manage to focus on something quite different, which gets their minds off their unmet

---

Hence the numbering of A5–6 used here is inconsistent with earlier publications, but the meanings are unchanged. I hypothesise that the A5 category will correspond closely to the ICD-10 diagnosis 'disinhibited attachment disorder of childhood' F94.2. Recently Crittenden has suggested the A5 and A6 categories can both be further divided into 'social' undergroups and 'sexual' for A5 or 'isolated' for A6. The latter two appear to correspond to those with psychopathology.

† Categories A3–8 are usually viewed as 'cannot classify' or 'disorganised' according to alternative classificatory systems.

needs. They seek out alternative people to be close to, in the expectation that some closeness is better than none. What characterises these attempts is that they prematurely share intimate details about themselves, and appear to make themselves vulnerable and so elicit care before they have reason to trust the other person to handle these issues sensitively. By the time of puberty these attempts may make use of sexualised closeness as a substitute for intimacy,[2] but even earlier some children are on the look out. On a paediatric ward some children make attempts to get to know mothers of other patients within a short time of coming to the ward. In the same way they may appeal to many nurses simultaneously – they are also often found to be very appealing children. Some children distract themselves with hectic exploration of their new situation on the ward, getting into the investigation room, checking the content of all the cupboards, turning on the ECG machine, as part of an unending frantic search. Their desire for comfort is overwhelming, and dominates their unresolved fears and anger. Stevenson-Hinde and Marshall found that the least-inhibited children in their research were all boys who had developed an avoidant attachment strategy (Stevenson-Hinde, Marshall, 1999).

With either an ignoring or direct disapproval of the expression of emotion, children's display of their emotion, including dis-ease, will be minimised through a shaping of their behaviour. This is especially so when their need for comfort predominates, such as with disease. The children will have greater problems regulating their affect because of their experience of lack of assistance from their parents. They will have few words to label their emotions or feelings of illness (Cicchetti, Ganiban, Barnett, 1991).

Parenting and lack of continuity of strategy

Parents use their own coping strategies and can find it difficult or impossible to put their needs to one side and focus on their children from the children's own perspectives. Some of the ways these parents cope will function as threats to their children's safety (the higher As), and the children develop strategies to minimise and cope with those threats. What is transmitted is not the solution to coping with threat and danger, but instead the pattern of contingencies created by the way the parents respond to how they see the dangers in the situation. For example, parents who developed the A4 strategy of compulsive compliance will expect their children to follow the same rules. This will not necessarily happen. The children of some of these adults will cope by exaggerating their show of anger, instead of developing strategies that take more care of their desire for comfort.

If they had shown their fear, they would have mobilised the parents' awareness that they were failing to meet their children's needs for care, and so this is hidden or disguised. Strategies involving biased use of displays of anger are covered in the next chapter.

Some parents, who exaggerate their displays of helplessness (see preoccupied type C4 strategy of feigned helplessness in Chapter 6), may elicit a caring response in their children (compulsive caregiving A3), who thereby gain maximal closeness to their parent. When dismissing type A strategies are mixed with preoccupied type C strategies (see Chapter 6) in families, it can lead to superficial harmony, and underlying disharmony. The same state of affairs can arise when choosing a marriage partner, in which case a marriage of this form is described as complementary, a meshing of two complementary sets of strategies. The cognitive strategies of one are complemented by the affective strategies of the other, providing superficial harmony. But as they understand the underlying issues on totally different premises, it is as if people speak totally different languages, without an interpreter to try to negotiate a peace agreement. Similar issues can arise in teams working in the health service. A classical example is the sort of dynamic which can arise when a psychiatrist, focusing on the patient's emotions and illness experience, meets a surgeon focusing on the disease and cognitive challenges, attempting to be a fast active problem-solver. Cure and healing need to go hand in hand, but they are not always integrated parts of the health service. Healing takes more time than cure.

The dismissing strategy, illness behaviour and keeping healthy

Box 5.4 summarises the dimensions important for developing illness behaviour and keeping oneself healthy.

Parents will be predisposed to reply to questions about their children's illnesses with generalisations. These cannot necessarily be elaborated on, should doctors request examples to which they were referring. These parents follow rules and have better access to their semantic memory, compared to their episodic memory. They will often reply in relation to a stereotype that they have in mind, as the particular details of their children's condition have not concerned them so much. More often than expected they will tend to answer vaguely that they do not know the answer. Sometimes the stereotype used comes from reading the literature on bringing up children, and so can seem highly appropriate. Application of a mugged up model of good parental practice shows up in the parents' timing, as it is less in tune with their children, appearing as a cliché of good practice.

Box 5.4 Mothers' ways to reinforce their children's dismissing strategies for keeping themselves healthy

- through what they have learnt about keeping their children and themselves safe;
- through which symptoms are salient for *them*;
- through how they protect their children, including their hygiene rules and how they implement them;
- through their cognitive information about the dangers of diseases,
    - the 'when' of danger more than the 'where';
- through their ignoring of their children's affective signals, especially of negative affect, and misinterpreting negative affect signals positively,
    - attributing sickness from their perspective;
    - ignoring their children's discomforts of illness;
- through non-containment of the negative affect associated with disease,
    - their own low emotional expressiveness;
- through functioning otherwise according to the interpersonal strategies listed in Box 5.1.

Parents who describe doing all the 'right' things can easily be seen as competent parents, whom we would expect to facilitate their children developing balanced attachment strategies. The tendency to ascribe competence is heightened through their appearance of being relaxed and little stressed. Two points need noting. People reveal their underlying attachment strategies when they are stressed, when demands are being made which stretch them. Parents with predispositions to use dismissing type A strategies can often appear to be balanced until they are under strain. Appearances are deceptive – the higher the A category the more deceptive the appearance. Adults with dismissing strategies are to be expected to correspond to those who say they feel calm, but who at the same time show biological signs of arousal (McLeod, Hoehn-Saric, Stefon, 1986).

A major problem with the stress literature is that there is often an underlying presumption that if people say they are not stressed, then this is recorded as a valid description of their total state – a correspondence between their own verbal description of their state and their physiology.

Box 5.5 Dis-ease, memory systems and learning

	Memory system	Learning
Physiology of disease	Implicit imaged memory	Behavioural learning principles
Cardiovascular system		Conditioning – instrumental and operant
Immune system Endocrine system		
Illness behaviour	Implicit procedural memory	Behavioural learning principles
Vocabulary	Semantic memory	Cognitive learning principles
Subjective experience	Emotional and imagined memory	Cognitive-emotional learning principles

What one believes one has conveyed, reflects which memory systems are integrated in working memory at that time.

There should not be any expectation of a general one-to-one correlation between people's physiology, the way they present their dis-ease, talk about it and experience it.

Understanding organisation of memory systems, and how signals of distress have been responded to, makes clear that this assumption is not warranted (see Boxes 5.5, 2.2). Each memory system appears provisionally to store information preferentially according to particular learning principles. Through identifying which sort of learning has been distorted in which way, it should be possible to increase the chances of approaching the lack of integration of memory systems as methodically as possible.

A perspective from AAI

When presenting the balanced strategy I did not describe details of the different categories of balanced strategy. The strategy seems intuitively 'right'. In contrast the different dismissing strategies need explaining in more detail. It is important clinically, as well as in research, to be aware of how people using dismissing strategies present themselves. In the AAI these people have difficulties finding episodes to confirm the relationship qualities they wish were true. I will go through different type A categories, so that it is possible to read the literature with a critical gaze, and devise research projects that can take notice of the discourse style in interpretation of findings. The presentation is based on the dynamic-maturational model of AAI (Crittenden, 1999–2002).

Critically, in all dismissing transcripts, there is an absence of the speaker's true negative feelings (i.e., anger, fear, and desire for comfort). The means by which these feelings are omitted from awareness varies by sub-pattern (Box 5.2). Subjects display positive affect, smiling faces for example, even if these are not felt. Many are fearful of being rejected if they showed their true feelings, and they are kept hidden. They can even come to describe situations involving them as if they were not present, in the passive tense or avoiding use of personal pronouns. These disguise their own responsibility and enable a continued belief in other people's view of the situation as true. Because some people blame themselves for not being good enough, many AAI transcripts are coloured by statements about responsibility, and especially statements about failing to meet one's responsibility. Continued lack of integration of information prevents recognition of personal vulnerability, and so indirectly facilitates coping but hinders development.

People relate on the predispositions of their working model of expectations of how people are. The way of being together is revealed in procedural memory, and so is preconscious and not immediately open to introspection. Clinically one expects patients to relate according to their working models of relationships, and for these to be revealed in the *form* of discourse. People using dismissing strategies tend to have limited involvement with the interviewer.

The form of answers found in AAI dismissing transcripts suggests that if one was to take a history of their diseases and psychosocial development one would expect a reasonably clear presentation, albeit with few details or images of comfort or distress. Surprisingly though this will not be complemented by easy access to personal memories of their illnesses. If one asks specifically about how they were cared for as children when ill, they more often than expected report that they were 'never ill'. This could even be said in the same breath as they told you about a sequence of serious hospital admissions. This is not to be understood as them lying, but as providing information from different memory systems, which are not integrated. Giving the answer 'never ill' saves them from questions about how they were looked after when they were ill. Such questions would have potentially shown their caregiver in a bad light, and so are sidetracked. In an AAI transcript, procedural discourse markers typical of a dismissing discourse include limited procedural involvement with the interviewer, avoidance of negative affect, and positive wrap up when concluding a description of an episode, which was on the way to not conforming to the idealised description of the attachment figure. When these are present, one nearly always finds that the questions addressing need for comfort, such as 'how did your parents respond when you were hurt or ill', are answered in ways that suggest that the need for comfort was never acknowledged. Semantic memory also gets distorted, and on reading AAI transcripts it appears that crucial information is lacking as the interviewees' conclusions about their good-enough parenting are not supported by the information provided. The medical history, or research interview, is also to be expected to lack information to support the conclusions to which the subject hopes you will come.[3]

Changing strategies: a clinical perspective

Dismissing patients undergoing long-term treatment can come to show other sides to their personalities after an initial settling-in period. Initially negative affect – their frustration and negative feelings about being ill – is kept to themselves, but after a while their continuing feelings of vulnerability in the face of their disease are no longer coped with by denial. It appears as if their personal vulnerability, instead of being reacted to as something for which they were to blame, and so kept to themselves, becomes something coped with by getting angry with those around them associated with an impression of invincibility. It is tempting to relate this to experience of the caregiving on a ward where they experience that there is room for including the negative emotions without risking being rejected. Their desire for comfort is still relatively disguised, but the emphasis on displaying anger nevertheless reduces their anxiety. This strategy is believed to be a step on the way from one way of relating to another. It is helpful for patients that staff recognise that the person with whom the chronic patient is getting angry is usually the one who has best met the patient's desire for comfort. It is not then the time to back out, and hand over to another if the patient is to make a more general transition in their way of relating.

This display of anger towards others is different from the display of anger to things around them, which can occur for children with the dismissing strategies as a form of displacement activity.

The 'compulsive' strategies: the dismissing type A3–8 strategies

These people have been predictably rejected, in contrast to the predictable rejection of the *attachment behaviour* found with the development of the A1–2 strategies. The higher the classification coding, the more demanding the situation with which they have had to cope during critical periods of their lives. These more demanding situations are those I hypothesise as being more likely to be associated with particular vulnerabilities for disease, and more deviant illness/symptom 'strategies'.

These people describe themselves through the eyes of their parents. The idealising of parents, typical of the A1–2 strategies, is no longer the main characteristic of the compulsive patterns. They tend to exonerate their parent of responsibility for their actions.

It is particularly difficult to get a picture of their illness experiences; instead clinicians hear about what their parents say they saw was wrong with their child. As they are used to seeing things from the perspective of parents who have intimidated them in more or less subtle ways, they easily enter into analytical discussion with 'powerful' clinicians, seeing things from the clinician's perspective, rather than entering into a dialogue where their own experiences come to light.

The compulsive caregiving strategy

This interactional style is very clear with the compulsive caregiving, A3, strategy (Box 5.3). They exonerate their parents for letting them down, and still manage to see them as competent. Their parents can have been depressed, and then the parent is absolved of their responsibility through being seen as sick – an allocation of the classical sickness role. Through protecting their parents and meeting their needs for comfort, they could maximise their closeness to their parents. At the same time their own needs were not being met by the sick parent. They can therefore appear to be in synchrony with other adults, dancing a common step, but it is the adults' dance they are in step with, rather than being helped to learn their own dancing repertoire. They are used to self-sacrifice so that others' needs are met, and soldier on with a smile on their faces – the false positive affect. It is difficult to open up new ways of coping for patients who are wedded to their well-tried patterns. It is hardly the time to experiment with challenging new ideas about tackling stress when you are about to lose your only child to a deadly disease. Such families are likely to soldier on as before and not consult.

If clinicians work with colleagues who have this background, they may find some confusing developments as the temperature rises on a hectic ward. Such staff put in enormous efforts for their patients, but they are vulnerable to burn-out. Their false positive affect disguises encroaching limitations on their heroic role. Usually without warning, their threshold for coping is passed without their colleagues being able to help them out, and they are on sick leave. In keeping with the dismissing type A strategy they are unlikely to blame their burn-out on their work conditions, instead taking self-blame for not being good enough at their job. At a time of serious financial squeeze on health services, system errors are not going to be in the minds of these staff. They will identify with the need to save money, rather than what it has done to their health. They are the idealised employees, just as they have idealised the powerful others in their lives. Compulsive caregiving adults are often particularly adept at working with people who do not know how they feel, or who need more than usual support and structure. In group settings they often enable others to feel comfortable enough to function productively.

Individuals using these strategies are believed to be at special risk of psychosomatic illnesses (Crittenden, personal communication). Suppression of anger, a key habit of these people, is associated with a resetting of 'pCO$_2$ norms', the acceptable standard level of carbon dioxide in the blood. Other homeostats are also believed to be readjusted. Associated with these readjusted settings of central physiological standards are consequences for developing psychosomatic illnesses, such as asthma. The chance of developing asthma does not determine whether the symptoms will be used functionally. If those with type A3 strategies develop asthma, for example, they do not use their symptoms to gain care and attention from their parents, or control what their parents, or nurses and doctors do.

The compulsive compliant strategy

Compulsively compliant A4 speakers are excessively aware of the effects of their behaviour on others. Their compliance appears to develop as a way of retaining closeness to those making excessive demands on them (Box 5.3). They appear less aware of how others affect them, or of how things could be different as they grow older or circumstances change. They are highly vigilant to signals of impending danger, having learnt that knowing the affective state of their parents meant they could protect themselves through knowing what was coming. This is believed to extend to vigilance to the affective state of those caring for them in hospital.

Children often know the affective state of their parents before their parents are aware of it themselves – just as parents know that of their children (a consequence of the biology of implicit memory). Hospital staff would be well advised to strive for honesty in recognising their own feelings, and not believe that strategies for disguising their feelings are effective, especially for these patients (Main, 1957).

Comfort has not come from being with someone, but instead from soothing qualities of a particular place or music. Using images of a relaxing place can be expected to work particularly well for such patients to help them cope with a stressful medical procedure. The lack of modulation of their distress through being looked after by attuned parents is associated with them finding it difficult to identify changes in their somatic symptoms in tact with changing circumstances. They fail to connect somatic dis-ease symptoms to their psychological source.

The compulsively promiscuous strategies

The compulsively promiscuous A5 speaker illustrates a strategy that is first available after puberty in its full form, although hints of it can be seen in childhood with undiscriminating attempts at physical contact with strangers – the social variant rather than the sexually promiscuous form. Having apparently given up on getting enough comfort from their parent, they idealise the potential of strangers to meet their unmet needs. This reflects more serious neglect between child and parent during development. The parent has to an even greater extent seen the child as 'organism', a relatively mindless person for whom their appearance has taken on greater significance. Bodies have become divorced from the personhood of integrated psyche/soma humanity. People have become reified, and treated as relatively emotionless packages. Their 'caregivers' have been the source of their danger, as well as the people they have had available to turn to.

The term 'Stockholm syndrome' was first used to describe the predicament of hostages who identified with a hostage-taker; their safety was dependent on identifying with the person who had put them in danger. The same process predisposes to the A5 strategy. Danger and pain become confused with safety and comfort. The hostage-taker or abuser can be idealised, whilst those who have attempted to protect can be denigrated. Some people who injure themselves and present repeatedly to emergency rooms have this strategy. Understanding the memory distortions and their likely experiences may facilitate meeting these frustrating patients with compassion. The help offered by doctors and nurses can be rejected, just as the hostages in Stockholm felt most threatened when the police intervened.

Dismissing type A strategists tend to refer to their own bodies and body parts without reference to them being a *part* of them as people. It is as if they have become psychologically disembodied. They can have emotionally charged images which awaken traumatic memories, leaving them in exceptional need of comfort, without them being clear what sort of memory it is or where the memory comes from. Such awakenings can lead to repeat cycles of promiscuous attempts at closeness when their need for comfort is greatest, with repeat chances of being further traumatised as the closeness is not associated with intimacy. Images of comfort have long since become confused with dangerous or non-protective people in their working models of relationships.

The compulsively self-reliant strategies

The compulsively self-reliant person is believed to be particularly vulnerable to depression (Crittenden, personal communication). As they are compulsively self-reliant, they will not immediately take kindly to suggestions to extend their social network to cope with their depression. Many diseases are found more often amongst people who are depressed, and those with minimal social networks are especially vulnerable. As a potential factor of importance for understanding the morbidity and mortality of cardiovascular disease, one needs to understand what can drive people to opt for a compulsively self-contained existence where social contact is eschewed. These people have given up trying to meet the standards of other people, and have opted to avoid depending on others. They have either been exposed to similar traumatic processes to the compulsively promiscuous, or a parent has been absent at a critical period of development (this could involve parental hospitalisation or psychological absence such as with major depression). In the end, they appear as if they have given up hope that contact with others could meet their needs, instead seeing themselves as unworthy and fundamentally bad. Their memories are not integrated, and their avoidance of dependence is not open to introspection. They continue to have a distorted balance between their semantic and episodic memories, with even greater degrees of falsified affect than found for the A1–4 subcategories.

Delusional idealisation and externally assembled self strategies

The A7 and A8 strategies have newly been identified (Crittenden, 2000a, and personal communication). They include markedly pathological delusional processes in order to retain the illusion of a good-enough caregiver, and those who appear like chameleons, as they seem to change their personality depending on whom they are with. We do not yet have enough experience with these classifications to elaborate on them constructively here in relation to the language of dis-ease.

Childhood and the dismissing type A classification

> Every function in the child's cultural development appears twice: first, on the social level, and later, on the individual level; first between people (interpsychologically), and then inside the child (intrapsychologically).
>
> (Vygotsky, 1978: 57)

Scoring infants up to 14 months on their *behaviour* in SSn can be done using the dismissing 'avoidant' A1–2, and there are the first signs in a few of a tendency to the higher As, termed a 'pre-compulsive' A+. The *strategies* used by preschool children include up to A3–4. Their A1–2 strategies have become the dismissing 'socially facile/inhibited' strategies we have noted for adults. A1–4 strategies are termed as a group 'defended' preschool children (Crittenden, 1992–2001). It is first at adolescence that the dismissing 'compulsively promiscuous' and 'compulsively self-reliant' A5–6 strategies are possible, related amongst other things to their developing sexuality; the dismissing A7–8 strategies have so far only been identified amongst adults (Crittenden, personal communication). This is partly a function of the method, as scoring of the AAI is not yet developed for scoring the transcripts of adolescents.

There is a long tradition in psychology of understanding development as the result of internalising interpersonal processes. George Herbert Mead was one of the first when he wrote that 'The self is not so much a substance as a process in which the conversation of gestures has been internalised within an organic form' (Mead, [1934] 1962: 178). Children develop expectations concerning themselves, their relationships to others, and regulation of emotions, which all derive from patterns of regulation experienced within their primary attachment relationships. Aroused emotions of dismissing children are not necessarily being expressed, accessed or acknowledged. Interpretation of their emotions (Boxes 2.2, 2.3, 2.4) has failed, so that their feelings of emotions are confused and confusing. They have learnt that displaying emotions is counter-productive. Signs of disease may nevertheless be productive, although illness symptoms are less likely to be so.

Infants differ in at least three qualities, influenced by physiology, that contribute to a susceptibility to the universal capacities for surprise, uncertainty and fear. These three include:

1   preparedness to detect subtle discrepancies;
2   reactivity of the amygdala and its projections; and
3   degree of visceral feedback to limbic sites, which influences the intensity of a conscious fear state (Kagan, 1994: 101).

It is possible that infants more disposed to experience fear will be more disposed to develop 'insecure' patterns of interaction. But there is currently no evidence for this. From an attachment perspective, the issue concerns the strategic use of attachment behaviour, not the threshold for mobilising attachment behaviour.

Those newborn who are particularly irritable could be predisposed to develop non-balanced, non-B, attachment patterns. The irritability can be associated with a variety of biological factors. Crockenberg found an association between neonatal irritability and insecure attachment at 12 months – but only for those with mothers with reduced sensitivity, who additionally had little social support (Crockenberg, 1981). It appears as if the prime cause of developing a type A pattern (or other non-B patterns described in Chapter 6) resides in the form of the relationship rather than factors in the infant.

Anxiety is for the infant a confusing mixture of physiological changes, ideas and behaviours. Balanced infants turn to their mothers when physiologically aroused, and this enables them to return to a composed state. In contrast Spangler and Grossman found that infants who had developed an A pattern looked only to their mothers when their arousal was *not* high (Spangler, Grossman, 1993). They are having to master modulation of their arousal more on their own. It is no longer just parents who are less available to respond to their needs, but their needs are being presented less often to their parents. The pattern begins to be self-perpetuating, and will from now on be part of the working model presented to clinicians and researchers.

Parental lack of availability is one aspect of reduced sensitivity. Substantial amount of non-parental care during the child's first year is a form of lack of parental availability (Belsky, 1988, 2001), which is associated with elevated rates of insecurity, aggression and non-compliance. There is another side to lack of sensitivity too. Parents can become intrusive and press their own understanding onto their children. They stimulate children from their own points of view, rather than understanding the need to respond to the children's attempts to engage them, however tentative and faltering these may be. In Norway there has been general encouragement to stimulate children, which has unfortunately been flawed advice. It has encouraged parents to take the initiative and interpret their children from the adults' perspective, just as type A strategy parents tend to do. But we do know that insensitive intrusive parenting can be enough to stress children to such an extent that their cortisol levels become easily raised in a variety of situations (Hertsgaard, Gunnar, Erickson, Nachmias, 1995). Some of these parents are impressive 'textbook' parents in the doctor's surgery.

Parental misinterpretation of the non-verbal communications of their infants and direct mislabelling of their children's feeling states, such as that they must be hungry (or cold, or tired), regardless of the children's own experience, encourage children to mistrust the legitimacy of their own feelings and experiences, leading to 'interoceptive confusion'. This is a necessary consequence of intrusive parenting, which is not attuned to children's actual subjective experiences but instead is imposed, and hence arbitrary from the children's perspectives.

Studies of dismissing attachment pairs have shown that words are used without correlation with non-verbal components of communication (Beebe, Lachman, 1988). This makes it difficult to learn a coherent vocabulary to convey discomforts, especially when taken together with their probable interoceptive confusion. For balanced children, verbal representations help them organise and integrate affective experiences, and reflect on their subjective states and plan affect-regulating strategies (Bretherton, Fritz, Zahn-Waxler, Ridgeway, 1986; Dunn, Brown, 1991; Stern, Hofer, Haft, Dore, 1985). The same is believed to occur with experience of illness. Once children have started out on a 'dismissing' developmental pathway, their difficulties in learning vocabulary for their internal states maintains their trajectory. Although they become emotionally illiterate, in the sense of not being able to talk about the *feeling* of the emotion, or disease, they will not be emotionally naïve. The language of dis-ease is compromised.

Wellman, Harris and Bannerjee showed that 2½-year-olds understand private feelings that are distinct from the situations that elicit them, and particularly that they are distinct from facial expressions of emotions (one can feel sad and not cry) (Wellman, Harris, Banerjee, Sinclair, 1995).

The theory of mind which children with A strategies develop includes knowing this about emotions and feelings. With this awareness pre-school children develop strategic use of their attachment behaviour, in contrast to the behavioural patterns characteristic of the infant. They are emotionally responsive, but unable coherently to describe their feelings of emotions. Their expertise is at procedural levels of competence, rather than semantic. This lack of integration of their competence in different memory systems leads to poorer socio-emotional functioning, and reduced capabilities, as the information held in the different systems is not available as a whole. These children will be anticipated to show low level of engagement with hospital staff, and make little use of the toys available in the ward playroom to cope, as their pretend play is impoverished (Fonagy, Target, 1997). Nevertheless, toys may be used as simple distracters to cope with unpleasant experiences, and they can also be used to structure play with an otherwise intrusive parent – for example board games or jigsaws. Their play is likely to be most complex when parents are not present, in contrast to the reverse for balanced children.

Their relatively poor socio-emotional functioning does not imply poor cognitive functioning. Although parents may reject and devalue their children's attachment needs, they may notice and praise their cognitive achievements, leading to a self-reinforcing cognitive loop (Scarr, McCartney, 1983).[4] Academic achievement facilitates closeness to parents and compensates for the rejection of the attachment needs. Parental interest, approval and positive regard may also be given if children show independence, task competence, and physical prowess. Some compulsive caregiving children can be expected to facilitate their coping through maximising their academic performance. From this group it would be natural to expect recruitment to medical schools.

Ill children

Ill children with dismissing type A strategies are likely to be confused by changes in basic emotions associated with disease, and potentially misinterpret them or delay acknowledging them. They will potentially have discrepant views about these emotions compared to their parents. There is evidence of low correlation between parent and child views of somatic complaints. Children who have the most difficulty communicating their problems are more likely to have parents who underestimate their child's health problems (Meade, Lumley, Casey, 2001).

When they have a disease they are going to want their parents with them. They fear the rejection of not being noticed. Although the parents have not been able to help them modulate their stress, they are part of their familiar milieu. The predictability of their parents' responses is in itself reassuring, even if they are neglectful. They are more likely to view the hospital ward as benign if their parents are with them, but they will not reveal their desire for comfort through clinging to their parents to make sure they are there. Even if they attempt to get close to relative strangers on the ward, they are unlikely to try to use that contact to solve their emotional dilemmas.

They will be unlikely to attempt to negotiate alternatives with the ward staff, or through the intermediary of their parents. Parents might try to push through their view of what an appropriate solution might involve. Instead children will be likely to monitor their attachment figures' behaviour and affect in order to infer their plans, rather than communicating directly with them regarding these plans. They adjust their own behaviour, and minimise or exaggerate aspects of reality to increase the chance that their parent will respond as they wish. This should not be seen as a manipulative move, but a result of how their responses have been shaped through years of experience. This maximises the chance of getting some care. When using false positive affect, the apparently smiling face that is characterised by a toothy smiling mouth and non-smiling eyes, which evolves from and at the same time disguises their fears, staff may view them as really happy and coping well, just as Ainsworth did originally. Yet these same children can go so far as to simulate involvement of their attachment figures by carrying on a monologue directed rhetorically toward them, to soothing or giving care to their attachment figures to cheer them up, whilst the children's needs go unmet.

With their confusion of danger and safety the children with higher A strategies will not be able to tell when the comfort they experience is actually safe. They do not have the basis in experience to trust their feelings that the ward staff might not also be dangerous. If secure attachment is the outcome of successful containment, insecure attachment may be seen as the infant's identification with the caregiver's defensive behaviour. Proximity to the caregiver is maintained at the cost of a compromise to reflective function (Fonagy, Target, 1997).

Risk, danger and insecurity

When children are ill they respond to their various discomforts based on how their behaviour has been shaped through how they have been cared for with similar discomforts previously. The parent's responses will have been moulded through how they have evaluated the dangers inherent in that particular illness, and their repertoire of responses to children in distress. In this chapter we have been concerned with the attachment behaviour of infants and the strategies of children and adults, which develop when parents are predictable in their responses or lack of response to children in distress. The parents tend not to identify and respond to children's emotions as a salient part of their caring strategy. Some of these children will have been at risk through parental negligence (predictable lack of response in dangerous situations), others not.

Although the dismissing strategies of type A attachment have often been referred to as insecure strategies, not all people who develop dismissing strategies have grown up at risk. The A1 and A2 strategies are found in children who have parents who do not respond to the attachment appeal of their distress behaviour (Box 5.1), but they are not in danger; the parents respond to the risky situations their children get into. It is just that the children's signals of distress are not what release parental caring. The signs of emotional distress of their children are less salient for these parents.

When people develop dismissing strategies they will seldom have had parents who have bothered about accurately interpreting their emotions for them, or checking whether their interpretations fitted. They are likely to have a poor vocabulary for feelings. Their reading of their internal body cues will be a hazardous enterprise, and small manipulations in the context will likely be associated with misinterpretation of internal signals. This is because the external cues are the ones that have been most reliable, when trying to understand what is going on for them.

The usual risks to which developmental psychologists refer are those associated with not meeting children's needs for care and protection. These include situations in which children experience overwhelming emotion, which parents have not been able to help modulate. The children's discomfort remains unaltered. There is no soothing response, hug or lullaby. Children's cries signal their distress, and they have gone unanswered. When children cry they are not always in danger, but they have learnt that the situation they are now in reminds them of a previous time when they had difficulties. Perhaps they have met a doctor in a white coat, and the last time a doctor in a white coat gave them a sharp pain with their triple immunisation – alternatively the room might have the same smell. Parents have to decide whether they should ignore their child's crying because they have evaluated the current situation as safe, or whether they should respond because the child is in 'danger'. In this way parents can help their children not to overgeneralise from one setting to another.

We can only guess at the dangers to which Pamela had been exposed. Learning to handle danger involves getting to know about the contingencies of the situations when one is in danger. Where does it occur, what happens before and what are the consequences? What is the risk – how likely is the danger? People learn such information early in life before they learn more comprehensive conscious evaluations of their situation. Pamela's experience will have moulded her preconscious behaviour, so that she reacts spontaneously as a result of simple behavioural conditioning to signals of importance. She will also have learnt the contingencies determining when carers are likely to respond, or not respond. Eventually she will have learnt their response thresholds. Her developing brain will have been affected, and her stress response thresholds and setting of her HPA axis adapted. Specifically for those who inhibit the display of their anger, whilst at the same time they feel vulnerable (as found in those with dismissing attachment strategies), they hold their breath to some degree. This results in a resetting of the set point for pCO_2, which results in changes in arterial blood vessel thickness and blood pressure increases (these are associated with increased cardiovascular risk).

Health rituals and routines

Household routines are part of the taken-for-granted way of life in families. At the moment we can only hypothesise about the specific characteristics that household rituals will play to prevent the risk of disease in the life of families characterised by 'dismissing' strategies. The aspect to parenting, which leads children to develop a dismissing strategy, is that parents do not respond to their shows of distress. I hypothesise that we can expect these parents to emphasise general rules of hygiene, especially parents of the safe A strategies (A1–2). This does not mean that children will necessarily follow the same strategy. They will be likely to be interested in establishing routines, which one could expect to be implemented somewhat rigidly, independent of how people feel from day to day. They will be founded in custom, and followed somewhat pedantically. At the same time children gain comfort more from the circumstances they are in than the response of the people they are with. Routines increase the sense of control and predictability, and can help them feel better. Rituals symbolically identify a place as a safe place. There will be a sense of security associated with having health rituals, greater than being close to their VIPs.

The needs of children with higher A strategies are more often neglected when distressed. These households can either be characterised by a lack of routines and customs, or rigid unswerving imposition. I hypothesise that the routines can be over-elaborate verging on the compulsive, with floor washing daily, to the frankly compulsive with washing basins and taps, door handles and hands many times each day. In the case of either extreme practices or neglected routines, it is not to be expected that simple advice to either implement routines, or modify well-established routines, will be followed. These habits are part of practice stored in procedural memory, which is not immediately available for cognitive reflection. Asking people to change what they do, when they believe* their safety depends on it, threatens their view of what is necessary for survival. If people do not believe that change can possibly make any difference, they will not bother. First they would need to experience that what they could do made a difference to their own situation. This is less likely if they have learnt that, whatever they do, it makes no difference. Predictably, they have felt powerless when with parents. This can be understood from the dynamic described in Box 5.1.

Health professionals have not always considered what it is like for people who have rigid health rituals which they cannot continue when in hospital. If your health depends on having the window open at night, and the hospital windows are closed, how do you cope with that? What do you think of the knowledge of professionals who have not learnt the basics of good housekeeping, and their importance for making people better? I have previously described nursery school children who reject the health knowledge of doctors because they know that eating sugar is wrong, at the same time as doctors gave them sugar cubes with their polio immunisation.

There is often a heavy moral compunction to carry out health rituals, and people gain moral superiority when they abide by expectations. Times have changed from a single bath before Christmas, to the 'need' for a daily shower. People then feel morally superior. Health rituals are usually not open to introspection or change, especially amongst those who have developed dismissing strategies. The ways in which the strategies are induced and maintained often involve emotional arousal and potential threats, such that not carrying out the proscribed ritual reactivates the associated emotional memory. Use of severe punishment can lead to children withdrawing, or instead of 'flight or fight', freezing to the

---

* 'Believe' conveys a cognitive learning, whereas my intention here is learning which includes procedural learning; that is, preconscious learning according to behavioural learning principles.

spot. Health rituals are not more or less helpful in various circumstances, but obligatory. We see the same sort of dynamic in health practices in hospitals, with often rigorous adherence without reflection, and righteous imposition of sanctions for lack of fulfilment. As the majority of hospital routines have not been subjected to controlled trials, there remains lack of clarity about which circumstances demand which sorts of practice, so such disapproval is usually inappropriate. The important issue, as for parents with their children, is distinguishing when danger from not carrying out the rituals *is* present.

When children become ill, they can be subjected to a round of questions to find out whether the families' particular protective routines have been followed or not. Did you have your hat on when you went out? Did you wash your hands after you had been to the toilet? As a result the parent can attribute blame, and also be more insistent the next time the routine has to be followed, depending on the anxieties raised in the parent. For the development of dismissing strategies the allocation of blame is not of as such central importance as it is for the preoccupied type C strategies (covered in Chapter 6). The focus is on the moral obligation to carry out the order.

Additionally people using the odd-numbered A strategies, who do not take the blame for their predicament, will attribute causes of their condition to external factors, what is termed an 'external locus of control'. Attributing bad events to global causes, corresponding to an external locus of control, predicts mortality, especially accidental and violent deaths (Petersen, Seligman, Yurko, Martin, Friedman, 1998). We now need to explore the intervening variables that can account for this observation. I believe these should be looked for in the interpersonal self-protective strategies found amongst dismissing individuals.

Moral obligation, and emotional and disease responsiveness

The parents' experiences lead them to associate particular threats and anxieties with their children's symptoms. Parents of children who have developed dismissing strategies have not often laid much emphasis on identifying the children's emotions, or modified their caregiving in response to them. The children have grown up in a climate of strict obligations. One consequence will have been that the children's behaviour will have been shaped, so that the emotional aspect is not well developed. They will give unclear signals about their discomforts early in the course of their disease. They will be somewhat under-responsive and less flamboyant emotionally. In more extreme situations some will also be relatively insensitive and uncommunicative about pain, although this does not mean that their physiology shows no sign of arousal. This developmental sequence will make the parents' job more difficult, because the children, when ill, can appear to have few discomforts and so the parents may fail tentatively to identify their ambiguous symptoms. Eventually, though, their basic emotions will be overwhelmed by the change in their proto-self and their symptoms will 'break through', often rather late in the day in the eyes of those who are more in tune to people's emotions. This is a consequence of their developmental history, and clinicians need to respond sensitively, rather than reinforcing their patients' 'failings' through an emotional outburst. Such outbursts can be reminiscent of the response they have had throughout the years when they have failed to follow prescribed orders in the family.

The psychosocial classification of diseases (Box 1.2) can be used to look at the sorts of threat different diseases are likely to represent, and different sorts of challenge for those who do not have highly tuned skills for identifying changes in emotions. People with dismissing strategies are less likely to respond to subjective symptoms, compared to objective signs. This will mean that of the diseases characterised by 'attacks' (for example asthma, diabetes and epilepsy), those which have objective signs early in their course will be those which they tackle most effectively – whereas responding to those with early warning subjective experiences will present a greater challenge, unless trained to identify associated small objective signs. It will be easier to live with the uncertainty of epilepsy, compared to that of diabetes, which requires the patient to identify subjective experiences in order to abort a forthcoming hypoglycaemic attack. It will be easier to oversee the coughs associated with asthma as these can be ascribed to everyday illnesses of little significance. People with dismissing strategies will find it more of a challenge to develop self-monitoring strategies to cope with their disease. The emphasis on objective signs can lead to a focus on the body as object, a divorce of the body from its subjectivity. Instead of the body as experienced, responses are to the body as viewed by others. Those cultures that encompass the values of the dismissing strategies, the self-made, self-sufficient values of the USA and the public school culture in the UK, for example, can be expected to disproportionately emphasise people's bodies and appearances.

Poverty, depression and stress

Poverty makes good parenting more difficult. It is not the economic factors as such, but the constraints imposed on parental flexibility in responding to the needs of their children. In addition the dangers likely to be present in the local area where the family lives will be greater, and that includes the chances of getting disease or injury. Parents are more likely to be frustrated, and either more unpredictable or relatively unavailable for the children. These proximal risk factors[5] in reducing parental competence are associated with a greater chance of developing one of the less secure attachment strategies. Within each range of strategies for the A and C types, dismissing and preoccupied, the chance of one of the higher categories (A3–8 or C3–8) is expected to increase with increasing poverty and frequency of danger in the local environment. Onset of poverty is believed to increase the chance for a change in developmental trajectory with a change in attachment strategy. Poverty can affect both the form to the language of dis-ease and the chance of disease.

A shift towards strategies for living with greater insecurity is associated with a greater chance for less intimacy in marital relationships, and more strain on marriages. Lower marital satisfaction prior to the birth of a child predicts a greater chance of having a child with 'insecure' attachment (Wood, Klebba, Miller, 2000). A mother's emotional state during pregnancy may affect brain development of the foetus (Trevarthen, Aitken, 2001). We know that maternal anxiety leads to constriction of the uterine artery and hence the food supply to the foetus, potentially leading to a smaller baby (Teixeira, Fisk, Glover, 1999). After birth post-natal depression appears to have a direct effect on the development of neuro-transmitter systems in the infant's brain.

Poverty and depression are found together. Depression is the fourth most important determinant of the global burden of disease, and the largest determinant of disability. Depression has been suggested as being more likely amongst those with compulsive self-reliant A6 strategies (see p. 135) (Crittenden, 1999–2002). Depression increases the chance of affected parents being less available for their children or, alternatively, that their behaviour may become more unpredictable. The former is more likely associated with developing dismissing type A strategies in their children, whereas unpredictability is believed to lead to children developing preoccupied type C strategies.

The association between depression and disease may potentially account for gender differences in mortality and morbidity. Depression comprehensively affects how parents talk to their children (Trevarthen, Aitken, 2001), as well as to each other. Gender differences become particularly noticeable. Boys seem to be especially vulnerable, receiving more negative comments than girls, less maternal attention and, in infancy, being believed by depressed mothers to be less capable. These effects are durable, as five years later, in their sixth year, the boys' views of themselves as effective capable people, who could get things done, were still reduced. This *only* correlated with how they were spoken to in the first months of life (Murray, Cooper, 1997). But we must not forget that gender differences can also reflect family value systems and stereotypes, specific needs of the parent, and special characteristics of the children. These gender-determined risks or protections are not visible in group comparisons (Radke-Yarrow, 1998: 152).

Language use changes with increasing poverty. In the USA parents receiving welfare benefits for their children gave them twice as much discouragement, and five times less encouragement, compared to children of professionals (Hart, Risley, 1995). The real issue becomes the way in which this discouragement is mediated. The elements in the dismissing strategies (Boxes 5.1, 5.2) have not been specifically included in analyses of how poverty could increase the chances of particular kinds of poor parenting. Whatever the final consensus, the actual words being used by parents have profound effects on children, which they can come to retain throughout life. For example, gut tone can become conditioned to words associated with anxiety and anger (Blomhoff, Reinvang, Malt, 1998). This implicit learning according to behavioural learning principles is preconscious, and will be a component of the individual's illness behaviour of which they are unaware. Children and adults who complain of abdominal pain need to be investigated with this in mind.

When poverty leads to withdrawal and neglect of infants' needs, it may lead to reduced experience-expectant brain maturation. Severe deprivation could even lead to early onset pre-programmed cell death: apoptosis. Abuse would be more likely to affect subsequent experience-dependent processes. Both could therefore affect subsequent brain functioning (Glaser, 2000). I do not wish to be taken as suggesting that abuse and neglect are limited to conditions of poverty, but they are associated with conditions making competent parenting more difficult.

Poverty and danger often go hand in hand, so making a study of poverty and attachment strategies important. I will not cover the literature on poverty and illness. Rather, I will limit myself to placing poverty on the map in relation to attachment theory and how issues of learning to handle danger can arise in one's local arena, which facilitate developing strategies used later when meeting health professionals. Poverty and its effect on parenting may turn out to be an important element in understanding gender differences. Similar processes contribute to the greater chance of developing antisocial behaviour in areas of poverty (Rutter, 1999).

Early experiences exert long-term effects stemming from their influences in both making negative experiences more likely to occur later and through rendering individuals more vulnerable to such experiences (Rutter, 1999). Although poverty may increase the strain on a family, and specifically their parenting, I will consider stress independent of poverty. Poverty is a predicament, which to a degree has to be lived with, whereas stressful events have to be handled. Stress has to be considered in relation to the parent's coping resources, and how they can be overwhelmed by particular demands on them. Their ability to cope will also depend on their access to their memory systems in an integrated way, so that they can make use of all they know. Greatest access comes to those with the balanced B strategies, but they will nevertheless not be resilient in all situations. Those with strategies for handling less secure relationships will reach their limits in different ways and at different times in superficially similarly demanding situations.

Life stress and negative family events are associated with poor health in children (Meade, Lumley, Casey, 2001). They correlate positively with symptom complaints among children and predict the continuation of unexplained abdominal pain (Walker, Garber, Greene, 1994). This association between family stressors and children's somatic complaints can be moderated by the quality of the children's relationships outside the family. Such influences can lead to change in the strategies which children adopt, although in other circumstances life experience can be just as important for encouraging children to go on using the interpersonal strategies they already use. Stress may just as likely enhance or accentuate pre-existing psychological characteristics as make them different. It is important to remember that influences in children's environments tend to make children within the same family different, rather than similar. Brown and Harris have emphasised that stressful events have to be evaluated knowing the individual's current and past circumstances (Brown, Harris, 1989). It may be more important whether a particular child is scapegoated in the family or treated disparagingly in relation to his sibling, rather than that the home as a whole is a quarrelsome one. The crucial issue as regards attachment is not whether parents are stressed, poor or depressed, but how their way of coping with particular stressors alters how they meet their children's needs for support. The parental strategy can be a risk factor for the child – if parents cope by withdrawing from their dependent children, they are putting them at risk. It is even more demanding if the whole family is stressed, so that all attachment behaviour systems are activated at the same time, compared to just a child or one parent.

The dismissing cognitive illness dialogue

Dismissing type A strategists are used to monologues, and may well elicit a monologue from their doctor – the tendency to engage in relationships with the same form as one is used to is associated both with satisfaction at its predictability and frustration that it could not be different. The dismissing style is largely incompatible with collaborative working relationships, and such individuals visit health professionals less often (Feeney, Ryan, 1994). Affect regulating problems are, in part, a consequence of parental disapproval of the expression of affect, and failure to teach them words to label emotions and other inner states (Cicchetti, Ganiban, Barnett, 1991). Children learn to soothe themselves through autosensual activity, such as self-rocking, excessive thumb sucking, hair twirling, and masturbation. When they become emotional their faces are less expressive (McLeod, Hoehn-Saric, Stefon, 1986). We should expect the same with systemic diseases, with the exception being where particular signs of disease empower close attention (I am not here suggesting strategic use of illness behaviour which is presented in the next chapter). In contrast, patients who report higher levels of emotional distress at the time of diagnosis and treatment have lower rates of recurrence and death (Bakal, 1999: 172). This constellation is confusing for the unsophisticated. Their communication strategies do not just make communication with others about their dis-ease more challenging, they also affect the outcome of the treatment they receive, they make poor use of the treatment offered and reject those who provide treatment. It is more complicated to have a productive dialogue.

For patients with diabetes this can result in worse treatment (Dozier, 1990), their taking of medication to lower their blood sugar is poorer and they are ineffective in monitoring their blood glucose (Ciechanowski, Katon, Russo, Walker, 2001). Detailed medical knowledge does not preclude a poor response to your own symptoms, as vividly illustrated by Tsjekov's denial of his symptoms of tuberculosis, and the survey of renowned cardiac specialists who had had heart attacks which showed that they waited for up to 48 hours before acknowledging their condition (Julian, 1996). Self-deception can be evolutionarily adaptive (Trivers, 2000).

The most demanding personal challenge is provided by diffuse, ambiguous, irregular and unpredictable physical sensations (Cioffi, 1991). These are best met by sensory monitoring strategies, which are those least available to individuals with dismissing strategies. These are the sorts of sensation found with stress, and when stress needs to be discriminated from other 'under the weather' states. Dismissing individuals find it particularly difficult to identify states of arousal, and may well say they are feeling calm, whilst they show biological signs of arousal (see also Kagan [1994: 143]). They have problems identifying levels of muscle tension, and what they report of tension level is not highly related to actual measurements of muscle activity. This difficulty contrasts with others who describe themselves as anxious, without there being any corresponding indicators in their heart rate, blood pressure or levels of catecholamines (those amines, such as noradrenaline, released into the blood when geared up for fight or flight). It is hypothesised that they will have preoccupied type C strategies, covered in Chapter 6.

Ambiguous states, such as half-illness states with unclear symptoms, can provide a solution of sorts for some people who have developed dismissing type A strategies. Katon and colleagues have proposed that for some children who do not have their emotional signals responded to there remains a window of opportunity whereby they receive more close-ness and understanding for their somatic complaints (Katon, Kleinman, Rosen, 1982). Discomforts, which can be attributed to somatic causes, are then acknowledged by parents and become especially salient in the absence of parental responses to other signs of dis-ease. Ambiguity is resolved in favour of an attribution of a physical illness, even if the cause was to be found in a stressful event. This can then form a basis for understanding somatisation, which I further elaborate in Chapter 7. The even numbered As, who attribute their condition to their own 'failings', will be more disposed to somatisation.

Disease and illness susceptibility

People may develop few close social ties and avoiding coping strategies, or a sensitivity to rejection as a consequence of the dismissing type A strategies. These characteristics are associated with a greater susceptibility to disease, and duration of illness. The definitive studies in relation to defined attachment classifications have not yet been done. A few suggestive studies relating to viral infections, such as the common cold, and cancer illustrate some of the research going on. I then discuss cardiovascular complaints and asthma specifically.

Stress is associated with increased occurrence of upper respiratory infections in children. If people lack social support, even low levels of life events are associated with infections. Children who cope by avoidance suffer more following frequent daily hassles. Colds come about three weeks later. Only psychological coping, such as using problem-solving and cognitive restructuring, reduced the duration of the illness episodes. High avoiders had longer episodes of illness than low avoiders (Turner Cobb, Steptoe, 1998). Susceptibility to colds decreases in a dose-response manner with increased diversity of the social network. Being introverted increased the susceptibility (Cohen, Doyle, Skoner, Rabin, Gwaltney, 1997). It may turn out that some of these introverted vulnerable children also use preoccupied type C strategies.

The key dilemma for someone who has developed dismissing strategies is coping with potential rejection. Either their attachment signals have been rejected (A1–2), or they have been rejected as individuals (A3–8). Cole, Kemeny and Taylor showed that people with HIV, who scored high on a rejection sensitivity questionnaire,[6] had definite signs of more rapid disease progression (Cole, Kemeny, Taylor, 1997). Although this can relate to type A strategies, it is also coherent with preoccupied type C strategies, if they should use complaining about being rejected in a strategic way, in order to play on another person's guilt to get them to respond as desired. More research addressing this issue is required.

It is easy to recognise characteristics of the dismissing strategies from both the compulsive caregiving and compliant categories in Temoshok's description of the 'type C coping style' of 'rationality-antiemotionality', believed to be associated with predisposition to cancer:

> being 'nice,' stoic or self-sacrificing, co-operative and appeasing, unassertive, patient, compliant with external authorities, and inexpressive of negative emotions, particularly anger.
>
> (Temoshok, 1990: 209)

Avoidance was found to be a predictor of cancer progression in young adult men and women, in addition to their intrusive thoughts and psychological symptoms (Epping-Jordan, Compas, Howell, 1994). A group of women with breast cancer were found to be significantly higher on type A attachment strategies (Tacón, Caldera, Bell, 2001). Graves and Thomas found a proneness to cancer in a prospective study associated with a pattern of relatedness in which emotions are controlled and rather restricted. This could also be associated with dismissing type A strategies (Graves, Thomas, 1981). The same study came up with the finding that closeness to parents was associated with cancer proneness. It is difficult to reconcile this with their degree of apparent emotional stunting, but it could be interpreted as the avoidance of criticism or exoneration of parents found amongst the lower dismissing type As. It is uncertain whether this is warranted.[7] There appear to be similarities to another attempt at identifying a cancer-prone personality type (Grossarth-Maticek, Eysenck, 1990; Eysenck, 1991). Grossarth-Maticek and Eysenck, describe a 'type one' where individuals tend to suppress emotion, are highly dependent on a person, goal, or situation that is inaccessible to them, and react to losses with helplessness and hopelessness. I do not wish to be taken as ascribing to all Eysenck's work in this area, which has been ably criticised (see, for example, Pelosi, Appleby [1993]).

We are not bound to continue with our attachment strategies even though neurobiological research suggests a degree of embodiment and continuity. It is therefore of interest whether there is any research suggesting that change in attachment strategy might improve outcome. O'Regan and Hirshberg summarised the literature dealing with 1,386 cases of spontaneous remission of various forms of cancer (O'Regan, Hirshberg, 1993). The patients described a qualitative shift in the way they perceived themselves and their bodies, and in the way they lived life. They reported abandoning an extremely self-sacrificing lifestyle in favour of a self-soothing lifestyle in which they took care of themselves rather than others. Their adjustments generally included a change in core belief and value systems. The significant common denominator in cases of spontaneous remission is the extent to which individuals are able to make a complete break with their previous ways of thinking, behaving, and living (Lerner, 1994). It is possible that this is the sort of experience associated with a change in attachment strategy. Nevertheless, believing oneself to be self-sacrificing could also apply to some of the preoccupied Cs. There is no one-to-one correspondence between behaviour and classification, as behaviour is used strategically.

Cardiovascular illness

Understanding the dismissing type A strategies can help us make sense of some of the apparently paradoxical findings concerning heart complaints. Although it is customary to write about cardiovascular disease rather than illness, I will distinguish between experience of cardiac symptoms and underlying pathology. Acute clinical practice responds to patients referred because of their symptoms, their subjective illness; prevention hopes to identify non-symptomatic vulnerable people who can be expected to develop cardiovascular disease. Why is it that people differ so much as to their complaining of ischaemic heart pain? Some people appear to have few indicators of ischaemia, but a lot of chest pain; others endure long periods of ischaemia before complaining – and then of fatigue rather than chest pain (Freedland, Carney, Krone, Smith, Rich, Eisenkramer, Fischer, 1991). Patients with severe blockages of blood vessels to the heart often seem to avoid seeking medical attention until the disease progresses even further, whilst, conversely, individuals with little or no blockage often present early in the process. The greater the blockage, the lower the number of symptoms reported (Frasure-Smith, 1987). Even world-renowned cardiologists delayed seeking help for up to 48 hours after heart attacks (Julian, 1996).

Subjects with silent ischaemia had a greater tendency to minimise their bodily symptoms and a higher degree of anger control than the symptomatic subjects (Torosian, Lumley, Pickard, Ketterer, 1997). This would be coherent with some of the dismissing type A strategies.

This combination of not telling others about symptoms can be because the symptoms were insignificant, or because they did not believe that telling others about them was going to be useful. Saying that a symptom was insignificant needs elaborating. Insignificant for 'what' – a signal to yourself that action is needed, or that discomfort can come to really bother you? Each of these has at some stage in development involved the assistance of other people. The dismissing strategy leads to the evolution of a dismissing attitude to bodily signals; they have not led to significant changes in interpersonal relationships throughout development. The individual's behaviour has been shaped so that their procedural memory is coherent with an interpersonal strategy that emphasises self-reliance. Through lack of symptom amplification through emotional contagion, the degree of discomfort will not be increased; and, using self-reliant strategies to modulate their own discomfort, the degree of felt discomfort is kept low. The high degree of anger control found in the low 'A' categories, where conflict is avoided, might be another aspect of an association between dismissing attachment strategies and cardiovascular disease, with minimal subjective feelings of cardiovascular illness. I would then expect the main difficulty of primary prevention campaigns to reduce the mortality of cardiovascular disease, through identifying such silent patients, to be to facilitate them participating actively in any preventive programme. The dismissing strategy is found in those who tend not to share their discomforts, minimise them, expect to manage alone and, if things start to go wrong tend to blame themselves for it. Even then they find it difficult to turn to another to help them. They are not the ideal target group for any initiative; although once they have decided to take action about something I would expect them doggedly to carry it through, as they take responsibility for themselves. Prevention must begin even earlier.

We know about several of the risk factors for cardiovascular disease. I hypothesise that several of them can be related to dismissing type A attachment strategies. Hypertensive patients have a high prevalence of alexithymia, which means that they have not developed a practice of sharing their distress with others, and appear not to have a well-developed psychological vocabulary for sharing their discomforts. This we would expect to result from the dismissing strategy, and it will be discussed further in Chapter 7 when discussing ambiguous somatic symptoms. When patients with high blood pressure attempt to recognise whether their blood pressure is high or low from their daily symptoms, they use symptoms such as headaches and a flushed face which co-vary more reliably with emotions and moods than blood pressure, to decide whether they should adjust their medication (Baumann, Leventhal, 1985). Their ability to recognise emotions, so that they could use the feelings of specific emotions to monitor their condition, appears jeopardised. This is to be expected for individuals with dismissing type A strategies. They then struggle to make use of their relatively undifferentiated, and for them originally 'meaningless' and confusing internal signals – their interoceptive confusion. These have been of little salience for individuals using dismissing strategies throughout their life.

Another suggestive study, potentially linking dismissing strategies and raised blood pressure, showed that how men and women handled anger affected their breathing patterns in different ways (Anderson, Chesney, Scuteri, 2000). Their resulting carbon dioxide levels affected respectively their diastolic and systolic blood pressures. The way we breathe can contribute to long-term challenges for blood pressure regulation. Because several of the dismissing strategies depend on handling anger by redirecting it away from caregivers and people in authority, it is to be expected that a link will be found between dismissing strategies and high BP.

Low birth weight predicts cardiovascular disease, diabetes and high blood pressure in about 30 per cent of cases. These diseases are only found in about 6 per cent of those with normal birth weight. Disease develops primarily in those who become obese in adulthood (BMI >27). This suggests that identification of the factors which lead to members of this group getting fat is important. It may be their strategy for coping with their threefold increase in risk for depression, which is also associated with a low birth weight – such as self-soothing eating. Alternatively it can be related to co-occurrence of depression and particular attachment strategies. Parental strategies for protecting low birth weight infants can determine a developmental pathway, and special structural coupling.

Low weight *gain* in infancy is associated with increased risk of cardiovascular disease – regardless of size at birth (Eriksson, Forsén, Tuomilehto, Osmond, Barker, 2001). Although much work has been directed at biological parameters, a severe degree of neglect can also lead to growth stunting in infancy. Neglect, as opposed to abuse, would be more likely to be associated with dismissing strategies. We do not yet know whether the hypothesised resetting of the HPA axis associated with foetal malnutrition and low birth weight can similarly occur during a period of low weight gain in infancy.

There is no doubting that low birth weight and low weight gain predispose to several physiological changes which can account for the occurrence of these diseases; the chase needs to be to find the salutogenic factors (the health-bringing factors) which prevent the diseases developing. I would like to suggest that those who develop balanced attachment strategies are more likely to avoid the complications of low birth weight, and that facilitating this could then be a prime preventive focus directed at early mother–child interactions amongst those with low birth weights. Low weight gain should be a warning signal at a well-baby clinic for the need for closer observations of infant attachment behaviour and maternal mental health.

The most consistently shown biological abnormality in major depression is increased activation of the HPA axis (Dinan, 1999). We have noted that depression is both associated with low birth weight and also with particular dismissing strategies. It is highly predictive of mortality. Among 237 healthy men recruited at college entry and assessed at the age of 70, 45 per cent of those who had suffered a depressive episode were dead at follow-up, compared with only 5 per cent of those in good psychological health. The differences in longevity could not be explained in terms of cigarette smoking, diet, or alcohol intake (Vaillant, 1998). In a similar 35-year study of 1,198 male university entrants Ford and colleagues found that major depression increased the risk of coronary artery disease, with a mean lag phase of ten years between the report of depression and the first report of cardiovascular disease (Ford, Mead, Chang, Levine, Klag, 1994). Depression and cardiovascular disease are each often deadly, and the combination is lethal. Hopelessness,[8] usually part of a formulation of the processes characterising depression, appears to accelerate cardiovascular disease (as seen in carotid atherosclerosis, the thickening of the carotid arteries) and increases mortality (Everson,

Kaplan, Goldberg, Salonen, Jukka, 1997). Depression is particularly associated with central obesity, which in humans is also associated with low birth weight. Central obesity can also be a result of social processes. In primates it is found in those low down in the social hierarchy (Shively, 2001). Identifying the common factors affecting biological and social processes leading to cardiovascular illness is a challenge. I suggest that there might be a common mediating factor in their dismissing type A attachment strategies, with development of balanced strategies being the most important salutogenic factor.

Asthma

Asthma, a disease on the increase in the industrialised world, is associated with much morbidity, as well as mortality, with which health services are striving to find helpful approaches. All diseases need to be considered for the role attachment strategies play in their presentation and course, and so affect the maintaining factors. We have only suggestive evidence that 'classical' psychosomatic illnesses, such as asthma, have associations with attachment strategies.

Pamela's parents are not hearing of her early asthma symptoms. To emphasise with repetition, Pamela with a dismissing type A strategy will be more reticent, and find it difficult to be specific about her discomfort. She will be likely to provide more details after a crisis has passed. She will not be used to a dialogue with powerful others, parents or doctors, instead being on the receiving end of a monologue in which she has played an unwitting role. She will not find it easy to negotiate, potentially being as stubborn as others might have been with her. Being uncertain whether she can rely on the comfort received, she will continue to be on her guard in case the situation is potentially deceptive (this is especially so for the higher As). Taken together these contribute to dismissing strategists being late to both identify and present their discomforts. They may be well into an asthma attack, and so it may be difficult to help them get control of the situation. An understanding of attachment suggests we can learn about the course of the disease and the illness experiences. Potential causal influences related to attachment need to be understood in the light of the biological factors presented in Chapter 2, and how attachment strategies are embodied.

One-third of young people with asthma are not identified, and, of these, two-thirds do not report their symptoms to a doctor. Lack of diagnosis is more common when there are serious family problems. A cough is the most common symptom amongst those with undiagnosed asthma, so that the prime symptom is easily overlooked as part of everyday life, especially as these undiagnosed asthmatics are often passive smokers (Sierstad, Boldsen, Hansen, Mostgaard, Hyldebrandt, 1998). The cough will be normalised and of no significance to both parents and doctors. Asthma is a disease which requires vigilance, first by parents of their children and, subsequently, by the patient (see the psychosocial classi- fication of disease – Box 1.2). The dismissing strategy is just one way of coping through maximising self-protection. An understanding of this strategy helps account for these findings.

Asthma treatment requires regular use of prophylactic medicines, usually inhalers, to be taken daily. With exacerbations it is important to take additional action as soon as possible to prevent a full-blown attack. Nevertheless, 75 per cent of those with mild asthma and 65 per cent of those with moderately severe asthma, who were eligible for treatment, were reluctant to visit their general practitioner or to comply with follow- up in a Dutch study (Thoonen, van Weel, 2000). The European Community Respiratory Health Survey (Cerveri, Locatelli, Zoia, Corsico, Accordini, de Marco, 1999) found that compliance was poor worldwide, being poorest in the USA at 40 per cent, and, even under exacerbations of the asthma, patients were only taking the medicine prescribed in 72 per cent of cases. The total cost of incomplete treatment adherence for all diseases in the US healthcare system was estimated to be $100 billion/year in 1993 (Shaw, 2001). It does not appear as if this group comes from the 'compulsively compliant' A4 subgroup!

The dismissing strategy is associated with interoceptive confusion, difficulties discriminating between different sorts of discomfort. This is a characteristic of those with asthma. Many asthmatic individuals fail to recognise both the presence of anxiety within themselves and early changes in airflow obstruction (Yellowlees, Kalucy, 1990). Overlap between anxiety and asthma creates a problem both for patients and their doctors since neither seems to be very good at telling the difference (Keeley, Osman, 2001). A group of physicians tended to interpret the personality characteristics of patients as reflecting illness severity, and confused psychological and physiological distress.

Asthma symptom 'minimisers', minimising their shortness of breath when they have significant airway resistance, present themselves as being in control of their feelings, efficient, and highly ethical in manner. They may have similar characteristics to those who minimised their cardiac ischaemia. These characteristics could correspond to a subgroup of the As.

Nevertheless, there is another group of patients who may be over- reacting to perceived airway resistance (Bakal, 1999: 79). It may be that asthma patients are a homogeneous group as regards their attachment strategies, with this latter group having type C strategies, described in the following chapter. This is supported by unpublished findings of Crittenden (personal communication). This would be expected if the condition arose on the basis of a heavy genetic component, but in living with the predicament of a susceptibility to asthma the symptoms were incorporated into each family's developing attachment strategies. The maintaining factors would be best addressed by identifying the attachment processes, although vulnerability factors and initial precipitating factors could be independent.

Stress is important for the prognosis of asthma. High levels of stress predict higher morbidity in children, and under some conditions the onset of asthma. It makes it especially important that they have effective coping strategies, and this would be expected to be associated with balanced use of affective and cognitive strategies which they can choose between, depending on circumstances. As we know that excessive parental anxiety, poor coping and lack of childcare skills predict the onset of asthma by the age of three years in children genetically at risk (Sandberg, Paton, Ahola, McCann, McGuiness, Hillary, Oja, 2000), it is unlikely that these vulnerable children have balanced strategies. High levels of parental criticism of their children increase the severity of asthma (Fiese, Wamboldt, 2000). Gustafsson and colleagues have shown that early onset asthma and atopic diseases, such as eczema, have a four times greater chance to disappear by the time the child is three years old if the family is functioning well, and they have a good social network (Gustafsson, Kjellman, Björkstén, 2002). Happiness appears to effect autonomic patterns that would tend to relieve airway constriction (Miller, Wood, 1997). Sadness evokes patterns of autonomic nervous system influence on the airways consistent with cholinergically mediated airway constriction. Feelings of hopelessness can do the same.

It is difficult for patients with asthma to follow standard treatment regimes. This may be related to their developmental experience, stress and/or sadness. Unfortunately the call for a more patient-centred, patient-negotiated plan, as the cornerstone for asthma care in the community (Jones, Pill, Adams, 2000), is unlikely to be successful if a significant proportion of patients have characteristics of the dismissing strategies.

Alternative treatment approaches need to be explored. Fiese and Wamboldt recommend and provide supportive evidence for the creation of regular family routines, which can serve to assimilate asthma management into the stream of everyday activities. They specifically view family management as the conscious use of strategies, which, to be effective, need to be sensitive to developmental changes in the family, involve multiple family members, and be deliberately planned (Fiese, Wamboldt, 2000). They work directly with processes that may turn out to be central for modifying attachment strategies. Families that created predictable routines had children who performed better in school; those who developed a ritualised household became more socially competent. Some families were developing routines for the first time and felt an enormous sense of accomplishment. Such approaches, which empower patients and their families, avoid scapegoating parents. Parents had been seen as one of the causes of the children's problems, following research which showed that removing *parents* from the home where children were allergic to dust mites led to the children having fewer asthma attacks (Knapp, 1969). This research had made it clear that interpersonal processes were of major importance for the course of the disease. But it proved contentious to retain a focus on the interpersonal dimension, when the genetic and biological aspects were clearly so prominent. I would suggest that the understanding provided by attachment theory, both the dynamic-maturational model and the 'psychobiological theory of attachment' (Kraemer, 1997), enables us to look again at the place particular interpersonal processes have in the course of asthma in a more compassionate way.

In order to address the role which stress has played in the past lives of these patients yet other approaches need to be employed. There is now some evidence that a simple task, such as writing about the most stressful thing that has happened to you, can lead to marked reduction in clinical problems in people with asthma (Smyth, Stane, Hurewitz, Kaell, 1999). Writing about negative experiences has a beneficial effect on immune function (Pennebaker, Kiecolt-Glaser, Glaser, 1988). The task may also prove useful when given to the parents of patients with asthma, as those who have histories of trauma and post-traumatic stress disorder (PTSD) have children who are less likely to adhere to their treatment (Shaw, 2001). Writing, rather than head-on interpersonal discussion, is likely to suit the dismissing type A characteristics (Box 5.1).[9] Health diaries (Stensland, Malterud, 1999) can fulfil a similar communication purpose.

In addition help is needed to aid recognition of the early symptoms of airway constriction. Newly diagnosed patients with diabetes are taught the symptoms of low blood sugar through inducing a hypoglycaemic attack with extra insulin. In the same way it is essential that this patient group, who more often seem to have problems identifying early symptoms, can experience such symptoms in the secure confines of a clinic. Those who have tried this have found it can be dangerous, and the ideal approach needs to be found.

Approaches to facilitate co-operation are the key to bridging the gap between the efficacy and effectiveness of asthma care (Thoonen, van Weel, 2000), and it is essential to understand the dismissing type A strategies in order to do this.

Some provisional implications for clinical practice and health promotion: compliance and collaboration

Patients with dismissing type A strategies are difficult to engage in treatment and care for. They suffer stoically. They seem to lack trust that they can be understood on the basis of their own needs. They have been used to others defining their needs, admitting to their knowledge being omnipotent. When coming to a doctor's surgery they will less often have taken the initiative to come but rather have been sent. They will probably be 'visitors', rather than 'customers' or 'clients' interested in shopping for something to help them. Recognising this dilemma can help the clinician approach the challenge as being to help the shy visitor become interested in what is on offer. This is in itself likely to be a problem, as the visiting patient does not know what they really want, just that something is 'up'. The standard reply from such patients to the enquiry about 'what is the matter' is likely to frustrate the clinician, as they may well say 'they do not know'. This is a very honest reply to a question, which for them can be exceedingly difficult given their interoceptive confusion.

Patients with dismissing type A strategies will more often have been exposed to the power tactics of their parents, paternalism and prejudicial 'maternalism', over-intrusive caregiving from the parent's perspective (not limited to mothers, just as paternalism is not limited to fathers), a power tactic disguised as 'sensitive' caring. It is important to avoid the processes associated with establishing the original patterns of communication in the clinical interview. They can, though, be mobilised below the clinician's level of awareness through a form of structural coupling. If health workers have chosen their vocation because of a fit of compulsive caregiving strategies to the demands of the job, their structural coupling to such patients can produce a tight fit, from which they will find it hard to extricate themselves. Some nurses can impose their 'ideal' care, supported by what they have been taught as good practice, with a moral righteousness, which provokes such patients into retreat unless a degree of compulsive compliance leads to their acquiescence. Old-fashioned general practitioners who always knew 'best', imposed advice under the guise of benign paternalism. They participated in a pattern of interaction, which was too similar to that experienced developmentally by this patient group to help them develop new ways of coping. They played on the patients' tendencies to compliance.

It is not easy to develop practices that facilitate reflective function and collaboration. This is necessary for enabling them to ask critical questions about their past and evaluate those who have been closest to them, and the part they have played themselves. This includes a critical appraisal of their health care, and the power tactics of doctors and intrusive nursing care. Through facilitating choice, empowerment grows. The goal is not to make the patient do something, but to provide information and help them to become aware of the causes, consequences and cures of their problems or concerns.

This may be helped through enabling them to learn for themselves through homework exercises between appointments. This would be coherent with an underlying wish to be able to manage on their own. The explanations, which are seen as helpful and satisfying, are those perceived by patients as tangible, exculpating, and involving. These explanations are empowering (Salmon, Peters, Stanley, 1999). This work starts from the reality of patients' symptoms as they experience their illness, however distorted this may seem to others. The explanations will also need to include the patients' theories of what can bring about change, although it will probably be very difficult for these patients to articulate it. Biofeedback may prove to be particularly useful for patients using these dismissing type A strategies, as it provides very concrete feedback, independently of an expert's interpretation (easily experienced as being the wrong sort of interpretation if they have experienced intrusive parenting).

Poor adherence to treatment can be seen as a challenge to health professionals' authority and expertise, seen from patients' positions as power tactics. This is similar to the confrontations adolescents' parents might get engaged in. It is likely to be more productive to avoid attempts at compliance, and conceptualise patient oppositionality as behaviour, which, paradoxically, can elicit care through expressing dependency (Shaw, 2001). Oppositionality in adolescence can be a step towards greater parental involvement. How would the adolescent know, though, that the parents were available with a different sort of care to that which had been provided previously – and, by analogy (or, in the framework of attachment theory, application of their 'working model of relationships' in relation to someone else), that which the health professionals could provide? In one study only 32 per cent of adolescents had thought of discussing their problems with their parents (compared to 64 per cent of a non-clinical control group), and even smaller proportions considered seeking assistance from institutions and professional helpers (17 per cent and 9 per cent respectively) (Seiffge-Krenke, 1993).

Anorexia nervosa is perhaps the ultimate challenge to parents' and health professionals' omnipotence – they rapidly feel helpless. Forty years ago Bruch described the difficulties these patients had in knowing what they felt, as being due to their mothers always 'knowing' how they felt (Bruch, 1962). Although this does not cover all patients with anorexia it is essential that experts develop the expertise required to know when not to know, but to have some ideas. Hospital routines to force more compliance can end in disaster. That means knowing about and recognising the dismissing type A strategies.

The past is fixed, but its meaning is rewritten every time it is recalled. Maturation is the means, and mental integration the process, through which future functioning can be expanded to field a nearly infinite range of human possibility. The dismissing type A strategists have poorer access to their episodic memory. Through enabling them to question what they have been told, and make use of what they have experienced (not what they have been told they have experienced), their mental integration will be aided. But health promotion strategies must not expect people with such experience to rely on the information they are given about their vulnerabilities for diseases. They have been misled too often in the past through information that was not coherent with what they had experienced.

The real challenge for health promotion is to succeed in inviting individuals who aim for self-reliance into a partnership for health. These individuals are vulnerable to disease, experience little illness, and can be expected to die younger. They comprise the populations that earmarked limited initiatives need to engage with, and yet they are to be expected to be the last ones to be tempted into such a partnership.[10] The seeds of such a style are embedded in their life and cultural history. There is a difficult question to answer about whether it is to the individual's advantage or society's to make them aware of the costs of their strategy, which has otherwise served them reasonably well. Helping someone to be aware of the strategies they employ can give them choices to do things otherwise, but we do not have a right to demand that they do so. The tortoise has to decide when to stick its neck out, but it cannot take a step forward without doing so. Its need for safety is balanced by its need to move on.

> Stop it at the start; it's late for medicine to be prepared when disease has grown strong through long delays.
>
> Ovid, *Remedia Amoris*

Notes

1 Even if the advice from the doctor is not given as a command, it is likely to be experienced as such by someone who has repeatedly experienced a communicative style based on an adult's perspective, where additionally the adult, if in doubt, uses the perspective of powerful others to decide what should be done.

2 The sexualised contact of the compulsively promiscuous A5 strategy corresponds closely to the mental condition previously diagnosed as 'moral insanity', alternatively as a patronising term for precocious sexual awareness.

3 Grice's maxims are not met.

4 Scarr and McCartney (1993) suggest a model whereby an intelligent parent has a child that is receptive for intellectually valuable information; that is, a child that is mentally advanced. This parent also plays in an intellectually stimulating way, and the child's responsiveness for this kind of information reinforces the parent for the effort. It seems to be rewarding for both partners to use their cognitive abilities. But this does not relate to any particular attachment dimension.

5 Proximal risk refers to the first of Tinbergen's questions: Why now?

6 This research field is very difficult to interpret. Sometimes written questionnaire studies give more valid results than interview studies because the impersonal situation enables those who are not used to sharing intimate details in interpersonal relationships to do this. It may therefore be the case that the sensitivity to rejection questionnaire is especially suited to identifying the sort of rejection complaints experienced by those with dismissing type A strategies.

7 Preoccupied strategies may also predispose to cancer. In the Johns Hopkins prospective study of medical students there was a group of students characterised by an ambivalent style of relating, with emotional lability, who were also cancer prone (Graves, Thomas, 1981), and these might have had the characteristics described in Chapter 6.

8 The hopelessness of depression is not used as in the manipulative play on helplessness found with the preoccupied type C attachment strategies to be described in the next chapter. Superficially the hopelessness of the powerless depressed person can seem similar to the functional use of an exaggerated display of hopelessness. It is a similar display, but the interpersonal strategic function is different.

9 See note 6.

10 For example, the sexual behaviour of those with compulsively promiscuous A6 strategies is the vulnerable node in the network of contact tracing at sexual diseases clinics. They are not just at risk themselves, but are the key sources to contact in order to contain outbreaks. Health education programmes should identify and target such well-connected people.

Chapter 6

'My pain is really terrible. What are you going to do about it?'

The 'preoccupied' type C attachment strategies, and other classifications

> We all know the truth: the difference is how we distort it.
>
> Woody Allen

As Pamela reached adolescence she struggled with bullying at school. She was still bothered by her tummy aches. Her asthma attacks increased in frequency, and several times left her breathless in the school playground. She was only left alone when acutely short of breath. She appeared to play on her asthma when the demands on her increased, and would inadvertently cut out prophylactic use of her inhaler. She was otherwise coy and demurring. She became preoccupied with worries about whether she might get a cold, which might trigger her asthma. From time to time she surprised her friends and family by erupting at them, just when they thought they were getting on well, and quite in contrast to her placid temperament of childhood. Her parents were getting quite confused.

In her adolescence Pamela changed tack. She was no longer quiet and compliant. Puberty is a time of changed motivations and potential turmoil. The males and females in Pamela's network of friends have changed, preoccupied with other interests. Sexuality and power issues drive the adolescent group. Power struggles in the family and at school are now expressed in alternative ways. Their emotions are raw and near the surface; issues of keeping face demand a different kind of face work to that used in childhood. In such a context, behavioural patterns, which have been picked out, become used in the service of all for new strategic purposes, given the preoccupations of adolescence. Adolescence is one of the times to expect change in attachment strategy (Crittenden, 2001). Strategies are thought to be automatically employed, brought into play from procedural memory, and need not be in any way conscious for the individual (Main, 1990). Eventual attribution of malingering to Pamela's strategic use of her asthma is missing the central point about how strategies come to be embodied in procedural memory, learnt according to behavioural learning principles, and preconscious.

Pamela has adapted fast. She has accidentally discovered that her asthma attacks can also be functionally adaptive, helping to abort the bullying at school. This is not something that she set out to manage in that way; it is procedural learning at a preconscious level. Her parents have got much more worried about her because of the attacks. Taking a *laissez-faire* attitude to her prophylactic medication has resulted in an increased chance of getting attacks of asthma. She experiments with her aggression; her anger has been under wraps throughout childhood, her aggression first being brought into service in her adolescence. She is trying to establish another form of relative independence from her parents. In a way it felt to her parents as if she was punishing them by getting them worried. She found that her symptoms had power, both productive and unproductive. But these deviously assertive moves did not reflect any diminished fear for what might happen. She became preoccupied with whether her attacks might get out of control, but she does not tell anyone about her fears. She was still concerned that the adults might get angry with her, a relic of her dismissing type A strategy of childhood. With her developing sexuality and the models available to her in the media, she found that coy behaviour worked wonders at reducing the chance of open conflict. Her attachment strategy moved from dismissing type A towards a preoccupied type C – and could later end up as an earned B/BO (B other). Both A and C strategies had been functionally adaptive (Hinde, Stevenson-Hinde, 1990), given her situations in childhood and adolescence – and both had costs.

The third major attachment strategy is the preoccupied type C classification. This chapter will also cover other current classifications, albeit in less detail. These either involve preoccupied type C strategies as part of their repertoire (e.g. A/C or AC – see Box 6.5), or the strategy is classified as 'disorganised' (DX[1]) because there is no evidence of current strategic use of attachment behaviour. The disorganised strategy in the dynamic maturational model is a classification-by-default, and can only be made on a comprehensive understanding of the A and C strategies. As knowledge about the dismissing and preoccupied strategies increases, the criteria for being classified as a disorganised DX will change (Crittenden, 1999–2002).

The focus for understanding the preoccupied strategies is how the behaviours are organised with regard to the relationship with the attachment figure. What is their function? The same behaviour can be present in dismissing and preoccupied strategies; the distinction lies in the different ways in which the patterns recur – different antecedents and consequences. The brain's way of working is ideal for learning about patterns and sequences of behaviour. It is predisposed to identify emotions in other people.

In medicine one is taught to identify what precipitates disease, what maintains it (why you do not get better), and what factors made one vulnerable to disease in the first place. The preoccupied group of strategies, as they influence dis-ease, have much to do with maintaining factors, as they are concerned with the manipulative use of symptoms. Symptoms are also used functionally to keep face. In order to see how they work I will present them as if they ran true in families, but Pamela's story shows that this is not always the case. Her history also illustrates how chance happenings can lead to temporary solutions to a predicament, which can then be further incorporated into a model of relationships. Understanding memory systems and learning clarifies that this is not necessarily a conscious process. Clinicians might be provoked through what they experience as planned manipulation, and then enter into a power struggle with their patients in order to get them to abort the manipulation. It is only to be expected that such an approach will lead to escalating conflict, and alternative solutions need to be found.

Other patients who use type C strategies manoeuvre into position through dissimulating; for example, they withhold some information which parents or clinicians require in order to get the necessary complete picture. It can easily feel as if one is in a power struggle, when one identifies that they are being economical with the truth.

> In every man's remembrances there are things he will not reveal to everybody, but only to his friends. There are things he will not reveal even to his friends, but only to himself, and then only under a pledge of secrecy. Finally, there are some things that a man is afraid to reveal even to himself, and any honest man accumulates a pretty fair number of such things.
>
> Dostoevsky

Adulthood, parenting and the preoccupied type C classification

Many people develop similar attachment strategies to those of their parents. They can continue over several generations (Benoit, Parker,

1994). The details of these processes will be described to increase general awareness of how familial and culturally approved interaction strategies can lead to the development of particular ways of sharing discomforts, and particular use of a language of dis-ease. Besides the hypothetical pathway for Pamela in her adolescence, or developing the same strategy as one's mother, there are also alternative pathways.[2]

Amongst infants the preoccupied type C behaviour is least common. It increases in frequency as a strategy at 18–36 months old and is generally higher in the preschool years. This suggests that some aspects of parenting which increase in frequency during this time may have a role to play in the transition from the use of attachment behaviour in infants to the preoccupied type C strategic use of such behaviour by the time they begin at school. It also corresponds to the time when children can handle more complex information. During this period children develop their theory of mind and modify their behaviour, in strategic ways, to accommodate to how they anticipated their parents' and others' responses. A particular dilemma of parents, which arises in relation to their sick children during this period, illustrates one half of the dynamic. Illnesses are a potent time for attachment learning as they are emotionally charged times of threat to children, parents are handling the threats, and the children experience their relations with their parents as being particularly important to them. Parents who facilitate their children developing preoccupied type C strategies are reacting especially to what they believe are their children's subjective states, albeit unpredictably. These episodes are therefore of much greater importance for the children described here than for those who develop dismissing type A strategies (their parents having overseen minor signs of discomfort).

Parents need to decide how poorly their children are. In Chapter 1, Pamela was described as not wanting to go to school. The processes parents use to decide whether children are ill or not open up the children's way of knowing about different sorts of discomfort, and clarifying the emotional discomfort particular symptoms arouse in their parents. They are not usually in a position to discriminate between the discomfort induced in a parent because of their current state of health, from the consequences of their state of health – for example, for eventual changes that the parents have to make to their routines. If decisions about whether children are ill can lead to parents having to abort important work commitments, it will be a more emotionally charged encounter than if parents were going to be at home anyway. Consequently there is a different dynamic around getting the decision 'right', rather than the decision being more or less helpful for ensuring the child's safety. Parents decide if children are pretending, upset or ill (Prout, 1988; Wilkinson, 1988), the same primary challenge faced by doctors with patients with unaccounted-for somatic complaints (for further discussion of the issues raised by ambiguous symptoms see Chapter 7).

Young children learn about pretence with their siblings, friends, and at nursery. They find that their parents begin to suspect them of potentially exaggerating their discomforts. By four years old children are clear about this (Wilkinson, 1986; Harris, 1994). They learn that symptoms can be presented with more or less elaboration, as they either aspire to remain healthy and get to that birthday party they wanted to go to, or avoid that visit to the clinic for their next immunisation. Deception of themselves and others is an important survival skill (Trivers, 2000). By the time they are eight years old they are very clear about the negotiating value of symptoms (Wilkinson, 1988), and this depends to a degree on the demands being made of them. Children's needs to negotiate are greater if there are more chores they have to do. All children enter into such negotiation, but develop different strategies depending on how they have been responded to and what they have experienced as effective (Wilkinson, 1988: 175–200).

The time of increasing use of preoccupied type C strategies corresponds to greater importance in the parents' ability to set clear limits for their children and negotiate with them about expectations of their capabilities in varying situations. This includes children's competencies to handle minor dis-ease on their own, or make use of varying degrees of closeness to their parents (this will depend on their age and developmental history).

In a similar way to that used with describing the development of the dismissing strategies, I will now describe the things that many adults are doing (Box 6.1) which lead to their children developing preoccupied type C strategies, before describing the C classification in more detail (see also note 2).

This detailed list in Box 6.1 encompasses more than the focus on signs of systemic disease, corresponding to change in basic emotion. The different points correspond to the same themes in previous figures (Boxes 4.1, type B, and 5.1, type A) – style of communication, ability to take different perspectives, use of own developmental history, effect on empathy and consequences for their child. These details enable generalisation to various types of illness, given the psychosocial classification of the illness, and the parents' experience of illness. In regard to recognising Pamela's tummy ache in childhood, a typical preoccupied type C parent would have recognised that something was the matter, but not what was the cause deduced from relevant antecedents and consequences. Her emotional arousal, secondary to the change in her basic emotion, her

Box 6.1 Preoccupied type C attachment figures

These figures:

- *Communicate unpredictably*; there is intermittent attunement and synchrony with their children. Non-verbal signals, such as signs of anger and fear, may be deceptively exaggerated for their functional effect, and only partially coherent with what they say and feel. When mixed emotions are present, the emotional behaviour that has been shaped through having the greatest probability of eliciting the desired response is the one displayed. The communicative style can be described as manoeuvring or, in the more extreme, manipulative, even deceptively so.
  - Feelings are unavailable to help clarify the issues; instead the communicative style is directed to coping with the unmodulated general arousal of the basic emotions. The feelings of the emotions are likely to remain confused, and poorly differentiated, as caregivers have had diffi- culties in reliably identifying them, and therefore not been able to respond to them contingently. This leads to interoceptive confusion.
- *More easily respond to the emotions of others than their expressed thoughts and stated feelings*; their responses are often feeling what others feel, although unable to clarify what emotion they are feeling. This often generates enmeshment with those close to them, in which their own needs become most prominent. Although blaming others for their difficulties, they are often strongly influenced by their feelings of guilt and anxiety. They find it difficult to know what caused what, instead relying on their antennae for picking up the emotional music of the situation. Poorly modulated arousal around changing affective states exaggerates the confusion of their causal reasoning.
- *Attempt to bring their children up differently to how they were brought up, believing that they know the real feelings that are important to bring forth in their children*. As they find it difficult to identify the causal sequences in interpersonal relationships that facilitate the outcomes that they desire, they get easily frustrated and slip out of the role they are attempting to

continued

employ. They can then oscillate between being too under-standing, and losing their temper, or withdrawing when they do not succeed. Negotiating with them risks becoming embroiled in recriminations, and threats, or alternatively a play on their helplessness or seductive coyness. There is likely to be little room for compromise, and if things do not work out blame will be allocated to the other part. With their feeling of being out of control of the situation, they become preoccupied with the power dimension to relationships.

- *Become over identified with their children's discomfort, losing the distinction between the children's pain and their affective responses.* They can become overwhelmed by emotional contagion, unable to modify their attunement to become available for their children. Under duress they will look for who was responsible for their discomfort, and expect them to do something about it – in extreme cases this could even be the children who 'reminded' them of their pain.

These responses facilitate *children* developing highly tuned affective coping strategies, relying on identifying the dangers and threats associated with settings. But they lack an understanding of causal temporal relations in interpersonal relationships. People seem unpredictable. Although they cannot rely solely on the emotional signals they pick up and their undifferentiated feelings, they nevertheless provide the best chance of identifying situations where they might be less safe. The emotional dimension is attended to, but because it is distorted their response often misses the mark. Because their discomfort is an emotional reaction to other people they expect others to put it all right through changing the situation, and they cling to them with this expectation. If the adults' emotional states resonate too closely to theirs as a form of emotional contagion, they will fail to modulate their dis-ease (see also note 2).

Produced with assistance of Pat Crittenden.

disease, would remain raised, as her parents' diffuse responses would not have helped her modulate her affect. She could have a somatic imaged memory of the occurrence. Her parents would not have found it easy to identify the sequence of events leading to her discomfort. Under stress, such as balancing work demands and parenting, parents on occasion get frustrated and potentially lose their temper. When parents are unpredictable, and children cling more to them, as their best bet for comfort, without being certain that they will be comforted, such clinging can make the eventual final separation from a parent, who decides that she will nevertheless take her preoccupied attached child to nursery, distressing for both. In the final struggle parents may blame children for pretending and 'laying it on thick', so that pretence becomes a moral category, rather than part of the process whereby illness behaviour is shaped, and takes a strategic quality in the context of the interaction (Wilkinson, 1986; Jureidini, Taylor, 2002). In the end these children remain in discomfort, whether or not they were sick originally.

A dilemma for children like this is that their attachment behaviour system will still be mobilised when they have achieved parental attention, even though that contact does not reduce their discomfort. The availability of their parents has been unpredictable, and this has the effect of an intermittent reinforcement schedule, which leads to a form of highly durable implicit learning in procedural memory. Children learn that their parents are more likely to be available, if they only raise the stakes. This means exaggerating various aspects of their behaviour to which their parents are most responsive (a preconscious shaping process of behavioural learning). Acting the feeling repeatedly leads to the feeling being felt more intensely and being released in similar situations – similar because they elicit the same emotional response (Laird, Apostoleris, 1996). They become preoccupied with appearances. The parents' dilemma, in deciding what sort of problem this is, rapidly becomes a real challenge.

The psychosocial classification of disease points out that those diseases associated with relapses, or 'attacks' – such as epilepsy or diabetes – demand that the parents be on their guard. This vigilance means that signs, which could have been overlooked, can come to make the parents doubt the state of their child, and with uncertainty and ambiguity there will be room for 'potential symptoms' to be used in family negotiation. Epilepsy is associated with a greater frequency of 'insecure' attachment, potentially both dismissing type A and more probably preoccupied type C (Marvin, Pianta, Britner, in Pianta, Marvin, Morog [1999]). Pseudo-epileptic attacks are found most often in those who have epilepsy. Those who have asthma, have available knowledge about how to simulate a pseudo-asthma attack. Parental vigilance, which may be required for helping children cope with their disease, can be intense, such as with haemophilia. The potentially extreme anxiety about their child's condition, and danger of bleeding to death, has led to this hypervigilance being called the Damocles syndrome. It is often associated with a pattern of over-control and enmeshment of parent and child, ensuring the child's physical safety at a psychosocial cost. The following metaphor may help explain this:

'Feedback hum pain'
The following metaphor was useful for understanding excruciating abdominal pain in a young teenager. If there is a sudden piercing noise from the speakers at a discotheque, it is referred to as feedback hum. The noise is very real, very painful. It arises because of the natural noise in the electronic system, noise to which we do not normally pay attention. If the microphone is placed too near the speakers, it picks up this noise, and provided the amplifier is turned up high enough (depending on the distance between microphone and speaker), it then makes the noise audible, and the noise rapidly (virtually instantaneously) becomes a deafening sound of which everyone must take notice. Parents can be too close, and pick up the natural 'noise' (insignificant signals) from their child, and through their own sensitivities, such as own previous illness histories and ways in which they have been responded to, magnify what they are picking up.

Mothers of children who develop preoccupied strategies more often show emotional contagion, rather than being attuned with their children. They tend to be overwhelmed by their children's feelings. Such parents often make poorly timed attempts to engage their children. The attempt is from the adult's perspective, and so inconsistent and unpredictable from the child's perspective. These interfere with the children's initiatives, and shift the children's attention to what their parents might get up to next. The pattern of behavioural interaction in infancy is self-perpetuating, and develops into the strategies of the older children.

When patients have had their suffering for some time we are not just interested in the precipitating factors but also in the *maintaining factors*. The complaint has become embedded in the daily lives of these patients and become the *predicament* with, and even by, which they live. The therapeutic issue involves identifying who is most concerned with there being change. It can be that there is more visible concern in the parents of patients with anorexia nervosa, than in the adolescents. Who owns the problem is an important place to start. Many of these teenagers have worked hard at getting rid of the 'complaint', including self-deception (Trivers, 2000), by getting someone else to take it on. Some of these families appear to play pass the parcel continuously: 'Do not let the rotten problem stop at me, it's not my fault.' They develop strategies for dealing with guilt feelings. Shame is part of the currency. The types of transactions, which go on in families who use the coercive preoccupied type C strategies, are like some of the 'games' which Berne describes in transactional analysis. Their internal working models correspond to the scripts to which he refers. He suggests that children pick up relationship games from their parents (Berne [1964: 52]; see also Byng-Hall [1995] who describes 'Rewriting family scripts', which concerns the application of attachment theory to family 'games'). I describe here how they do this.

In summary these children learn to pay attention to the emotions associated with the situation. There will additionally be associative behavioural learning whereby the situation they are in releases emotions they have previously experienced in similar situations. Because of their parents' inherent unpredictability – from the child's perspective – they do not overly attend to what their parents are doing, or to temporal sequences of action, or successfully deduce causal sequences for how they come to feel as they do. They continue to feel uneasy, becoming dependent, angry and/or fearful. They focus on signs of danger, things that might be threatening given their experience, and show affective arousal. The affect shown will have been shaped through interactional sequences during development. Preoccupied type C children will distort their display so that either the anger shows as aggression, and their fear and desire for comfort is inhibited, or they display their fear and desire for comfort, and inhibit their display of anger, their aggression (Box 6.2). This leads to a complicated classificatory system of paired codings, in which, although paired, the odd or even score predominates. The alternative paired strategy is available for use when required. The rapid shifts of strategy, from showing coy behaviour to aggression and back again, are confusing for those around, and are designed to maintain close enough contact when one or the other strategy is on the point of leading to a break up of the contact. As the forms of interaction described in Box 6.1 can be more or less comprehensive, there are graded codings (Box 6.2). The preoccupied type C1–2 children have been primarily safe, whereas the categories C3–8, referred to as the 'obsessive' categories, or higher Cs, reflect the results of varying degrees of threat and increasing use of distorted affect and false cognition (Box 6.3).

Box 6.2 Preoccupied type C strategies

Characterised by aggression

Behaves aggressively towards attachment figures as this attracts their attention, and makes self less preoccupied with their fears and elicits compliance with own desires. Elicits others' negative affect, which may mean the need to shift to placating coy behaviour, with the potential for lowering arousal of those involved (see column to the right). Preoccupied with hierarchy in relationships, and appearance of being dominant.

Characterised by signals of desire for comfort and fear – coy behaviour

Behaves disarmingly towards attachment figures in order to attract their attention, be less preoccupied with own anger and elicit caregiving. Can shift to aggression if attachment figures become angry, or frustrated by degree of involvement desired, as this retains their attention and yet introduces differentiation between people (see column to the left). Preoccupied with hierarchy in relationships, and appearance of being submissive.

Both strategies involve distortions of affect as all people experience some mixed feelings.
The degree of distortion increases with increasing classification code.

C1 *Threatening*
Instrumental display of threatening behaviour to elicit predictable attention and compliance from willing, but inattentive, attachment figures. Fluid shifts to disarming attachment figures' anger with coy behaviour. Preoccupied with gaining attention.

C2 *Disarming*
Instrumental display of appealing charm to elicit predictable attention and nurturance from willing, but inattentive, attachment figures. Fluid shifts to aggression to minimise attachment figures' demands to be competent. Preoccupied with gaining attention.

C3 Aggressive

Uses aggression, alternating with brief flashes of incompetence, as part of a strategy to force compliance with desires from reluctant attachment figures. Aggression is exaggerated, and display of fearfulness and desire for comfort minimised in order to appear invulnerable. Preoccupied with gaining control for the sake of protection.

C4 Feigned helpless

Exaggerate appearance of helpless vulnerability,* in alternation with brief flashes of anger, to force caregiving from reluctant attachment figures by exaggerating their desire for comfort and fearfulness, and hiding their anger in order to appear powerless or incapable. Preoccupied with gaining protection by using submissive control.

C5 Punitive

Obsessed with revenge† that is plotted with, or against, both attachment figures, and also friends. Defines others as being for or against them, and coerces support by threats, blame, and manipulation of information about safety (false cognition). Expects treachery because people recruited under false pretences often defect. Dramatically incongruent shifts to seductive behaviour directed towards former targets of aggression. Preoccupied with defining friend and foe and maintaining control.

C6 Seductive

Obsessed with rescue by both attachment figures, and also friends, from dangers they have created. Defines others as being for or against them, and coerces support by threats, guilt induction, and manipulation of information about danger (false cognition). Expects treachery because people recruited under false pretences often get angry. Dramatically incongruent shifts to focused and obsessive revenge against partners and friends. Preoccupied with enlisting protection and maintaining control.

---

* And therefore not to be equated with comprehensive helplessness, although their failure to try to protect and comfort the self ultimately yields a lack of skills compared to more self-reliant peers.

† Having acted aggressively one is predisposed to feel more anger. The effects are additive so that displaying more aggression leads to one feeling more anger, and instrumental aggression goes over to being hostile aggression (see, for example, Laird,

continued

C7 *Menacing*

Obsessed with unfocused revenge directed to all possible enemies, but deceives others regarding intentions (false cognition). Prepares to defend self with deceptively pre-emptive aggression. No longer trusts people who offer comfort because comforting people have, in the past, been deceptively dangerous when most needed. Usually driven into a loner position in which the self is good and everyone else is bad or potentially false. Anger and fear combine to create motivating feeling of hatred. Preoccupied with protecting the self through deceptive attack and generating unfocused fear/ dread in others.

C8 *Paranoid*

Obsessed with unfocused fear of deception and treachery, especially when situations appear safe (false cognition). Defends self with pervasively wary withdrawal. No longer trusts those who offer comfort because comforting people have, in the past, been deceptively dangerous when most needed. Usually driven into a loner position in which the self is good and everyone else is bad or potentially false. Fear and anger combine to create motivating feeling of dread. Preoccupied with protecting the self through exaggerated vulnerability and submission and generating unfocused anger/hate in others.

Although one half of the strategy usually predominates, all type C individuals make use of both the odd and even numbered parts of the strategy (in contrast to the As). Without alternation the strategy is stuck and no longer functions coercively. If previously preoccupied with displaying their internal distress and eliciting attention, type C individuals can rapidly switch to directing protest at those who do not respond as desired. A person at one level may on occasion show aspects of the next higher or lower level; the even-odd alternation is sometimes across levels (e.g., C4–5). The C1–2 and C7–8 strategies are the most nearly integrated, whereas the C3–4 and C5–6 sub-patterns are more firmly split. Low numbered

---

Apostoleris [1996]). There is no reason to suppose that the same developmental process does not affect instrumental display of helplessness and seduction.

sub-patterns can accept comfort, whereas people using higher numbered sub-patterns fear deception when comfort is displayed by others; in the higher patterns, comfort is associated with danger.

Produced with assistance of Pat Crittenden.

Box 6.3 Transformations of information: characteristics of the preoccupied type C

Age	Affect	Cognition
	Type C	Type C
Infant		Omit temporal information
Preschool with theory of mind	Split and distort negative affect	
School age with theory of mind		Falsify causal information

In addition it is possible to come to *erroneous* conclusions due to coincidence, and to *truly* predictive cognitive or affective information.

The preoccupied type C strategies (C1–2) of essentially safe children

Parents who have children using these strategies have usually (see note 2) been varyingly attentive to their children, and the children have been essentially safe. The children use behaviour strategically to gain their parents' attention when they want it. It has not been easy for the parents to decide whether attention was needed, or the complaint could helpfully be overlooked as there was no real threat. They become emotionally drawn in to their children's distress. This has the effect of leading these children to overgeneralise the emotional response, and remain unsettled. Their own contribution to the joint emotional discomfort is unclear. Their parents' lack of containment of the children's emotion can also result in the children feeling that their parents *caused* their distress. This effect is made more probable because of their difficulties in learning about the temporal contingencies associated with their escalating emotional discomfort. Their strategic play on the sensitivities of their parents as a necessary way of coping with their situation entails them avoiding drawing conclusions about their own role in the situation. Their parents become both the potential source of soothing, as well as being unable to be totally effective in comforting their children. The children deny that they have played any role in the development of this situation.

In a healthcare setting we would expect such children to cling to their parents, and yet not be effectively soothed. Regrettably this marked clinging has at times been incorrectly described as 'strong' attachment. They would be likely to become conditioned to the settings where painful procedures were carried out, so that they generalise that distress to other settings too. They would be unlikely to be able to use information about what will happen, because their preferred way of coping has been an emotional awareness. They will often turn to others to see how they appear to feel about what is being done to them, and ascribe similar feelings to their own poorly differentiated emotional arousal. They will be acutely in tune to any distress which their parents feel, and maybe it is primarily from this group of patients that Skipper and Leonard (1968) found that pulse and blood pressure in children changed with their mothers'. As these parents will be showing only part of their feelings at any one time – for example, attentiveness to their children's need for care or their fear, whilst their anger that invasive investigations are being carried out on their children remains hidden – the children will be relying on distorted parental affect to guide them.

Children who develop a preoccupied 'disarming' type C2 strategy could well have parents who conveyed a sense of concern, even when there was no real threat. This may play a role in sensory amplification – the way in which particular responses to symptoms amplify them rather than contain them, such as with feedback hum. Minor somatic upsets could then get the status of symptoms, and a state of being 'under the weather' or half ill becomes an illness. These patterns can then be carried forward into adulthood, with the potential for repetition in the next generation. Predispositions for pain in particular parts of the body run in families (Wilkinson, 1988: 198), but this does not mean that the cause is genetic – and an hypothesis about this being related to preoccupied attachment strategies is not yet tested.

The preoccupied 'obsessive' type C strategies (C3–8)

As with the higher type A strategies, these are found when people have been exposed to increasing danger during their development. Parents have not ensured their children's safety, or enabled them to modulate their level of arousal. Danger can include threatening procedures in hospital, and time in isolation. What constitutes a threat is partially dependent on personal experience. In the 1950s and 1960s the information sheet given to all parents of children admitted to the children's ward at the largest hospital in Oslo, Norway, specified that no visiting was allowed during the first three days of admission, and then twice a week for a maximum of one hour each time for those under three years, rising to three times a week for those older. This was defended by referring to good hygiene practice. The staff was most concerned about outbreaks of infection which might prove difficult to control. Parents of children recently admitted to the children's wards may well have experienced such routines themselves, and these will have sensitised them both to what to expect in hospital and what to 'fight against'. In relation to the prognosis of specific diseases, experience is bound to be out of date, and the past influences the future.

The column entries in Box 6.2 illustrate the various dynamics that are employed in the service of the sub-strategies. These reflect various working models of what is effective in managing relationships. These are then also used when patients meet health professionals. There is an increasing degree of suspicion and collusion, with more leveraged use of distorted displays of affect in order to get control of the situation as the C coding increases. This reflects the sort of attention they had been used to getting with their experience of relationships. The emotions aroused when having to depend on other people, as when ill in hospital, will be coloured by the emotions associated with depending on other people when they were growing up – feeling comfortable can even function as a warning of danger when parents have been dangerously unpredictable. As the emotions are available in implicit memory, their origins are not necessarily available for introspection.

Should patients have conditions which necessitate them being in hospital for a reasonable time, there is the chance of them experiencing people looking after them in alternative, and for them surprising, ways. This is an opportunity for personal development.

I was called to an intensive care ward because the staff was concerned about a teenager who had been run over by a motorboat. His chest had been badly injured by the propeller. He had been a tough, often aggressive, daredevil. He had become depressed – in many ways not surprising, albeit not coherent with his tough image. The origin of his depression appeared to be that when on the intensive care ward all his bodily functions had to be looked after by the nursing staff. He was well cared for, as they were sensitive to his needs for privacy at the same time as they identified what he needed from small tentative signals. He did not have to make a fuss to get attention and the service required; the staff did not get too involved. He had no option but to be forcibly looked after in a way he had never experienced before. As the care lasted for a long time, he experienced alternative relationships, which he could use as a starting point for alternative working models of relationships. He showed aspects of the alternative aspect of his preoccupied type C strategy, the display of his vulnerabilities. Through tolerating the apparently contradictory aspects in close conjunction, he could begin to integrate disparate aspects of himself, whilst he experienced a different sort of responsiveness from the staff.

The higher preoccupied strategies are associated with poor modulation of affect, and potentially poor modulation of other parameters of stress, such as cortisol levels in the blood. The situation is especially confusing for these individuals because they have received labels for their feelings that have only been partially correct. A parent will tell the preoccupied aggressive C3 child that he is angry, as a response to his display of aggression, and not identify the inhibited feelings, the associated unmet fears and need for comfort. Children's understanding of their subjective state becomes very imprecise. Engaging in exercises to write about their feelings as a way of coping, which is otherwise effective (Pennebaker, 2000), cannot be expected to be as helpful for those exposed to such selective attention, *and* who selectively present from their discomforts (this is a process of co-evolution involving both child and caregiver – they become structurally coupled in an imprecise affectively charged 'bop', dancing up and down on the spot).

Some people will be predominantly angry when they are aroused, others appear fearful and in need of comfort when they are also angry (the odd compared to the even C strategies). This is a confusing mix for health workers trying to meet the needs of patients whom they expect to feel in need of care and attention. The preoccupied patient may instead be predisposed to one of the odd-numbered preoccupied strategies where aggression is preferentially displayed. Care staff may not be aware that many preoccupied obsessive patients will have generalised their experience from previous threatening situations to new situations. When they then encourage these patients to overlook their anticipated fears of the new situation (as there is no threat actually involved), they will find this very difficult as situations have been unpredictable and their parents inconsistent (from the child's perspective). In these responses to 'threat', patient and staff are likely to get frustrated with each other, and after a while revert to type – the patient experiences a repeat of the unpredictability of their parents, as the staff get frustrated and alter tack just as parents did of old. Staff will vary in how soon they get frustrated, and conflicts in the staff group may get quite heated, especially with the obsessive higher Cs as patients. These processes were brilliantly described by Tom Main for the effects 'special' patients had on staff groups, including decisions about when to medicate (Main, 1957). The staff on the intensive care unit needed to know that their competent care had precipitated my patient's depression, and at the same time opened new possibilities for him. Previously he had been an angry young man, with a classical conduct disorder; and they die young.

> Staff can also use coercive strategies to get compliance from patients, as I myself experienced when my son was investigated in an ear, nose and throat department. He was only two years old when placed in the examination chair. The doctor used surprise as his main tool to examine the back of his throat. I was not quick enough to notice that the nurse had taken up a position behind the chair, and the team were prepared for what was about to happen – but not my son and I. He learnt that doctors were unpredictable, and that sitting in that stool was dangerous. Subsequent investigations became difficult, and the senior consultant in the end asked me what was up with my son that made him co-operate so poorly with the necessary investigations. The doctor who performed the initial investigation did not learn from the long-term effects of his strategy, and was instead rewarded with a quick, efficient, and 'dirty', inspection of my son's throat. Honesty and openness are the best enemies of such coercive practices.

Instead of detailing the particular phenomena found with each sub-strategy, I refer the interested reader to Crittenden's descriptions of the preschool strategies and adult attachment strategies (Crittenden, 1992–2001, and 1999–2002). She has helped with the condensed formulations in Boxes 6.1 and 6.2. These do not do justice to the descriptions available in the original references.

The characteristics of the preoccupied type C strategies lead to difficulties in designing health promotion strategies, which can tap into the emotional learning that guides such people's coping strategies. They tend to cope with responsibility by either appearing incompetent (the higher even Cs), or invincible and in no need of health advice (the higher odd Cs). This is a difficult starting point for enabling individuals to take responsibility for their own futures, and identifying alternative ways of coping. They are likely to frustrate health staff interested in prevention. It is necessary to help them avoid overgeneralising, and learn about causal sequences and the 'when' of danger.

Some of the higher Cs (C7–8) probably correspond to some of the vulnerable people described by other researchers as disorganised (Solomon, George, 1999), and who appear to be at greater risk of developing disease. The processes listed in Box 6.4 are especially important to have in focus when devising health promotion strategies for type C individuals. At the moment we have no answer to how to achieve better health promotion in this group. The intermittent reinforcement schedule (Cassidy, Berlin, 1994), which has led to the deeply ingrained preoccupied type C strategy being maintained, is hard to extinguish.

Health promotion depends on people owning a responsibility to do something about their own situation, yet type C individuals are often preoccupied with allocating blame to others – the worst possible starting point for empowering people to find solutions for their own discomforts. Type C strategists account for children's lack of responsibility as a function of immaturity, powerlessness, and lack of knowledge, but they also tend to carry this forward unchanged into their adolescence and adulthood. The vulnerable population of higher Cs who employ these strategies can be expected to include a greater-than-expected number who have a history of psychosomatic disorders, hyperactivity, sleep disorders, and conduct problems (Crittenden, 1999–2002). They are likely to present more often to the emergency departments, and be a challenge to the doctor who is working hard at establishing a 'patient-centred' approach. With their focus on feelings, parents have often responded in similar ways to both important and inconsequential events. They have also responded in different ways to the same behaviour. The emergency department patient is expecting the doctor to behave similarly. Such patients do not have experience of constructive goal-directed and corrected alliances. Those who have been least at ease, the highest Cs, will find being taken care of the most unsettling of affective states, because trust in comfort could lead to vulnerability in the event of covert danger, given their previous experience with totally unpredictable danger when they had thought they

---

Box 6.4 Mothers' ways to reinforce their children's preoccupied strategies for keeping themselves healthy

- by doing what they feel is right for keeping their children/ themselves safe;
- by deciding which symptoms are salient for their children;
    - predominantly their children's feelings rather than signs of disease;
- by how they protect their children, including their hygiene rules and how they implement them;
- by their affective information associated with the dangers of diseases:
    - feeling the discomforts of illness *with* their children,
    - being preoccupied with diffuse, all-pervasive potential causes of disease such as germs and 'stress';
- by their willingness to respond preferentially to their children's emotional complaints without clarifying the contingencies which lead to them arising:
    - leading to difficulties distinguishing different causes of changes in proto-self,
    - their predisposition to emotional responsiveness, going over to contagion;
- by attributing responsibility for discomfort to others and not assisting in containment of the negative affect associated with systemic disease:
    - being easily swayed by their children's discomforts of illness;
- by functioning otherwise according the interpersonal strategies listed in Boxes 6.1 and 6.2.

---

were safe. Will supportive health information be seen as dangerous because it provides a false sense of security, whilst one is manoeuvred into a trap?

Gender issues

Parents see what they expect to see in their children's behaviour. Parents of small children interpret their crying children differently. In identical situations in a Western society research project boys were more often said to be angry and girls were said to be frightened. Interestingly we have here the two major distinctions between the even and odd preoccupied type C strategies. The way in which the children's behaviour was interpreted affected the form of support that the children elicited from their parents, and the development of the behaviour so that it became integrated in a coherent strategy. Cultural differences in how the various vulnerabilities of the different sexes are responded to give the functionality of the differing preoccupied strategies its gender bias. British and Norwegian children are likely to be divided up with more girls amongst the even Cs and boys amongst the odd Cs. The paradox is that the boys are the vulnerable group, dying earlier than the girls, whereas the girls experience more discomfort throughout their lives. The girls need to be helped to distinguish the body signals which they really must pay attention to, from those which become well developed as part of the care-eliciting coy behaviour of the preoccupied even C strategies, who exaggerate their vulnerability through symptom display.

There is an interesting interaction between children's gender and the state of the mother after birth. Mothers who were depressed (at the moment we do not know their attachment status, or theory of mind with regard to their children's attachment), responded differently to their sons and daughters. They were less focused on their sons' needs, especially when they showed distress, whereas they tended to be highly focused on their daughters' needs. They did not differ in the extent to which they were either behaviourally intrusive or withdrawn from their infants. They used motherese, the adaptation of speech to make it easily understood by infants. But they did show signs of being especially sensitised to their children's negative affect, and primarily in relation to their sons they became locked into cycles of mutually responsive negativity. These were only aborted when the child cut off the interaction. At the moment it remains to be seen whether these children were disorganised (see pp. 191–194), or whether this was the start to alternating between even and odd type C strategies (Box 6.2).[3]

Boys of depressed women perform significantly worse, cognitively, than boys of well women, whereas the girls of depressed women perform rather better (Murray, 1998a). This suggests that boys will not easily be able to use cognitive skills to master the over-learnt procedural interactive dance, which has characterised their interaction with their mothers. Children of depressed mothers see themselves as more helpless, and less personally effective. In other words they are beginning to describe themselves as developing the cognitive style associated with depression (Abramson, Seligman, Teasdale, 1978), although as noted here they may be learning the *effective* strategic use of displayed helplessness, and asserted lack of effectiveness associated with the preoccupied feigned helpless type C4 sub-strategy.

Other classifications

A/C and AC

Children appear able to develop initially up to three or four different attachment patterns in infancy. As they consolidate their strategic use of these behaviours during the preschool years they appear to develop a predominant strategy, which is usually that which they have developed in relation to their mother, even if that strategy was either dismissing (A) or preoccupied (C), and the strategy used with father was balanced (B). Nevertheless some children and adults switch between A and C strategies. Depending on the specific demands of the situation they employ either a dismissing strategy, or a preoccupied strategy. In order to qualify for a reliable coding according to the dynamic-maturational model, the strategy needs to fulfil the criteria for at least three memory systems in relation to the specific situations. This alternating A/C mixture was first described by Crittenden in children (Crittenden, 1985), and has since been described in relation to adults. The full range of sub-strategies can be employed from both the dismissing and preoccupied strategies (for further details see Crittenden [1999–2002]). If they had available the balanced B strategy, they would have been able to employ the cognitive and affective elements of the A and C strategies in a balanced way across all situations, and see things from both their own perspective and that of their parents. Those employing a preoccupied strategy see things predominantly from their position, and those using dismissing type A strategies from the other's position.

Mixing dismissing and preoccupied strategies adds an extra complication to understanding the language of dis-ease, the strategic use of illness behaviour, but one that can be understood by making use of the descriptions provided so far. Patients with borderline personality disorder more often appear to have an A/C strategy. They can be particularly difficult to manage wherever they are hospitalised, either because of somatic complaints, self-injury, or psychiatric problems. A/C combinations are probably also common in the process of psychotherapy as change takes place, as well as during adolescence when there are shifts from one strategy to another, as for Pamela.

Box 6.5 Other classifications

Strategies	Modifiers of strategies
A/C – Oscillations between A and C strategies depending on the demand characteristics of the situation	UI/tr – Unresolved loss/trauma
AC – Integrated use of false affect and false cognition in strategic ways (psychopathic)	R – Reorganising
DX – Disorganised; no current effective strategic use of cognitive or affective strategies	Dp – Depression.* This modifier identifies cases where the child or parent believes no change is possible and no one can help; aware that no strategies work
A/C can be further differentiated on the basis of the classifications for A and C (e.g. A3/C1)	Loss is further specified in relation to who, and which strategy, is employed for handling it

---

When an individual uses both pervasive false cognition and false affect, they can integrate a comprehensively falsified view of the world along both dimensions. This is regarded as typical of psychopaths, and notated as the blended 'AC' strategy (Crittenden, 1999–2002). They understand the observer's perspective so well that they are able to construct an appearance that closely matches the observer's expectations and desires (cognitively in values and affectively in feelings). They can *appear* to become structurally coupled, but retain their suspiciousness and make use of others who become their 'victims' – the ideal being a trusting naïve balanced type B person.

Unresolved

Is there a way of understanding how Pamela's mother could have got embroiled in a preoccupied type C strategy with her daughter in

---

*   This modifier is not well established and will not be further discussed.

adolescence? We have only theory to guide us, and a few findings from the research literature. Theoretically we need to postulate that Pamela's mother's theory of mind about her daughter's attachment needs was mobilised in a different way for this daughter at this point in time, given the development in her behaviour during adolescence. The relevant dimensions would be likely to involve the salience of particular behaviour in adolescence, which could relate to her own adolescence, or to particular experiences she had had, which alter her view of what is a threat. If Pamela's mother had had a sister who had died during an asthma attack when she was 15 years old we would expect situation-dependent preferential retrieval of memories from this time when her daughter with asthma approached the same age. If the threat which occurred in the past is allowed to colour the current situation, in spite of there being no other signs that the situations are in any way similar, we refer to an unresolved loss (Ul). If a previous loss was 'resolved', Pamela's mother would have learnt from the death of her sister, so that what happened in the past be kept in the past, and her new learning employed in a balanced way for the future without overgeneralisation.

Unresolved loss is classified with both a descriptor of who died and the strategy that is used to cope with the loss. For example, if Pamela's mother lost her sister we write $Ul_{(sister)}$ and follow this with a preoccupied strategy marker, 'p', (or for example 'ds' for dismissing) – for details of available strategies and scoring refer to Crittenden's manual for the AAI (Crittenden, 1999–2002). Trauma is similarly described (Utr), followed by a key word for the trauma (it has to involve a threat to the person, although it can be vicarious if it involves your child or parent) and the strategy used ('p' or 'ds', etc.).

An unresolved loss for Pamela's mother could then affect her ability to contain the affective distress in her daughter. The danger was that she would shift from her previous emotional attunement to resonating with her daughter's distress as in emotional contagion. This would be especially likely if she was preoccupied with the unresolved loss (in contrast to Ul_{ds}). Themes of loss and trauma need always to be explored in medical histories, and provide bridges from the loss of one generation to the next (Fonagy, 1999). In the hypothetical case of Pamela's mother we note generalisation of her experience of loss in childhood to another situation in the future. The teenager with the feedback hum pain had a parent with an unresolved loss, who acted like the amplifier turning up the tuning to the unresolved symptoms of dis-ease resonating between parent and child, where the loss of the patient's grandparent following similar symptoms set the scene.

The important distinction for parents in relation to their ill children, or for clinicians in relation to their patients, is to distinguish the inherent threat in a disease, from the threat associated with the emotional response of dis-ease, the subjects' illness experiences. Symptoms can become amplified through emotional contagion, especially if the threat of the discomfort is not distinguished from the threat of the underlying condition. This can be both more difficult because of unresolved previous loss or trauma, and also because of preoccupied type C strategies. The resulting feeling of lack of safety can generate too much anxiety for effective thought and action, or make it too difficult to focus sufficient attention on the threat. Dismissing strategies will be associated with diminished identification of danger, and over-attribution of own responsibility, whereas preoccupied strategies will over-predict danger and view themselves as having little responsibility.

TRAUMA

Trauma, as conceptualised in the dynamic maturational model of attachment, is a psychological reaction to a perceived self-endangering circumstance. This can be a hospital admission, for example. Early trauma or abuse usually appears to be associated with lack of resolution. Because of the child's age and other factors, early memories are often unavailable for recall. The psychological response to the event is the critical feature, rather than the event itself. The response affects the ease with which resolution can be achieved, and which strategies are adopted to cope with the unresolved trauma. The central question is 'does the danger (or dangerous loss) affect mental functioning in general, either through what is omitted that is needed or what is retained that is not needed for identification, prevention, or protection from future danger' (Crittenden, 1999–2002). If the trauma has been inflicted by those to whom one turns for help, either parents, siblings or health professionals, it will have enduring consequences of major importance for the person's future health and development. Their attachment strategies will reflect this insecurity, and the unresolved trauma compounds their dilemmas. The attachment strategy developed prior to the trauma is probably the single most important determinant of long-term damage following a *natural* disaster (McFarlane, 1988).

Trauma leads to biological and psychosocial consequences. They interact and co-evolve in a complex interplay. I am limiting my focus to the attachment issues.[4] Extraordinary demands are made on attachment relationships after trauma. Traumatised people have difficulties finding words to convey their discomforts secondary to neuro-anatomical changes due to the trauma (van der Kolk, 1996), and so the natural dialogue of a balanced relationship loses one of its pivotal strengths. It also makes it more difficult to nurse such patients. A particular form of trauma within the health service concerns experiences on Intensive Care Units. These are reported to be responsible for some patients losing their ability to articulate their discomforts. This is referred to as secondary alexithymia (Freyberger, 1977; Taylor, Bagby, Parker, 1997: 37).[5]

Trauma can be predictable, such as abuse each time father is drunk, or unpredictable. When it is unpredictable and inescapable, children or adults, depending on the attachment strategies they already have to cope with it, may even turn to the person who has inflicted the trauma. Predictable trauma is associated with the higher script dismissing and preoccupied strategies already described (covered also by some researchers' use of disorganised – see pp. 191–194). Staff on paediatric wards should not necessarily believe that children are securely attached to their parents because they turn to them when they are faced with major crises in their illnesses. The old expressions of strong and weak attachments have no place in modern understanding of attachment. A 'strong' attachment may describe the intense clinging of a preoccupied abused child to her unpredictably abusive parent.

People who have been traumatised in their own families may have great difficulty taking care of their own basic needs for hygiene, and protection, at the same time as they are exquisitely responsive to other people's needs. This can be very confusing for health service staff, especially so if it involves their colleagues, who can be highly tuned to the needs of their patients and yet grossly neglecting their own care.

Vigilance to the state of others is part of the survival strategy found with the compulsive caregiving A4 strategy, as well as the emotional attunement of the higher preoccupied type C strategies. Health staff can be especially confused if traumatised patients use false affect and false cognition, which distort the validity of the information provided in the medical history so that it is very difficult to understand what is going on. When patients turn to those who have traumatised them for 'comfort' rather than to safe others (the Stockholm syndrome), their attachment behaviour can be difficult to follow. The sequence needs to be seen in the light of the biological embodiment of attachment strategies, whereby the predictability of the abusing relationship contains less uncertainty than being exposed to the risks of an unknown response from a stranger. You would expect deception from the stranger after your experiences with abuse, and trust is fundamentally skewed. Health workers are not initially perceived as dependable and trustworthy. It can take a very long time before such perceptions alter. Since many of these patients have not learned to negotiate with people who are in a position to hurt them, they tend not to give clear signals when the reality of the therapeutic relationship itself becomes a violation.

A particularly complex sort of trauma, which affects illness behaviour directly, occurs when a parent directly induces signs of disease in their child, so that the child is presented as if they had that disease – a strategic use of another's 'disease behaviour'. This is termed 'factitious illness', previously termed 'Munchausen syndrome by-proxy' when somatic symptoms are fabricated, or 'Ganser syndrome by-proxy' for psychiatric symptoms.[6] There is then going to be a major distortion in the affected person's understanding of the causes of their symptoms, and the relationship between their symptoms and the care available from that parent. The deception involved leads me to believe, on theoretical grounds, that the affected person would develop high number preoccupied obsessive type C strategies, as well as unresolved trauma. The exact strategies will depend on many factors, including the age of the child when the trauma took place.

Trauma can also be indirect, transmitted over several generations. It is revealing to note the processes that appear to be involved, as they illuminate intricate details in distortion of attunement. Fonagy has described a process whereby parents could show cognitive and affective irregularities in their attunement with their child, whenever the trauma theme is activated (Fonagy, 1999). Parents might confuse past and present, have slips of the tongue and appear distant. This can appear unpredictable from the child's position, as the traumatic reactivation need not be in relation to objective signs, but subjective or even implicit,[7] occurring in preconscious memory and so unavailable for identification by the child. In such unpredictable situations the child becomes emotionally aroused, at the same time as the parent is no longer psychologically available for them. The loss of attunement has precipitated mobilisation of the attachment behaviour system, and also prevented resolution of the distress. At the same time the parent sees the fear of the child, and this compounds the fear that had been mobilised with activation of the trauma theme. Parent and child develop an emotional contagion characterised by fear around a theme, which has not been identified or talked about. Preconscious implicit memory has been mobilised, and because this is not available for conscious introspection parent and child can 're-traumatise' each other. Parental dissociation, whereby there is no integrated access to the involved memory systems, will lead to their children also dissociating in relation to a theme of which they are unaware, and which has been transmitted over generations. A taboo becomes profoundly capable of influencing development in subsequent generations. Health professionals need to be aware that taboos about inherited diseases in families can predispose to similar processes, related of course to the degree of trauma and threat to those involved. I propose that they can predispose to dissociation and disorganised attachment.

Dissociation is understood in several different ways (see Chapter 2). I use it specifically in relation to problems in making use of more than two memory systems in synchrony.[8] In other words it shows itself through there being dys-synchrony between, for example, procedural and semantic and/or episodic memory, and limited functionality of working memory. This has the consequence of there being a disruption in the normal integration of cognition, affect, behaviour – and ultimately a sense of self. Dissociation is here used to describe a process which results from severely frightening traumatic experiences and to which people appear to be vulnerable if they have either a higher dismissing type A strategy or higher preoccupied type C strategy. In very young children there may be particular physiological changes, such as activation of the parasympathetic nervous system's vagus nerve, which leads to a slowing of the heart and drop in blood pressure (Perry, Pollard, Blakely, Baker, Vigilante, 1995). The acute change in state of the child becomes a trait secondary to implicit learning. Subsequently, when the same state arises the memories associated with the state are reactivated. This may be due to preconscious memories, which guide patterns of behaviour. Traumatised patients can be very difficult to understand. Through their difficulty in integrating all that happens around them it becomes especially difficult to keep a treatment alliance going through the various challenges that a hospital admission can present.

Disorganised

The process of dissociation is believed to predispose to the development of a disorganised attachment strategy (DX). Elements of strategy are present but they are not used comprehensively in an integrated effective strategic fashion. Main and Hesse reported a link between disorganisation of infant attachment behaviour and unresolved traumatic attachment experiences of the mother (Main, Hesse, 1990). Traumatised mothers were assumed to exhibit frightened or frightening behaviour in specific situations, which then caused disorganisation in infant attachment behaviour. Crittenden has criticised an extended use of the disorganisation classification, and notes that in the neurological literature fear is conceptualised as leading to a rapid, efficient organisation of preconscious self-protective behaviour (Crittenden, 2001). Possibly the difference in understanding lies in the failure to differentiate 'organised' from 'integrated'. Preconscious behaviour is unlikely to be fully integrated, but it may be highly organised. When classifying attachment strategies, their organisation determines the allocation of strategy. It is required that the strategy is coherent across at least three memory systems. The application of modifiers, such as 'unresolved loss/trauma', together with a higher coding of dismissing or preoccupied (e.g. $Ul_{(p)}$ C6), can account for many case descriptions of 'disorganised attachment'. This leads to problems in presenting the literature in a coherent way so that it is possible to make sense of illness languages and behaviour.

Theoretically it is likely that an inability to organise a strategy to make effective use of attachment relationships will be associated with greater disturbance in regulating homeostasis, and modulating affect. Disorganised strategies are not effective for helping people protect themselves from danger. Their behaviour will be seen as flitting from one form to another, so that it becomes difficult to predict what their needs are, and how they can best be responded to. The details of the disorganised behaviour of preschool children and a detailed description of disorganisation in adults according to the dynamic-maturational model can be found in Crittenden (1992–2001 and 1999–2002), and according to an alternative understanding in Solomon, George (1999).

Changes in behaviour do not correspond predictably to changes in demands. Nevertheless it is possible to describe their lack of organised strategy to take account of the elements of A and C strategies which one finds – e.g. DX (A5) (disorganised compulsively promiscuous dismissing strategy), or DX (C3) (disorganised aggressive preoccupied strategy). Disorganised may be limited to the experience of trauma and then notated as $Utr_{(dx)}$.

> A man had grown up with a father who had been tortured during the Second World War. His father had been presented to the firing squad several times without being killed. During this man's childhood he had repeatedly woken up at night to the sound of his father screaming as he lived out his nightmare. His AAI was disorganised.

The disorganised attachment strategy is not to be seen as an attachment disorder (Solomon, George, 1999). Evidence suggests that disorganisation is not a result of neurological damage (Barnett, Hunt, Butler, McCaskill IV, Kaplan-Estrin, Pipp-Siegel, 1999), unless such damage means that the person is without a theory of mind. That would mean that their behaviour could not become strategically organised. Their behaviour is then best scored provisionally using infant patterns of behaviour, rather than preschool or adult strategies. Nevertheless the presence of a neurological handicap precludes the formal allocation of a disorganised classification with the AAI.

When parents of children born with congenital neurological conditions were classified as unresolved, their infants were more than three times as likely to be classified as non-balanced – that is, dismissing (A), preoccupied (C) or disorganised (DX) in the Strange Situation – than those whose parents were resolved (Barnett, Hunt, Butler, McCaskill IV, Kaplan-Estrin, Pipp-Siegel, 1999). Children born after there had been a stillbirth were more likely to develop disorganised attachment if the mother had an unresolved loss (Hughes, Turton, Hopper, McGauley, Fonagy, 2001), and unresolved loss was more likely if she had seen the dead foetus. There are various reports of failure to thrive in children born subsequent to a stillbirth in the family, and this necessitates working with an understanding of how attachment develops in children and the role of the mother's unresolved loss. This recent research will hopefully lead to evaluation of alternative practices after stillbirth. Currently mothers are encouraged to see their stillborn children.

When children are born with serious disability or a threatening medical condition, this is a vicarious trauma for the parents. It threatens the potential security of the infants' attachment through affecting the parents' abilities to be attuned with their infants (Pianta, Marvin, Morog, 1999). Parents are reported as acting fearfully or frighteningly towards their children in situations that required their availability for their children's security.[9] Only when the psychological response to the trauma is resolved enough to facilitate their ability to put their own needs to one side can they meet their children as they are. When the course of the medical condition can be predicted, resolution is more likely. Theoretically, according to Main and Hesse, such fear could predispose to children developing disorganised attachment (Main, Hesse, 1990), although Crittenden would theoretically expect such children to organise, albeit not in an integrated way.

At the moment we do not know if some children are transiently disorganised on their way to integrating experience in new ways. Patterns of infant disorganised behaviour such as

- freezing, stilling and slowed movements and expressions
- sequential display of contradictory behaviour patterns

- simultaneous display of contradictory behaviour patterns
- undirected, misdirected, incomplete or interrupted movements and expressions (Main, Solomon, 1990),

may give the infant more time to gather and digest information. It may be that we are seeing an attachment correlate of the developmental processes described by Piaget as accommodation and assimilation (Piaget, Inhelder, 1969: 6). Instead of being able to assimilate new information to current working models, children have to go through a relatively chaotic process whereby they integrate conflicting information to accommodate in a new way, as it was not possible to assimilate the new experience to their existing working model of relationships.

Childhood and the preoccupied type C classification

Amongst infants the smallest proportion are classified as type C, yet this rapidly changes in the early preschool period so that they become the most frequent classification in the preschool years using the PAA classificatory system. Remember that it is primarily strategic organisation of attachment that has predictive validity from as early as 24 months, rather than the infant patterns of behaviour (Vondra, Shaw, Swearingen, Cohen, Owens, 2001). There have been a variety of names used to describe preoccupied attachment in children, and so as not to be too confusing when relating to other literature here is a summary of some of them, with the changes from infancy to school age:

- Scoring infants, 10–14 months, on their *behaviour* in SSn includes the preoccupied 'resistant/passive' C1–2 pattern.
- The *strategies* used by preschool children and scored with the PAA include in addition preoccupied 'aggressive/feigned helpless' C3–4 strategies.
  - The preoccupied type C1–2 categories as strategies become 'threatening/disarming'.
  - The C1–4 preschool children have been termed as a group, 'coercive' preschool children.
- Older school age children are capable of using preoccupied 'punitive/ seductive' C5–6 strategies, but not yet the 'menacing/punitive' C7–8 strategies of adulthood.

The primary issue for young children with preoccupied attachment strategies is the apparent unpredictability of their parents. This is associated with fear. As the children get older their preoccupied strategy has enabled them to regulate their parents' behaviour, through the push-me-pull-you system described in Box 6.2, but this has not led to the ability to self-regulate. Closeness to their parents has not led to successful modulation of their discomfort. These children are not at ease. When ill they will fail to adjust through using closeness to others. It may well be that it is these children who grow into adults with persistent hypochondriasis (Robbins, Kirmayer, 1996). People who were close to persistent hypochondriacs failed to normalise their symptoms, and through somato-sensory amplification, similar to emotional contagion, could exaggerate their discomforts. This would be coherent with the processes described in the figures in this chapter.

Children and their parents have different views about what is wrong with the children, especially the subjective dimension to their experiences (Notaro, Gelman, Zimmerman, 2001). This sort of disagreement is widespread, not limited to preoccupied attachment relationships, although it is a natural result of the dynamic described here. This has important implications for practice and research. Parents will be unreliable informants on their children's internal worlds, especially for children with preoccupied attachment strategies. Nevertheless these parents' focus on their children's states can lead them to believe they are expert informants. Research workers need to know that discomforts are presented for their functional effect in handling preoccupied relationships and they do not necessarily correspond to how a child would describe their own state to a neutral third party. The description provided depends on the demand characteristics of the context.

When these children are ill, theoretically we can expect them to show threatening and blaming behaviour alternating with childish supplications for nurturance – similar to the situation seen with patients with anorexia nervosa. In contrast to infants, children understand that deliberately avoiding behaviour leads to their parents feeling rejected, and so avoiding behaviour can be used as part of a preoccupied strategy to force parents to attempt to get close to them. It disguises their anger. Preoccupied children minimise or exaggerate reality to create an appearance that will motivate the attachment figure to behave as they desire. Some will respond more to threats, others to withdrawal, others to coy behaviour. For nursing staff these alternating behaviours are often seen as patterns of behaviour, without the chance to step back a bit and note the strategic use of the behaviour to handle their needs for their parents. The pattern can often appear confusing and make their nursing difficult unless they can follow the dynamic which has given rise to this pattern. The working model of important relationships is enacted with the nurses, and often frustrates them – leading to the repeating form of relationship, of which the children have previous experience. My hope is that understanding this alternating pattern can reduce their confusion so that they do not 'swing' with the children.

Children try forcibly to get from their parents what they want. 'Pester power' describes rather nicely the challenge laid out for parents. One in five families in the UK are described as having battles over food nearly every mealtime. Children nag their parents to buy food they have seen advertised. Pester power is not solely nourished through the media. The dynamic arises in the family and is part of the culture, which becomes a new norm. Children appear to pester more in Sweden, where advertising aimed at children is banned,[10] compared to Spain where it is deregulated. Children can effectively play on parents' tender spots in order to force their wishes, but the pattern persists as it is not inherently satisfying.

> A mother hit her child as a result of the following sequence. The infant sat in his high chair. It was teatime. He asked for a slice of bread, she promptly gave him exactly the spread he asked for. When she gave it to him he asked for cake instead. She had some in the house, and came up with that too. When he asked for chips instead, she hit him.

Children begin to experiment with the household rules as they get older. Hygiene rules are some of the first to be tinkered with. How is a preoccupied attachment strategy likely to influence this? Children will be attentive to their parents' reactions to breaking the rules. The parental response will be of primary interest, rather than the adolescent independently asserting that this is how they will do things, or coming to some kind of compromise between their wishes as an adolescent and the household routines decided upon by the parents. They will identify which risks they feel exposed to through noting the emotional reactions of those around them, making less use of cognitive information. Depending on their basic predispositions they may break the rules so as to emphasise their vulnerability. This would be done in such a way as to minimise the chance of being held responsible for what they did, and disguise their anger. An alternative would be to threaten to contaminate the household, a dirty protest for example, coherent with the odd-numbered Cs. They are clearly aware of the hygiene rules, and through 'accidents' they challenge the rules to manipulate parental involvement. Through the way in which they focus on handling the emotions raised, they oversee the details in the sequences that lead to the reactions, and fail to learn from what happens.

Risk and preoccupation

Preoccupation with risk can be catastrophic. Instead of facilitating coping, somato-sensory amplification exaggerates existing discomfort. Closeness to those near us does not lessen discomfort. Obsessive thoughts about risk drive attempts at a solution, but with their lack of clarity about temporal sequences and causal relationships, preoccupied individuals are left relying on their emotional antennae. Meeting the gaze of worried associates, be it friends, parents, nurses or other family members, does not help them handle the feeling of being in danger. It is now that the residual anxiety when with their parents, generalised to their new relationships, takes its toll. The pragmatism and instrumentalism, which have characterised their attempts at durable closeness, have become fiends of love and care. They are likely to mull over the forthcoming operation, or go repeatedly through the newspaper reports of the latest influenza epidemic, without ever successfully coming to terms with the issues involved. They will be the easy prey of media hysteria.

Their internal musings, verging at times on catastrophic thinking, focus on somatic images. These arise from body signals, the origins of which they lost sight of long ago. They will be predisposed to feedback hum. The somatic images will become overlaid with the bodily changes associated with fear. Their preoccupation with their bodily signals also means that preoccupied people are seldom satisfied with their bodies.

When people are not there, there is no enmeshment, no emotional contagion. Although their desire for closeness is still activated, they are less troubled by the contagious affect and find a degree of comfort in relaxing settings. Their need for control when under strain can make them possessive and vigilant about comings and goings in their territory. Even when they have found an apparently safe corner, it tends not to be as satisfying as they had hoped. They still feel vulnerable.

Household routines are designed to keep the house as safe a place as possible. The dangers of dirt are tamed. Fresh air drives out the bad. It does not matter that we do not really know what fresh air is, it does its job as a concept that organises routines, destined to keep us healthy (see also Wilkinson, 1988: 48–49, 144–149). Such routines help establish a sense of security in that 'safe corner' which preoccupied individuals are looking for. But because they are not clear about the causal relationships between events, they are most concerned with the feelings engendered by carrying out the routines, rather than the characteristics of 'dirt'. Carrying out household chores can also be a form of moral face-work, designed to assert one's moral rectitude in the neighbourhood. A clean household places one above criticism, and is part of a strategy for handling guilt, shame and anxiety. Challenging such routines, when this is a driving force in the family, can be an effective way of getting parents involved, such as the odd numbered Cs – just try emptying the contents of the vacuum cleaner in the bathroom.

Children can also get parents involved in another way when they feel at risk. Perhaps they have a niggling somatic feeling that they cannot quite place, which has got them worried. They may then display their vulnerabilities and helplessness. These can include adapting the tentative symptoms as if they were definite precursors of illness. A heading in *The Independent*, 19 October 2000, put it this way 'I pretend to be ill, therefore I am'. Uncertainty is banished through getting control over the symptoms, and giving them a name as signal of disease. Parents who care for their children according to the premises in Box 6.1 will find it particularly difficult to distinguish between leveraged use of symptoms and bona fide diseases. Their preoccupation is with their children's illness experiences, not with the antecedents or consequences of disease. The disease models which are likely to make most sense to their way of experiencing such illness episodes involve contagion, the chances of being contaminated by either germs, miasma, air pollution or evil spirits. These are diffuse and intangible and feed their obsessive way of thinking. Their vigilance leads to them being especially vulnerable to the strains associated with children having diseases, such as epilepsy and diabetes, requiring added vigilance from them. Their vigilance also gives their children a powerful tool to manoeuvre with on the family playing field, as slight hints of a forthcoming attack can be effective in getting attention.

Preparing such individuals for an anticipated risky outing, such as with a hospital admission, is not going to succeed if you use the same approach as for a dismissing individual, who can make good use of information about what is likely to happen. Preoccupied individuals get their information from the faces of those close to them. They are monitoring them for *their* affective reaction to what is about to happen to 'the patient'. It will be essential to take care of the emotional needs of those accompanying preoccupied patients to the hospital in order to take care of the coming patient.

The preoccupied affective illness dialogue

> To be preoccupied with health is the greatest obstacle to a good life.
> Platon

It is not easy for preoccupied people to accept their sick role and concentrate on getting themselves well again. It can be as difficult to know when one is well again, as when one was ill. The preoccupation that parents have had with getting to know their children's state has become the children's own preoccupation with how they are. It is not just parents who find it difficult to know when their children are putting it on, children get confused too. The half-ill states of being under the weather become all-embracing diseases. The distinction between being at risk and being ill is unclear, as the emotional response they meet can be similar in both situations. Screening programmes, which highlight risk for breast or prostate cancer, or cervical dysplasia, can be counter-productive for this group of patients.

Although ambiguity maintains preoccupation, the ability of signs of illness, or telling of symptoms to manipulate attention from reticent and unpredictable carers, means that apparent illness can also be turned to advantage. The danger is that people get carried away with their own performance, and lose the distinction in the drama they are enacting (Jureidini, Taylor, 2002). Darwin described it so, 'a frequently repeated effort to restrain weeping, in association with certain states of the mind, does much in checking the habit. On the other hand, it appears that the power of weeping can be increased through habit' (Darwin, [1872] 1998: 155). Even the simulation of an emotion tends to arouse it in our minds (ibid.: 365). The performance, which appeared to provide liberation through its functionality in modulating the relationship, has also trapped them. Symptoms can have both advantages and disadvantages.

Fear and anger are two central affects that predominate in the experience of preoccupied patients. There is a normal developmental sequence for fear (Marks, 1987). Theoretically we should expect that instead of the naturally occurring fears disappearing as children get older, they have been maintained through the processes described in this chapter. Fear of blood is of special interest for those working with patients. When found in adults it has probably been present since childhood, and beside the fear of animals is the fear most likely to persist. It may well have a larger genetic loading than other fears.

Fear and anger may have specific sensitising effects on the alimentary system, and we can expect preoccupied strategies to be more common amongst people with a variety of gut symptoms. Fear leads to less upper gastrointestinal tract motility, whereas anger leads to an increase, associated with increased release of the hormone secretin and blood flow to the region. Both fear and anger increase motility in the colon (Mayer, 2001). There arise special conditioned intestinal responses to words associated with trauma based on learning in implicit memory (Blomhoff, Reinvang, Malt, 1998). It remains to be seen exactly how different disorders may fit into this pattern. Provisionally we know that patients with irritable bowel syndrome (IBS) have marked increase in tension in colonic musculature, that is in the large bowel, in response to anger. Attachment dynamics may prove to play an important role in both symptom origins and maintenance. If one gives patients with IBS exaggerated feedback on the degree of gut distension, their degree of subjective discomfort rises. In other words the degree of dis-ease depends on the external feedback they are receiving, to a larger extent than the feedback from the stretch receptors in the gut. We need to find out what sort of attachment strategies IBS patients have been using. On theoretical grounds one would predict a preoccupied type C attachment pattern, probably C3/5.

Fear and anger also have important different effects on the cardio-vascular system, which are best discriminated through changes in heart period and blood pressure (Kagan, 1994: 148). It remains to be seen whether the preoccupied type C strategies will in consequence predispose to cardiovascular disease,[11] and whether the gender biases in Western culture which make it more acceptable for males to use the odd C strategies characterised by displays of aggression, and females the even Cs with displays of fear and desire for comfort, can explain any of the difference in cardiovascular morbidity. As women in Norway increasingly adopt the 'male' strategies, will their morbidity and mortality from heart attacks increase – or will changes correlate better with changes in other habits such as their relative increase in smoking and dietary changes?

Similar phenomena to those described for IBS are found with blood pressure. Providing an illness label, or putting an illness hypothesis in mind, causes some people selectively to search for sensations associated with that illness, and to interpret incoming sensory information relative to it. After a group of college students were told that their blood pressure was 'a little high for their age', they reported having experienced more blood pressure symptoms in the previous three months (Cioffi, 1991). After a heart attack some patients fail to distinguish between the arousal of exercise, emotion and sexual excitement. They cannot discriminate when they are at risk, and instead adopt a strategy of avoiding arousal-inducing behaviour. They are on the way to chronic disability

(Taylor, Bandura, Ewart, Miller, DeBusk, 1985). My hypothesis is that these patients will more often have preoccupied attachment strategies. Understanding the dynamic which has given rise to their illness behaviour will make it easier to meet them constructively and to anticipate the other aspects of their language of dis-ease.

Medical student syndrome (also see Chapter 7), whereby students come to believe that they have the same disease as they are currently learning about, may arise on the basis of this phenomenon to which type C individuals are especially predisposed.

A healthcare system responds to the symptoms and signs presented by patients. There is an enormous potential for facilitating the elaboration of the complaints presented, so that illness behaviour becomes strategic. Repeated presentation increases the chances of elaboration. Individual performances become sophisticated and intractable with time and in rehearsal with doctors. In a prison health service the potential gains from the functional display of symptoms can lead to very elaborate and highly refined displays to negotiate the rigid power hierarchies. A doctor who fails to contain the emotions, instead nourishing the somato-sensory amplification, is an effective inducer of disability. Investigations and technology play their part in this elaboration, which can result in the confirmation of a disorder. A dubious conviction about whether one is ill has become a certainty as the illness behaviour has become shaped in the interaction with the health profession and their interest in particular symptoms (Jureidini, Taylor, 2002). It seems unfair in such a situation to say that the patient has a factitious illness. Illness symptoms, the feeling of being ill, are real enough. Their elaboration and exaggeration, and increase in suffering, arose in the dynamic of the interaction, not in either participant alone. If anything we should refer to this as a failure of the system. The way in which consultations are influenced by the health-care system's guidelines for good practice affects to what degree symptoms and signs are investigated. Fear of litigation provides fodder for both lawyers and illnesses. Physicians nurture somatic symptoms, psychiatrists and psychologist can nurture psychological discomfort. Heightened bodily awareness is a negative attribute,[12] that not only leads to poorly perceived health but also to excessive use of healthcare systems (Bakal, 1999: 30). Preoccupied attachment strategies exacerbate this problem.

My main focus has been the characteristics of the preoccupied attachment strategy for its effect on the general form of the illness dialogue. Disorganised attachment 'strategies' appear to have an association with the phenomenon of dissociation described in Chapter 2. This makes it difficult for these individuals to make full use of their memory potential. Trauma may have been the cause of their dissociation, and we noted above that this in itself can be enough to limit patients' access to words for describing their subjective state. It may be that this explains the observation that alexithymia is associated with dissociation (Taylor, Bagby, Parker, 1997: 136), and so by extrapolation we should be expecting that individuals with disorganised attachment have a confused access to words for describing their illness experiences, and may well lack a competent vocabulary for conveying their psychological discomforts. There is also a strong association between PTSD and alexithymia, and it may be that unresolved loss and trauma are associated with difficulties with their illness language.

Other twists to the language of dis-ease

In Chapter 5 I described how attachment strategies could be seen as predisposing to various ways of presenting complaints, ways which were characteristically found for certain illnesses. But this does not mean to say that the illness symptoms associated with those diseases are necessarily only found with the dismissing strategies. I used the example of Pamela taking into service her symptoms of asthma to illustrate this chapter's focus on the functional use of symptoms, although I also described characteristics of asthma under the dismissing strategies. This functional application of symptoms has been written about as the 'tyranny of the asthmatic child' (Nocon, 1991). It is important not to draw premature conclusions that particular illnesses are 'caused'/'predisposed' by particular attachment strategies. Understanding the particulars of each patient's developmental history helps us to understand which types of relationship are likely to unfold with health staff, which types of vulnerability are likely to release particular forms of response, how we can best prepare different patients for the demands likely to be made of them during their treatment – and just perhaps it may turn out that the biological consequences of the interpersonal dance which has been internalised in all of us are important for understanding the development of particular diseases. Attachment strategies may turn out to be as important for understanding disease as for the language of dis-ease.

Parents who facilitate the development of preoccupied patterns are focusing on the subjective state, the emotional distress, of their children. The primary effect is in relation to the non-specific illness dimensions of pain and ambiguous somatic symptoms, which can just as well be symptoms of distress as of disease. These include aches, tiredness, changes in feeding habits – all those small details which parents are keeping an eye on when trying to decide whether their child is well enough to go to school or not. The symptoms become woven into a web of interpretations, and in all likelihood elaborated as described above. They are then part of the strategic repertoire employed in the service of maximising attachment with a preoccupied strategy. In order to obtain more reliable research results we need to await the development of methods that do not just note the presence of hostility or fear, pain or illness symptoms, but whether their presentation is strategically organised.

A focus on feeding habits is normal, and yet holds the potential to develop into something more malign. A young child's appetite when claiming to be ill is often regarded as an important indicator of their state. Eating disorders with characteristics of anorexia nervosa are found in two- to three-year-olds who already seem to have found power over others through not eating. In a reciprocal dance of fear and anger with their parent, the stopping eating has escalated out of control – there has been no containment of the infective emotional contagion of fear; the angry aspect (remember the pairing with the odd Cs) appears to be hidden, but secretly felt in 'angry' confrontations around the meal table.

There has been some preliminary exploration of the attachment strategies of women with anorexia nervosa. Various strategies are found, including both dismissing and unresolved loss and trauma, as well as preoccupied type C strategies. The preoccupied women with anorexia, who reported feeling depressed, played up feelings of anger, as well as emphasising their vulnerability. Both aspects of the C strategy were in use. Rates of reported symptoms, whether of minor illnesses, mental health or relationship difficulties, tend to be highest for those with anorexia classified as preoccupied (Cole-Detke, Kobak, 1996).

It is especially in relation to preoccupied attachment strategies that the functionality of symptoms is relevant and important to explore. Although my focus has been on a combination of affective and somatic elements in the language of dis-ease, anxiety as a disorder is found especially often amongst those with preoccupied attachment strategies. This is independent of maternal anxiety and temperament variables (Warren, Huston, Egeland, Sroufe, 1997).

Pain and strain

Discomforts can grow into pains depending on how they are met, both by the patients who are suffering and by the very important others (VIPs). Small niggles which would have been best ignored become significant in the educated gaze of the 'expert' – be that parent of their child, or doctor of their patient. The educated eye is not just looking for associated signs in order to determine the significance of the symptom; they will be more or less vigilant, depending on their concerns. It is not just a neglectful parent who ignores symptoms; it can be the most appropriate thing to do if the child is not in danger. People adopt the strategies that have been used with them during their development. If parents have been especially vigilant, and not helped identify releasing factors which precipitated the episode of pain and soothing strategies which terminated it, children may be left with vigilance as the only strategy to employ when discomforts arise. Their preoccupied type vigilance then nurtures the complaint's potential to become a pain. When the threat value of the complaint is greatest, there will be the greatest contribution of the attachment strategy to the outcome. Unpredictability of the discomfort also leads to more vigilance.

Engel reported the characteristics of patients referred with chronic pain that did not respond to conventional treatment. Many of the life history details he obtained are coherent with descriptions of what goes on in families where preoccupied attachment strategies have developed. For example:

- A parent who was cold and distant except when the child was ill or in pain (illustrating the functionality of the symptom for regulating closeness).
- Having had a parent who punished severely and then overcompensated (illustrating the unpredictability of the parent – which could, but need not necessarily be, associated with preoccupation).
- An inhibited aggressive drive (may be understood as predominant display of the even numbered C strategies – or as part of one of the dismissing strategies such as A3 or 4).
- A patient who as a child was aggressive and hurtful to others until suddenly forced to abandon this behaviour, with associated guilt (may represent a characteristic of the odd-numbered Cs who can apparently unpredictably switch over to the complementary aspect of the strategy) (Engel, 1959).

The discomfort/pain of childbirth is subject to the same phenomena. Women reporting *excruciating* pain during early labour go on to have a mean labour length over twice as long as women who reported pain as *discomforting* (Wuitchik, Bakal, Lipshitz, 1989). My hypothesis is that they also have internalised the vigilance to the internal signals of the preoccupied type C attachment strategies.

Recurrent pain of various kinds is common in childhood and accounts for an enormous load for the first and second levels of health services (Walker, Garber, Smith, Van Slyke, Claar, 2001): 10–30 per cent of children and adolescents report weekly or 'frequent' headaches, 10–25 per cent recurrent abdominal pain (RAP), and 5–20 per cent complain of musculoskeletal pains. About 5 per cent of paediatric consultations are due to abdominal pain and headaches (Egger, Costello, Erkanli, Angold, 1999). Gender difference in pains first becomes prominent at adolescence – and continues into adulthood. Females report more somatic symptoms. The hypothesis needs to be explored that this is secondary to the preferential sensori-amplification of females' discomforts, given their form of attunement to their VIPs, and the sorts of threats and vulnerabilities which they are assumed to have. The original vulnerabilities attributed to girls are responded to as if their vulnerabilities continued and extended at adolescence. Theoretically I expect this to be predominantly involving those with preoccupied attachment strategies, who do not change their expectations with the children's age. The girls' depression and anxiety is a predictor of their likelihood of headaches (four times greater in depressed girls, 2.6 times greater with anxiety), and musculoskeletal pains (13 times greater in depressed girls, and 3.4 times greater with anxiety) (Egger, Costello, Erkanli, Angold, 1999). They have general difficulties modulating their dis-ease. Children with high negative affectivity may interpret stressors as more threatening, doubt their coping abilities, and use passive coping strategies that are less likely to be effective. This results in physiological arousal and emotional distress. The relation between daily stressors and somatic symptoms is stronger for patients with RAP, who have higher levels of trait negative affectivity (Walker, Garber, Smith, Van Slyke, Claar, 2001).

Some provisional implications for clinical practice and health promotion: collaboration and conflict

Patients' expectations in a consultation build on the working model of relationships that they apply to the doctor or nurse; that is, expectations based on a dispositional representation rather than a cognitive one. Patients with preoccupied type C attachments are expected to differ from the dismissing type A patients in several ways:

*   Preoccupied strategists seek help from their doctor or nurse early in the course of their illness. They pick up on small symptoms of

dubious significance, and present these to others for scrutiny. Those with the even C strategies, characterised by desire for comfort and fear, will do this to the greatest degree. They primarily expect others to get them better, minimalising their own responsibility.

- The contact they establish with their health professional will not be as satisfying as they had hoped. They expect to establish and maintain contact through their symptoms. They have not usually found closeness to VIPs inherently satisfying due to their experience with unpredictable parents. They have repeatedly had to work at getting their attention. When they have got their attention, the emotional contagion of the relationship has not enabled them to modulate their own distress. They are noticed, but not helped with their dis-ease.

- They have not learnt about causal relationships, instead being primarily aware of the emotional distress. The form of response to which they have been used has not picked up on the antecedents and consequences of their condition, instead being directed to their subjective state. Their experience of their distress is such that they feel more discomfort, rather than less, because during development the parents' response did not contain their distress but magnified it as they were too identified with it.

- They will remember many colourful episodes, which can illuminate their case history, but they will find it difficult to organise a clear sequence of these. They will be keen to tell all the details in order to convey the emotional qualities, which they have found so necessary with their parents. Nevertheless some of the episodes are likely to be fragmented and by the time one is dealing with a higher C strategy they are likely to be distorted or blatantly false. By the end of the interview you are likely to disagree with the picture the patient has painted of their life history. Demanding a clearer focus from them at the interview stage runs counter to their hopes and expectations based on previous experience. Their semantic memory is much poorer than for the other attachment patterns.

- They are likely to involve clinicians, in contrast to the dismissing patients who attempt to keep them at arm's length. Their strategies for involving others may be problematic, such as using either threats or seductive approaches (especially C5 and 6). The seductive aspect can be quite subtle, such as using 'approved' psychobabble when with a psychotherapist in order to retain their interest and involvement, conveying the idea that progress is coming soon.

- Many of them retain an idealised optimism for the future, learning little from how things have gone previously. They come back for more, still in hope that the 'closeness' they achieved last time can be more satisfying next time, as their attachment behaviour system is still active.

It is not surprising that these patients are frustrating. Clinicians can easily get into conflict with them. Yet it is particularly important in clinical practice that clinicians do not enter a relationship in which the same strategic use of these behaviours to maintain the relationship is repeated. Repeated presentation of somatic symptoms of unclear origin is likely to induce the same use of strategy. There is some suggestion that the otherwise highly acclaimed model of 'patient-centred practice' can do just this in some cases. A personal and understanding relationship was associated with 'greater symptom burden' (Little, Everitt, Williamson, Warner, Moore, Gould, Ferrier, Payne, 2001). Patient centredness, when it includes emotional over-involvement or does not retain a reflective position, cannot be expected to lead to change, and is inherently dissatisfying for both patient and practitioner. The patient's hopes and expectations are a long way from the tradition in which a doctor has been educated, as causal relationships are confusing and antecedents of little inherent interest. Attempts to find out about what *caused* the difficulties open up a new field of enquiry. This is different to what the patient had been expecting, and can be felt as inherently threatening at a time when they most expected to be met with deep-ploughed understanding. It is essential that all practitioners understand this dynamic, as it appears to be associated with some of the least satisfying consultations in the health service.

Clinicians have to meet patients with their illness experience before deciding on the presence or absence of disease/disorder. The emotional contagion between patients and their caregivers has confirmed sickness, and even exaggerated the sickness as a step in referral to a health service (the initial two-person version of this sequence has been internalised by adulthood).[13] The doctor's challenge is to retain clarity about the differences in illness, disease and sickness, and how these are affecting different memory systems. A doctor needs to acknowledge the subjective discomforts, and yet shift the dialogue to an area that provides information about disease and for treatment planning. This is inherently challenging for these patients.

Symptoms have both their pros and cons; they can be used strategically. For preoccupied patients both of these are important to identify, and yet the process of doing this can feel threatening to such patients unless clinicians retain their neutrality.[14] The main aim is to help patients develop their *own* causal models, which can account for their discomforts in alternative ways. What are the repeating sequences, the patterns in their lives as seen by those who are not engulfed in those patterns? What did those sequences result in, how were intentions attributed?[15] The patient is helped to monitor what happens when he tries different approaches to helping himself get better, and he repeats these again and again with necessary modifications of his own to confirm that the sequences occurred and lead to the benefits he was wanting. He becomes an active participant in his own treatment. In order to retain attunement with the patient without contagion, one has to keep a fine balance whenever the patient attempts overly to involve the clinician. Identifying the patients' own theories about how change has come about previously is another way of maintaining engagement on the patients' premises, without remaining in a state of emotional high alert, going nowhere.

In order to maximise collaboration between practitioner and patient the following points must be taken note of:

- The patient's interpretations of the pros and cons of their illness symptoms
- Facilitating the patient's sense of being in control
- Enabling acceptable and attainable targets for change
- And taking account of the patient's attitude to change

(Butler, Rollnick, Stott, 1996)

Treatment goals are specified in small, concrete, specific and behavioural terms. The abstractness of undifferentiated dis-ease must be avoided for preoccupied patients. In contrast to the temptation for a 'paternalistic' approach to the dismissing patients, these patients induce a 'maternalistic' approach, here characterised by intrusive definition of patients' subjective symptoms on their behalf, whilst at the same time the patients only present a part of their strategy (hiding the anger and presenting their coyness, or the opposite) so that this approach can never be more than half right.

Preventive work with such patients is especially difficult given their lack of causal awareness. Information campaigns are unlikely to be effective, as they are directed to their intellect rather than the emotions, which are guiding their behaviour. Exhortations to pay attention to children's needs, which are suitable for a dismissing type A parent, will be counterproductive and potentially exaggerate further the focus of preoccupied type C parents on the subjective world of their infants. Health promotion strategies need to be radically different to cater for the differences in the cognitive and affective strategies of dismissing type As and preoccupied type Cs. I do not have research to point to on which we can build models of good practice, but hope that understanding the processes involved will facilitate trials of goal-directed health promotion.

An aspect of preventive work which has received much attention has been debriefing after traumatic events – or 'defusing' for a process with a similar aim occurring within the first few hours after trauma. The follow-up research has not confirmed that debriefing provides the benefits hoped for (Kenardy, 2000). Currently the debriefing process is not varied depending on the attachment strategies of those attending, or whether they have current unresolved trauma experiences already affecting their response to the current trauma. It is unlikely that that could ever be the case. Yet an attention to the subjective experiences of preoccupied type C individuals risks exaggerating their distress, as has been found with follow-up studies of debriefing. The aim is to avoid development of the unresolved trauma response, which would mean that the trauma affected future processing of information with an inappropriate overgeneralisation to new situations. The ideal debriefing routine remains to be found. It must take account of the different information processing strategies described here, and the way in which information is stored and accessed differently in memory systems.

> There is only one way to happiness and that is to cease worrying about things which are beyond the power of the will.
> Epictetus, *The Golden Sayings of Epictetus*

Notes

1 Initially the A, B, C classification system was used for children, and D was used to describe dismissing adults (E and F being used for the other main adult categories). I am here using the ABC system throughout, and, to avoid confusion with earlier use of D, I use DX for disorganised.

2 Some people develop preoccupied strategies to cope with the dismissing strategies of their parents. If mothers are depressed and withdrawn they will have a chance of getting more attention by getting angry (possibly one of the odd-numbered preoccupied type C strategies), as an alternative to taking care of her in order to get as close to her as possible (compulsive caregiving, A3). Some adults who have developed compulsive compliant strategies, where they have seen things from the point of view of powerful others, attempt to do better for their own children. This can mean becoming aware of their children's negative affect, the anger which had no place in their own childhood relation with their parents. They then attempt to see things from the children's position and focus on their children's feelings rather than their own (this was also what they had done before – focusing on the other's feelings). Through focusing on the children's feelings their children have the

potential to use their display of feelings strategically in negotiation with their parents.

Another way in which dismissing type A parents can bring up preoccupied type C children is through consciously deciding to demand less of their children than was demanded of them, and to be more accepting of the negative affect from their children. These children's parents are still likely to feel uncomfortable with close bodily contact, as the dismissing type As, and so the attachment behaviour employed by the children will mean that their wishes are also partially unrequited, and they will remain frustrated. When the parent neither punishes nor rewards negative affect, the child will tend to organise as a preoccupied threatening type C1. The parents of preoccupied C1 speakers have often been unpredictable, but usually not dangerous (Crittenden, 1999–2002).

3   This may also be the precursor of the development of the ICD-10 diagnosis 'Reactive attachment disorder of childhood', F94.1. The conceptualisation of attachment strategies as being disorders is nevertheless not coherent with the conceptualisation used in this book of attachment strategies being adaptive to the conditions where they were first developed. They represent predicaments, rather than disorders, when employed in situations with different characteristics later in life.

4   See van der Kolk, McFarlane, Weisæth (1996) for further elaboration of the details involved in understanding trauma.

5   There are documented biological consequences of trauma, which on their own are sufficient to account for alexithymia. The data suggest that alexithymia is influenced by the severity of the precipitating trauma, the intensity of the PTSD symptoms, and the chronicity of any physical injury caused by the traumatic event. When people with PTSD are exposed to stimuli reminiscent of their trauma, there is an increase in perfusion of the areas in the right hemisphere associated with emotional states and autonomic arousal. Moreover, there is a simultaneous decrease in oxygen utilisation in Broca's area – the region in the left inferior frontal cortex responsible for generating words to attach to internal experience (van der Kolk, 1996).

6   Virtual support groups on the 'web' are particularly risky areas where people can cause havoc making up serious illnesses to manipulate others in the group.

7   Conditioned responses are preconscious. Similarities in the room, which preconsciously are identified with similarities to the room where they themselves experienced acute distress with their parents, can be enough to release the response. An example, which relates to trauma rather than intergenerational transmission, explains what I mean.

> An eight-year-old boy became impossible to handle each time he sat down on the sofa on the ward. The texture of the sofa was identical to the texture on the sofa where he had been sexually abused for three years from the age of four.

8   The definition of the American Psychiatric Association includes a failure of 'integrative processes of identity, memory, or consciousness' and is I believe

coherent with my use in relation to memory systems (American Psychiatric Association, 1994).

9 At the same time, living under chronically stressful conditions, in which comfort is rarely present, contributes to congenitally healthy children developing neurological damage (Dawson, Grofer Klinger, Panagiotides, Spieker, Frey [1992] and Levine, Johnson, Gonzalez [1985] in Barnett, Hunt, Butler, McCaskill IV, Kaplan-Estrin, Pipp-Siegel [1999]).

10 There are suggestions that Sweden has a greater than expected number of people with preoccupied strategies (Crittenden, 2000b).

11 The development of the autonomic nervous system can take a slightly different course, with various balances between sympathetic and parasympathetic activity, depending on the demands made at critical periods of development (Beauchaine, 2001). We do not yet have definite knowledge pointing to attachment patterns in infants, and strategies in older children and adults. Hypotheses need developing and testing, and can be expected to be fruitful.

12 Panic-prone individuals are one specific patient group known to possess a heightened sensitivity to bodily sensations associated with anxiety (Asmundson, Norton, Wilson, Sandler, 1994).

13 Attention to symptoms is preferable to distraction, especially when the stressor is chronic and when the strategy focuses on the concrete characteristics of the physical sensation (somatic awareness) rather than on diffuse physical states, such as fatigue or tension, or on emotional or cognitive responses (Suls, Fletcher, 1985). Herein lies the crucial distinction for meeting preoccupied type C patients productively. The focus has to be on the concrete details, not the diffuse basic emotions. The goal behind somatic awareness is symptom attenuation, rather than symptom elimination. It is especially difficult for them to grasp the distinction between preoccupation with their symptoms, in contrast to their bodily reactions as somatic awareness. They need help to identify the sequences that give rise to bodily *reactions*.

14 Current treatment strategies for older patients with anorexia nervosa can include encouraging patients to 'Write a letter to your fiend anorexia, and to your friend anorexia'. This is a way of exploring the coercive dynamic of which the symptom has become part, and the patient's motives.

15 Finding out about maintaining factors can be done by asking patients to gain control of their symptoms by elaborating them, being affected at particular times, and generally encouraging symptomatic behaviour so that the double sided nature of the coercive strategies can be personally investigated. This is not to be seen as a paradoxical injunction, which was the rage in family therapy some time ago, but facilitating a genuine exploration of the symptom, with genuine questions. As soon as genuineness is lost the question or advice will be interpreted within the coercive paradigm, and be seen as a manipulation (as many paradoxes used in the name of therapy were – the power of the therapist to trick the patient into getting better). The real paradox is to be found in the discrepancies in patients' own memory systems. Treatment is directed to helping them explore these.

Chapter 7

Ambiguous symptoms and the attachment strategies of health professionals

> Care more particularly for the individual patient than for the special features of the disease.
> William Osler, *The Quotable Osler* (Silverman et al., 2002)

Pamela continued to be troubled by her tummy aches, and at times her asthma attacks seemed quite dramatic. Her regular general practitioner had known her for some time, and helped her and her parents manage most of her attacks. When the newly appointed partner was called out late at night she decided that Pamela, now 16 years old, needed to be admitted to hospital. This leads to a debate between all the partners about how to manage Pamela's escalating use of the practice with an ever-increasing spectrum of complaints.

This chapter looks at how ambiguous symptoms can play a special role in the evolution of attachment relationships between healthcare workers and their patients. Ambiguous symptoms are open to many interpretations; in particular they can be seen as having physical and/or psychological explanations, and their presentation can be part of a person's desire for comfort. They are a fertile ground for personal interpretation, as they may or may not signify 'danger'. Attachment strategies will be revealed, in part depending on how their overtures are responded to.

Children develop their attachment behaviour and subsequently their strategies, depending on the particular sensitivities of those who are close, their VIPs. These developmental processes enable the ambiguous signs and symptoms of childhood, such as crying and tiredness, to gain functional effects for eliciting closeness with a preoccupied type C strategy, or the symptoms may be regarded as unimportant and overseen (in spite of objective signs of disease) by a less-attuned mother. Her child will be more likely to develop a dismissing type A strategy, and ignore those forms of discomfort to which the parent is particularly unresponsive. A balanced type B strategy would be best able to establish a balance, both whether there was a need for response and which skills needed to be used.

I hypothesise that the diagnostic processes carried out by clinicians will be characterised by the same issues of varying attunement and differential responsiveness. The results of their deliberations will play a major role in patients learning how to convey their discomforts effectively, so that their suffering has the best chance of being met. Clinical discourse styles will depend on the predominant attachment strategies of those working in the various branches of medicine. Patient symptoms evolve in the clinical discourse, so that they have the greatest chance of being effective for them (see also Wilkinson [1986] for a parallel description of the same process for children in their families). The discourse starts from the expectations the patients bring – their attachment strategies that they have used for maximising their chances of being taken care of, and the strategies that doctors, nurses or other health professionals also employ.

Medically unexplained symptoms, which can be indicators of serious problems or appropriate to overlook, fulfil the same role as crying and tiredness did for parents of distressed children – and for the children it included their desire for comfort. Coughing can be appropriate to overlook, but it is also the most commonly overlooked symptom of asthma in children. This particular distinction is usually easily resolved, in contrast to headaches and backaches, or chronic fatigue, without associated bodily changes to account for them. Patients' subjective dis-ease meets the gaze of clinicians looking for disease.[1] The search for objective signs to resolve a dilemma concerning the weight to be attached to patients' subjective distress becomes a moral dilemma to a greater degree than a clinical dilemma (providing the doctor is primarily preoccupied with his instrumental role as a curer of disease, rather than a carer of those with unmet desire for comfort).

There is greater potential for conflict amongst those who work with these patients, because ambiguous symptoms are open to many inter-pretations. Within families there is greatest potential for conflict around the half-ill states of being a bit poorly. For some people disease is something you either have or do not have, whereas for others dis-ease is part of a continuum.[2] Parents and health professionals can quarrel viciously about whether a child or patient should be afforded the benefits of the altered demands of the sick role – the adolescent, whom father thinks was skipping school, and mother regarded as ill. Illness behaviour and strategies are partly the result of the outcome of such decision-making and discussion (Wilkinson, 1988). The partners in the practice looking after Pamela need to find out how they are making decisions about responding to Pamela, and note eventual consequences for Pamela's way of presenting her complaints to them.

Such 'dubious' symptoms of uncertain moral value lead to the largest expense borne by health services. People with multiple unexplained symptoms use inpatient and outpatient services up to nine times as often as the general population (Smith, Monson, Ray, 1986). Twenty-five per cent of all general practice consultations concern physical symptoms without a discernible medical cause, and about 50 per cent of hospital outpatients have unexplained medical symptoms (Mayou, Sharpe, 1997); the rate is especially high in gastroenterology and neurology clinics, and low in dermatology. Escalating health service costs are directly related to this group of patients to a much greater extent than the escalating costs of high-technology medicine. These patients suffer, and their health service bears the brunt of their distress, incurring the costs (see Bass, Murphy [1990] for details of costs) without alleviating the suffering. These patients spend between 1.3 and 4.9 days in bed each month, compared with patients with major medical problems who average one day or less. They are the bane of a health minister's life, and seldom the interest of research institutes.

Treatment of ambiguous symptoms requires that clinicians operate with an integrated understanding of mind and body. Adopting an attachment perspective enables a focus on how to understand their complaining, but it does not address the question of veracity of disease as a precipitant of their suffering. We are now essentially back to where we started in Chapter 1. There we looked at the way in which parents decided about a child's crying, and from their interpretation they decided if the child was sick, but not what sort of disease the child had. The same interpretative dynamic is guiding clinicians. Patients are suffering, but initially it is unclear whether their discomforts reflect disease, psychological discomfort that requires treatment, or dis-ease which has to be lived with and needs comfort – a predicament. Just as parental strategies for handling their distressed children lead to the children developing strategies for complaining effectively and maximising their coping with their parents (and concurrently parents with their children), the same processes occur between clinicians and patients. Patients have theories of mind concerning their doctors and nurses, based both on previous working models of relationships and more specific models based on experiences with doctors – and doctors and nurses have them of their patients and each other.

Just as parents tend selectively to perceive and organise their children's signs and symptoms on the basis of their own models of what is meaningful and the pattern of their lives together, it is likely that doctors do the same. This will mould the illness behaviour that predominates in that doctor's practice. Mechanic pointed out that mothers experiencing stress symptoms assumed that their children were experiencing the same symptoms (Mechanic, 1964). We must expect that both parents and doctors will influence their children and patients to label and report symptoms in ways similar to themselves. It is already beginning to seem as if patients' ways of coping with illness are looking more like those of doctors (Christie, 2001). There is nothing inherently right in either the parents' or doctors' way of seeing things; it is more or less helpful for that particular child or patient with their particular history of being looked after. Symptoms mean different things to different people. In one study (Pennebaker, 1982: 61) not one of 18 symptoms was described in an identical way by all subjects. Nevertheless, symptoms that are reported within any given culture tend to be similar. Symptoms are socially constructed and used in strategic ways, which depend on each individual's theory of the other's mind and their attunement capability.

Presentation of somatic symptoms, regardless of their cause, is associated with greater levels of social and psychiatric morbidity, independent of culture (Kisely, Goldberg, Simon, 1997). The high symptom reporter makes frequent use of health services, but their frequent consultations do not have any enduring effect on symptoms. Consultations do not reduce their frequency of subsequent attendance with acknowledgement of their ineffectiveness for effecting cure (although we cannot exclude it having a role in relation to desire for 'comfort care'). Through exploring the fit between somatic presentations, the likely dominant attachment strategies employed by health professionals and those employed by these patients, it may be possible to use attachment theory to analyse this form of illness strategy in fruitful ways, so that the distress of these patients can be met helpfully. Because we are here looking at an intersubjective fit of patient and doctor, the focus will be on the language form and content, and not on the veracity of the symptoms.[3] In the process I hope to extend the field of applicability of attachment theory in relation to understanding the language of dis-ease.

Ambiguous symptoms

Everyday symptoms can signify a wide range of diseases. Some of them are part of the pattern of symptoms found with life-threatening diseases, and yet others are found as part of a pattern of disorder, a syndrome without associated diagnostic pathognomy. A doctor's role is partially as a gatekeeper to the rights that a society gives to those who have officially approved disorders. Patients are acknowledged, and afforded the rights of being sick – but not acknowledged rights to consult a doctor with unmet desire for comfort. Yet there is no reason for a correspondence between these dis-ease states, and in the final count ambiguous symptoms arouse a political debate about the rights being afforded the sufferer, and how the gatekeeper should handle the role. A family equivalent in a traditional family is how a housewife decides whether her children should attend school or not. Her gatekeeper function on behalf of the family can be a problem in her relation to school and husband.

Through looking at the pattern found with various of these symptoms it may be possible to develop hypotheses about links to particular strategic use of these symptoms and differing attachment strategies. In order to find out about these possibilities we need to note the *precipitating* factors – when is the presentation of the complaint relevant, and what are the associated vulnerabilities or *predisposing* factors which make such presentations more likely, and likely to take specific form. By following this up with an exploration of how health professionals respond to symptoms of unknown provenance, maintaining or *perpetuating* factors may be discerned related to the interactional pattern. Together there is a co-evolution of strategy, where the response can maintain the vulnerability, and yet paradoxically facilitates the effectiveness of a way of complaining. If the response is only partially appropriate to the needs of the patient, there may be a particularly strong predisposition to retain the behaviour. The type C attachment behaviour meets some of the person's needs, but not all. It is strongly retained with an intermittent reinforcement schedule, which can appear to an outsider as a particularly 'strong' sort of attachment.

Different attachment strategies are associated with different distortions of information (see Box 7.1, p. 234). These will both concern what sort of information is presented for consideration by the health professional, and what information the health professional makes use of in decision making. The presentation of a symptom means that a particular form of complaint 'behaviour' is available in the person's vocabulary, but it does not tell us how it might be used strategically. This requires an interpersonal perspective. We ought not to expect a one-to-one correlation between symptom and type of attachment strategy. The '*valeur*' of the symptom will differ depending on the experience of those who can come to respond (for a theoretical discussion of *valeur* see Harré [1991: 227]). The *valeur* is in the eye of the beholder and their preconscious dance with the patient, and gets transmitted to the patient, without them knowing exactly what is going on at the preconscious level. Values are conveyed in the non-verbal interaction.

The more symptoms people have the more likely they are to get a medical response as if they had a disorder; the chance of discerning pattern is greater (in this context not a pattern of usage in a defined context, but an aggregation of symptoms found together in a syndrome). Pennebaker described the characteristics of those who get multiple symptoms, in comparison to those who get few symptoms (Pennebaker, 1982: 139). They tend to be self-conscious and anxious with low self-esteem. They are likely to be young women from lower socioeconomic backgrounds. At home there are likely to be many conflicts, and people are socially insecure and anxious. More often they seek to please and be close to members of the opposite sex. They make frequent use of medical services and self-medicate with painkillers. Their lifestyle is less healthy than those with less frequent symptoms. Those who spontaneously complain without holding back have a particularly poor outcome, as do those who do not even temporarily respond to assurance.

We know that poverty makes good parenting more difficult, and that there is a bias towards higher scores for both type A and C attachment strategies, as well as unresolved loss and trauma. Such people would be expected to be more anxious and socially insecure, although willing to share this to markedly differing degrees (Boxes 5.2, 6.2) – the self-sufficiency and avoidance of the type A strategies suggest they will keep away from health professionals with all sorts of complaints, the Cs will be preoccupied with their condition and make greater use. Use of the preoccupied strategies would be coherent with the spontaneous complaining and ineffectiveness of assurance. Nevertheless we need to look at specific disorders (patterns of symptoms) in order to explore whether patient forms of complaining, with various somatic symptoms, can be expected to have any special relation to attachment strategies.

Although backache and chronic fatigue syndrome[4] have been much researched, I will concentrate on 'somatisation disorders' with their diversity of symptoms, and somatisation as a process. As is frequent for enigmatic disorders there is also little agreement about what constitutes somatisation between those on both sides of the Atlantic. This enigma needs its decoder. My interest is not to explore the objective diagnostic criteria and their validity, but to look at the way in which the strategic use of symptom presentation (or withholding of presentation) can be understood within an attachment paradigm. My interest is therefore to present some of the characteristics of those who preferentially present disease with language of potential somatic disease. I subsequently look at the attachment strategies of those working in health services to see whether there can be a fit or mismatch between patient and professional which can lead to some of the problems for this large group of expensive patients. When the attachment strategies of the doctor meet those of the patient, there arise peculiar difficulties for establishing a goal-directed and corrected partnership, depending on the match of attachment strategies.

Somatisation: somatic dis-ease

Somatisation has been seen as a cultural and historical product of Western medicine; it was the evolution of the notion of medical illness, in contrast to psychiatric, which allowed the emergence of somatisation (Fabrega, 1990). Indeed, there is no place for such a concept in cultures that make no distinction between physical and psychological sickness, and that have no technology for establishing objectively that somatic dysfunction exists.

Somatic awareness emphasises the mental processes by which we perceive, interpret, and act on information from our bodies, our basic emotions.[5] The basic emotions are not directly available for consciousness, but are interpreted and give rise to feelings of somatic awareness. The process of interpretation becomes embodied. The interpersonal process of interpreting the child's state is carried forward as the child's reality of the nature and value of those states – the way of being with the child more or less meets his desire for comfort. The affect associated with the state is deduced from the gaze of those looking after them. The proto-emotions associated with stress, disease and bodily needs, such as hunger and tiredness, present ever-changing, unpredictable and diffuse physical sensations which need to be identified and responded to. Some will be filtered out so that consciousness never needs to take notice of them. Imagine what it would be like having consciously to monitor and adjust respiration. Other symptoms are either subsequently overlooked or acted upon. The difficulty is to know what is required. Those looking after us can need help with identifying when action is imperative, probably necessary, or irrelevant. Coming to a consultation can be part of this process. Professionals are then drawn into deciding with the patient, and/or their parents, whether the condition can be normalised and lived with, requires further clarification, or must be acted upon. As they are under a potential threat, the patient's attachment strategies will be mobilised in the consultation.

There is maximum uncertainty for a professional who depends on identifying somatic signs of diagnosis, until such signs are clear. The predominant mind/body dualism amongst Western healers exaggerates this dichotomy, and they often cope with this by ignoring that there is no direct correlation between physiological parameters and dis-ease. It is possible to feel highly stressed without associated physiological changes, and to have the changes without discomfort. It is possible to have behaviour corresponding to high stress, without feeling stressed or having physiological signs (Box 3.1). Looking for objective signs provides a false sense of diagnostic security. The problem remains making sense of patients' illness, as regardless consultations have to start with their dis-ease, and subsequently note the pattern of relation to other parameters.

When patients come to a consultation it is often found that their emotional reaction, or level of function, does not relate to the clinician's view of the seriousness of the condition. Nevertheless there is no doubting the *potential* seriousness of the symptoms. The most common somatisation symptoms seen in medicine are dizziness, dyspnoea, and chest pain, which may make people worry about their heart. These three symptoms are also the core symptoms of anxiety,[6] although they are seldom presented to a psychiatrist first. Anxiety feeds worry, and anxiety is worry (Box 2.4).[7]

Having a disease is also likely to make people more concerned, and be more predisposed to additional signs of anxiety. The subjective discomfort of the dis-ease of illness needs to be the prime focus as it is the motivating force for the consultation, treatment and prevention, even though specific treatment methods and health promotion literature will more often be directed to disease processes.

Somatisation is probably most helpfully seen pragmatically as a process characterising a spectrum of disorders with a spectrum of severity (Katon, Lin, von Korff, Russo, Lipscomb, Bush, 1991). What are relatively stable for the long term are patients' propensities to have (or not have) multiple medically unexplained somatic complaints (reanalysed data from Simon, Gureje [1999] in Gara, Escobar [2001]).

Kirkmayer and Robbins suggest that somatisation amongst patients presenting to primary care can involve three different processes:

- Functional somatisers, who have no sign of depression or apparent overconcern about their symptoms which are employed functionally.

- Somatic presenters, who have current major depression or anxiety, and are open to psychological interpretations of their somatic distress.
- Hypochondriacal somatisers, who have high illness worry in the absence of serious illness or depression (Kirmayer, Robbins, 1991). (I return to hypochondriasis on pp. 221–223.)

It is necessary to note a fourth group of patients presenting from cultures without a differentiation between somatic and psychological disease languages, for which the above distinctions do not apply.

Much research has not explicitly discriminated between these categories, yet I am interested in retaining them because it is tempting to hypothesise different attachment processes in relation to each of the subgroups. The preoccupied type C attachment strategies are functional, and the even-numbered C strategies preoccupied with eliciting caregiving and appearing submissive (Box 6.2). This might continue until their caregiver (or health professional) became overly involved and enmeshed with them, at which time they might temporarily shift to being aggressive, and a complementary odd-numbered strategy. In contrast people developing dismissing type A attachment strategies would be expected to have had parents who neglected the nuances in their discomforts, and with a lack of interest in their subjective discomforts they would have had little chance of learning the words for psychological discomforts. These feelings would not have elicited any extra care and attention. Instead a minimal parental responsiveness when disease began to affect the child might have had a special place in sensitising the person to the effectiveness of complaining with bodily complaints, and meeting their desire for comfort in that way. It is worth a provisional hypothesis that functional somatisers make use of preoccupied type C strategies, and somatic presenters type A strategies.[8]

Why should those who somatise have such persistent problems, and make such frequent use of health services, without apparently being helped? Their visits to clinicians appear as exceedingly necessary, yet inherently unsatisfying and mutually frustrating, just as do the 'recharging' approaches carried out by children who seek their parent to whom they have developed a preoccupied type C attachment strategy. They come back for more, yet complain that the consultation did not help. What keeps the consultation tango going when they appear to be stepping on each other's toes all the time?

The illness triad: somatisation, depression and anxiety

Part of the lack of satisfaction of the consultation is the confusing presentation. The surface message does not convey all the music. Somatisation is the most common way for psychiatric disorders to present. Although depression and anxiety colour the picture of the somatic presenters group, the National Institute of Mental Health Epidemiologic Catchment Area Study in the US suggested that anxiety[9] and panic were probably the most important determinants of somatisation (Simon, von Korff, 1991). The details get confusing because of the lack of agreement about which are valid subgroups to investigate, and even the central characteristics of the somatising group as a whole. The important issue is that psychiatric disorders and somatisation often occur together.[10] Some recent work suggests that depression (here including dysthymia, a form of chronic low mood), anxiety and somatisation are all part of a distress syndrome. The difference seems to be that those who present somatic dis-ease feel more incapacitated by the physical symptoms, and those who present psychological symptoms feel more incapacitated by their depression or anxiety. There are different attributions of the distress (Henningsen, Jakobsen, Schiltenwolf, 2001). The situation is similar for children, with an association between unexplained pain and depression (Egger, Costello, Erkanli, Angold, 1999). It is important to identify co-morbid psychiatric disorder and treat it. The presence of co-morbid psychiatric disorder is associated with a good outcome; indirectly this suggests that the functional somatisers may have the worst prognosis.

Hypochondriasis

Every change in basic emotions can be a signal of threat. They signal that something is wrong, but not initially what it is, or whether it really needs attention. With risk of serious danger it is more important to take action than to wait and find out whether it was really necessary. The psychosocial classification of diseases (Box 1.2) discriminates a key group which requires vigilance. Several of this group have symptoms that can be linked to such diseases as can be expected to be the predominant concern in hypochondriasis, such as fear of heart attack. Attachment systems of behaviour will be mobilised.

People learn the somatic cues that need to be taken care of, and those that can be ignored. We adopt strategies to make use of other people based on our working models of relationships. Hypochondriasis involves the conviction that the person has a disease, is worried about it and seeks help for it, but no disease is found. Such patients have illness without disease, and receive a disorder diagnosis and are regarded in many societies as having a sickness, although a second-rate one. Doctors are also tempted to abet the process as they often ascribe disease, even though they cannot be specific about the physical changes purportedly observed corresponding to signs of the disease (Gureje, Üstün, Simon, 1997).

Medical student syndrome is a form of hypochondriasis, which doctors may have experienced.[11] Yet they fail to make use of this experience when attempting to understand their patients. Many qualified doctors report that their medical knowledge still makes them prone to swing between panic and denial when they experience symptoms (Thompson, Cupples, Sibbett, Skan, Bradley, 2001). The contributory factors involve bodily symptoms, which the student fails to identify as they have detailed but incomplete and diffuse information of the disease, at the same time as they are anxious and socially stressed (Mechanic, 1972). It needs an integrated mind/body to meet the challenge, and complaints need to be placed in their social context.

Hypochondriacal worries also occur in patients with definite disease. Their fears appear exaggerated, being regularly presented and yet not responding to assurance given in a language coherent with the patient's own understanding of how their disease is affecting them. Their preoccupation with their symptoms can also be regarded from an attachment perspective, especially in regard to preoccupation with somatic images (to be discussed on p. 227), and an unmet 'desire for comfort'.

Patients with hypochondriasis tend not to confide in others about distressing personal experiences (Barsky, Wool, Barnett, Cleary, 1994). This makes it less likely that errors in processing of information will be corrected. It is also suggestive that hypochondriasis will be associated with attachment strategies that emphasise self-sufficiency, such as compulsively self-reliant A6. But this need not be the case, as the attachment issue, once people have a theory of mind, is the eventual strategic use of the symptom – the symptomatic behaviour having evolved in VIP relationships. If the 'lack of confiding' was demonstratively waved in front of potentially interested people, such as demonstratively appearing to be in discomfort, but not opening up to people about it, this could be part of a type C strategy. The flagged discomfort could be in order to get them to enquire about what was troubling the patient (an even-numbered type C strategy playing on helplessness and lack of responsibility for their own condition). Beware also the distinction between what support a patient says is available and what is available. A person using a type C strategy would be likely to play on their own helplessness when conveying their 'plight' in a research investigation. Conversely the potentially available other, if part of the preoccupied dynamic will exaggerate their own ability to be that confidant, and so assist in the blame for failure of the relationship residing with the presenting patient. Because a type C strategy is associated with only partial presentation of negative affect – fear without anger, or anger without fear – a person with such a strategy will be unlikely to rely on any assurance given, as they will be used to this being only half of the truth; their parents will more often have been 'economical with the truth'. For such individuals assurance is worth a try, but reassurance should be avoided until one knows why they could not rely upon the assurance.

We do know that patients with persistent hypochondriasis have people close to them whom they believe would find it difficult to normalise their symptoms, and also be less likely to have encouraged them to see a doctor (Robbins, Kirmayer, 1996). In contrast, those with temporary illness fears reported that their significant others supported their decision to see the doctor, and would act to normalise new symptoms. By normalising new symptoms, those close to them redefine new illness episodes as non-threatening. Again, a more detailed analysis of attachment strategy could help elucidate the nature of the belief, and the interpretation of advice, and how it should inform future research or a clinician's approach.[12] Although their major presented concern is their worry about disease, they are nevertheless at increased risk of major depression or anxiety (Robbins, Kirmayer, 1996). This places this group also in the triad of somatisation, depression and anxiety. Just like other somatising patients, they cost the health service a lot. They are more likely to be no-shows for clinic appointments, and instead go doctor shopping. Overall they are at increased risk for over-investigation. And they still suffer.

It is possible that the prognosis for individuals with hypochondriasis relates to this distinction between types A and C. Patients with a good outcome had an illness of shorter duration when first referred, whilst patients with a poorer outcome tended to have had longest duration (Pilowsky, 1997: 54). The potential explanation being that assurance could work for those with a type A self-reliance, and a reliance on cognitive information given by a doctor who did not convey any affective uncertainty. In contrast, those with a longer history might have a functional use of their helplessness as part of a type C strategy, and reassurance for them did not alter the context in which the symptoms lived their independent life, and they continued to search for comfort.

A developmental perspective

To understand Tinbergen's second question: 'How did the person grow to respond this way?' we turn to developmental research. The twin research within this field (somatoform disorders) shows the importance of a familial explanation, and yet highlights the importance of influences from the environment rather than genetic influences (Torgersen, 1986). I suggest that these are especially the developmental processes associated with children developing the various attachment strategies, which occur within their families. This is supported by the work of Magai, who has found that the ways in which children attribute meaning to ambiguous affective stimuli depend on their early relationships with their parents, which have established their expectations (Magai, 1999). The attachment strategies of health workers have a role to play in further evolution and maintenance of the difficulties,[13] and the dominant strategies in the culture will affect frequency.

The dismissing type A strategies are associated with people learning causal sequences with their contingencies – antecedents and consequences[14] – but failing to balance this with an understanding of affect, which for them can provide erroneous information. One thing appears clearly to lead to another, although coincidental occurrences can lead to erroneous beliefs about causal sequences. They also learn that negative affect directed to those looking after them can make it difficult to get close to them, or even elicit a punitive response. This can also paradoxically result in an idealisation of those one depends upon, and yet an avoidance of intimacy. When attunement between parent and child has been so reduced that the children's care has been jeopardised, these individuals will seldom have been responded to for the nuances in their states of discomfort. It would therefore be a natural consequence that they developed an ineffective language for conveying their discomforts to others. Many maltreated children fail to differentiate, label and understand emotional expressions in other people; their range of feelings also appears rather limited and blunted (Beeghly, Cicchetti, 1994).

Their attempts, from initial simple crying, can gradually have faded out through a process of contingent shaping of behaviour. Occasionally, though, chance events open up new avenues, such as a serious illness in the family, which may be sufficient to mobilise some caregiving. A subgroup of somatising individuals may consist of people who have learnt that presenting somatic complaints can succeed, where presentation of other forms of discomfort was never enough. This should not be regarded as a conscious process, but a shaping of behaviour according to the learning principles of implicit memory. We do know that children only need to see illness behaviour once to have got a good enough idea of what it involves to repeat it later; they can also build on their own previous experience of illness (Mullins, Olson, Chaney, 1992), as is found with pseudo-epilepsy attacks being most common amongst patients with epilepsy, and possibly asthma attacks amongst those with asthma.

In addition we know that particular pains run in families.[15] If parents tend to have backaches, the children develop backache more often – similarly for headache, and toothache, without there necessarily being signs of disease matching the discomfort being presented (Wilkinson, 1988: 198). The condition is familial, but not genetic. Parents are sensitised to respond to the same discomforts that they have been bothered by. Once something is noticed, it gets a label as part of the coping process. The label comes from the vocabulary available. Only when parents are less stressed are they more open to acknowledging relatively unknown discomforts, which are not from their own realm of experience. Part of the doctors' dilemmas become distinguishing the familial from the genetic, especially if they are preoccupied with a moral superiority of physically based suffering. Family members can also be interested in creating scapegoats who have not arrived in their current predicaments through family processes, in order to assert their own moral superiority over the involved family members.

Does any additional research on somatisation support such an analysis? A consistent finding is that somatisation is more common amongst those who have grown up deprived of material resources during the first twelve years of their life, whereas the depression arm of the triad is more common amongst those exposed to life events, and when the deprivation has occurred when they were older (Portegijs, Jeuken, van der Horst, Kraan, Knottnerus, 1996). If we then return to the predisposing, precipitating and perpetuating factors model for understanding disease, we have a potential non-specific vulnerability factor of early deprivation, which cannot explain why a particular behaviour should be shown at a particular time (Tinbergen's first question), or retained; and a precipitating factor of a life event, which can potentially explain both 'why now?' and associated maintaining factors in someone vulnerable because of their deprivation. Deprivation and life events do not explain, but are associations that point in the direction of, further investigation of interpersonal processes which are modified under threat, be it material or personal. Attachment theory, which accounts for developmental biases that arise under threat, can explain these phenomena, but it remains uncertain whether it is warranted to account for somatisation under such circumstances in this way.

An attachment perspective can help us to understand why individuals with somatisation convey their discomforts as they do – the form to their complaining as opposed to the content of their complaints. In the way they use health services, taken with the way they are responded to, lies the greatest hindrance to effective use of health service resources. Interventions, designed to help people with chronic need for medication to take it regularly, are not usually effective. Only about 50 per cent of those who require regular medication take it, and this includes those dependent on it for survival, such as after a transplant. Interventions to enable people to maintain changes in lifestyle are carried through by under 10 per cent (Haynes, Montague, McKibbon, Brouwers, Kanani, 2001). The chances of those with somatisation disorders succeeding in these areas will probably be even less, given their frequent non-attendance.

The conundrum involves looking for an explanation for why a group of patients go frequently to their doctor, get followed up with a large number of outpatient appointments, may be admitted for further investigations, appear content, yet retain their complaints – and come back for new rounds of protracted investigation and advice, now complaining about the treatment they received the previous time. Their hope for a future solution, and preoccupation with their somatic discomfort, is not lessened.

A dismissing type A strategy would not carry on like this, whatever disease they had. The exception amongst those who somatise are a group who have transient somatising, make use of assurance, manage to reattribute the origins of their dis-ease from a physical cause to a psychiatric disease – and hopefully with adequate treatment of their depression or anxiety get well. Kirmayer and colleagues described the agreeableness and conscientiousness of some of the somatising patients (Kirmayer, Robbins, Paris, 1994). These personality attributes could be coherent with dismissing type A compulsive compliant or compulsive caregiving, A4 and A3, classifications for example, or could be part of the leveraged display of helplessness characteristic of the even-numbered type C strategies. Remember that the even-numbered type C strategies are part of pairs, which involves the individual at times flipping over to displays of aggression. Not until the strategic use of the illness display is analysed can the terms help us distinguish the attachment issues.

Illness vocabulary: words for feelings or alexithymia

People learn their vocabulary for their internal states dependent on how their states have been responded to by those close to them (Box 2.2). Later on vocabulary is enlarged in meetings with others, through the media and especially health professionals. People depend on their parents' attunement, such that they identify that something is up, and put a name to it. The various attachment strategies are associated with various degrees and forms of attunement (e.g. emotional resonance and alignment). They are associated with differing transformations of information, and so the words attributed to the states that are noticed will be more or less complete or accurate. For instance a child who is distressed may have their facial grimace ignored, but the parent may later respond to the child's complaint of tummy ache. Type A strategy holders have no preoccupation with experience of their bodies, but are dependent on how their body signals are seen or ignored, which gives them a sort of distance between body and subjective experience. When people say that they are stressed, we only know that describes the state they were in when others provided that label. Symptom labels are often misleading in ways that vary with attachment strategy. For example, people using preoccupied type C strategies will often only convey *some* of their feelings (and then to an exaggerated degree), and so the clinical picture remains incomplete.

When parents' statements do not reflect children's experience, or when the statements are inaccurate (usually because the parent wants the child to believe something), children's emerging semantic representation of reality will be incongruent with their procedural and imaged understanding. They learn that semantic information, such as the words being used of them, can be false, but will not necessarily be enabled to acknowledge this difference. They will experience paradoxes when they attempt to integrate information from all their memory systems.

Preoccupied individuals often use images as a substitute for words for their feeling states, and organise their speech on the 'affective logic' inherent in the images rather than with cognitive (temporal/causal) logic. These images, particularly the somatic images, appear to function to make past events seem real, present, and immediate; thus, they focus the individual's attention on the situation associated with the image (Crittenden, 1999–2002). It may be that patients who somatise are repeatedly being troubled by their somatic images of distress, for which they have no reliable words to convey effectively. They are preoccupied with their body sensations, and dissatisfied with their bodies. Words and labels for these states are slippery stuff. The somatic images often reflect emotions of fear and vulnerability, whereas contextual images can convey comfort or arousal associated with territorial vigilance and possessiveness.

The special difficulty associated with the preoccupied type C strategies, and their use of words for feelings of dis-ease, is that words describing overtly expressed feelings are associated with inhibited feeling states as well:

> Association of words for conveying feelings with displayed affect confuses the meanings of those words when the internal experience includes *inhibited* feelings; for example, telling a type C child that he is 'angry' when he displays exaggerated anger while concurrently inhibiting display of feelings of fear and desire for comfort reduces the precision of semantic language. This explains the vague and inaccurate use of semantic descriptors by type C speakers. They learn that semantic information can be false.
>
> (Crittenden, 1999–2002, Chapter 7, p. 5)

In contrast, compulsively dismissing type A speakers both provide affectively intense images and, at the same time, fail to acknowledge the affect represented in the image; indeed, if queried, they deny experiencing that affect. In these cases, the image functions to represent the forbidden feelings of the speaker (Crittenden, 1999–2002).

Whatever the feeling, we all search for a name for it, and are limited to the vocabulary we have learnt. Psychological language, to a patient who somatises, is like Norwegian to the average Englishman. There is close correlation between presence of somatisation and alexithymia. Alexithymia describes difficulty in identifying feelings, and distinguishing between feelings and bodily sensations of emotional arousal (Taylor, Bagby, Parker, 1997: 29).[16] I refer the reader who particularly wishes to explore the connection between this construct and somatisation to Taylor *et al.* op. cit. (see also glossary for definition of alexithymia). The important point for my purpose is that the characteristics of individuals with alexithymia can be understood using a developmental perspective and the dynamic-maturational model of attachment. This includes reports from clinicians that alexithymic individuals tend to establish markedly dependent relationships, but that these relationships are highly inter-changeable, or alternatively that they prefer to be alone and to avoid people altogether (Taylor, Bagby, Parker, 1997: 44). Taylor suggested application of the dynamic-maturational model as a fruitful future research direction in 1997 (ibid.: 41). In order to understand the complexity we need to make use of a variety of attachment strategies, but this should not be surprising as symptomatic behaviour needs to be understood strategically – the same behaviour being employed in various strategies.[17]

In the series of clinical vignettes on Pamela's life, it is provisionally uncertain to what extent her experiences with her well-enough-attuned adopted mother can compensate for her early traumatic influences.[18] Beeghly and Cicchetti found that children who had experienced severe neglect and abuse used less internal state language and talked less about their own thoughts, feelings and actions, than did non-maltreated toddlers. They were also less able to differentiate between different feelings (for example, being confused between their feelings of sadness, anger and fear – a form of 'interoceptive confusion') (Beeghly, Cicchetti, 1994). Acute somatisation in adults is associated with a history of early parental neglect, indifference, and abuse (Craig, Boardman, Mills, Daly-Jones, Drake, 1993). By the time they are six years old children who have developed 'insecure' attachments show more somatic complaints (Lewis, Feiring, McGuffog, Jaskir 1984). Transcripts of the language used by somatising patients had been investigated prior to the current knowledge about memory systems and scoring of AAI (Oxman, Rosenberg, Schnurr, Tucker, 1985). They were characterised by a lack of references to other people, both family and friends. The apparent isolation of the patients was striking. Social isolation can be associated with several attachment classifications (Boxes 5.2, 6.2). It limits use of words and the chance of learning new ones.

The developmental cycle can be perpetuated as the children, when grown up, attribute meaning to their own children's complaints and signs of dis-ease using their own limited vocabulary. Research has shown a positive relationship for alexithymia between young adult children and their mothers (Meade, Lumley, Casey, 2001). In order to enable greater coping, it is not necessary that everyone learns a psychological vocabulary, but it is necessary that maltreatment of children and deprivation be reduced. Psychological language is a relatively new 'language', and is not necessary for conveying all dis-ease (Kirmayer, 1984). It is necessary to get in tune with people who have not had people 'feel with them'. It is helpful to think of somatisation as a sign of 'system error', to use management language. The fault does not lie in an individual, but belongs to their ecology of development. The doctor needs to avoid furthering the error.[19] Somatisation survives with medical complicity. Through enquiring of the children of their adult patients who somatise, clinicians can improve their lot. They are a particularly vulnerable group who are more often maltreated, hospitalised, develop psychiatric disorders and attempt suicide (Livingston, 1993). In order to get the whole picture, and enable sympathy for a group of patients who are frustrating, ask about their families of origin too (remember the caveat from Chapter 5 that many who have been neglected idealise their parents). The key questions need to distinguish between an answer from a person's semantic memory – an adjective, which idealises a parent perhaps, and a description from episodic memory which can confirm the adjective used.

Should patients be helped to accurate descriptions of their state, clinicians find that verbal communication of affective distress appears to protect against somatisation through reducing the level of autonomic arousal, which gives rise to the emotions feeding the feelings of distress, whereas continuing alexithymia is associated with poor treatment outcome. The difficulties patients have in conveying their feelings to others, either in words or with accurate expressive facial dialogue or gestures, maintain their difficulties, as it is more difficult to enlist help – even if mobilisation of their attachment strategy had disposed them to make use of others.

Clinicians' main difficulties are usually in establishing the sort of relationship whereby

• they avoid the pitfalls of confirming or denying a patient's reality of their suffering from the clinicians' privileged position (confirming their 'headache' or 'recurrent abdominal pain'), and instead
• identify the music which the patient is 'dancing' to – the form of their complaining rather than the notes used.

Just as parents need to learn the dance of their child when they attune to the child, so clinicians need to have a broad enough repertoire to be able to get attuned with their somatising dancing partners, and dance their tune. Once the dance has started, there arises the possibility to add new notes and learn new steps. In order to get started doctors need to be aware of their own attachment strategies for the part they play in their attunement with their patients, and the limitations they can impose on their understanding of languages of dis-ease.

The attachment strategies of health professionals

The doctor–patient relationship results from what both parties bring to the relationship, their hopes, expectations and fears (their dispositional representations in their working models of relationships). Doctors' attachment strategies are one bit of this equation. Health professionals do not appear to be a cross-section of society, and we ought not to expect them to have the same distribution of attachment strategies as found in their local community. It is nevertheless to be expected that the general characteristics of physicians or nurses from one country will not be the same in another.

Researchers need to address the complexity of the doctor–patient relationship, given the greater complexity of current understanding of bio-psychosocial development. As I said above, I regard the perpetuation of somatising behaviour and its leveraged use in medical consultations in many Western health service practices as a sign of system error. System errors are being looked at through the theoretical approaches of complex systems theory, and chaos theory, as in a recent Institute of Medicine report in the USA (Institute of Medicine, 2001). They see human behaviour as being influenced by 'strange attractors', which are often hidden or poorly articulated values or needs.

Improving the service so that the doctor–patient relationship does not breed illness or foster sickness entails understanding and using the values and needs of those who directly care for patients (Kelley, Tucci, 2001). One way of doing this is to look at the attachment strategies which predominate in health services. Such strategies reflect articulated values, as well as implicit values and the needs of those working there. The suggestions here will hopefully lead to increased curiosity, so that health professionals will be interested in knowing themselves in sufficient detail to make flexible and helpful use of their strategic biases.

Understanding of attachment behaviour is still evolving. We do not have a detailed knowledge base concerning health workers' attachment strategies to report on, just recurring relationship patterns and personality characteristics described in the literature. These characteristics are very important for treatment outcome – even up to three times more so than applying evidence-based treatment approaches in some disciplines (Luborsky, McLellan, Woody, O'Brien, Auerbach, 1985). There is some evidence that having a 'secure' attachment strategy makes for a better 'therapist' (Dozier, Cue, Barnett, 1994). Yet physicians are not typical of the general population (Vaillant, Sobowale, McArthur, 1972), and they have their special characteristics whenever they have been investigated. For instance Krakowski found that physicians were obsessional, had reduced ability to express care, were perfectionists, demanded that others acted as they did, were workaholics, and productive at the expense of having fun (Krakowski, 1982). A similar list was drawn up by Gabbard and Menninger: perfectionism, a susceptibility to self-doubt and guilt feelings, a chronic sense of emotional impoverishment, difficulties managing dependency and aggression, and a limited capacity for emotional expressiveness (Gabbard, Menninger, 1989). Not much fun to be married to, and their marriages suffer (Vaillant, Sobowale, McArthur, 1972).

Although lack of closeness to another would have visibly distressed some people, many of these physicians were described as avoidant by nature, and coped more often on their own – and that included coping with their own illnesses, both physical and psychiatric, for which they sought no help and avoided taking sick leave (Aasland, 2001; Rosvold, Bjertness, 2001).[20] They appear to regard illnesses as 'destructive', in Herzlich's terminology (she contrasts this perspective with illness as an 'occupation' where one works at getting better, and illness as a 'liberator' where freedom from social obligations is much appreciated) (Herzlich, 1973).[21] This constellation suggests a denial of their vulnerability and weaknesses, which if transmitted as an attitude to their patients will prevent them being genuinely attuned to their suffering, and instead tend to concentrate on the technical aspects of medicine (Vaglum, Falkum, 1999). Having presented the characteristics of the attachment strategies, I hope that one gets a sense that these characteristics of doctors may be coherent with various aspects of the attachment strategies as described – excluding the balanced type B strategy.

Doctors seem to be tenuously distinguishable from those who somatise, including those with hypochondriasis. Many physicians have had deprived childhoods, and have also been exposed to serious life events in their childhood, especially serious illness in a family member (Johnson, 1991). Instead of going repeatedly to the doctor, they have become that doctor. But it is highly unlikely that they will identify themselves with their somatising patients, even though doctors in Vaillant's follow-up study developed hypochondriasis more often than controls (Vaillant, Sobowale, McArthur, 1972). They fail to be curious about the 'health clinic atten-dance dance', and whether their competent clinical practice could have any role in maintaining such attendance without improvement. Doctors are missing out on the opportunity to learn about themselves and the patient role through experience in that role.

We now return to Pamela's Health Centre and the discussion between the practitioners. There is some research into the ways in which doctors of various levels of 'sensitivity' respond to patients with asthma. Low-sensitivity doctors tend to interpret the personality characteristics of the patients as reflecting illness severity and they confuse psychological and somatic distress – reminiscent of somatising patients with interoceptive confusion. Moderate-sensitivity doctors appear to be able to distinguish between psychological and somatic distress, and base their judgement of illness severity more on their patient's pulmonary function results. In contrast the decisions of high-sensitivity doctors deviate from this balanced appraisal and are again influenced by patient personality vari-ables (Yellowlees, Kalucy, 1990).[22]

Our interest in the dynamic-maturational model of attachment is that it enables us to go much further than 'sensitivity', employing developments from developmental social psychology. Sensitivity can be a similar concept to attunement, but also potentially emotional contagion. If this was to prove the case, the high-sensitivity doctors may be over-involved, employing a form of emotional contagion which often characterises those with a preoccupied type C attachment. The low-sensitivity doctors may be employing a dismissing type A strategy as found amongst those who have experienced less attunement whilst they developed their working models of relationships.

Is it possible to make use of the basic A, B, and C distinctions, and Unresolved loss/trauma, when understanding the different sorts of partnership which may arise in the doctor–patient relationship? How is Pamela likely to respond to the doctors in the practice? What is it that both parts are sharing when they establish a treatment relationship? The patient usually comes at a time when their attachment system is mobilised, as they feel under 'threat' – their health is at risk. Doctors should ideally feel secure enough so that their attachment behaviour systems are not mobilised. It is important to note that with increasing frequency doctors' attachment behaviour systems are mobilised prior to their consultations, due for example to expectations of physical abuse by patients, risk of catching infection, and being found wanting and not up to the standards demanded.

The doctor has a responsibility to make patients feel comfortable enough to share their complaints, and their wishes for treatment. What will be comfortable enough for a balanced type B patient can be a threat to a person with an extreme type C strategy. Doctors need to be flexible enough to adjust their attunement to the signals they are receiving from their patients – just as a mother adjusts to her child. In the extreme this can mean that doctors need to watch and wait. Patients who have expectations of a type A strategy dance will be expecting a doctor who does not attempt to establish a shared relationship, but presents himself as the expert who has the solution. They will be accepting of an intellectual explanation of what is going on, and what needs to be done. But this would be inherently dissatisfying for type C expectations. Such patients would be wanting to draw their doctors into a discussion about the affective aspects of their discomforts, even if they do not have a very clear language for conveying these, albeit many, somatic images. I would expect them to succeed in involving their doctors. Their doctors would find it difficult to get enough distance from these patients to make a considered evaluation. They will struggle to identify the pattern to the

Box 7.1 Summary of transformations of information

Age	Affect		Cognition	
	Type A	Type C	Type A	Type C
Infant	Omit negative affect			Omit temporal information
Preschool with theory of mind	Falsify positive affect	Distort negative affect		
School age with theory of mind			Distort temporal information	Falsify causal information

In addition it is possible to come to *erroneous* conclusions due to coincidence, and to *truly* predictive cognitive or affective information.

relationship, and link that to causal explanations of the patient's dis-ease. A 'somatocentric' doctor will suit the type A strategy holder, whereas the C will be ambivalently attached. A 'psychocentric' doctor will not get to grips with the A patient's starting point and the A patient will be dissatisfied, whereas a patient with C strategies will feel understood, although not necessarily helped.

The sequence of interaction in a consultation is co-evolving, based on the fit between different strategies. This question of fit has been described as involving either 'matching' or 'meshing'. We can envisage a doctor using the transformations of information processing found with dismissing type A (Box 7.1), treating a patient with type A strategies, in which the relationship would involve matching expectations. Both would in all probability be satisfied with a predominantly cognitive approach – but there may be joint blank spots of which they never become aware. In all likelihood these would involve negative emotions, which they found it difficult to identify and talk about in any meaningful way. They might both be taken in by displays of false positive affect.

Similarly, a type C match would involve a consultation with the same sorts of transformation of information from both parties, so that they would regard themselves as being 'on the same wavelength'. Due to their mutual preoccupations they would maybe not see the wood for the trees, and risk getting enmeshed in a long unfruitful series of consultations, which may culminate in unexpected intrusion of outbursts if the enmeshment became overwhelming. This can happen in some long-lasting psychotherapy treatments – there are suggestions that psychotherapists seem more often to have type C strategies (Crittenden, personal communication).

A meshing of patient and doctor involves a situation whereby the complementary skills of the type A and C strategies try to make sense of each other's worlds. Together they cover the full spectrum, without being aware of why they seem to have major problems in understanding each other due to their differing transformations of information. Employing a paternalistic medical consultation strategy with a patient with type C strategy risks being provocative, and the doctor will be confused about why his strategy, which worked for the previous patient, failed dismally for the next.

With a balanced awareness of the emotional and cognitive dimensions to relationships (both implicitly and explicitly, i.e. in all memory systems) a professional with a mature balanced type B strategy will be able to adjust flexibly to the varying demands. A naïve type B may not notice the transformations of information employed by the most extreme A and C classifications, and so be in danger of being misled (a particular problem within high security prison health services). As a patient lives through the course of a chronic illness an initial paternalistic approach may need to change. A type B strategy would be flexible enough to change over to an information-based approach, in which the patient becomes an active participant in their treatment planning.

A consistent finding is that doctors who adopt a warm, friendly, and reassuring manner are more effective than those who keep consultations formal and do not offer assurance (Dixon, Sweeney, 2000). These qualities would be expected to be found with balanced strategies. A combination of emotional and cognitive care has been found to produce the most consistent treatment effects (Blasi, Harkness, Ernst, Georgiou, Kleijnen, 2001). Hippocrates wrote that 'the patient, though conscious that his condition is perilous, may recover his health simply through his contentment with the goodness of the physician'. Doctors are left with the need to facilitate this sense of contentment, and maximise the chance of the doctor being good enough. The doctor's first necessity, regardless of the branch of medicine, is 'gnotis auton' (know yourself), as the ancient

Greeks encouraged – where I suggest that all health professionals need a level of conscious reflective function which depends on them having an insight into the attachment issues described here.

Contentment is not bought at the price of the doctor suppressing his genuine affect. William Osler's advice that the doctor should show 'an infinite patience and an ever tender charity', has not been shown universally to give good results. Physician expression of negative affects, such as frustration or tension, has been positively associated with treatment response (Scovern, 1999). I assume that it is important that expression of these 'negative' affects is not done coercively (as part of a preoccupied type C strategy), but part of the genuineness that characterises a balanced relationship.

In the longitudinal study reported by Vaillant, they had available information about the subjects' childhoods at the time they entered the study in the 1940s. The work stress of the doctors turned out to be predicted by the degree of stability in their childhoods (Vaillant, Sobowale, McArthur, 1972). The workload, although demanding, did not explain the doctors' vulnerabilities. The hypothesis that their childhood experiences related to their attachment strategies needs formal testing, but it is very suggestive, when the other characteristics noted above are taken into account. A later study found that the main predictors of job stress for doctors were self-criticism and father's age, and these were independent of job attitudes, which were predicted by the doctor's relationship with their mother. Job stress was not predicted by objective measures of work demands. The chronically stressed doctor also made significantly more mistakes (Firth-Cozens, 1992). The issues seem to be similar for clinical psychologists (Cushway, Tyler, 1994).

The sorts of mistakes made by doctors have often been attributed to work pressure and hospital environment, but the above research suggests that attributes secondary to their childhood development may have played a more important role. This may be especially prominent with the type of situation which can arise, whereby an especially highly tuned vigilance, acquired as a survival skill in childhood, and potentially showing as 'excessive interpersonal sensitivity', is not accompanied by a sense of empathy, intimacy and trust. Such professionals may misuse their power in ways which victimise patients; for example, medicating them against their will, unthinkingly switching treatment contacts whom patients have come to rely on, instituting force feeding and raging against patients. The doctor unwittingly recreates the misuse of power and lack of attunement to which he was exposed during his formative years (van der Kolk, 1996).

In these ways early trauma and dissociation amongst clinicians, associated with probable disorganised attachment strategies, or higher type A and C strategies, can seriously jeopardise patients. It is not just patients who find it difficult to face unresolved loss and trauma; these can also affect health professionals' ways of behaving, without them being aware of them. Trauma and dissociation have profound implications for how clinicians integrate the information available to them from their memory systems, much of which is preconscious and only available from implicit memory. Doctors' patients may well know more about their doctors than their doctors know about themselves, as they experience how doctors relate to them – not just the words they use. Negative experience of illness within their own families when growing up is associated with subsequent occupational stress, and it may be that reactivation of traumatic memories affecting preconscious functioning has affected the non-verbal aspect of their relationship with patients.

What people fail to allow themselves to experience, they will also fail to notice in others. This is the same process as described within families, which affects development of somatisation. Some illness experiences, personal or vicarious, which doctors had experienced within their families during their childhood, may have been taboo, and though not talked about, transmitted to the next generation through the processes described previously (Fonagy, 1999). If a doctor and his patient have had similar experiences they will not find the blind spots – for example, a match of attachment strategy coupled with similar unresolved loss or trauma coped with by the same process (e.g. $Ul_{(ds)}$) prevents a resolution. The danger is that they will resort to technological medicine or a focus on practical problem-solving to avoid the affective experiences; the intersubjective dimension of the art of medicine will be missing, and not used to advance the patient's treatment. Health professionals need to be aware how their experience of loss and trauma, and serious threats to which they have been exposed, affect their ability to respond flexibly and make use of these experiences to their patients' advantage.

A focus on problem-solving (especially prominent in the USA [Payer, 1996]), often blinds physicians to emotional issues in their patients and in themselves. In the worst case scenario a blind following of evidence-based approaches, which are not the result of an integrated psychosocial-somatic understanding, will further the system error which I believe perpetuates the extent of somatising as the major cost of Western health services.[23] The clinical practice of some doctors is believed to express covert resentment to giving patients the care they believe they never got as a child, prompting unreasonable anger towards overly dependent patients (Vaillant, Sobowale, McArthur, 1972). They tend to rely heavily

Box 7.2 Level of medical care

Level

Abdication

0   Doctors/nurses do not know what they do or are incoherent

0.5   Doctors/nurses defer to others or echo their views

Egoistic reasoning

I   Doctors/nurses make decisions based on self-interest

I.5   Doctors/nurses behave the way they would have wanted if they were the patient

Conformist reasoning

2   Doctors/nurses decisions are based on normative standards

2.5   Doctors/nurses modify normative standards on the basis of some characteristic of the patient (e.g. age or sex)

Individualistic reasoning

3   Doctors/nurses select their own behaviour in response to unique aspects of the patient

3.5   Doctors'/nurses' reasoning includes more than one level, but is not individualised

Integrative reasoning

4   Doctors'/nurses' reasoning is based on the integration of information from lower levels, including the unique characteristics of the patient

Source: Adapted from Crittenden (2000: 222)

on intellectualisation (Lamberg, 1999), which is coherent with a keen adherence to the apparent objectivity of the EBM trend.

Box 7.2 is adapted from a figure used to illustrate levels of parenting skills, and is modified and included here to show a classification of levels of doctors' or nurses' competence to provide medical care. For example, a doctor who expected to be able to 'match' his patient, rather than flexibly adjust his level of responding, is only at level 1.5. It is possible that a nurse who uncritically adopts a compulsive caring A3 strategy, which may meet his fit without taking into account the patient, is at level 1. In adulthood the A3 sub-pattern is often combined with the compulsive compliant A4 sub-pattern (Crittenden, 1999–2002). Such doctors and nurses can make high achievers and, interpersonally, are able to work effectively with very demanding or difficult people.[24] But such a strategy can also be associated with a dependence on patients, at the same time as the doctor is divorced from his own feelings (Vaillant, Sobowale, McArthur, 1972; Johnson, 1991). Such a dependency can also be a vulnerability for later burn-out – typically in someone who has previously been unaware of his vulnerabilities[25] – driven by a compulsive drive to help (Falkum, 2000). EBM seems to be attempting to ensure that practice moves from a potential level 2 towards level 4 – but it is only with time and easy access to search facilities that even level 3.5 can be reached.

Patient expectations are partially politically and culturally determined. They have a right to expect doctors to function over level 1.5. In order to get the relationship balance on the right footing the *British Medical Journal* has suggested the need for a new contract between patients and their doctors. This seems to presume balanced type B capabilities.

The new contract
Both patients and doctors know:

- Death, sickness, and pain are part of life
- Medicine has limited powers, particularly to solve social problems, and is risky
- Doctors don't know everything: they need decision making and psychological support
- We're in this together
- Patients can't leave problems to doctors
- Doctors should be open about their limitations
- Politicians should refrain from extravagant promises and concentrate on reality

(Smith, 2001: 1073)

Training needs

Training ought to aim for enabling health professionals' flexibility to meet patients employing a wide range of attachment strategies. This will be a challenge that requires that they include learning about their own strategies, and perhaps how their own traumatic experiences can come to affect their capabilities. A competent clinician needs to be capable of meeting unexpected challenges (Fraser, Greenhalgh, 2001). Through supervision directed to the intersubjective dimension of clinical practice, the art of medicine will be able to flourish and inform the evidence-based science of medicine. Attachment strategies are opened up for new learning through a secure enough relation to a supervisor, in which recurring patterns of relatedness, both with patients and in relation to the supervisor, can be explored so that implicit procedural learning reveals itself and becomes open for change.

In the future is it too much to expect all branches of medicine, or nursing, to devote an increased amount of training to the interpersonal? The aim is not to produce psychotherapists but to ensure patient safety, minimise risk and system error, and enable some future health professionals eventually to find other outlets for their interests than they had perhaps first thought. For example, Firth-Cozens found that depressed medical students seemed preferentially to choose either psychiatry or laboratory-based specialities such as pathology. Those choosing laboratory-based specialities were content with their choice and functioned well, whereas those who chose psychiatry were in difficulty (Firth-Cozens, 2001). Vaillant had found that those who went into branches of medicine where they did not have primary responsibility for patient care came from a similar background to the controls, and had less problems than clinicians (Vaillant, Sobowale, McArthur, 1972) – but I do not understand why they included surgeons in the group which did not have primary responsibility for patients. Training a doctor is a very expensive business, and identifying these vulnerable individuals early is appropriate use of expensive resources such as supervision.

Training needs to help students identify the variety of transformations of information (Box 7.1), including those that the students themselves use without being aware of them. If they are to develop their reflective self-function and 'mind-reading' skills, which will be necessary for adapting to the attachment strategies of their patients, results from developmental psychology suggest that this is best achieved through pretend play in conflict situations with peers. All problem-based learning groups should have as part of their agenda an awareness of an integrated mind/body understanding, and a chance to enable the group to facilitate development of the above competences.[26]

Wright and colleagues asked junior doctors at four university departments to name senior doctors whom they regarded as good role models. The role models used more than 25 per cent of their time teaching juniors, they more often pointed out the importance of the doctor–patient relationship, more often emphasised the psychosocial factors, and gave more specific personal feedback to the junior doctors. There was no difference as regards age, gender or academic position (Wright, Kern, Kolodner, Howard, Brancati, 1998). This study puts supervision where it belongs – in the centre of training. Only in supervision, which directly addresses the art of medicine whilst evidence is in focus, can patient care be maximised. Patients know more about their doctors than their doctors are likely to know about themselves (through the way in which implicit memory works). Supervision can minimise this shock for new doctors, and helps them use this awareness. Attachment theory bridges the gap between the art and science of medicine.

The Canadian Medical Association policy now includes a call for doctors to acknowledge their duty to help each other stay well. The vision is of a healthcare system led by example, where the doctors are as healthy as they wish their patients to be. They aim for an occupational environment with clearly defined limits to doctors' duties, training for medical students and graduates in maintaining well-being, and specialised health promotion services (Yamey, Wilkes, 2001). This attitude needs to be introduced in supervision from the start of training. I believe that it will entail an understanding of the role attachment strategies play in human suffering. The list of a doctor's duties begins with 'make the care of your patient your first concern'. A duty of self-knowledge and self-care should underpin this (Thompson, Cupples, Sibbett, Skan, Bradley, 2001). Medicine only becomes a strain when the doctor asks himself to give more than he has been given (Vaillant, Sobowale, McArthur, 1972).

> Experience is not what happens to a man, it is what a man does with what happens to him.
> Aldous Huxley (1894–1963), *Texts and Pretexts*, 1932

Notes

1 Those familiar with Foucault's use of '*le regard*' will appreciate that I am trying to convey the same process.
2 Within medicine there is also discussion about whether a dimensional approach or categorical approach is most appropriate when distinguishing normality and pathology (Harrington, 2001).
3 Within social anthropology the dominant research paradigms have shifted between a primary focus on the individual or society. There are current attempts to adopt a third way which emphasises the processes going on between people (Samuel, 1990). The attachment paradigm lends itself to this development, as it bridges the individual and society through a focus on their intersubjective attunement and the patterning of their interpersonal dance.

4 The political process whereby a diagnosis gets official approval for general use is illustrated by the 'Report of the CFS/ME working group' (2002) and the government response www.doh.gov.uk/cmo/cfsmereport/response.htm (accessed 10 March 2002). Chronic fatigue syndrome became part of the disorder to be known in the United Kingdom as 'CFS/ME' (Chronic fatigue syndrome/Myalgic encephalomyelitis). The work on the report led to the resignation of both professional and lay members of the working group, as the evidence accumulated through scientific enquiry and patient experience became a battleground for moral supremacy.

5 A distinction is frequently made between somatic awareness and preoccupation with feelings of somatic change. Somatic awareness reflects the threshold for acknowledging somatic feelings, whereas preoccupation reflects the attention devoted to them once they have reached consciousness. The latter would be coherent with an even-numbered type C strategy.

6 Anxiety comes from the Latin '*angere*', to choke or to strangle, and so is directly associated with the symptom of dyspnoea, or shortness of breath.

7 'Look, it's much worse than you think. And if you think it's much worse' (Carl Whitaker).

8 A recent study attempted to look at attachment amongst a group of somatising patients but did not use a detailed enough analysis of their attachment status to assist with the distinction here believed important. Their conclusion was that 'presentation to the doctor with unexplained physical symptoms is associated with both higher levels of psychiatric symptoms and abnormal attachment style when compared to presentations with organic physical symptoms' (Taylor, Mann, White, Goldberg, 2000).

9 Fear involves the accurate perception of danger and, depending on the context, a flight, flee or freeze response. In contrast anxiety can be defined as a fear response in the absence of threat.

10 In one study of 106 adult general practice patients with high consultation frequency the overlap between somatisation, depression and anxiety was largely accounted for by just 16 patients with a triple problem: somatisation and depression and anxiety (Portegijs, Jeuken, van der Horst, Kraan, Knottnerus, 1996).

11 Although it has long been thought that medical students were especially prone to this form of hypochondriasis, recent research suggests that they may be less prone than other student groups (Ellingsen, Wilhelmsen, 2002).

12 Research that does not take account of which memory systems are being addressed in a survey, and then interprets the results without referring to such issues, fails to assist in an integration of knowledge relevant for practice.

13 I adopt the distinction of a problem as requiring action, and a difficulty as requiring to be lived with (Watzlawick, Weakland, Fisch, 1974). These map onto diseases, where action can be necessary, and predicaments, which need to be lived with as helpfully as possible. Presentation of desire for comfort in the disguise of a symptom requiring action confuses a difficulty and problem, and induces system error.

14 Antecedents serve as signals, which indicate when manifestation of the behaviour is *potentially* reinforcing. Consequences serve as *direct* reinforcement for exhibition of the behaviour (Mullins, Olson, Chaney, 1992).

15 Engel's classical study of chronic pain, referred to in Chapter 6, described

the type of family experience which often troubled these patients, and personality traits which were accentuated. It is relatively easy to see the importance of these themes for development of dismissing or preoccupied attachment strategies (the following list illustrates other themes than those specifically relevant for the preoccupied type C strategy, and is nevertheless not complete):

Family experience
- A history of having been reared by physically or verbally abusive parents.
- Having had a parent who punished severely and then over-compensated.
- A parent who was cold and distant except when the child was ill or in pain.
- A patient who as a child felt responsible or guilty for the pain experienced by a close family member.
- A patient who as a child was aggressive and hurtful to others until suddenly forced to abandon this behaviour, with associated guilt.
- A patient who as a child deflected the aggression of a parent towards others onto the self.

Personality traits
- Prominence of guilt.
- A predisposition to use pain to atone.
- An inhibited aggressive drive.
- A tendency to use pain as a replacement for loss.

(Engel, 1959)

16 There is preliminary evidence that alexithymia is not a culture-bound construct. Cultures which do not use a well-developed psychological language can nevertheless distinguish between basic emotions secondary to arousal and those secondary to disease (Taylor, Bagby, Parker 1997: 36).

17 We should be expecting that individuals with disorganised attachment, who more often dissociate and have been exposed to trauma, will have a confused access to words for describing their illness experiences, and may well lack a competent vocabulary for conveying their psychological discomforts (see Chapter 6).

18 A comprehensive British follow-up study of children adopted from Romanian orphanages is exploring the degree and form of improvement that can be expected after serious early deprivation (Rutter *et al.*, 1998).

19 An attempt to find common ethical principles to guide all health workers has led to guidelines called the Tavistock principles. As somatisation involves deprivation and child maltreatment, the health of the extended family is at issue. Deprivation and its consequences is a necessary priority.

The Tavistock principles
- Rights – People have a right to health and health care
- Balance – Care of individual patients is central, but the health of populations is also our concern

- Comprehensiveness – In addition to treating illness, we have an obligation to ease suffering, minimise disability, prevent disease, and promote health
- Cooperation – Health care succeeds only if we cooperate with those we serve, each other, and those in other sectors
- Improvement – Improving health care is a serious and continuing responsibility
- Safety – Do no harm
- Openness – Being open, honest, and trustworthy is vital in health care

(Berwick, Davidoff, Hiatt, Smith, 2001: 616)

20 In contrast the US doctors in Vaillant's follow-up study had made use of psychotherapy significantly more often than a control group (Vaillant, Sobowale, McArthur, 1972).

21 In acknowledgement of the importance of denying their vulnerability Thompson and colleagues drew up the following hypothetical contract for a new partner in a Health Centre:

> *Informal shadow contract*
> I undertake to protect my partners from the consequences of my being ill. These include having to cover for me and paying locums. I will protect my partners by working through my illness up to the point where I am unable to walk. If I have to take time off, I will return at the earliest possible opportunity. I expect my partners to do the same and reserve the right to make them feel uncomfortable if they violate this contract. In order to keep to the contract I will act on the assumption that all my partners are healthy enough to work at all times. This may mean that from time to time it is appropriate to ignore evidence of their physical and mental distress and to disregard threats to their well-being. I will also expect my partners not to remind me of my own distress when I am working while sick.
>
> (Thompson, Cupples, Sibbett, Skan, Bradley, 2001: 730)

22 The authors of this research note the dearth of research into the doctor–patient relationship in relation to specific conditions, and attribute it to researchers and doctors using the same intellectual approaches, rationalisation and denial. They appear to be suggesting a possible bias towards a shared dismissing type A strategy between clinicians and researchers.

23 Up until now the prevalence of somatising has been lower in the UK. This has been attributed to the National Health Service organisation, which through earmarking a general practitioner to function as the individual patient's entry port to specialist services has attempted to address some of the system errors which exaggerate the problem more in the US. With the growing EBM culture it may be that the necessary prerequisites for GPs to maintain fruitful relationships with these patients will break down.

24 Providing physical care for incapable parents who, nevertheless, retain the adult role psychologically (i.e., they remain in authority and provide comfort to the child), is not role reversal. Experience of serious illness in parents

and providing care for them is not the same as the compulsive quality of A3, which more often arises in a situation where the child inhibits his own feelings, and displays false positive affect as a way of maximising access to a depressed or neglecting parent (dismissing type A), or an incompetent child-like parent who exaggerates her helplessness (preoccupied type C4).

25 The *Washington Post* carried two articles (23 and 27 March 2001), which described a Harvard-trained surgeon who claimed: 'Surgeons are built differently (to other people) and become impervious to exhaustion.' His own frightening schedule included meeting his juniors every Sunday morning at 8.30 a.m. to listen to their grievances. He dismissed complaints about fatigue as 'whining' (reported in *British Medical Journal*, 7 April 2001, p. 874).

26 Students are very interested in this. I had to work with the staff on a paediatric ward to help them see the connection between the way their patients thought and the physiological consequences. I took to the ward a collection of Biotic Bands™, which enable one to see small changes in temperature on a fingertip. The staff was asked to try and warm up or cool down their hands through thinking of an appropriate situation where their hands would get colder or warmer. I lost 80 per cent of the bands on 'permanent loan', as an excited group of nurses got hold of the message, which was otherwise excluded from their training at that time.

Chapter 8

Goal-corrected partnerships for health

The best-laid schemes o' mice an' men
Gang aft a-gley,
An' lea'e us nought but grief an' pain,
For promis'd joy!

Still thou art blest, compar'd wi' me
The present only toucheth thee:
But, Och! I backward cast my e'e.
On prospects drear!
An' forward, tho' I canna see,
I guess an' fear!
                    Robert Burns, 'To a Mouse'

As a young adult, newly pregnant, Pamela is reflecting on her own origins, the culture of her parents, the traumas they must have endured, her mothers – and especially what she takes from her relationship with them into her forthcoming role as mother. How can she enable her child to be as healthy as possible throughout life? Her adoptive mother sits on the sidelines with hopes and fears for her grandchild.

This chapter concerns health and one particular aspect of attachment theory, the goal-corrected partnership, which I believe will help develop patient–clinician communication in new directions. In some ways this chapter summarises the previous chapters as they can be applied in a clinical setting. This will include a brief look at the issues raised through the major differences in morbidity and mortality depending on gender and culture, and the importance of associated attachment strategies for health. My hope would be that Pamela and her offspring could experience goal-corrected partnerships, which ensure their health for generations to come.

Throughout this book suffering has been the defining characteristic of patients. Attachment strategies, developed primarily in early childhood, but open to change, maximise people's chances of modulating their level of dis-ease. These strategies are adopted when under threat of illness, identified as a feeling of basic emotion, not immediately modifiable like other conventional emotions. The first-level consultation is with someone close, your personal VIP; subsequently other levels of expertise are drawn in.

This emphasis on modulation of affect, and interpersonal relationships as a means to this end, leads to my definition of health as 'the ability to modulate your own dis-ease, either alone or with the assistance of a trusted companion, such that you feel comfortable'.[1] This definition encompasses the ability to feel healthy, which is important for actual mortality (Idler, Angel, 1990; Heistaro, Jousilahti, Lahelma, Vartiainen, Puska, 2001). With this definition one can paradoxically be reasonably healthy whilst one has a disease. Health and disease are seen as two different but related dimensions to the human state. With disease it can be impossible to achieve health; without disease people are not necessarily healthy.

Summarising from Chapters 2 and 3, modulation of affect results from an internalised ability to modulate one's own distress dependent on how you have been looked after. Health is a competence, founded in interpersonal relationships, and characterised by a primal partnership between 'mother' and child, which enables the growing child to manage her own discomforts on the basis of the preceding attunement between mother and child.[2] Health services attempt to replicate elements of this primal partnership. They distinguish those for whom the lack of health means that they need to diagnose disease or disorder. A health service shall reduce suffering – and distinguish those for whom their suffering and lack of health, in the sense of failure to modulate their own distressed feelings, stem from a fundamental difficulty between mother and child. For some children their attachment strategies are not sufficient for minimal health. It is a political decision where the limits are drawn between the health concern of social services, and the health concern of health/disease services. Given the growing evidence of the biological consequences of poor care, people should not expect a clear boundary.

Healthcare systems

Attachment theory has moved on from formative political issues, such as the condition of children moved out of London during the Second World War (Bowlby, 1951), and the condition of children separated from their parents when admitted to hospital (see Robertson, Robertson [1971] for a description of the films they made illustrating, amongst others, the admission of a child to hospital). The children in these situations were distressed on separation from their parents. Attachment theory informed the change in policy which led to parents retaining contact with their children on paediatric wards. The current focus in the dynamic-maturational model is the *strategies* developed to maximise access to those who are perceived as being in a position to help them modulate their distress – their self-protective stategies. Situations, which are seen as threatening, will reflect both acknowledged and taboo subjects. This will depend on cultural history and family history; the threats will have their roots in the past and be transmitted into the future. Health systems need to be organised so that patients, whatever their attachment strategies, their personal and cultural background, can be cared for, as well as treated.

Goal-corrected partnerships for health are multilevel phenomena, in which each system level can hopefully enable the relevant culture of partnership for common goals. The same processes occur, whatever the 'distance' from the patient's suffering. Those responsible for healthcare systems are influenced by the same interpersonal processes as those they manage, and those who decide on their budgets and political priorities. It is not possible to illuminate attachment dilemmas for the doctor–patient relationship, without at the same time illuminating the relationships between health administrators and their employees, or within political parties. Does the administration run on coercive principles, as illustrated by preoccupied type C strategies, where the issue is to leave responsibility with someone else, monitor the affective response in the staff carefully, and use fear and aggression to drive the team?[3] An alternative could be the leadership of a dismissing type A leader who isolated himself, ignored the feelings engendered in his staff by his dictates, demanded uncomplaining allegiance, and prided himself on his endurance and rigorous intellectually logical analyses of the causes of problems.

Leadership appears to enable best results from teamwork when the leader makes use of balanced type B attachment strategies, using both cognitive and affective information flexibly. The Institute of Medicine Committee on quality of health care in America, suggest the following guidelines for a healthcare system:

- Care is based on continuous healing relationships
- Care is customised according to patients' needs and values
- The patient is the source of control
- Knowledge is shared and information flows freely

- Decision making is evidence based
- Safety is a system property
- Transparency is necessary
- Needs are anticipated
- Waste is continually decreased
- Cooperation among clinicians is a priority

(Plsek, Wilson, 2001: 748)

These are coherent with themes identified from developmental research within the attachment paradigm, such as the need for continuity, individual attunement, being proactively responsive to needs, management of the feeling of control and a secure setting (a temporary 'secure enough base' within the treatment setting). These rules should enable patients to experience health care fitting balanced type B expectations. Nevertheless there remains a real challenge to carry this out in practice, because of the tendencies for staff to react when under stress according to their attachment strategies. Patients, when under threat of disease, will not immediately be able to feel comfortable with a system characterised by processes with which they are unfamiliar (good care and comfort can feel threatening: Box 6.2). The healthcare systems guidelines can set the scene for goal-corrected partnerships with patients, and patient-centred care. But they will require a flexible responsiveness of clinicians to patients with other attachment histories (and of employees for clinicians).

A brief return to memory systems illustrates the dilemmas involved in attempting to make the knowledge about attachment strategies applicable to healthcare systems. Our ways of relating – the non-verbal habits – are played out from our procedural memory for learned patterns, learnt and shaped through behavioural principles. This preconscious learning cannot be expected to change on the basis of a presentation of facts in a book.[4] It may be that Bowlby's presentation of Attachment and Loss (Bowlby, [1969] 1982, 1973, 1980) would not have achieved such wide influence if it were not a part of a dual assault on the health professionals and the public with the films of the Robertsons. The films have been, and still are, a particularly powerful tool. They appeal directly to the viewer's sense of attunement with the suffering child.

Systems are characterised by their relationship patterns, and how they perceive and handle threat (see Bruggen [1997] for examples from the NHS in the UK). Systems can effectively maintain the status quo, evolve or be thrown into chaos – they can be dismissing of affect or preoccupied with the feelings of their staff. A complex adaptive systems model is being used to understand healthcare systems (Institute of Medicine, 2001). It is now time to challenge healthcare systems to move from aiming for the level of normative standards (Box 7.2, level 2) to a higher level. This can be achieved through a return to the relationship which makes up the basic unit of each health system – the doctor–patient relationship. The goal of partnership at all levels is to ensure patient safety, support healthy habits, and strive with patients for health. The supportive apparatus should be just that. The clinical relationship has to aim for being a secure base for the patient so that together they can create a 'goal-corrected partnership' with the aim of enabling patients to maximise their health. Patients primarily need responses to their illness during the initial contact as the foundation for the treatment alliance, and only subsequently will clinicians introduce eventual disease issues and treatment plans (and all within 20 minutes perhaps).

The cultural expectations of what constitutes good practice, the rituals and ways of talking about complaints, lead to the accepted forms of discourse for the illness encounter. To understand group systems of discourse four basic questions need to be answered:

1. What are the historical/social/ideological characteristics of the group? (ideology)
2. How does one learn membership and identity? (socialization)
3. What are the preferred forms of communication? (forms of discourse)
4. What are the preferred or assumed human relationships? (face systems)

(Scollon, Scollon, 2001: 110)

These are relevant at all levels of the healthcare system. I return to the first point under the headings of gender and culture. This chapter primarily discusses the forms of discourse that arise when attempting to enter into goal-corrected partnerships with patients who employ a wide variety of attachment strategies. Attachment strategies are seen both as ways of preferentially presenting dis-ease, as well as being ways of keeping face in close encounters – both coping and complaining.

Patients and clinicians make use of their psychological resources to maximise the potential of the clinical encounter for health. Politicians and health service administrators have had a preference for supporting the materialistic resources required for a service. It requires an understanding of the complexity of psychological processes in order to make full use of them for patients. Antonovsky pointed out the lack of value placed on psychological resources for promoting health, and the situation has not improved. The other factors he identified for promoting health are encompassed within a patient-centred, goal-corrected partnership – a salutogenic orientation involves the challenge being 'understandable, manageable and meaningful' (Antonovsky, 1987).

Unless a health service is psychologically minded, aware of its reflective function, it is unlikely to meet the needs of its patients in a balanced way. This is not a question of funding psychiatric services but of an understanding of the wholeness of patients who suffer, who present to all branches of the service with complex pictures of suffering. Health services appear to foster predominant ways of presenting discomforts, given their own histories and what makes for an effective appeal for treatment. Patients learn strategies to get the most out of such systems. Is a dismissing type A strategy better suited to living with an 'under-funded' NHS in the UK? Is a preoccupied type C strategy best cared for with the Norwegian emphasis on understanding people's suffering, and their priority of psychiatric provision relative to the UK?

> Sitting in on case allocation at an outpatient department in England it appeared as if the general practitioners had found that the only way to get through the clinic's tight priorities was to imply in the referral letter that the patient was suicidal and could benefit from either medication or another time-limited approach which only those specialists could manage.

We do not yet know if the differences in prevalence of disorders between countries reflect differences in strategic use of health services. Disorders depend on objective signs[5] and behaviour, such as expressed threat of suicidal behaviour, not their strategic use, such as to gain access to limited resources. Current ways of obtaining official statistics cannot answer such questions. On theoretical grounds we would expect that changes in health service systems could alter patterns of complaining, and disorder prevalence. These may just be ways of disguising suffering, which takes on a chimeral quality as it presents in different guises in order to be strategically effective – provided that the suffering was not adequately responded to. The problem will be greatest when suffering as part of the person's predicament is presented as if it required treatment – somatic dis-ease (i.e. unmet need for care). The issue is not just a replay of symptom substitution at the social level, but understanding the complexity of when change should be expected and when it should not. An understanding of the complexity of goal-corrected partnerships can help elucidate this.

Goal-corrected partnerships

> God, give me courage to accept the things I can't change, courage to
> change the things I can, and wisdom to know the difference.[6]
>
>   Prayer

Responses to the question, 'Do you think that most people would try to
take advantage of you if they got the chance?' predicted age-adjusted
mortality rates better than measures of income differentials (Stewart-
Brown, 1998). Can this situation relate to consequences of the attachment
strategies that the subjects employ? Can a clinician develop a trusting
alliance with a new patient if such a view is the patient's starting point?

The term 'goal-corrected partnership' comes from attachment theory.
Infants show goal-directed behaviour, which is supported by their parents.
In the preschool years they develop an understanding of the way in which
achievement of their goals is easiest to achieve in partnership with their
parent. They develop a theory of mind that includes how other people are
likely to view the goals they are working towards, and what makes a
particular difference to them. Their behaviour then develops the strategic
quality, which takes into account how other people view it, and may
respond.[7] The way they work towards their goals is modified to take
account of their theory of the other's mindfulness – at the same time they
respond so that their relationship will not be jeopardised, but strategically
adapted for their purposes (Marvin, Britner, 1999).

Recent research into the doctor–patient relationship has been under
the umbrella of 'patient centred approaches' (Stewart, Brown, Weston,
McWhinney, McWilliam, Freeman, 1995). These arose as part of a move
away from 'paternalistic approaches' – doctor-directed 'partnerships'
where doctors knew best what patients required. They now put the patient
clearly in the centre of the consultation.[8] Patients' goal-corrected partnerships with clinicians for the sake of their health is one way of translating
this into attachment terms. The rights of the participants in the consultation
change. A new moral order is established with different rights and ways
of showing respect (Harré, 1983: 243–246).

In some ways this involves a return to the values of the classical
Socratic relationship style:

*   Speak the patient's language
*   Respect the patient's individuality
*   Be collaborative
*   Be honest
*   Be curious

- Be focused
- Be systematic

This puts the patient in the centre, and emphasises the need for collaboration – a partnership. Note that the same qualities are necessary for establishing secure relationships, and for valid qualitative and quantitative research.

But people do not always expect that their doctor will hear/notice their needs, or be genuinely curious about them as individuals. Will a doctor understand that they did things as they did because of their history of how important people had heard their needs in the past, the challenges, threats and dangers that they had been brought up with? Patients cannot be expected accurately to access all sorts of information from all memory systems. Yet clinicians need to maximise their possibilities of accurately hearing from their patients about their subjective discomforts, so that consultations begin with balanced presentations of their patients' illness experiences. A consultation cannot be patient-centred, and build on patients' languages of dis-ease, unless clinicians have learnt enough about how sharing of discomforts is modified according to attachment strategies – both the form and content.

Patients are hypothesised to transform information they present to their doctors in ways similar to the ways in which they have been exposed to transformations of information during their development (see Box 7.1). These will be reasonably coherent within the different attachment strategies. They need to be identified and accepted without moral judgement. Clinicians who understand the attachment dynamic, of which they have become a part during the consultation, can then become sensitised to which mistakes of interpretation they might be disposed to. This depends upon clinicians being aware of their own preconscious biases to transform information along exactly the same dimensions – omitting, distorting and falsifying affective and cognitive information, as well as making errors of prediction based on coincidence.

Treatment implications

The prerequisite for successful treatment is a secure enough base (Bowlby, 1988: 138). When attachment strategies are mobilised, they involve particular ways of telling about dis-ease, as well as potentially predisposing for particular disorders, and even diseases. Until a secure base is achieved there will be difficulties in achieving an honest discourse about subjective states, and patient care and cure will be jeopardised. Care and cure are intimately related; attachment theory is a means for understanding this relationship. Survival strategies will predominate, even though their costs for health can be high, as shown by conditions such as anorexia nervosa. The predicament is how best to live with the capabilities of those people available – a depressed mother, for example, who can jeopardise her child's development and health.

In a goal-corrected partnership each person is responsible for reaching the goal, and they monitor progress and continually adjust. This runs counter to both the expectations and hopes of the A and C strategy 'holders'; the A believing that they are responsible alone, whereas the C holder believes that someone else is responsible if things go wrong. A balanced B strategy is associated with recognition of the role of both in enabling improvement or perhaps failing to improve, with the respective roles of clinician and patient being comprehensively available for inspection.

Clinicians have to have a broad enough repertoire to be able to interpret the widest possible array of discomforts, with attunement to their patients, which enables them to discriminate and identify the significance of their patients' discomforts. Clinicians, parents and researchers see initially what they know. Patients' basic emotions will have been interpreted according to the possibilities which their caregivers had available, and with their degree of sensitivity to nuances in dis-ease. These limited possibilities have led to information being omitted, distorted and falsified. Similarly, clinicians and researchers will have some difficulties entertaining a full range of possibilities.

Omitted cognitive information can appear relatively easy to handle. It may look as if one only has to ask for it. Yet it is only the patient who can identify possible precipitating events, and events that they have found out terminate the presenting discomfort. The clinician can ask about events, and introduce their relevance into the discourse. A preoccupied type C person needs help to focus on causal sequences and attribute relevance to them – a process that can seem irrelevant from their perspective of how they have previously handled threat through sensing which situations might be dangerous.

Omitted affect in someone employing a dismissing type A strategy may seem equally easy to introduce into the discourse, but we have already seen that the affect has been excluded for very good reasons. Suggestions of words for feelings can feel like an intrusion of little relevance, even threatening. Due to this approach having had little relevance for solving problems it will not be straightforward to enquire with 'strange' words of feelings of little significance. In Antonovsky's terminology it is neither understandable nor meaningful. It is relatively easy for someone providing labels for feelings to get it wrong when the patient concerned is vague about feelings. This can be experienced by patients as very intrusive if their parents have been defining what was 'wrong' with them, rather than feeling with their suffering.

Affect is not just omitted but also wrongly attributed, which can result in the fear smile being interpreted as a positive smile. This distortion of meaning then further complicates the consultation, as clinicians may view the smiling patient as if they were smiling warmly. Causal relationships are distorted for preoccupied type C strategy holders. Falsifications and erroneous information make the situation more complicated – but this is the complexity we know from personal experience. Such transformations are also employed to keep face, and lubricate the clinical consultation, but with the costs that the honesty of presentation of disturbed emotions, the dis-ease, may be misinterpreted and not afforded its due significance.

Expectations of dishonesty and manipulation do not initially have anything to do with the clinician; they come from the past. The clinician is dependent on accurate information, and has a dilemma about how to obtain it. Immediately one asks a question one is perceived according to the apparent honesty of the question. Loaded questions invite evasive answers (Tschudi, 1977). This dilemma is well known in qualitative research, and addressed by the critical sociologists (McCarthy, 1973). The questions which tend to be asked by clinicians who are type C strategy holders are rapidly identified as only half-honest, especially by patients attuned to that style of questioning. Coercion has no place in clinical practice. It spreads like wildfire on a ward, and trust is precarious. Trust needs time.[9] Trust needs non-judgemental questions.

Evaluation of the genuineness of a clinician or researcher includes an evaluation of their emotional expression. This involves their whole body, and can be perceived directly even before an individual is aware of his own feelings. Only A-strategy-holder clinicians could perhaps fail to show their feelings, whereas C strategy holders would be likely to confuse patients by displaying some of their feelings, and then albeit to a misleading degree. I believe it is essential for clinicians genuinely to not-know, and nurture their curiosity, in exactly the same way as researchers.[10] Whether it is in the clinical or research setting, it is necessary not to respond in kind to the response elicited but to *retain* a genuine curiosity. Patients need to be enabled to have a genuine curiosity. Attachment strategies are associated with particular limited use of information available, which is often distorted. Only if they can retrieve their original curiosity can they find their own answers. The researcher or clinician's genuine curiosity is a guide stone.[11]

Empowerment

Treatment should be empowering so that next time there is a greater chance of a patient managing with the help of their own network. Empowerment will not be covered directly (see Bandura, 1998). Instead I will point to the function of empowerment for the A and C strategies. The 'insecure' strategies are associated with feelings of powerlessness.[12] Those employing both strategies will be expected to be interested in any approach which has the stated aim of 'empowering' them – but they need quite different approaches. The compulsive compliance of an A4 strategy is associated with following directives, and putting the lid on negative affect. Dismissing people may misleadingly appear as rugged self-contained individualists (A6 perhaps), who have no need for empowerment. Nevertheless they need room to become active participants, sharing their suffering and using the full range of their capabilities.

In contrast, type C strategies make use of leveraged displays of affect. They appear powerful to those around them, whereas they themselves will often describe themselves as powerless, responding to the misuse of power of those around them. Theoretically attempts to empower these patients could be limited to the half of the strategy that they are not employing at that time – for example, the anger of a woman 'playing on' her helplessness and need for comfort (C4). But they nevertheless are already hypothesised to have a complementary C3 strategy available for use (Box 6.2). They are preoccupied with the power of leveraged use of feelings. The aim needs to be to reduce their affective preoccupation and empower their ability to follow causal logic, and manage to cope on their own when required. I am not aware of any empowerment literature that distinguishes between these respective needs, and how the strategy which works for one may be counterproductive for the other.

Attribution and narratives

Teaching patients reattribution of their symptoms may seem like a good idea, a reinterpretation of their emotions so that feelings are different. But it can prove difficult in practice. The first step is crucial; the patients must feel understood within their own paradigm for handling dis-ease. I suggest that an understanding of attachment theory is essential to enable clinicians to do this. This involves recognition of the full complexity of the range of attachment possibilities. The next step is to change the agenda so that one can introduce the new elements that have been ignored, and do this so that links are made to the patients' original discomforts (Goldberg,

Gask, O'Dowd, 1989). Retaining a focus on what brought them to the consultation with each step maintains the goal-corrected partnership, but the introduction of new elements, foreign to their language and understanding, can be very threatening. Regular monitoring and correction makes the challenge manageable, and more meaningful.

In contrast, talking about what you might do about your suffering theoretically leads to changes in semantic memory. For the cognitive changes to lead to change in practice, people who are suffering need to work at doing things differently. They need to be motivated to apply what they have learnt in a different way.[13] The stories we tell ourselves, about why we have come to be as we are, differ depending on the attachment strategies we are employing. Narrative-based medicine, which helps people look at the stories they have been told for their usefulness in their current predicament (Grenhalgh, Hurwitz, 1998), is theoretically particularly suited for those who have discrepancies between what they have been told about their lives and their own experiences. They can be expected to be useful for those with dismissing type A strategies who are likely to have discrepancies between their semantic and episodic memory.[14]

When distortions and omitted information have been reviewed, new stories can be created from the information available, which help them change. New meanings of events and experiences can make them more manageable – meaningful from their own perspective, and not just from the perspective of, for example, powerful others from the patient's childhood. This can be especially important when the patient's network attributes the patient's sickness to a physical cause, but where the clinician finds only dis-ease, such as with many cases of chronic fatigue syndrome, or historically with telegraphist's hand or 'nostalgia' (Johannisson, 2001). Continued attribution to ongoing physical disease is associated with poor prognosis (Powell, Bentall, Nye, Edwards, 2001).

Attribution and narrative are closely related. One is telling a story about something. It is necessary to address the attributions of feelings to emotions directly, as otherwise doctors may unintentionally foster anticipatory disability (Cioffi, 1991). The key interpretation being made by a recuperating cardiac patient is whether the arousal being experienced is secondary to a further cardiac problem, or to the benign basic emotions associated with excitement, other positive or negative emotions, or even the arousal associated with exercise. The outcome of their rehabilitation is more closely associated with their beliefs about what they can accomplish, than their actual cardiac capacity. This process is not itself solely a quality of the patient's own attributions, as was found when the spouses of recovering heart attack patients were involved in an ergometric bicycle test, so that they also got a feeling of what their spouse could accomplish. It was not enough to tell them about it, they actually had to participate in the same bicycle test before their husbands improved significantly (Taylor, Bandura, Ewart, Miller, DeBusk, 1985). Narratives are not enough. It is uncertain whether the greater tendency for a type C strategy to be associated with preoccupation with internal somatic images, without identifying their origin, makes them especially disposed to unsuccessful use of narrative approaches, requiring instead active participation for learning.

Explanations

More effective explanation probably uses a three-stage process model, whereby mood is identified, and the associated physiology described for the way in which it can account for the symptoms. From an attachment perspective it is possible to credit this model as being suitable for a person using a preoccupied type C strategy, which would facilitate stage one of emotional engagement if their feelings were genuinely acknowledged; it is more difficult to believe it could be applied to a person adopting a dismissing type A strategy as they would be unlikely to feel understood, and at least be sceptical should the clinician appear to get it almost right. The antecedents and consequences are clearer for dismissing individuals, who would not have any problems with the last step – making the link; in contrast, a preoccupied individual could be quite challenged by this final step.

Relaxation and information

Relaxation approaches will also on theoretical grounds be quite different for A and C strategy 'holders'. People who are preoccupied find comfort in images of comforting places. They will find it relatively easy to conjure up images. The challenge is very different for an A strategy holder, who can theoretically be expected to find relaxation with use of images difficult. If they fail to relax, they will probably attribute their failure to their own failings rather than to a failure of those offering the technique to adapt it to their personal competencies. Their coping will more often be based on cognitive strategies, appreciating lots of information about the approach being offered. The more they know, the more they think they will be at ease; but they often get disappointed when they find out that the more they know, the more they know they do not know – especially as regards affective attunement.

Clinicians, patients and administrators (and researchers) have to learn how to live with their lack of knowing. 'Not-knowing' groups can reveal new opportunities for them. This may seem a strange concept, but it is a goal-directed approach for those who find it difficult to cope without knowing more. It has been included in the medical curriculum at the University of Utah, and is I believe a particularly useful ingredient in a medical curriculum for doctors who may be predisposed to meet their patients with primarily cognitive approaches, and be unaware of how they use facts to cloud over their difficulties with subjective engagement with their patients. A key requirement for participation in a 'not-knowing group' is that people who participate be on an equal footing as regards not knowing.[15]

Treatment involves helping patients manage their dependence on others in new ways. Throughout life their attachment strategies have enabled them to live with their vulnerabilities. Some of those strategies can be stretched at times of dis-ease. Many will not have had a balanced dependence on others, having either clung to their VIPs or attempted to get by on their own. These strategies will have made it more difficult for them to help their doctors be helpful. They will find it difficult in varying ways, depending on their attachment strategies, to accept that

- their doctor does not know all about what is troubling them without them telling him,
- the other person cannot know whether what they did helped or not unless you tell them honestly,
- you need to be very concrete as words are slippery stuff,
- compliments are not necessarily something to do with them, but the person who gave the compliment,
- you can never be certain that another person is ill.

In clinical settings only the recipient of the clinician's power can tell whether it was a helpful or poor experience. Sometimes, though, patients feel forced to go their own way, and yet retain a façade of a goal-corrected partnership. They have given up trying to correct the way they were going together. Does monitoring of outcome reveal 'lack of concordance', compliance, or collaboration?

Compliance and collaboration

> Of all tyrannies, a tyranny sincerely exercised for the good of its victims may be the most oppressive.
>
> C.S. Lewis, *God in the Dock* (Hooper, 1970: 292)

The low frequency with which medicines are used as prescribed has been conceptualised as a lack of compliance (within a doctor-directed 'partnership'). With a conceptualisation of the medical consultation being part of a patient-centred partnership, compliance is undesirable. Collaboration between clinician and patient results in greater concordance between the doctor's and patient's views of the outcome of the consultation (Mullen, 1997). The degree of concordance is used to describe the degree to which prescribed medicine is taken, or lifestyle has changed. Understanding the issues of compliance and concordance within an attachment perspective will also illuminate one of the areas for health promotion strategies.

How does concordance develop? Concordance between infant and parent looks like compliance, because of the clear differences in power between parent and child. It is most often found amongst the children of sensitive mothers (Ainsworth, 1985) ('consent' comes from the Latin for 'feeling with'). It looks as if those children who develop apparent compliance with sensitive parents go on to establish relationships with high concordance with clinicians. Lack of concordance is an important issue for health services, and some developmental research casts light on this. Belsky has now followed up and confirmed his controversial finding that children who make use of non-maternal care, such as with nursery placement, are less 'compliant'. Early, extensive, and continuous non-maternal care is associated with less harmonious parent–child relations and elevated levels of aggression and non-compliance. The effects are such that the large variation within families means that the overall effects will show up at the societal, rather than individual, level (Belsky, 2001). I believe that understanding attachment strategies can help understand this phenomenon, and inform clinical practice.

Clinicians can be expected to get consent from their patients when they are feeling with them. Not in the sense of emotional contagion, but in a balanced way so that they can identify the patient's subjective sense of dis-ease, as well as objective signs of disease. With clinician attunement comes the possibility of identifying which level of responsibility patients are able to take for their condition, and distinguish this from *willing* to take. Clinicians who are A and C strategy holders will find this more of a challenge. Just as patients with these strategies will be predisposed to give misleading messages about what they are prepared and capable of taking responsibility for, so, I hypothesise, do clinicians find it difficult to strike the balance.

Learning to take responsibility for one's actions is part of growing up. To take responsibility for an active role in decision-making is part of the goal-corrected partnership, the precursor of which evolves as part of the attachment strategy between child and parent. As pointed out for the preoccupied type C strategies, handling of responsibility evolves in a particular direction within a coercive interpretative framework. This is to be seen as a consequence of the long train of events described in Chapter 6. The bottom line for them is that the responsibility is not theirs.

The processes leading to the dismissing strategy form their attitude to responsibility. Many will take responsibility when it is not realistic that they should have taken it alone. Instructing an irresponsible adolescent to 'be responsible' is a paradox for the adolescent, and should be for the parent, teacher, or exasperated clinician.[16] Yet this is the temptation for the powerful clinician or parent who has fostered type A strategies in their child. Responsibility is not something that one has or does not have. It grows in secure relationships. Responsible decision-making is influenced by emotions, experience and social context. It depends on being able to share reliable information (security/attachment strategy-dependent) without distortion or falsification. In a secure situation collaboration and consent evolve together; when A and C attachment strategies are mobilised, consent may feel like compliance. Each culture has its own expectations of when children are responsible for various decisions affecting their future, their health, etc. These have varied throughout the centuries and are cultural determinants of the context in which families determine the responsibilities to be delegated to children (Ariès, 1960). Active participation in a treatment alliance is one element in a goal-corrected partnership, is predictive of outcome, and is relevant for all age groups.

The alliance depends on the clinician responding flexibly to the patient, with respect for the patient's communicative biases. There are four components (Hubble, Duncan, Miller, 1999), of which two appear to have a relation to attachment processes – 'the patient's affective relationship with the clinician' and 'the clinician's empathic understanding and involvement'. Outcome depends on the patient experiencing the alliance as positive. This latter is a challenge which I believe can best be met with respect for each patient's individual life history through an attachment perspective. Through realising that attachment strategies have evolved to maximise patients' survival in their environments of development, and have then been generalised to new settings of clinical encounters, it is possible to work out how best to meet patients so that the affective relationship and attunement with clinicians is as helpful as possible. Theoretically one would expect such compassion to be easiest if clinicians had developed balanced type B attachment strategies. Recognition of complexity requires the balanced cognitive and affective understanding one obtains with a view of the world coloured by balanced type B strategies.

Motivational interviewing

> People are generally better persuaded by the reasons which they have themselves discovered than by those which have come into the minds of others.
>
> Blaire Pascal, *Pensées, Section I*

Patients may well be ambivalent to treatment. Motivational interviewing has been developed to address these issues. It was initially formulated to help those with substance misuse problems, and has been taken up in the treatment of eating disorders, and further expanded in the treatment of adolescents whom clinicians perceive as being especially ambivalent about their problems. This should not be surprising, because adolescents strive with issues of autonomy. Whose problem is it anyway? Is it a problem or a difficulty? Who has to live with what; who has to change what? Who is suffering and hence the patient; who is asking for assistance and is a client? Until these questions are answered it is difficult to work at creating a goal-corrected partnership for the doctor–patient relationship. Motivation is the key ingredient in all medical partnerships, both the doctor's motivation and the patient's.

Neither goals, without knowing how one is doing, nor knowing how one is doing without any goals, has any motivational impact (Bandura, 1998). Motivation for change can be understood within an attachment perspective. The goal for the partnership in a clinical consultation may not be what it appears to be. Somatic dis-ease may be presented as if it corresponded to the paradigm 'treat the disease causing the symptom', but needs to be understood within the paradigm 'care for my suffering as if it was caused by disease'. The partnership may have difficulties explicitly agreeing on the goals. A preoccupied type C strategy holder may exaggerate fear and desire for comfort, and deny other feelings. A dismissing type A strategy holder may lack presenting complaints as part of a language of dis-ease, as he suffers in silence alone. Emotions, and hence feelings of illness, are slippery stuff, whatever the words used. Until these are agreed upon the outcome of the partnership is uncertain (just as the outcome of qualitative research is uncertain until the words are clarified – and one can never be certain with subjective states).

A dismissing strategy involves observing, but not being affectively preoccupied. Affective engagement is the building block of the treatment alliance. A preoccupied strategy can lead to patients being affectively involved, without a perspective of what seems to be the sequences of what is happening and leading to their distress.

Patients can be ambivalent in different ways, which become clear when clinicians attempt to involve them in discussion of both the causal sequences leading to their disorder and the subjective discomforts associated with the disorder in an integrated bio-psychosocial model of medicine. Ambivalence is theoretically minimal when the doctor and patient match their strategies – a focus on causes and somatic treatment for a dismissing patient, or a psychotherapist's focus on the subjective world of his preoccupied patient. In that situation important blind spots remain (the subjective discomforts of the dismissing patient and clarity about precipitating causal events for preoccupied patients), and an episode of illness cannot be a transition in development from one attachment strategy to another associated with more integration.

Motivational interviewing involves a clinician:

1 Validating the patient's resources
   - as healthy enough, capable and competent to bring about change;
   - as autonomous and having a right to choose;
   - recognising successful outcome as dependent on the patient's resources;
   - making active patient participation central to all.
2 Minimising the importance of the clinician's interventions
   - by being responsive with expertise (rather than stimulating), after the patient has taken the first step.[17]

Resistance to change often follows confrontations.[18] Unless clinicians reduce their time in confrontation with patients one can expect little change. Repeating the message leads to stalemate. The clinician has the responsibility to solve the deadlock.

The following qualities:

- understanding the other person's frame of reference,
- expressing acceptance and affirmation,
- filtering the patient's thoughts so that motivational statements are amplified and non-motivational statements dampened down,
- eliciting the patient's self-motivational statements,
- matching processes to stage of change,[19]
- affirming the patient's freedom of choice and self-direction,

are identified as characterising a good motivational clinician (Rollnick, Miller, 1995). They are also coherent with the qualities expected of a mother who facilitates her child developing a balanced type B attachment. The child exposed to such attunement appears 'compliant' to others because mother and child regularly agree to do the same things, but as the child gets older the apparent compliance is better seen as concordance. The only difference to the attunement associated with a balanced type B strategy is the specific emphasis on amplification of motivational statements.

It is important to get a picture of what the patient believes will lead to change, their views of the pros and cons, their sense of control, the acceptable and attainable targets for change and their attitudes to such change (Butler, Rollnick, Stott, 1996). In order to do so questions need to be seen as genuine, and not part of a manipulative type C dialogue which the patient might expect to conclude with apportioning blame. Examples of change need to be found, amplified, and attributed to the patient's efforts.

If clinicians are dependent on confirming their view of their own self-worth through attributing all patient change to their efforts – I hypothesise more often to be expected in clinicians with some of the dismissing strategies – this will work against the motivational approach. The motivational approach begins by accepting informed patient decisions, even if they run counter to current medical wisdom. The aim has been to agree mutually acceptable plans, the goal-corrected partnership. It is coherent with the patient-centred clinical approach. Decisions made by the person affected are most likely to result in long-lasting change (Butler, Rollnick, Stott, 1996).

Hope, placebo and expectancy

The placebo effect is one of the most powerful and under-utilised aspects of treatment in medicine.[20] How does it fit into a goal-corrected partnership? Do attachment strategies play a part in the degree to which individuals are placebo responders or not? The dilemma is how one conceptualises the placebo phenomenon – is one *manipulated* into thinking that one is better, or is one actually improved? For the sake of honest enquiry we need to ensure that placebo effects are accounted for in ways that are warranted, and my purpose here is to suggest potential associations to attachment functioning.

Placebo effects are found most often amongst those who show some degree of acquiescence, and have high anxiety scores – the greater the degree of anxiety the stronger the placebo response. In addition the patient needs to have a positive attitude towards the treatment and the clinician

(Shapiro, Shapiro, 1997: 235). Other factors about the clinician play a role. The success rate of placebo is reportedly much greater when medication is given by a doctor compared to a nurse (70 per cent compared to 25 per cent) (Tjomsland, Ekeberg, Saatvedt, 2001). Whether these are gender issues or role expectations is unclear.

The effects of expectancy and hope are similar to placebo. Treatment guidelines should include specifically the need to nurture hope. Hope-lessness accelerates the progress of ischaemic heart disease and increases patients' mortality (Everson, Kaplan, Goldberg, Salonen, Jukka, 1997). Ways for therapists to facilitate hope and positive expectations for change include forming strong therapeutic relationships, identifying goals, and incorporating clients' strengths into the treatment (the goal-corrected partnership). What does count in facilitating hope and positive expectations for change is challenging or modifying the pessimistic assumptions clients have about the future, and making that future more salient to the present.

Is there to be expected any specific pattern of hope for the future amongst those with various attachment strategies? Theoretically preoccu-pied type C strategy holders will appear to have inappropriately optimistic hopes for the future, given their circumstances. A dismissing type A strategy holder will be cautious in his evaluation of what the future holds.

Double blind studies of medication are highly influenced by expectancy effects, and context. For example one study found that when a new analgesic was compared to a placebo, the placebo response was about 70 per cent amongst those who were patients in a small group room, whereas on the larger ward there was no placebo response (Kjær-Larsen 1956). Expectation that a medicine will be helpful is affected by how it is introduced. If a patient with asthma is given a drug which can 'open up their airways', the effect can be totally negated through a misleading message to the patient that the drug is one which can 'tighten up airways and make it harder to breathe' (Luparello, Leist, Lourie, Sweet, 1970).[21] Instructions also affect the blood levels of the drugs involved (Flaten, Simonsen, Olsen, 1999).

Until the placebo arm of a double blind trial is introduced with the clear message that it helps a significant number of those who take it – and especially those who are a bit worried about participating – we are carrying out a misleading double blind trial. The placebo effect should be maximised for the patient, not minimised for the sake of the inventor of the procedure or drug company. If a clinician cannot convey honestly the benefits of placebo I believe he is minimising his healing ability, and conveying, instead of containing, his doubts. The patient needs to make full use of an important healing process. The need to convey a particular view of reality as correct, denying a balanced view, suggests a predominant focus on the cognitive dimension, and potentially a dismissing type A attachment strategy, which idealises objective knowledge and ignores the subjective dimension, which is important for the placebo response.

Just as expectations can improve outcome, they can also make matters worse – the 'nocebo' effect (Kaada, 1989). A legal obligation to inform about risk can increase risk. The risk of getting an infection in hospital is significant (about 10 per cent in some Western European countries). A non-balanced understanding of risk mobilises attachment strategies and labels the hospital context as a threat to their health. Clinicians' compulsive wishes to do things right by the powerful lawmakers (dismissing type A strategy), can lead to the patients' needs being neglected, and the potential for their healing made worse if they are warned in advance of this risk. Their immune function may even be jeopardised so that they are the ones who become infected. Hospital routines, preadmission and on admission, need to minimise nocebo effects, and maximise placebo – the hope and expectant faith of restored health. How can one helpfully convey honest explanations and information? The full complexity is overwhelming; media-size 'bites' are necessary, but misleading.

Things going wrong and things going right

> I never trust air I can't see.
>
> Woody Allen

It has been the custom to attribute both health and illness to the air we breathe. It could either be not fresh enough, or the cause of poor sleep or tiredness. Alternatively one 'took the airs' to recuperate. Now more often people are held responsible for their own state of health.

If a treatment team fails to motivate a patient sufficiently to engage in treatment, it should be taken as the team's responsibility to identify and work on why they failed, and not to attribute the failure to the patient's lack of motivation (Wilkinson, 2001). Firth-Cozens (presentation Oslo, 2001) has reported that good teams produce more reports of errors. This can be seen as a sign of system health; there is the prerequisite secure-enough relation between the clinical team and the administration to be open and honest in a collaborative relationship to learn from experience. The team takes responsibility for things going wrong.

Alternatively, reporting of more errors can be a sign of major problems. But the Bristol paediatric cardiac surgery unit did not report on their 'errors' in the recent UK scandal. They did their best within their level of competence, but they were found not capable enough given the standards expected. Their failure to report their poor performance was severely criticised. An A type culture rewards those who manage on their own and do not make demands of their administrators – or report the intimate details which enable critical appraisal. I hypothesise that a C type culture fails to facilitate delegation of responsibility with adequate support. The balanced type B helps create the climate for good teamwork and effective feedback about performance indicators (see also Department of Health, 2000). System errors and individual responsibility are both open to scrutiny. A leader with balanced access to cognitive and affective information about the organisation will manage his team through errors, so that they learn most from such episodes.

Attribution of responsibility in a goal-corrected partnership needs to be done according to the special responsibilities that the clinician has for helping the patient feel better. I am an adherent of retaining the expression 'patient', as it is the patient's suffering (virtual or 'real') which must always be the focus of the consultation. Nevertheless, the clinician's responsibilities are well described with the description of patients as 'clients'. Ideally clinicians are responsible if patients' suffering is not relieved, and patients are responsible if they succeed. The attitude of type B doctors would be to achieve a balance between the contributions of the patient and the doctor to the outcome. Attachment theory suggests that clinicians who use type C strategies will be disposed to attribute failure to the patient, and the even-numbered type A strategies may be associated with taking the blame – they may also exonerate anyone from blame because of understandable failures which were outside their control. It would probably be more interesting if we changed the exercise and asked how we apportion 'blame' when things go right. It is just as difficult to give detailed concrete constructive credit (Ihlen, Ihlen, Koss, 1997).

The patient should be the judge of whether the doctor has been helpful or not. Doctors cannot know without having asked. They are nevertheless in a dilemma about the veracity of the replies they get, and need to have some way of knowing the limits of knowing. If patients are dependent on them for further treatment it will not be a patient with an A type strategy who would risk showing any negative affect involving criticism of the doctor. A patient used to the more coercive styles will find a way of complaining which can embroil him and the doctor in a perpetual dance. That sort of criticism can lead to doctors becoming more involved, rather than feeling rejected, or rejected in such a way that they will feel compelled to do something about it (such as manoeuvring politicians into the field of play). In contrast the veracity of the criticism from a truly balanced patient will have enough of the support necessary to enable doctors to tolerate the negative comments that reflect the need to work on some of their practice.

Gender

Men die on average 5–10 years before women in the UK. Men in the north of England die on average ten years before those in the south of England.[22] These are dramatic differences. The interesting question is why men and women do not appear to be more concerned about this discrepancy. The current attribution of the different frequency with which the sexes complain of illness is said to be that women are 'biologically the weaker sex', modified later to 'the biology of women makes them more sensitive to the signals from their bodies'. There is no equivalent attribution of men being the weaker sex in Western Europe to account for them dying earlier than women (Kraemer, 2000), although in Egypt, for example, mothers are considerably more careful with the health of their sons whom they say are weaker, and so justify spending more money on nourishing food for them (von der Lippe, Crittenden, 2000).

The relative frequency of suffering symptoms is a complex issue. For example, Pennebaker found that when *current* symptoms were being reported there were no consistent gender differences (Pennebaker, 1982: 7), but it was more that females took note and remembered their symptoms, whilst men were relatively inattentive (ibid.: 156; see also Courtenay, 2000a, 2000b). Yet the difference in male and female illness behaviour is socially constructed and depends heavily on how masculinity and femininity are constructed. These involve deadly male habits and painful female habits, deeply engrained in many societies' norms of acceptable behaviour for the different sexes. Women and men maintain each other's respective masculine and feminine stereotypes. Social practices that undermine men's health are often signifiers of masculinity, and instrumental in the way that men negotiate social power and status (Courtenay, 2000a, 2000b). Are attachment strategies playing a part? Are male doctors constructing femininity in unhealthy ways, and influencing the goal-corrected partnership in such a way that they respond in kind to the preoccupied play on helplessness as a manoeuvre in the consultation? Are female nurses, to borrow a stereotype, doing the equivalent for masculinity, and falling for apparent male 'toughness'?

Healthy habits, and dirty habits, are learnt and exploited from childhood onwards. They elicit praise and disgust. Eating forbidden things, such as earthworms and fag-ends, can signify belonging to the 'daredevils' at school, and doing what the adults forbid (Wilkinson, 1988: 138). Dirty habits can be employed coercively as part of a leveraged preoccupied type C dialogue, and also reflect a dimension to caregiving which has lost its meaningfulness – dirt has been neglected. Mary Douglas described the rituals involved for coping with the threats inherent in dirt, and their relation to cultural values and different religious practices. The interested reader is referred to her excellent description (Douglas, 1966). Our task here is to look at the themes associated with dirt from an attachment perspective, and especially the gender issues involved.

Attachment strategies develop in situations of threat, both real and perceived. Parental vigilance in relation to their boys and girls depends both on how the culture views the threats to boys and girls, as well as the particular family illness history. We do not yet know how the culture-specific perceived vulnerabilities of each gender become translated into particular parenting practices, and how these influence the development of attachment.[23] The vulnerabilities that are overlooked can lead to the children being presented with a distorted picture of their strengths and vulnerabilities, which they then take with them into adulthood.

Women predominantly determine the household rituals in Western Europe and in many other cultures. They still hold the last word on whether the children's bedroom windows shall be open at night, whether the bedding should hang out of the window to be refreshed, how often the floors should be washed, and if the carpets should be exchanged for polished floors in the interests of hygiene (the Greek goddess Hygeia, the health giver, was also female[24]) (Wilkinson, 1988: 136, 146). Changes in amount of time devoted by men and women to housework have little to do with whose values dominate, or more especially *how* the hygiene practices are used strategically in power struggles around making the home a 'safe' place. Strategies develop within families to cope with the controlling aspect of the usually female 'health giver' in the family, who can intrude into the pastimes of parent and child with moral righteousness to ensure cleanliness. Gender roles indirectly affect attachment strategies. The hygiene rules are followed with moral obligation. The duty to protect meets the subjective desire for attunement with those who are vulnerable. Dirt intervenes in the care dance, and influences the developing attachment strategy depending on how the child copes with the intrusions.

In general there are no clear differences in the chances of boys and girls developing the A, B or C strategies (van IJzendoorn, Kroonenberg, 1988), although this may not hold for the greater differentiation of classification provided with the development of the dynamic-maturational model. The situation appears also to be the same in China in spite of the different value placed on girls and boys, especially following the single-child policy (van IJzendoorn, Sagi, 1999) (but again the dynamic-maturational model was not used). There are suggestions that in some societies where the gender differences are very pronounced, for example Egypt, the balance changes (von der Lippe, Crittenden, 2000). The same may also be true in Italy (Crittenden, 2000b). Differences are to be expected on theoretical grounds in the distribution within the preoccupied type C strategies, where the exaggerated display of desire for comfort and fear, associated with the even-numbered C strategies, is more coherent with socially constructed aspects of femininity in many societies. The display of aggression and inhibition of signs of fear, the odd-numbered type C strategies, are more associated with the social construction of masculinity. Theoretically one expects an interaction between the frequency with which males and females develop type A and C strategies and culture (see p. 271). Gender-related issues may also influence the relative numbers affected by unresolved trauma, as risk-taking is also socially constructed as part of masculinity in many societies; women are more vulnerable to abuse of power leading to trauma.

Another influence concerns the specific details of how boys and girls learn about illness behaviour through differential reinforcement of particular aspects of the sick role. Exaggerated displays of helplessness and desire for comfort will affect how patients are responded to when ill. Boys and girls 'get away with' different degrees of expressed helplessness and aggression. The attribution responsibility to them is handled differently depending on the patient's gender. In general mothers encourage children to adopt the sick role more than fathers, especially for gastroenterological symptoms – and girls perceive their parents as more often acknowledging their sickness. Girls report more sympathy than boys when they are ill, and are excused more of their responsibilities (Walker, Zeman, 1992). Similar shaping of behaviour is continued into adulthood in medical consultations. Men receive significantly less of their doctor's time in medical encounters than women, and men are provided with fewer and briefer explanations – both simple and technical (Banks, 2001). Although such differential reinforcement of aspects of behaviour may affect the frequency of the behaviour, it says nothing about the role of attachment strategies in influencing how the behaviour is incorporated into strategies and indirectly the frequency. The important distinction is again between the illness behaviour and the strategy, just as between attachment behaviour and strategy. The behaviour will be part of the patient's repertoire, and will be part of their procedural memory, learnt according to behavioural learning principles. Only by gathering information about the strategic use of the presentation of symptoms and illness behaviour, and the coherence of the strategy across a minimum of three memory systems, as the criteria for allocation of an attachment classification (Crittenden, 1999–2002), will we get a clearer picture of the place of attachment strategy.

Although the distribution of attachment strategies is generally not skewed by gender, it is possible that other influences determine the later presentation of disease in men relative to women. Theoretically one would expect late presentation of discomforts to be related to dismissing type A strategies. Other processes, such as a perceived duty to protect the 'weaker sex' (female) through encouraging them to visit the doctor, and a greater preoccupation with appearance – socially constructed as part of femininity – may encourage earlier female presentation with dermatological conditions such as melanoma. Deaths from melanoma are 50 per cent higher in men than women, despite a 50 per cent lower incidence of the disease. Attachment theory has most to offer an understanding of later presentation in men when they have odd-numbered type C strategies. They will theoretically be expected to hold back on their desire for comfort and their fears, instead presenting an invincible 'coping' exterior. In this group information campaigns (directed at semantic memory) cannot be expected to be as effective. But it is important to note that virtually no health promotion literature is produced for men other than on sexual health (Banks, 2001).

Are the health promotion strategies that involve providing more information to women, and emphasising their needs for health screening, counterproductive? Are they associated with women's greater understanding of their vulnerability to diseases, and their greater morbidity, i.e. their increased complaining about deteriorating health? Is there a causal link to greater suffering without increased mortality? There are suggestions that screening produces anticipatory and post-screening dis-ease (for example, Sachs, 1995).[25] Is it better to be a man who presupposes invincibility until he dies, or the women who live significantly longer with their image of being of the vulnerable sex? Attachment theory cannot answer that question, but it suggests that the analysis of the complexities in gender differences in morbidity and mortality (Popay, Groves, 2000) can benefit from an attachment perspective. Early presentation of discomfort, or late presentation of dis-ease, differentially affects morbidity and mortality.

Culture

Culture appears to influence the relative frequency of type A and C strategies in social groups (Crittenden, 2000b; but see suggestions to the contrary based on findings from other models of attachment, which found greater within-country than between-country variation [van IJzendoorn, Kroonenberg, 1988]). The strategies that predominate, and are thought of as the ideal strategies, vary from group to group. Scorers of SSn, PAA and AAI, when learning the method, tend to score their own country's subjects as if they were more skewed to an idealised norm of a balanced type B strategy (the comfortable B3) (Crittenden, personal communication). The hypothesis that Crittenden presents is that each social group has developed ways of living with the threats peculiar to them, with their history, climate, geography, dominant religion,[26] and, for our particular interest here, threats of particular diseases.

Different attachment strategies may be preferred and come to dominate in different cultures, passed on with the family tradition of good-enough parenting, and maintained through media and network attitudes and values. Many themes are not even spoken of; the critical eye of the alma mater is sufficient to know that some limit has been crossed. Taboos are transmitted as much at the cultural level as the family level, with presumably the same effects as discussed earlier – culturally transmitted transformations of information can prevent the social group resolving historical threat/trauma and integrating information, so that their adaptive function changes (examples come to mind for both Germany and Israel).

Culture is characterised by what is taken for granted. An outsider can know more about the local culture than they do themselves, but initially the outsider does not even know what questions to ask to get the answers needed. In the process of an outsider articulating this 'taken-for-granted' knowledge, representatives of the culture can feel threatened. Such articulation has to be done with respect for why things are done as they are. Traditions and rituals fulfil some of the functions of attachment strategies – namely, protection against threat and danger. The origins may lie many years back in time, such as when miasma was a 'cause' of disease, and household routines developed around fresh air. A culture is as much a product of the lives lived at other times and other places by other groups. It is transmitted at both the individual, structural and systemic levels. This can be visualised in terms of the bio-psychosocial understanding of development, which is the cornerstone of attachment theory. In a microcosm, the environment within the egg determines how the genes will first be read and interpreted; the environment determines interpretation, and the structure determines the response and modifies the subsequent genetic 'reading'. The same co-evolution of genetic pool and environment occurs at the level of individuals and their environment of adaptedness, and between groups of individuals and their geography (for a further elaboration see Hoffmeyer, 1995b). Human biology appears to predispose for cultural learning (Trevarthen, Aitken, 2001).

Respect for people's choices depends on understanding their context on their premises. There are suggestions that the communist philosophy, encouraging connection to the community, was at the same time seen as suggesting that the mother–child bond was of less significance. Views of good-enough mothering were coloured by this, and maintained in the culture through all channels – media, official services (including clinicians' attitudes at well-baby clinics), etc. One consequence of this may be the distribution of patterns that were found in the old East Germany (GDR), and in Russia. There is hypothesised to have been an official encouragement to non-B, which led to types A and A/C bias in the GDR, and C in Russia. The difference can be understood with further appeal to other aspects of their histories, and especially the sort of danger for which those societies had to be prepared (Crittenden, 2000b). Such ways of accounting are understandable, but as yet it is uncertain they are warranted.

The principles in such a conceptualisation are not new. A comparison of Dionysian and Apollonian societies is interesting within an attachment perspective (Parrot, Harré, 1996). In the first, elaboration of emotions is valued, as one would expect in a society that had exalted preoccupied type C strategies; in the second, the management of emotions is important to achieve affective calm, as the majority of emotions are seen as threats to themselves and to the way their institutions function – a dismissing type A strategy predominates. In an Apollonian society emotions to do with anything other than enhancing the power of the established order are viewed negatively. Some emotions will be heard and others ignored; some behaviour will be forthcoming and other behaviour inhibited.

With this background I return to the classic paper of Zborowski, who is regularly cited as having demonstrated that 'Jewish' and 'Italian' patients in a New York hospital were more demonstrative ('played up their pain') compared to 'Old Americans' and 'Irish', who played down their pain (Zborowski, 1952). There are some suggestions from Israel and Italy that in these countries the preoccupied type C strategies predominate today, and Crittenden (op. cit.) hypothesises why that might be so. Depending on the sort of danger to which you have been exposed, you develop strategies to cope. If the danger is predictable, such as long dark winters in Finland, a type A strategy would facilitate coping (ibid.), but the unpredictable dangers to which Jews had been exposed would be better protected against with vigilance and a preoccupation with signs of potential danger. The leveraged display of their pain can be interpreted within such a hypothesis as part of a type C strategy, as was discussed for aspects of ambiguous symptoms in the preceding chapter. In contrast, the first settlers in the US valued self-sufficiency, a characteristic of the dismissing type A strategy, and Crittenden has suggested that Americans still have an overrepresentation of the A5 and A6 subgroups. For such strategies, a playing down of pain would be coherent with their other displays of emotion and their feelings about them. It would also be coherent with another characteristic of the Old American group, which was that they delayed seeking help for their pain. Other cultural histories of particular threats from disease could explain the cultural differences with which symptoms from various parts of the body are presented (Pennebaker, 1982: 7), and that symptoms reported within any given culture tend to be similar (ibid.: 146; Payer, 1996).

Zborowski's research included many immigrants, who in the families' near past would probably have experienced dangers outside the normal experience of the rest of their current socioeconomic group. The illness behaviour of refugees and immigrants can be difficult to interpret because they find it especially difficult to feel at ease with those to whom they present their dis-ease. Their illness vocabulary consists of even more slippery stuff than for those who have grown up within the culture.[27] Words for subjective feelings can never be objectively checked out on language courses for immigrants. There are also seldom one-to-one translations for words for feelings, and the mind–body wholeness is to varying degrees represented in the new language.

Contacts with people in flight or migration confront doctors with dimensions of human pain and vulnerability that cannot be understood from within the framework of their own culture. Nevertheless, attunement to immigrants' dis-ease is possible if clinicians allow themselves empathic closeness. From this perspective engagement must begin with the illness, before moving to disease models via an understanding of how sickness has been attributed. It is in negotiating sickness that patients are socialised into the illness culture of their new country, as they both learn the appropriate signs and the rights afforded the sick (the French 'spasmophilia' and English 'chilblains' are unheard of in the US [Payer, 1996]). Because of experiences of misuse of power and exposure to danger, their attachment system will be rapidly mobilised, and often predominantly coloured by issues of unresolved loss and trauma:

> The Western physician's carefully honed precepts of informed consent, beneficence, and autonomy do not prepare healthcare practitioners to understand the patterns of individual and community harm that can arise from experience of forced migration, mass

killings, torture, targeted abuse, systematic rape, loss of home and family, obliteration of culture, denial of political status or economic opportunity, and rejection of personal or group values. Good intentions are not enough. Acting from presumed beneficence but ignorant of what a person has endured before reaching the doctor's office may inflict further injury. Assuming patient autonomy in discussions with prisoners or torture victims may subvert the informed consent process. One must turn to the evolving notions of human rights to find a more comprehensive context in which to recognise how people are affected by power structures that have assaulted and harmed them. From the human rights perspective people are approached as persons who can claim rights from the state and must be protected from the predations of power.

(Leaning, 2001: 1435)

I include the above hypotheses so that potential links between danger, and social processes which maintain particular ways of coping and complaining, can be explored within an attachment paradigm. Theory is at the stage of generating hypotheses for further testing rather than being able to present hard facts.

Cultures support dominant strategies through their values, rituals, and socialisation practices, including the ways in which illness is responded to within health services. I explored a few of these previously when I described how health and illness behaviour develop (Wilkinson, 1988), but I did not have available a comprehensive and detailed model of attachment theory. Children are introduced to the same sort of ideas about what causes disease over the whole world. These ideas are then incorporated into interpersonal dynamics, which change character as children mature. For example, invisible agents affect them so that they lose control over their bodily functions. In Nepal it might be a '*deuta*' (a sort of spirit), in England it is a 'germ' (invisible and taken on trust in the adults' explanations), and was previously just as pervasively invisible as 'miasma'. The power of the invisible is used strategically. Children look for ways of explaining how this secret agent, known to the adults or experts, came to affect just them, at that particular time. In Scotland in 1980 they were relating transgressions of the family code for keeping healthy – going out without a hat on, or not washing their hands to get rid of those still-invisible germs after they had been to the toilet. They employed exactly the same sort of system as Evans-Pritchard described for the African Azande people (Evans-Pritchard, 1937).[28] A good formulation of a psychiatric disorder today employs the same elements – how the disorder evolved, why this patient and why presenting now.

Clinicians need to understand ways both of knowing the world and of feeling safe if they are going to have any chance of offering patients healing appropriate to their needs. In order to do this they can be helped by understanding attachment theory. There is nothing inherently right or better, with either cognitive (in the sense used in the dynamic-maturational model) or affective expertise. It is helpful, though, if clinicians can use either when needed. It will help them see the way in which coping and complaining evolve together.

This attachment-based analysis of how dis-ease is presented and responded to is a preliminary presentation, with predominantly theoretical deductions about what is to be expected with the different classifications. The dynamic-maturational system is complex, and not all details are presented here. It is continually evolving. Nevertheless it is my hope that it will be possible to use the analyses presented to devise research projects of both qualitative and quantitative nature. Because of the distinctions concerning transformations of information, and the consequences for health promotion and clinical consultations, it is possible to test out the theory in areas of major social concern. Attachment theory at this level of detail does more than provide a way of understanding; it suggests dimensions to interpersonal relations that have direct consequences for health, illness and disease.

The attachment paradigm poses a challenge to traditional scientific enquiry. The transition from objective description of behaviour, which is the basis of diagnostic systems, is extended to the strategic use of that behaviour, where the same behaviour can be used to serve various strategies (depression, for example, cannot be expected on this theory to be mapped directly onto one attachment strategy). Strategies presuppose deductions about other people's theory of mind and their intentions; subjectivity meets objectivity, and meaning arises in the room in between. Pattern becomes as important as phenotype, but also pattern across memory systems. Complicated – yes, but a necessary complexity to do justice to human nature. It would be tempting to appeal for more attention to the early years, but this would in my view be to misunderstand the adaptive function of children growing to live life to the full in that niche where they have been born. It is an appropriate priority to meet the suffering of all people[29] – parents, adolescents who will soon be parents, infants and young children, and grandparents who have so much experience in alleviating suffering, and who carry the traditions that their families need and understand their taboos from the inside.

I leave the last words to Darwin from his final paragraph in *The expression of the emotions in man and animals*:

We have also seen that expression in itself, or the language of the emotions, as it has sometimes been called, is certainly of importance for the welfare of mankind.

(Darwin, [1872] 1998: 366).

Notes

1 The World Health Organisation defines health as 'a state of complete physical, mental, and social well-being and not merely the absence of disease or infirmity'. Ivan Illich, in contrast, defined health as the process of adaptation to growing up, ageing, disease and death, using the coping mechanisms embedded in the culture and traditions of communities (Dixon, Sweeney, 2000: 23), which is more similar to what I propose.

2 Etymologically 'health' comes from the Anglo-Saxon for 'wholeness'. Good enough attunement of mother and child leads to a wholeness of integrated access to all memory systems, and a balanced type B strategy, which makes use of both cognitive and affective information without transformation, enabling open, clear and true communication about feelings and intentions.

3 The strategic nature of the relationship between leader and employees will first be revealed when the responses of the staff to these attempts at coercion are known.

4 Aristotle described two types of knowledge: (1) knowledge such as from reading and finding out facts, and (2) knowledge garnered by 'phronesis', a form of practical wisdom which could only be achieved through personal experience. This latter type of knowledge corresponds to 'learning by doing' or Wittgenstein's 'intimate knowledge'; all these seem to be covered by the learning stored in procedural memory.

5 The relationship between signs and habits evolves. Recurring habits successively become used as signs, which then elicit new habits and new signs etc. (see note 3, Chapter 1).

6 Although this is difficult for the non-balanced strategies, it is a particular problem for those with unresolved loss and trauma who struggle to discern whether the danger really is in the past or represents a continuous threat.

7 The following is a perspective from developmental biologists:

> If we know that our world is necessarily the world we bring forth with others, every time we are in conflict with another human being *with whom we want to remain in coexistence*, we cannot affirm what for us is certain (an absolute truth) because that would negate the other person. If we want to coexist with the other person, we must see that *his certainty – however undesirable it may seem to us – is as legitimate and valid as our own* because, like our own, that certainty expresses his conservation of structural coupling in a domain of existence – however undesirable it may seem to us.
>
> (Maturana, Varela, 1988: 245–246)

8 This is not new, but is having a renaissance. Balint described a similar approach nearly forty years ago (Balint, 1964).

9   It is suggested that at least 20 minutes are needed for involving a patient in decisions about treatment, giving them a sense of control, and asking them to take some responsibility for care. Doctors in both the United Kingdom and the United States believe that they have less time for each patient, yet time with patients is increasing in both countries (Mechanic, 2001).

10   There is a problem here for researchers who are trained to have a hypothesis to test. Their genuine curiosity has been violated at one level, and instead their curiosity is limited to one area of enquiry, without room genuinely to entertain other possibilities. Within the qualitative research tradition this should not be a predicament, which is why theoretically qualitative research should precede quantitative research. Otherwise the result is 'like pirates, sailing under flags of false objectivity and spurious science' (Main, 1977: 462).

11   Interestingly, this creates violations of the scientific paradigm. When I carried out qualitative research for my dissertation about twenty years ago amongst children 3–13 years old, they informed me that they had learnt a lot from my research questions. I had to double check that they were referring to their own learning through their curiosity, which had been nurtured through my questions and form of enquiry. They were not the same subjects after the research. They discovered for themselves things that did not hang together. Their experiences did not connect up to the information others had told them about illness and disease. They had solved some of their paradoxes:

> One should not think slightly of the paradoxical; for the paradox is the source of the thinker's passion, and the thinker without a paradox is like a lover without a feeling: a paltry mediocrity . . . The supreme paradox of all thought is the attempt to discover something that thought cannot think.
>
> (Søren Kirkegaard, *Philosophical Fragments*, 1844)

12   Murray found significant association between not attributing agency and intentionality to children at two months, and the development of depressive cognitions about the self at five years (Murray, 1998b). This can be mediated by the same processes described as important for development of insecure attachment strategies, and is an indicator of the importance of attributing intentionality and sense of agency to patients in a consultation.

13   As pointed out by Bandura:

> Habit change is not achieved through an act of will. It requires development of self-regulatory skills . . . [These again] depend on the fidelity, consistency and temporal proximity of self-monitoring . . . Self-observation serves at least two important functions in the process of self-regulation. It provides the information needed for setting realistic goals and for evaluating one's progress toward them.
>
> (Bandura, 1998: 633)

14   Incoherent narratives are more typical of preoccupied speakers who are following the logic of their imaged memory, as they lack clarity of temporal sequences. Siegel has hypothesised that this probably 'involves a resonance

of left- and right-hemisphere processes in both the teller and the listener'
(Siegel, 1999: 299). Through co-operative mutual activation of mind coherent
narratives emerge, and through this process the mind is able to achieve
maximal complexity and thus stable self-organisation. This is said to facilitate
a deep sense of internal coherence.

15   Such groups are asked to think of the following:

* All you know that you do not know,
* All that you do not know that you do not know,
* All that you think you know, but do not know,
* All that you do not know that you know,
* All that you do not know because it is too painful,
* Taboos, the dangerous and forbidden knowledge
                 (from the 'not-knowing' course at Medical faculty,
                                         University of Utah, USA)

The groups can operate as weekly gatherings

* to take up things that people do not know,
* where they meet together with other people who do not know,
* investigate how to ask fruitful questions,
* share their most productive mistakes.

16   English law affords minors the right to consent to, but not to refuse, medical
treatment, which suggests a right to agree with your doctors (Ford, Kessel,
2001), and it is left to the child to solve the paradox.

17   General practitioners tend to be responsive, whereas hospital practice
primarily tends to initiate.

18   For example, perhaps the oppositionality of the higher dismissing type A
strategies, for whom control and power are central issues in attempts to live
with an internal working model of a powerful adult who has abused their
power in relation to them, but often been exonerated.

19   I follow Bandura in being sceptical of the concept of there being stages to
change. A genuine stage theory is rooted in three basic assumptions: qualitative transformations across discrete stages, invariant sequence of change,
and non-reversibility. The stages-of-change scheme violates each of these
requirements (Bandura, 1998).

Examples of the sort of question used from the field of eating disorders:
What would have to happen for it to become more important for you to
change?
What are the good things about . . . – and some of the less good things
about . . .?
What concerns do you have about . . .?
If you were to change what would it be like?
What would make you more confident about making these changes?
How can I or anybody else help you succeed?
Is there anything you have found helpful in any previous attempts to
change?

What have you learned from the way things went wrong last time you tried?

What are the practical things you would need to do to achieve this goal – are they achievable?

Is there anything you can think of that would make you feel more confident?

(Treasure, Schmidt, 2001: 7)

20 It may appear rather peculiar that the ideal care for a patient should be a 'placebo'. Placebo means 'I will make someone more comfortable' – the ideal hope for a sufferer. Placebo had an original meaning of to help someone get a 'quiet mind' (Simpson, 1968). Placebo is in the future tense, it holds out hope for the future. Balint described the ideal role of the doctor as being like a drug that would make someone more comfortable – although he was keen to distinguish that role from negative moral connotations of placebo. He was referring to the non-specific factors for bringing about change, which need to become a part of the doctor's repertoire (Balint, 1964).

21 It appears as if recognition of drug effect is important for the outcome of placebo effects in double-blind trials of medication. Patients and physicians were both able to correctly guess the appropriate condition at high levels of accuracy (79 per cent and 87 per cent). Responders were more accurate than non-responders in identifying whether they had received an active drug or a placebo (Fisher, Greenberg, 1989). The effect of medication relative to placebo is significantly reduced when an active placebo (with noticeable side effects) is used.

22 Despite having had most of the social determinants of health in their favour, men have higher mortality rates for all leading causes of death. When greater affluence has come to countries it has usually led to reduction in female mortality, whilst male mortality has remained unchanged, so that the difference has increased. Sex mortality ratios (the male death rate divided by the female death rate) generally increased during the mid-twentieth century; during the transition towards a market economy, the sex differential in life expectancy at birth increased in all countries of Central and Eastern Europe (Waldron, 2000). Privilege does not prevent privation.

23 When parents are in severe conflict, they are more likely to quarrel in front of their sons than their daughters. Animal studies have shown that females are less likely to elicit damaging behaviour from others. Harlow's socially isolated monkeys were more likely to abuse and kill the male than their female offspring (Rutter, 1985).

24 Dixon and Sweeney explain the tradition:

In the Hygeian tradition health is a natural and normal way of things, derived from a state of inner equilibrium and balance. Treatment in this tradition is seen as a way of restoring equilibrium, and the role of the physician is to help to achieve this by re-establishing not only an inner balance between the individual's physical, emotional and spiritual aspects of illness, but also an outer balance between the person and the person's environment.

(Dixon, Sweeney, 2000: 22)

25 Campaigns designed to make people aware of the risk of a particular disease, and the ways they can effectively combat the risk, need to be run in goal-directed ways to reach different groups. Risk campaigns convey facts. Those at risk can come to take on a patient role, their vulnerability converted to a state of illness, whereby their attunement with the clinician has led to them taking on board the emotional associations of an 'as-if' disease. The pre-disease state, just like a primary emotion/dis-ease state, has led on to being an illness state, rather than an emotional state of uncertainty, which is a predicament that has to be lived with. In the USA only half of the population are happy with their health – and this proportion is reducing. Ninety-six per cent of them want to change something with their body (Falkum, Larsen, 1999)! Their future death is the ultimate predicament that they have to live with, although some deep-freeze mortician parlours seem to pander to those who don't like that paradox.

The role of technology in screening opens up another moral order. Self-management of diabetes is monitored by measuring the concentration of a form of haemoglobin in the blood, HbAlc. The test can now assume the function of a sign indicating moral qualities in the patient, and this has an impact on the clinical dialogue. This test-as-sign offers an illustration of how technologies may enter into people's understanding of themselves (Hilde, 2002).

26 The association between religion and attachment strategies will not be covered here, although there have been tentative beginnings to exploring religious behaviour within the attachment paradigm (Kirkpatrick, 1999), albeit not within the dynamic-maturational model. Mary Douglas (1966) has presented relations between religion, dirt and strategies for cleanliness. Ideally a presentation on attachment strategies and illness behaviour would cover the main characteristics of the world's religions for their influence on the relative frequencies with which the attachment strategies will be expected within each culture. The religious beliefs are central to how social groups attempt to live with threat and danger, and one would expect coherence with issues otherwise presented in this section.

27 'I know you think you know what I mean with what I write, but I am not sure whether you are clear that what you have read is perhaps not what I meant' covers a central dilemma with the use of language, such as with writing a book, which can be especially poignant for refugees.

28 Malinowski's analysis employed a different logic. He was concerned with the superiority of the sense of science in Western medicine, and contrasted this to the magic of approaches based on strong affect (Malinowski, 1948). The point that is of interest, given the distinction we have elaborated in the preceding chapters, is the way in which one strategy can be seen to be associated with the superiority of the cognitive and understanding tempero-causal connection, with associated activation of particular brain areas. The other strategy can be compared to the affective strategies of the preoccupied type C attachment strategy. The crucial issue is that he failed to obtain a balanced account where both aspects could be integrated.

29 Finally I bring to your attention two papers covering political consequences of recent social cognitive and developmental psychology, rather than developing the political agenda suggested by this attachment analysis. One

'promotes community self-help through collective enablement' as part of a detailed programme for health promotion (Bandura, 1998). The other is to include evaluation of maternal mental health during pregnancy and at well-baby clinics – with an awareness of attachment behaviour for the infants and the mothers' reflective function, attachment strategies and ability to see the world through the eyes of her baby (Dawson, Ashman, Carver, 2000). These initiatives can facilitate goal-corrected partnerships for health.

Glossary

Affective expression The way an emotional state is revealed.

Affects Composite states involving the subjective, neuro-physiological and motor-expressive dimensions of feelings and emotions, inter-twined with memories of experiences that give personal meaning to current feeling states. Many use the terms 'emotion' and 'affect' interchangeably.

Alexithymia Lack of a psychological language for presenting discomforts. It is composed of the following salient features: '(i) difficulty identifying feelings and distinguishing between feelings and the bodily sensations of emotional arousal; (ii) difficulty describing feelings to other people; (iii) constricted imaginal processes, as evidenced by a paucity of fantasies; and (iv) a stimulus-bound, externally orientated cognitive style' (Taylor, Bagby, Parker, 1997: 29). Constituted from the Greek for 'lack of words for affects'.

Alignment One component of affect attunement in which the state of one individual alters to approximate that of another. Alignment can be primarily a one-way process, or it can be bilateral.

Allostasis Maintaining balance by change.

Allostatic load The result of a body system being overused, or not shutting down to conserve itself.

Apoptosis Pre-programmed cell death.

Attunement, affect The ways in which internal emotional states are brought into external communication with each other within infant–caregiver interactions (Siegel, 1999: 280). It is a broader concept than alignment. It includes sensitivity to times when alignment should not occur. [See also *Alignment* and *Emotional resonance*.]

Autonoetic consciousness The ability of the mind to have a sense of recollection of the self at a particular time in the past, awareness of the self in the lived present, and projections of the self into the imagined future (Wheeler, Stuss, Tulving, 1997). This kind of consciousness is said to enable 'mental time travel'.

Background emotions   The textures of the shifts in brain state that are the results of both initial orientation and elaborative appraisal–arousal processes. Here they correspond to Siegel's use of 'primary emotions' (Siegel, 1999: 125).

Background feelings   See *Vitality affects*.

Body Mass Index   Weight in kilograms, divided by height in metres squared. It is used as a measure of obesity/thinness, which takes account of a person's height.

Ecphoric sensation   A clear sense that something happened when in fact it did not.

Emotional resonance/emotional contagion   Involves more than the alignment of states; it also includes the ways in which the interaction affects the individuals in other aspects of their minds. Resonance also continues after alignment has stopped. 'Contagion' and 'resonance' are used interchangeably.

Emotions, categorical   Differentiated states of mind that have evolved into specific, engrained patterns of activation (Siegel, 1999: 127), the equivalent of Damasio's use of primary emotions (Damasio, 2000: 50–51).

Enviromes   Environmental factors affecting how genes are read.

Epigenesis   Dependence of biological development on environmental circumstances.

Epigenetic factors   The ways in which experience directly influences how genes are expressed.

Equifinality   Multiple pathways can converge on a common outcome.

Exaptation   Features that initially serve one function, but are then refined in the service of a new function that may be quite different. For example, feathers initially served as an insulation device before enabling flight.

Fallibilism   The doctrine that our knowledge is never absolute but always swims in a continuum of uncertainty and indeterminism.

Feeling   Refers to the subjective, cognitive experiential domain of emotion response systems.

Genotype   Genetic constitution of an individual.

Internal locus of control   People see themselves as effective agents to bring about change, rather than being passive victims of external forces.

Interoceptive confusion   A mistrust of the legitimacy of own feelings and experiences based on interoceptive information.

Interoceptive information   Information from the muscles and viscera (guts).

Motherese   The adaptation of speech to make it easily understood by infants.

Negative affectivity   The tendency to experience and report negative self-states, including aversive emotions and problematic physical symptoms.

Phenotype   Set of observable characteristics of an individual or group as determined by genotype *and* environment.

Proto-self   The proto-self is a coherent collection of neural patterns which map, moment by moment, the state of the physical structure of the organism in its many dimensions (Damasio, 2000: 154).

Recruitment   Neuronal processes which selectively activate patterns of firing of other neural pathways, including within other brains. The infant both responds in the world of others and plays an active role in influencing how others respond. Thus when neuronal circuits become activated, they create and reinforce their connections with each other. Once established, such a pattern in neuronal activations will tend to recruit similar patterns in the future.

Referential decoupling   The ability to reflect back to infants their emotions in such a way that on one level the emotions are perceived as identical, but on another level there are additional signals that the adult is only pretending to experience the emotion.

Reflective function   Capacity for affect attunement communicated with facial expression, vocalisations, body gestures, and eye contact.

Salutogenesis   The creation of health, in contrast to the usual focus on what causes disease.

Secondary alexithymia   Alexithymia arising in the course of treatment for a life threatening disease.

Self   An internally organised cluster of attitudes, expectations, meanings, and feelings.

Sensory amplification   The way in which particular responses to symptoms amplify them, rather than contain them.

Social referencing   Children look to the facial expressions and other non-verbal aspects of their parents' signals to determine how they should feel and respond in an ambiguous situation.

Soma   A living, self-sensing, internalised perception of oneself – in contrast to 'body', which reflects how others perceive your physical form.

Somatisation   A tendency to experience and communicate distress in the form of physical symptoms. The somatic dis-ease is often presented for medical help.

Somato-sensory amplification   A tendency to amplify and hence misinterpret significance of bodily sensations.

Structural coupling   '[W]e speak of structural coupling whenever there is a history of recurrent interactions leading to the structural congruence between two (or more) systems' (Maturana, Varela, 1988: 75).

Vitality affects   The feelings resulting from background emotions and corresponding to background feelings, prior to their becoming specific feelings of emotions.

References

Aasland, O.G. (2001) Bakerens barn. *Tidsskrift for Norsk Lægeforening* **121**, 3504 (in Norwegian).

Abramson, L.Y., Seligman, M.E.P. and Teasdale, J.D. (1978) Learned helplessness in humans: Critique and reformulation. *Journal of Abnormal Psychology* **87**, 49–74.

Adolphs, R., Damasio, H., Tranel, D. and Damasio, A. (1996) Cortical systems for the recognition of emotion in facial expressions. *Journal of Neuroscience* **16**, 7678–7687.

Adolphs, R., Tranel, D. and Damasio, A.R. (1994) Impaired recognition of emotion in facial expressions following bilateral damage to the human amygdala. *Nature* **372**, 669–672.

Ainsworth, M.D.S. (1985) Patterns of infant–mother attachment: Antecedents and effects on development. *Bulletin of the New York Academy of Medicine* **61**, 771–791.

Ainsworth, M.D.S., Bell, S.M. and Stayton, D.J. (1974) Infant–mother attachment and social development: 'Socialization' as a product of reciprocal responsiveness to signals. In: P.M. Richards (ed.) *The integration of a child into a social world*, pp. 99–135. Cambridge: Cambridge University Press.

Ainsworth, M.D.S., Blehar, M.C., Waters, E. and Wall, S. (1978) *Patterns of attachment: A psychological study of the strange situation*. Hillsdale, NJ: Erlbaum Associates.

Aitken, K. and Trevarthen, C. (1997) Self/other organization in human psychological development. *Development and Psychopathology* **9**, 653–678.

Ali, N. and Cimino, C.R. (1997) Hemispheric lateralization of perception and memory for emotional verbal stimuli in normal individuals. *Neuropsychology* **11**, 114–125.

American Psychiatric Association (1994) *Diagnostic and statistical manual of mental disorders*, 4th edn. Washington, DC: American Psychiatric Association.

Ammaniti, M., van IJzendoorn, M.H., Speranza, A.M. and Tambelli, R. (2000) Internal working models of attachment during late childhood and early adolescence: An exploration of stability and change. *Attachment and Human Development* **2**, 328–346.

Anderson, D.E., Chesney, M.A. and Scuteri, A. (2000) Anger expression style mediates association of expired carbon dioxide level with resting blood pressure. *Journal of Psychosomatic Research* **48**, 271.

Antonovsky, A. (1987) *Unraveling the mystery of health: How people manage stress and stay well*. San Francisco: Jossey-Bass Publishers.

Ariès, P. (1960) *Centuries of childhood*. Harmondsworth: Penguin.

Asmundson, C.J.G., Norton, G.R., Wilson, K.G. and Sandler, L.S. (1994) Subjective symptoms and cardiac reactivity to brief hyperventilation in individuals with high anxiety sensitivity. *Behaviour Research and Therapy* **32**, 237–241.

Bakal, D. (1999) *Minding the body: Clinical uses of somatic awareness*. New York: Guilford Press.

Balint, M. (1964) *The doctor, his patient and the illness*. London: Pitman Medical.

Bandura, A. (1998) Health promotion from the perspective of social cognitive theory. *Psychology and Health* **13**, 623–649.

Banks, I. (2001) No man's land: Men, illness, and the NHS. *British Medical Journal* **323**, 1058–1060.

Barker, D.J.P. (1998) *Mothers, babies and health in later life*, 2nd edn. Edinburgh: Churchill Livingstone.

Barnett, D., Hunt, K.H., Butler, C.M., McCaskill IV, J.W., Kaplan-Estrin, M. and Pipp-Siegel, S. (1999) Indices of attachment among toddlers with neurological and non-neurological problems. In: J. Solomon and C. George (eds) *Attachment disorganization*, pp. 189–212. New York: Guilford Press.

Barr, R.G., Hopkins, B. and Green, J.A. (2000) *Crying as a sign, a symptom and a signal: Crying, emotional and developmental aspects of infant and toddler crying*. Lavenham, Suffolk: Mac Keith Press.

Barsky, A.J., Wool, C., Barnett, M.C. and Cleary, P.D. (1994) Histories of childhood trauma in adult hypochondriacal patients. *American Journal of Psychiatry* **151**, 397–401.

Bass, C. and Murphy, M. (1990) The chronic somatizer and the Government White Paper. *Journal of the Royal Society of Medicine* **83**, 203–205.

Bateson, P. and Martin, P. (1999) *Design for a life: How behaviour develops*. London: Jonathan Cape.

Bauer, P.J. and Wewerka, S.S. (1995) One- to two-year-olds' recall of events: The more expressed, the more impressed. *Journal of Experimental Child Psychology* **59**, 475–496.

Baumann, L.J. and Leventhal, H. (1985) 'I can tell when my blood pressure is up, can't I?'. *Health Psychology* **4**, 203–218.

Beauchaine, T. (2001) Vagal tone, development, and Gray's motivational theory: Toward an integrated model of autonomic nervous system functioning in psychopathology. *Development and Psychopathology* **13**, 183–214.

Bechara, A., Damasio, H., Tranel, D. and Damasio, A. (1997) Deciding advantageously before knowing the advantageous strategy. *Science* **275**, 1293–1295.

Beebe, B. and Lachman, F.M. (1988) Mother–infant mutual influence and precursors of psychic structure. In: A. Goldberg (ed.) *Progress in self psychology*, pp. 3–25. Hillsdale, NJ: Analytic Press.

Beeghly, M. and Cicchetti, D. (1994) Child maltreatment, attachment and the self system: Emergence of an internal state lexicon in toddlers at high social risk. *Development and Psychopathology* **6**, 5–30.

Belsky, J. (1988) Infant day care and socioemotional development: The United States. *Journal of Child Psychology and Psychiatry* **29**, 397–406.

Belsky, J. (2001) Developmental risks (still) associated with early child care. *Journal of Child Psychology and Psychiatry* **42**, 845–859.

Benes, F.M. (1998) Human brain growth spans decades. *American Journal of Psychiatry* **155**, 1489.

Benoit, D. and Parker, K. (1994) Stability and transmission of attachment across three generations. *Child Development* **65**, 1444–1457.

Benoit, D., Parker, K.C.H. and Zeanah, C.H. (1997) Mothers' representations of their infants assessed prenatally: Stability and association with infants' attachment classifications. *Journal of Child Psychology and Psychiatry* **38**, 307–313.

Berne, E. (1964) *Games people play*. New York: Grove Press.

Berwick, D., Davidoff, F., Hiatt, H. and Smith, R. (2001) Refining and implementing the Tavistock principles for everybody in health care. *British Medical Journal* **323**, 616–620.

Blasi, Z.D., Harkness, E., Ernst, E.G.A., Georgiou, A. and Kleijnen, J. (2001) Influence of context effects on health outcomes: A systematic review. *Lancet* **357**, 757–762.

Blomhoff, S., Reinvang, I. and Malt, U.F. (1998) Event-related potentials to stimuli with emotional impact in posttraumatic stress patients. *Biological Psychiatry* **44**, 1045–1053.

Bowlby, J. (1951) *Maternal care and mental health*. Genève: World Health Organisation.

Bowlby, J. ([1969] 1982) *Attachment and loss: I Attachment*. London: Hogarth Press.

Bowlby, J. (1973) *Attachment and loss: II Separation, anxiety and anger*. London: Hogarth Press.

Bowlby, J. (1980) *Attachment and loss: III Loss, sadness and depression*. London: Hogarth Press.

Bowlby, J. (1988) *A secure base: Clinical applications of attachment theory*. London: Routledge.

Brandon, S., Boakes, J., Glaser, D. and Green, R. (1998) Recovered memories of childhood sexual abuse: Implications for clinical practice. *British Journal of Psychiatry* **172**, 296–307.

Bretherton, I., Fritz, J., Zahn-Waxler, C. and Ridgeway, D. (1986) Learning to talk about emotions: A functionalist perspective. *Child Development* **57**, 529–548.

Bronfenbrenner, U. (1979) *The ecology of human development*. Cambridge, MA: Harvard University Press.

Brown, G.W. and Harris, T.O. (1989) *Life events and illness*. London: Guilford Press.

Bruch, H. (1962) Perceptual and conceptual disturbances in anorexia nervosa. *Psychosomatic Medicine* **24**, 187–194.

Bruggen, P. (1997) *Who cares? True stories of the NHS reforms*. Charlbury: Jon Carpenter Publishing.

Butler, C., Rollnick, S. and Stott, N. (1996) The practitioner, the patient and resistance to change: Recent ideas on compliance. *Canadian Medical Association Journal* **154**, 1357–1362.

Byng-Hall, J. (1995) *Rewriting family scripts: Improvisation and systems change*. New York: Guilford Press.

Cassidy, J. and Berlin, L.J. (1994) The insecure/ambivalent pattern of attachment: Theory and research. *Child Development* **65**, 971–991.

Cerveri, I., Locatelli, F., Zoia, M.C., Corsico, A., Accordini, S., de Marco, R., on behalf of the ECRHS (1999) International variations in asthma treatment compliance: The results of the European Community Respiratory Health Survey (ECRHS). *European Respiratory Journal* **14**, 288–294.

Christie, V.M. (2001) *Syk lege: En presentasjon gjennom 88 legers egne stemmer*. Oslo: UNIPUB forlag (in Norwegian).

Chugani, H.T. (1999) Metabolic imaging: A window on brain development and plasticity. *Neuroscientist* **5**, 29–40.

Cicchetti, D. and Rogosh, F.A. (1997) The role of self-organization in the promotion of resilience in maltreated children. *Development and Psychopathology* **9**, 797–816.

Cicchetti, D., Ganiban, J. and Barnett, D. (1991) Contributions from the study of high-risk populations to understanding the development of emotion regulation. In: J. Garber and K.A. Dodge (eds) *The development of emotion regulation and dysregulation*, pp. 15–48. Cambridge: Cambridge University Press.

Ciechanowski, P.S., Katon, W.J., Russo, J.E. and Walker, E.A. (2001) The patient–provider relationship: Attachment theory and adherence to treatment in diabetes. *American Journal of Psychiatry* **158**, 29–35.

Cioffi, D. (1991) Beyond attentional strategies: A cognitive-perceptual model of somatic interpretation. *Psychological Bulletin* **109**, 25–41.

Claussen, A.H. and Crittenden, P.M. (2000) Maternal sensitivity. In: P.M. Crittenden and A.H. Claussen (eds) *The organization attachment relationships: Maturation, culture, and context*, pp. 115–122. Cambridge: Cambridge University Press.

Cobb, J.M.T. and Steptoe, A. (1998) Psychosocial influences on upper respiratory infectious illness in children. *Journal of Psychosomatic Research* **54**, 319–330.

Cohen, S., Doyle, W.J., Skoner, D.P., Rabin, B.S. and Gwaltney, J.M. (1997)

Social ties and susceptibility to the common cold. *Journal of the American Medical Association* **277**, 1940–1944.

Cole, S.W., Kemeny, M.E. and Taylor, S.E. (1997) Social identity and physical health: Accelerated HIV progression in rejection-sensitive gay men. *Journal of Personality and Social Psychology* **72**, 320–335.

Cole-Detke, H.E. and Kobak, R. (1996) Attachment processes in eating disorder and depression. *Journal of Consulting and Clinical Psychology* **64**, 282–290.

Courtenay, W.H. (2000a) Constructions of masculinity and their influences on men's well-being: A theory of gender and health. *Social Science and Medicine* **50**, 1385–1401.

Courtenay, W.H. (2000b) Engendering health: A social constructionist examination of men's health beliefs and behaviors. *Psychology of Men and Masculinity* **1**, 4–15.

Craig, T.K.J., Boardman, A.P., Mills, K., Daly-Jones, O. and Drake, H. (1993) The South London somatisation study I: Longitudinal course and the influence of early life experiences. *British Journal of Psychiatry* **163**, 579–588.

Crittenden, P.M. (1985) Maltreated infants: Vulnerability and resilience. *Journal of Child Psychology and Psychiatry* **26**, 85–96.

Crittenden, P.M. (2000a) A dynamic-maturational approach to continuity and change in pattern of attachment. In: P.M. Crittenden and A.H. Claussen (eds) *The organization of attachment relationships: Maturation, culture, and context*, pp. 343–357. Cambridge: Cambridge University Press.

Crittenden, P.M. (2000b) A dynamic-maturational exploration of the meaning of security and adaptation: Empirical, cultural, and theoretical considerations. In: P.M. Crittenden and A.H. Claussen (eds) *The organization of attachment relationships: Maturation, culture, and context*, pp. 358–383. Cambridge: Cambridge University Press.

Crittenden, P.M. (1992–2001) *Preschool assessment of attachment: Manual classification of quality of attachment for preschool-aged children*. Miami, FL: Unpublished manuscript available from the author.

Crittenden, P.M. (2001) Organization, alternative organizations, and disorganization: Competing perspectives on the development of endangered children. Book review of J. Solomon and C. George (eds) (1999) *Attachment disorganization*, in *Contemporary Psychology: APA review of books* **46** (6), 593–596.

Crittenden, P.M. (1999–2002) *Attachment in adulthood: Coding manual for the dynamic-maturational approach to the Adult Attachment Interview*. Unpublished manuscript, Miami, FL.

Crittenden, P.M. and Claussen, A.H. (2000) *The organization of attachment relationships*. Cambridge: Cambridge University Press.

Crittenden, P.M., Lang, C., Claussen, A.H. and Partridge, M.F. (2000) Relations among mothers' dispositional representations of parenting. In P.M. Crittenden and A.H. Claussen (eds) *The organization of attachment relationships: Maturation, culture, and context*, pp. 214–233. Cambridge: Cambridge University Press.

Crockenberg, S.B. (1981) Infant irritability, mother responsiveness, and social support influence on the security of infant–mother attachment. *Child Development* **52**, 857–865.

Cushway, D. and Tyler, P.A. (1994) Stress and coping in clinical psychologists. *Stress Medicine* **10**, 35–42.

D'Esposito, M., Detre, J., Alsop, D., Shin, R., Atlas, S. and Grossman, M. (1995) The neural basis of the central executive system of working memory. *Nature* **378**, 279–281.

Damasio, A. (2000) *The feeling of what happens: Body, emotion and the making of consciousness*. London: Vintage.

Darwin, C. ([1872] 1998) *The expression of the emotions in man and animals*, 3rd edn. London: HarperCollins.

Dawson, G. (1994) Development of emotional expression and emotion regulation in infancy. Contributions of the frontal lobe. In: G. Dawson and K.W. Fischer (eds) *Human behavior and the developing brain*, New York: Guilford Press.

Dawson, G., Ashman, S.B. and Carver, L.J. (2000) The role of early experience in shaping behavioral and brain development and its implications for social policy. *Development and Psychopathology* **12**, 695–712.

Deacon, T. (1997) *The symbolic species: The co-evolution of language and the human brain*. London: Penguin Books.

Department of Health (2000) *An organisation with a memory: Report of an expert group on learning from adverse events in the NHS chaired by the Chief Medical Officer of Health*. London: The Stationery Office.

De Wolff, M.S. and van IJzendoorn, M.H. (1997) Sensitivity and attachment: A metaanalysis on parental antecedents of infant attachment. *Child Development* **68**, 571–591.

Dhabhar, F.S. and McEwen, B.S. (1999) Enhancing versus suppressive effects of stress hormones on skin immune function. *Proceedings of the National Academy of Sciences* **96**, 1059–1064.

Dinan, T.G. (1999) The physical consequences of depressive illness. *British Medical Journal* **318**, 826.

Dixon, M. and Sweeney, K. (2000) *The human effect in medicine: Theory, research and practice*. Oxford: Radcliffe Medical Press.

Douglas, M. (1966) *Purity and danger: An analysis of the concepts of pollution and taboo*. London: Routledge & Kegan Paul.

Dozier, M. (1990) Attachment organization and treatment use for adults with serious psychopathological disorders. *Developmental Psychopathology* **2**, 47–60.

Dozier, M., Cue, K.L. and Barnett, L. (1994) Clinicians as caregivers: Role of attachment organization in treatment. *Journal of Consulting and Clinical Psychology* **62**, 793–800.

Dunn, A.J., Antoon, M. and Chapman, Y. (1991) Reduction of exploratory behaviour by intraperitoneal injection of interleukin-l involves brain corticotrophin-releasing factor. *Brain Research Bulletin* **26**, 539–542.

Dunn, J. (1993) *Young children's close relationships: Beyond attachment.* London: Sage.

Dunn, J. (1994) Changing minds and changing relationships. In: C. Lewis and P. Mitchell (eds) *Children's early understanding of mind: Origins and development,* pp. 297–310. Hove, UK: Lawrence Erlbaum Associates.

Dunn, J. and Brown, J. (1991) Relationships, talk about feelings, and the development of affect regulation in early childhood. In: J. Garber and C.A. Dodge (eds) *The development of emotion regulation and dysregulation,* pp. 89–108. Cambridge: Cambridge University Press.

Edelman, G. (1989) *The remembered present.* New York: Basic Books.

Egger, H.L., Costello, E.J., Erkanli, A. and Angold, A. (1999) Somatic complaints and psychopathology in children and adolescents: Stomach aches, musculoskeletal pains, and headaches. *Journal of the American Academy of Child and Adolescent Psychiatry* **38**, 852–860.

Ekman, P. (1992) Facial expressions of emotion: New findings, new questions. *Psychological Science* **3**, 34–38.

Ekman, P., Levenson, R.W. and Friesen, W.V. (1983) Autonomic nervous system activity distinguishes among emotions. *Science* **221**, 1208–1210.

Ellingsen, A.E. and Wilhelmsen, I. (2002) Disease anxiety in medical students and law students. *Tidsskrift for Norsk Lægeforening* **122**, 785–787.

Engel, G.L. (1959) Psychogenic pain and the pain prone patient. *American Journal of Medicine* **26**, 899–918.

Epping-Jordan, J.E., Compas, B.E. and Howell, D.C. (1994) Predictors of cancer progression in young adult men and women: Avoidance, intrusive thoughts and psychological symptoms. *Health Psychology* **13**, 536–547.

Eriksson, J.G., Forsén, T., Tuomilehto, J., Osmond, C. and Barker, D.J.P. (2001) Early growth and coronary heart disease in later life: Longitudinal study. *British Medical Journal* **322**, 949–953.

Eriksson, P.S., Perifilieva, E., Bjork-Eriksson, T. *et al.* (1998) Neurogenesis in the adult human hippocampus. *Nature Medicine* **4**, 1313–1317.

Evans-Pritchard, E.E. (1937) *Witchcraft, oracles and magic among the Azande.* Oxford: Clarendon.

Everson, S.A., Kaplan, G.A., Goldberg, D.E., Salonen, R. and Jukka, T. (1997) Hopelessness and a 4-year progression of carotid atherosclerosis: The Kupio ischemic heart disease risk factor study. *Arteriosclerosis, Thrombosis, and Vascular Biology* **17**, 1490–1495.

Eysenck, H.J. (1991) Personality, stress and disease: An interactionist perspective. *Psychological Inquiry* **2**, 221–232.

Fabrega, H. (1990) The concept of somatization as a cultural and historical product of western medicine. *Psychosomatic Medicine* **52**, 653–672.

Falkum, E. (2000) Hva er utbrenthet? *Tidsskrift for den norske lægeforeningen* **120**, 1122–1128 (in Norwegian).

Falkum, E. and Larsen, Ø. (1999) Hva former befolkningens oppfatninger om helse og sykdom? *Tidsskrift for den norske lægeforeningen* **119**, 4488–4491 (in Norwegian).

Feeney, J. and Ryan, S. (1994) Attachment style and affect regulation: Relationships with health behavior and family experiences of illness in a student sample. *Health Psychology* **13**, 334–345.

Felitti, V.J., Anda, R.F., Nordenberg, D., Williamson, D.F., Spitz, A.M., Edwards, V., Koss, M.P. and Marks, J.S. (1998) Relationship of childhood abuse and household dysfunction to many of the leading causes of death in adults: The Adverse Childhood Experiences (ACE) study. *American Journal of Preventive Medicine* **14**, 245–258.

Fernald, A. (1992) Human maternal vocalizations to infants as biologically relevant signals: An evolutionary perspective. In: J.H. Barkhow *et al.* (eds) *The adapted mind: Evolutionary psychology and the generation of culture*, pp. 391–428. New York: Oxford University Press.

Field, T. (1994) The effects of mother's physical and emotional unavailability on emotion regulation. In: N.A. Fox (ed.) *The development of emotion regulation: Biological and behavioral considerations. Monograph of the Society for Research in Child Development*, **59** (Serial No. 240) (2–3), 208–227.

Fiese, B.H. and Wamboldt, F.S. (2000) Family routines, rituals, and asthma management: A proposal for family-based strategies to increase treatment adherence. *Families, Systems & Health* **18**, 405–418.

Firth-Cozens, J. (1992) The role of early family experiences in the perception of organisational stress: Fusing clinical and organisational perspectives. *Journal of Occupational and Organisational Psychology* **65**, 61–75.

Firth-Cozens, J. (2001) Interventions to improve physicians' wellbeing and patient care. *Social Science and Medicine* **52**, 215–222.

Fisher, S. and Greenberg, R.P. (1989) A second opinion: Rethinking the claims of biological psychiatry. In: S. Fisher and R.P. Greenberg (eds) *The limits of biological treatments for psychological distress*, pp. 309–336. Hillsdale, NJ: Erlbaum.

Fivush, R. (1994) Constructing narrative, emotion, and self in parent–child conversations about the past. In: U. Neisser and R. Fivush (eds) *The remembering self: Construction and accuracy in the self-narrative*, pp. 136–157. Cambridge: Cambridge University Press.

Flaten, M.A., Simonsen, T. and Olsen, H. (1999) Drug-related information generates placebo and nocebo responses that modify the drug response. *Psychosomatic Medicine* **61**, 250–255.

Fonagy, P. (1999) The transgenerational transmission of holocaust trauma: Lessons learned from the analysis of an adolescent with obsessive-compulsive disorder. *Attachment and Human Development* **1**, 92–114.

Fonagy, P., Steele, H. and Steele, M. (1991) Maternal representations of attachment during pregnancy predict the organization of infant–mother attachment in one year of age. *Child Development* **62**, 210–225.

Fonagy, P., Steele, M., Steele, H., Leigh, T., Kennedy, R., Mattoon, G. and Target, M. (1995) Attachment, the reflective self, and borderline states: The predictive specificity of the Adult Attachment Interview and pathological emotional development. In: S. Goldberg, R. Muir and J. Kerr (eds) *Attachment theory: Social, developmental and clinical perspectives*, pp. 233–277. Hillsdale, NJ: Analytic Press.

Fonagy, P. and Target, M. (1997) Attachment and reflective function: Their role in self-organization. *Development and Psychopathology* 9, 679–700.

Ford, D.E., Mead, L.A., Chang, P.P., Levine, D.M. and Klag, M.J. (1994) Depression predicts cardiovascular disease in men: the precursors study. *Circulation* 90 (suppl. I), I–614.

Ford, T. and Kessel, A. (2001) Feeling the way: Childhood mental illness and consent to admission and treatment. *British Journal of Psychiatry* 179, 384–386.

Fraser, S.W. and Greenhalgh, T. (2001) Coping with complexity: Educating for capability. *British Medical Journal* 323, 799–803.

Frasure-Smith, N. (1987) Levels of somatic awareness in relation to angiographic findings. *Journal of Psychosomatic Research* 31, 545–554.

Freedland, K.E., Carney, R.M., Krone, R.J., Smith, L.J., Rich, M.W., Eisenkramer, G. and Fischer, K.C. (1991) Psychological factors in silent myocardial ischemia. *Psychosomatic Medicine* 53, 13–24.

Freyberger, H. (1977) Supportive psychotherapeutic techniques in primary and secondary alexithymia. *Psychotherapy and Psychosomatics* 28, 337–342.

Fridlund, A.J. and Duchaine, B. (1996) 'Facial expressions of emotion' and the delusion of the hermetic self. In: R. Harré and W.G. Parrott (eds) *The emotions: Social, cultural and biological dimensions*, pp. 259–284. London: Sage.

Gabbard, G.O. and Menninger, R.W. (1989) The psychology of postponement in the medical marriage. *Journal of the American Medical Association* 261, 2378–2381.

Gara, M.A. and Escobar, J.I. (2001) The stability of somatization syndromes over time. *Archives of General Psychiatry* 58, 94.

Garraghty, P.E., Churchill, J.D. and Banks, M.K. (1998) Adult neural plasticity: Similarities between two paradigms. *Current Directions in Psychological Science* 7, 87–91.

Gergely, G. and Watson, J.S. (1996) The social biofeedback theory of parental affect-mirroring: The development of emotional self-awareness and self-control in infancy. *International Journal of Psycho-Analysis* 77, 1181–1212.

Glaser, D. (2000) Child abuse and neglect and the brain – a review. *Journal of Child Psychology and Psychiatry* 41, 97–116.

Goldberg, D., Gask, L. and O'Dowd, T. (1989) The treatment of somatization: Teaching techniques of reattribution. *Journal of Psychosomatic Research* 33, 689–695.

Goodyer, I.M. (2002) Social adversity and mental function in adolescents at high risk of psychopathology. *British Journal of Psychiatry* 181, 383–386.

Gopnik, A., Meltzoff, A. and Kuhl, P. (1999) *How babies think: The science of childhood*. London: Weidenfeld & Nicolson.

Gould, E., Beylin, A., Tanapat, P., Reeves, A. and Shors, T.J. (1999) Learning enhances adult neurogenesis in the hippocampal formation. *Nature Neuroscience* **2**, 260–265.

Graves, P.L. and Thomas, C.B. (1981) Themes of interaction in medical students' Rorschach responses as predictors of midlife health or disease. *Psychosomatic Medicine* **43**, 215–225.

Greenfield, S. (1998) Brain drugs of the future. *British Medical Journal* **317**, 1698–1701.

Greenhalgh, T. and Hurwitz, B. (1998) *Narrative based medicine*. London: BMJ Publishing.

Greenough, W.T., Black, J.E. and Wallace, C.S. (1987) Experience and brain development. *Child Development* **58**, 539–559.

Gregory, R. (1998) Snapshots from the decade of the brain: Brainy mind. *British Medical Journal* **317**, 1693–1695.

Grice, H.P. (1975) Logic and conversation. In: P. Cole and J.L. Morgan (eds) *Syntax and semantics 3: Speech acts*, pp. 41–58. New York: Academic Press.

Grossarth-Maticek, R. and Eysenck, H.J. (1990) Personality, stress, and disease: Description and validity of a new inventory. *Psychological Reports* **66**, 355–373.

Grossman, K.E. and Grossman, K. (1981) Parent–infant attachment relationship in Bielefeld: A research note. In: K. Immelmann, G.W. Barlow, L. Petrinovich and M. Main (eds) *Behavioral development: The Bielefeld interdisciplinary project*, pp. 604–699. Cambridge: Cambridge University Press.

Gunnar, M.R. (1998) Quality of early care and buffering of neuroendocrine stress reactions. Potential effects on the developing human brain. *Preventive Medicine* **27**, 208–211.

Gureje, O., Üstün, T.B. and Simon, G.E. (1997) The syndrome of hypochondriasis. A cross-national study in primary care. *Psychological Medicine* **27**, 1001–1010.

Gustafsson, P.A., Kjellman, N.-I.M. and Björkstén, B. (2002) Family interaction and supportive social network as salutogenic factors in childhood atopic illness. *Pediatric Allergy and Immunology* **13**, 51–57.

Hampson, J. and Nelson, K. (1993) The relation of maternal language to variation in rate and style of language acquisition. *Journal of Child Language* **20**, 313–342.

Harré, R. (1983) *Personal being*. Oxford: Blackwell.

Harré, R. (1991) *Physical being*. Oxford: Blackwell.

Harré, R. (1998) *The singular self: An introduction to the psychology of personhood*. London: Sage.

Harrington, R. (2001) Developmental continuities and discontinuities. *British Journal of Psychiatry* **179**, 189–190.

Harris, P.L. (1994) Understanding pretence. In: C. Lewis and P. Mitchell (eds) *Children's early understanding of mind: Origins and development*, pp. 235–259. Hove, UK: Lawrence Erlbaum Associates.

Harris, P.L., Johnson, C.N., Hutton, D., Andrews, G. and Cooke, T. (1989) Young children's theory of mind and emotion. *Cognition and Emotion* 3, 379–400.

Harris, P.L. and Saarni, C. (1989) Children's understanding of emotion: An introduction. In C. Saarni and P.L. Harris (eds) *Children's understanding of emotion*, pp. 3–26. Cambridge: Cambridge University Press.

Hart, B. and Risley, T. (1995) *Meaningful differences in the everyday experiences of young American children*. Baltimore, Md.: Paul H Brookes Pub. Co.

Haynes, R.B., Montague, P., Oliver, T., McKibbon, K.A., Brouwers, M.C. and Kanani, R. (2001) Interventions for helping patients to follow prescriptions for medications (Cochrane Review). In: *The Cochrane Library*, Issue 4, 2001. Oxford: Update Software.

Hebb, D. (1949) *The organization of behavior: A neuropsychological theory*. New York: John Wiley.

Heistaro, S., Jousilahti, P., Lahelma, E., Vartiainen, E. and Puska, P. (2001) Self rated health and mortality: A long term prospective study in eastern Finland. *Journal of Epidemiology and Community Health* 55, 227–232.

Henningsen, P., Jakobsen, T. and Schiltenwolf, M. (2001) 'Explanatory models, symptoms and diagnoses in patients with somatoform and related mental disorders', Paper presented at the 16th World Congress on Psychosomatic Medicine, Gothenberg, Sweden, August.

Herman, B.H. and Panksepp, J. (1978) Effects of morphine and naloxone on separation distress and approach attachment: Evidence for opiate mediation of social affect. *Pharmacology, Biochemistry and Behaviour* 9, 213–220.

Hertsgaard, L., Gunnar, M., Erickson, M.F. and Nachmias, M. (1995) Adreno-cortical responses to the strange situation in infants with disorganized/disoriented attachment relationships. *Child Development* 66, 1100–1106.

Herzlich, C. (1973) *Health and illness*. New York: Academic Press.

Hesse, E. (1996) Discourse, memory, and the Adult Attachment Interview: A note with emphasis on the emerging cannot classify category. *Infant Mental Health Journal* 17, 4–11.

Hilde, P.K. (2002) Technology and culture: The case of Hb A_{1c} and type 1 diabetes. *Tidsskrift for Norsk Lægeforening* 122, 69–72 (in Norwegian, with English abstract).

Hinde, R.A. (1982) *Ethology: Its nature and relations with other sciences*. Glasgow: Fontana.

Hinde, R.A. and Stevenson-Hinde, J. (1990) Attachment: Biological, cultural, and individual desiderata. *Human Development* 33, 62–72.

Hoff-Ginsberg, E. (1991) Mother–child conversation in different social classes and communicative settings. *Child Development* 62, 782–796.

Hoffmeyer, J. (1993) Biosemiotics and ethics. In: N. Witoszek and E. Gulbrandsen (eds) *Culture and environment: Interdisciplinary approaches*, pp. 152–176. Oslo: Centre for the Development and the Environment, Centre for Technology and Culture, University of Oslo.

Hoffmeyer, J. (1995a) The semiotic body–mind. *Cruzeiro Semiotico (special issue in honour of Prof. Thomas Sebeok)* **22/25**, 367–383.

Hoffmeyer, J. (1995b) The swarming cyberspace of the body. *Cybernetics and Human Knowing* **3**, 16–25.

Hoffmeyer, J. (2000) The biology of signification. *Perspectives in Biology and Medicine* **43**, 252–268.

Hubble, M.A., Duncan, B.L. and Miller, S.D. (1999) Directing attention to what works. In: M.A. Hubble, B.L. Duncan and S.D. Miller (eds) *The heart and soul of change: What works in therapy*, pp. 407–447. Washington, DC: American Psychological Association.

Hughes, P., Turton, P., Hopper, E., McGauley, G.A. and Fonagy, P. (2001) Disorganised attachment behaviour among infants born subsequent to stillbirth. *Journal of Child Psychology and Psychiatry* **42**, 791–801.

Idler, E.L. and Angel, R.J. (1990) Self-rated health and mortality in the NHANES-I epidemiologic follow-up study. *American Journal of Public Health* **80**, 446–452.

Ihlen, H., Ihlen, B.-M. and Koss, J.O. (1997) *Effekt: falske smil og ekte ørefiker (Effect: false smiles and real clips over the ear)*. Oslo: Cappelens Forlag.

Institute of Medicine, Committee on Quality of Health Care in America (2001) *Crossing the quality chasm: A new health system for the 21st century*. Washington, DC: National Academy Press.

Isabella, R.A., Belsky, J. and von Eye, A. (1989) Origins of infant–mother attachment: An examination of interactional synchrony during the infant's first year. *Developmental Psychology* **25**, 12–21.

Jacobs, B., Schall, M. and Scheibel, A.B. (1993) A quantitative dendritic analysis of Wernicke's area in humans. II Gender, hemispheric, and environmental factors. *Journal of Comparative Neurology* **327**, 97–111.

Johannisson, K. (2001) *Nostalgia*. Stockholm: Bonnier.

Johnson, B.H. and Hugdahl, K. (1991) Hemispheric asymmetry in conditioning to facial emotional expressions. *Psychophysiology* **28**, 154–162.

Johnson, W.D.K. (1991) Predisposition to emotional distress and psychiatric illness amongst doctors: The role of unconscious and experiential factors. *British Journal of Medical Psychology* **64**, 317–329.

Johnston, S.L. and Openshaw, P.J.M. (2001) The protective effects of childhood infections: The next challenge is to mimic safely this protection against allergy and asthma. *British Medical Journal* **322**, 376–377.

Jones, A., Pill, R. and Adams, S. (2000) Qualitative study of views of health professionals and patients on guided self management plans for asthma. *British Medical Journal* **321**, 1507–1510.

Julian, D.G. (1996) If I woke with central chest pain . . . *The Lancet* **348**, S29–S31.

Jureidini, J. and Taylor, D.C. (2002) Hysteria: Pretending to be sick and its consequences. *European Journal of Child Psychiatry* **11**, 123–128.

Kaada, B. (1989) Nocebo – the antipode of placebo. *Tidsskrift for Norsk Lægeforening* **109**, 814–821 (in Norwegian, with English abstract).

Kagan, J. (1994) *Galen's prophecy: Temperament in human nature*. New York: Basic Books.

Katon, W., Kleinman, A. and Rosen, G. (1982) Depression and somatization: A review: Part 1. *American Journal of Medicine* **72**, 127–135.

Katon, W., Lin, E., von Korff, M., Russo, J., Lipscomb, P. and Bush, T. (1991) Somatization: A spectrum of severity. *American Journal of Psychiatry* **148**, 34–40.

Keeley, D. and Osman, L. (2001) Dysfunctional breathing and asthma. *British Medical Journal* **322**, 1075–1076.

Kelley, M.A. and Tucci, J.M. (2001) Bridging the quality chasm: To improve health care we need to understand the motivation of those who work in it. *British Medical Journal* **323**, 61–62.

Kenardy, J. (2000) The current status of psychological debriefing. *British Medical Journal* **321**, 1032–1033.

Kendler, K.S., Walters, E.E., Truett, K.R., Heath, A.C., Neale, M.C., Martin, N.G. and Eaves, L.J. (1995) A twin-family study of self-report symptoms of panic-phobia and somatization. *Behavioral Genetics* **25**, 499–515.

Kirkpatrick, L.A. (1999) Attachment and religious representations and behavior. In: J. Cassidy and P.R. Shaver (eds) *Handbook of attachment: Theory, research and clinical applications*, pp. 803–822. New York: Guilford Press.

Kirmayer, L.J. (1984) Culture, affect, and somatization (part I). *Transcultural Psychiatric Research Review* **21**, 159–188.

Kirmayer, L.J. (1994) Improvisation and authority in illness meaning. *Culture, Medicine, and Psychiatry* **18**, 183–214.

Kirmayer, L.J. and Robbins, J.M. (1991) Three forms of somatization in primary care: Prevalence, co-occurrence, and sociodemographic characteristics. *Journal of Nervous and Mental Disease* **179**, 647–655.

Kirmayer, L.J., Robbins, J.M. and Paris, J. (1994) Somatoform disorders: Personality and the social matrix of somatic distress. *Journal of Abnormal Psychology* **103**, 125–136.

Kirschbaum, C., Prüssner, J.C., Stone, A.A., Federenko, I., Gaab, J., Lintz, D., Schommer, N. and Hellhammer, D.H. (1995) Persistent high cortisol responses to repeated psychological stress in a subpopulation of healthy men. *Psychosomatic Medicine* **57**, 468–474.

Kisely, S., Goldberg, D. and Simon, G. (1997) A comparison between somatic symptoms with and without clear organic cause: Result of an international study. *Psychological Medicine* **27**, 1011–1019.

Kjær-Larsen, A.J. (1956) Napatyl – et nyt analgeticum: Klinisk vurdering af N-acetyl-p-aminophenol med codein. *Ugeskr Læger* **113**, 1421–1425 (in Danish).

Knapp, P.H. (1969) The asthmatic and his environment. *Journal of Nervous and Mental Diseases* **149**, 133–151.

Kraemer, G.W. (1992) A psychobiological theory of attachment. *Behavioural and Brain Sciences* **15**, 493–541.

Kraemer, G.W. (1997) Psychobiology of early social attachment in rhesus monkeys: Clinical implications. *Annals of the New York Academy of Sciences* **807**, 401–418.

Kraemer, S. (2000) The fragile male. *British Medical Journal* **321**, 1609–1612.

Krakowski, A. (1982) Stress and practice of medicine, II: Stressors, stresses, and strains. *Psychotherapy and Psychosomatics* **38**, 11–23.

Laird, J.D. and Apostoleris, N.H. (1996) Emotional self-control and self-perception: Feelings are the solution not the problem. In: R. Harré and W.G. Parrot (eds) *The emotions: Social, cultural and biological dimensions*, pp. 285–301. London: Sage.

Lamberg, L. (1999) 'If I work hard(er), I will be loved.' Roots of physician stress explored. *Journal of the American Medical Association* **282**, 13–14.

Leaning, J. (2001) Health and human rights: The BMA's latest handbook on human rights challenges us all. *British Medical Journal* **322**, 1435–1436.

LeDoux, J.E. (1995) Emotion: Clues from the brain. *Annual Review of Psychology* **46**, 209–235.

LeDoux, J.E. (1996) *The emotional brain: The mysterious underpinnings of emotional life*. New York: Simon & Schuster.

Lerner, M. (1994) *Choices in healing*. Cambridge, MA: MIT Press.

Lewis, C.T. (1879) *A Latin dictionary*. Oxford: Clarendon Press.

Lewis, M. (1992) Individual differences in response to stress. *Pediatrics* **90**, 487–490.

Lewis, M., Feiring, C., McGuffog, C. and Jaskir, J. (1984) Predicting psychopathology in six-year-olds from early social relations. *Child Development* **60**, 831–837.

Little, P., Everitt, H., Williamson, I., Warner, G., Moore, M., Gould, C., Ferrier, K. and Payne, S. (2001) Observational study of effect of patient centredness and positive approach on outcomes of general practice consultations. *British Medical Journal* **323**, 908–911.

Livingston, R. (1993) Children of people with somatization disorder. *Journal of the American Academy of Child and Adolescent Psychiatry* **32**, 536–544.

Luborsky, L., McLellan, A.T., Woody, G.S., O'Brien, C.P. and Auerbach, A. (1985) Therapist success and its determinants. *Archives of General Psychiatry* **42**, 602–611.

Lumley, M.A., Stettner, L. and Wehmer, F. (1996) How are alexithymia and physical illness linked? A review and critique of pathways. *Journal of Psychosomatic Research* **41**, 505–518.

Luparello, T.J., Leist, N., Lourie, C.H. and Sweet, P. (1970) The interaction of physiologic stimuli and pharmacologic agents on airway reactivity in asthmatic subjects. *Psychosomatic Medicine* **32**, 509–513.

Lyon, M.L. (1999) Emotion and embodiment: The respiratory mediation of somatic and social processes. In: A.L. Hinton (ed.) *Biocultural approaches to the emotions*, pp. 182–212. Cambridge: Cambridge University Press.

McCarthy, T.A. (1973) A theory of communicative competence. In: P. Connerton (ed.) *Critical sociology*, pp. 470–497. Harmondsworth: Penguin.

McClearn, G.E., Johansson, B., Berg, S., Pedersen, N.L., Ahern, F., Petrill, S.A. *et al.* (1997) Substantial genetic influence on cognitive abilities in twins 80 or more years old. *Science* **276**, 1560–1562.

McEwen, B.S. (1998) Stress, adaptation, and disease: Allostasis and allostatic load. *Annals of the New York Academy of Sciences* **840**, 33–44.

McEwen, B.S. and Stellar, E. (1993) Stress and the individual. *Archives of Internal Medicine* **153**, 2093–2101.

McFarlane, A.C. (1988) The aetiology of post-traumatic stress disorders following a natural disaster. *British Journal of Psychiatry* **152**, 110–121.

McGaugh, J.L. (1990) Significance and remembrance: The role of neuro-modulatory systems. *Psychological Science* **1**, 15–25.

Macintyre, S., Ford, G. and Hunt, K. (1999) Do women 'over-report' morbidity? Men's and women's responses to structured prompting on a standard question on long standing illness. *Social Science and Medicine* **48**, 89–98.

McKenna, J.J., Mosko, S., Dungy, C. and McAninch, J. (1990) Sleep and arousal patterns of co-sleeping human mother/infant pairs: A preliminary physiological study with implications for the study of sudden infant death syndrome (SIDS). *American Journal of Physical Anthropology* **83**, 331–347.

McLeod, D.R., Hoehn-Saric, R. and Stefon, R.L. (1986) Somatic symptoms of anxiety. *Biological Psychiatry* **21**, 301–310.

McQuade, R. and Young, A.H. (2000) Future therapeutic targets in mood disorders: The glucocorticoid receptor. *British Journal of Psychiatry* **177**, 390–395.

Magai, C. (1999) Affect, imagery, and attachment: Working models of inter-personal affect and the socialization of emotion. In: J. Cassidy and P.R. Shaver (eds) *Handbook of attachment: Theory, research, and clinical applications*, pp. 787–802. New York: Guilford Press.

Maier, S.F., Watkins, L.R. and Fleshner, M. (1994) Psychoneuroimmunology: The interface between behavior, brain, and immunity. *American Psychologist* **49**, 1004–1017.

Main, M. (1990) Cross-cultural studies of attachment organization: Recent studies, changing methodologies, and the concept of conditional strategies. *Human Development* **33**, 48–61.

Main, M. (1991) Metacognitive knowledge, metacognitive monitoring, and singular (coherent) versus multiple (incoherent) models of attachment: Findings and direction for future research. In: C.M. Parkes, J. Stevenson-Hinde and P. Marris (eds) *Attachment across the life cycle*, pp. 127–159. London: Routledge.

Main, M. and Hesse, E. (1990) Parents' unresolved traumatic experiences are related to infant disorganized attachment status: Is frightened and/or frightening parental behavior the linking mechanism? In: M.T. Greenberg, D. Cicchetti and E.M. Cummings (eds) *Attachment in the preschool years*, pp. 161–182. Chicago, IL: University of Chicago Press.

Main, M. and Solomon, J. (1986) Discovery of a new, insecure-disorganized/disoriented attachment pattern. In: T.B. Brazelton and M. Yogman (eds) *Affective development in infancy*, pp. 95–124. Norwood, NJ: Ablex.

Main, M. and Solomon, J. (1990) Procedures for identifying infants as disorganized-disoriented during the Ainsworth Strange Situation. In: M. Greenberg, D. Cicchetti and E.M. Cummings (eds) *Attachment in the preschool years: Theory, research, and intervention*, pp. 121–160. Chicago, IL: Chicago University Press.

Main, T.F. (1957) The ailment. *British Journal of Medical Psychology* **30**, 129–145.

Main, T.F. (1977) Traditional psychiatric defences against close encounters with patients. *Canadian Psychiatric Association Journal* **22**, 457–466.

Malinowski, B. (1948) *Magic, science and religion and other essays*. Boston, MA: Beacon.

Marks, I. (1987) The development of normal fear: A review. *Journal of Child Psychology and Psychiatry* **28**, 667–697.

Marvin, R.S. and Britner, P.A. (1999) Normative development: The ontogeny of attachment. In: J. Cassidy and P.R. Shaver (eds) *Handbook of attachment: Theory, research, and clinical applications*, pp. 44–67. New York: Guilford Press.

Maturana, H.R. and Varela, F.J. (1988) *The tree of knowledge: The biological roots of human understanding*. Boston, Mass.: Shambhala Publications.

Mayer, E. (2001) 'Brain gut interactions in functional GI disorders', Paper presented at the 16th World Congress on Psychosomatic Medicine, Gothenberg, Sweden, August.

Mayou, R. and Sharpe, M. (1997) Treating medically unexplained physical symptoms: Effective interventions are available (editorial). *British Medical Journal* **315**, 561–562.

Mead, G.H. (1962) *Mind, self and society*. Chicago: Chicago University Press.

Meade, J.A., Lumley, M.A. and Casey, R.J. (2001) Stress, emotional skill, and illness in children: The importance of distinguishing between children's and parents' reports of illness. *Journal of Child Psychology and Psychiatry* **42**, 405–412.

Mechanic, D. (1964) The influence of mothers on their children's health attitudes and behaviour. *Pediatrics* **50**, 444–453.

Mechanic, D. (1972) Social psychologic factors affecting the presentation of bodily complaints. *New England Journal of Medicine* **286**, 1132–1139.

Mechanic, D. (2001) How should hamsters run? Some observations about sufficient patient time in primary care. *British Medical Journal* **323**, 266–268.

Scrimshaw, N.S. (1997) The relation between fetal malnutrition and chronic disease in later life: Good nutrition and lifestyle matter from womb to tomb. *British Medical Journal* **315**, 825–826.

Seifer, R., Schiller, M., Sameroff, A.J., Resnick, S. and Riordan, K. (1996) Attachment, maternal sensitivity, and infant temperament during the first year of life. *Developmental Psychology* **32**, 12–25.

Seiffge-Krenke, I. (1993) Coping behavior in normal and clinical samples: More similarities than differences? *Journal of Adolescence* **16**, 285–304.

Sergent, J., Ohta, S. and MacDonald, B. (1992) Functional neuroanatomy. *Brain* **115**, 15–36.

Shalev, A.Y., Rogel-Fuchs, Y. and Pitman, R.K. (1992) Conditioned fear and psychological trauma. *Biological Psychiatry* **31**, 863–865.

Shapiro, A.K. and Shapiro, E. (1997) *The powerful placebo: From ancient priest to modern physician.* Baltimore, MD: Johns Hopkins University Press.

Shaw, R.J. (2001) Treatment adherence in adolescents: Development and psychopathology. *Clinical Child Psychology and Psychiatry* **6**, 137–150.

Shields, S.A. and Simon, A. (1991) Is awareness of bodily change in emotion related to awareness of other bodily processes? *Journal of Personality Assessment* **57**, 96–109.

Shively, C. (2001) 'Experimental evidence for stress-induced abdominal fat deposition, pathophysiology, and disease in primates', Paper presented at the 16th World Congress on Psychosomatic Medicine, Gothenberg, Sweden, August.

Siegel, D.J. (1999) *The developing mind: Toward a neurobiology of interpersonal experience.* New York: Guilford Press.

Sierstad, H.C., Boldsen, J., Hansen, H.S., Mostgaard, G. and Hyldebrandt, N. (1998) Population based study of risk factors for underdiagnosis of asthma in adolescence: Odense schoolchild study. *British Medical Journal* **316**, 651–657.

Simon, G.E. and von Korff, M. (1991) Somatization and psychiatric disorders in the NIMH Epidemiologic Catchment Area Study. *American Journal of Psychiatry* **148**, 1494–1500.

Simpson, D.P. (1968) *Cassell's Latin dictionary.* London: Cassell.

Skipper, J.K. and Leonard, R.C. (1968) Children, stress, and hospitalization: A field experiment. *Journal of Health and Social Behaviour* **9**, 275–287.

Smith, G.R., Monson, R.A. and Ray, D.C. (1986) Patients with multiple unexplained symptoms. Their characteristics, functional health, and health care utilization. *Archives of Internal Medicine* **146**, 69–72.

Smith, R. (2001) Why are doctors so unhappy? *British Medical Journal* **322**, 1073–1074.

Smyth, J.M., Stane, A.A., Hurewitz, A. and Kaell, A. (1999) Effects of writing about stressful experiences on symptom reduction in patients with asthma or rheumatoid arthritis: A randomized trial. *Journal of the American Medical Association* **281**, 1304–1309.

Solomon, J. and George, C. (1999) *Attachment disorganization*. New York: Guilford Press.

Sontag, S. (1979) *Illness as metaphor*. New York: Vintage.

Sontag, S. (1989) *AIDS and its metaphors*. New York: Farrar, Strauss & Giroux.

Spangler, G. and Grossman, K.E. (1993) Biobehavioral organization in securely and insecurely attached infants. *Child Development* **64**, 1439–1450.

Squire, L.R., Knowlton, B. and Musen, G. (1993) The structure and organization of memory. *Annual Review of Psychology* **44**, 453–495.

Sroufe, A.L. (1995) *Emotional development: The organization of emotional life in the early years*. Cambridge: Cambridge University Press.

Steele, H., Steele, M. and Fonagy, P. (1996) Association among attachment classifications of mothers, fathers, and their infants. *Child Development* **67**, 541–555.

Stensland, P. and Malterud, K. (1999) Communicating symptoms through illness diaries: Qualitative evaluation of a clinical method to expand communication. *Scandinavian Journal of Primary Health Care* **17**, 75–80.

Stern, D.N., Hofer, L., Haft, W. and Dore, J. (1985) Affect attunement: The sharing of feeling states between mother and infant by means of inter-modal fluency. In: T.M. Field and N.A. Fox (eds) *Social perception in infants*, pp. 249–268. Norwood, NJ: Ablex.

Stevenson-Hinde, J. (1991) Temperament and attachment: An eclectic approach. In: P. Bateson (ed.) *The development and integration of behaviour: Essays in honour of Robert Hinde*, pp. 315–329. Cambridge: Cambridge University Press.

Stevenson-Hinde, J. and Marshall, P.J. (1999) Behavioral inhibition, heart period, and respiratory sinus arrthymia: An attachment perspective. *Child Development* **70**, 805–816.

Stewart, M., Brown, J.B., Weston, W.W., McWhinney, I.R., McWilliam, C.L. and Freeman, T.R. (1995) *Patient-centred medicine: Transforming the clinical method*. Thousand Oaks, CA: Sage Publications.

Stewart-Brown, S. (1998) Emotional wellbeing and its relation to health: Physical disease may well result from emotional distress. *British Medical Journal* **317**, 1608–1609.

Suls, J. and Fletcher, B. (1985) The relative efficacy of avoidant and non-avoidant coping strategies. *Health Psychology* **4**, 249–288.

Tacón, A.M., Caldera, Y.M. and Bell, N.J. (2001) Attachment style, emotional control, and breast cancer. *Families, Systems and Health* **19**, 319–326.

Taylor, C.B., Bandura, A., Ewart, C.K., Miller, N.H. and DeBusk, R.F. (1985) Exercise testing to enhance wives' confidence in their husbands' cardiac capability soon after clinically uncomplicated acute myocardial infarction. *American Journal of Cardiology* **55**, 635–638.

Taylor, D.C. (1989) Hysteria, belief, and magic. *British Journal of Psychiatry* **155**, 391–398.

Taylor, F.K. (1979) *The concepts of illness, disease and morbus*. Cambridge: Cambridge University Press.

Mechanic, D. and Volkart, E.H. (1960) Illness behaviour and medical diagnosis. *Journal of Health and Human Behaviour* **1**, 86–94.

Miller, B.D. and Wood, B.L. (1997) Influence of specific emotional states on autonomic reactivity and pulmonary function in asthmatic children. *Journal of the American Academy of Child and Adolescent Psychiatry* **36**, 669–677.

Miller, P.J., Potts, R., Fung, H., Hoogstra, L. and Mintz, J. (1990) Narrative practices and the social construction of self in childhood. *American Ethnologist* **17**, 292–311.

Milner, B., Squire, L.R. and Kandel, E.R. (1998) Cognitive neuroscience and the study of memory. *Neuron* **20**, 445–468.

Morris, D.B. (1998) *Illness and culture in the postmodern world*. Berkeley, CA: University of California Press.

Mullen, P.D. (1997) Compliance becomes concordance: Making a change in terminology produce a change in behaviour. *British Medical Journal* **314**, 691–692.

Mullins, L.L., Olson, R.A. and Chaney, J.M. (1992) A social learning/family systems approach to the treatment of somatoform disorders in children and adolescents. *Family Systems Medicine* **10**, 201–212.

Murray, L. (1998a) Contributions of experimental and clinical perturbations of mother–infant communication to the understanding of infant intersubjectivity. In: S. Bråten (ed.) pp. 127–143. Cambridge: Cambridge University Press.

Murray, L. (1998b), 'Impact of parental mental ill-health on child development', Paper presented at the National Centre for Child and Adolescent Psychiatry Conference on Mentally Ill Parents and their Children, Oslo, Norway, May.

Murray, L. and Cooper, P.J. (1997) *Postpartum depression and child development*. New York: Guilford Press.

Nachmias, M., Gunnar, M., Mangelsdorf, S., Parritz, R.H. and Buss, K. (1996) Behavioral inhibition and stress reactivity: The moderating role of attachment security. *Child Development* **67**, 508–522.

Nelson, C.A. and Carver, L.J. (1998) The effects of stress and trauma on brain and memory: A view from developmental cognitive neuroscience. *Development and Psychopathology* **10**, 793–810.

Nelson, K. (1993) The psychological and social origins of autobiographical memory. *Psychological Science* **2**, 1–8.

Nobre, A.C. and Plunkett, K. (1997) The neural system of language: Structure and development. *Current Opinion in Neurobiology* **7**, 262–268.

Nocon, A. (1991) Social and emotional impact of childhood asthma. *Archives of Disease in Childhood* **66**, 458–460.

Notaro, P.C., Gelman, S.A. and Zimmerman, M.A. (2001) Children's understanding of psychogenic bodily reactions. *Child Development* **72**, 444–459.

O'Regan, B. and Hirshberg, C. (1993) *Spontaneous remission: An annotated bibliography*. Bolinas, CA: Institute of Noetic Sciences.

Oxman, T.E., Rosenberg, S.D., Schnurr, P.P. and Tucker, G.J. (1985) Linguistic dimensions of affect and thought in somatization disorder. *American Journal of Psychiatry* **142**, 1150–1155.

Parrot, W.G. and Harré, R. (1996) Overview. In: R. Harré and W.G. Parrot (eds) *The emotions: Social, cultural and biological dimensions*, pp. 2–17. London: Sage.

Parsons, T. (1964) *Social structure and personality*. London: Collier-Macmillan.

Payer, L. (1996) *Medicine and culture: Varieties of treatment in the United States, England, West Germany, and France*. New York: Henry Holt.

Pelosi, A.J. and Appleby, L. (1993) Personality and fatal diseases. *British Medical Journal* **306**, 1666–1667.

Pennebaker, J.W. (1982) *The psychology of physical symptoms*. New York: Springer-Verlag.

Pennebaker, J.W. (2000) Telling stories: The health benefits of narrative. *Literature and Medicine* **19**, 3–19.

Pennebaker, J.W., Kiecolt-Glaser, J.K. and Glaser, R. (1988) Disclosure of traumas and immune function: Health implications for psychotherapy. *Journal of Consulting and Clinical Psychology* **56**, 239–245.

Penrose, R. (1989) *The emperor's new mind: Concerning computers, minds, and the laws of physics*. Oxford: Oxford University Press.

Penrose, R. (1994) *Shadows of the mind: A search for the missing science of consciousness*. London: Oxford University Press.

Perry, B.D. (1997) Incubated in terror: Neurodevelopmental factors in the 'cycle of violence'. In: J. Osofsky (ed.) *Children in a violent society*, pp. 124–149. New York: Guilford Press.

Perry, B.D., Pollard, R.A., Blakely, T.L., Baker, W.L. and Vigilante, D. (1995) Childhood trauma, the neurobiology of adaptation, and 'use-dependent' development of the brain: How states become traits. *Infant Mental Health Journal* **16**, 271–291.

Pert, C.B., Ruff, M.R., Weber, R.J. and Herkenham, M. (1985) Neuropeptides and their receptors: A psychosomatic network. *Journal of Immunology* **135**, 820s–826s.

Petersen, C., Seligman, M.E.P., Yurko, K.H., Martin, L.R. and Friedman, H.S. (1998) Catastrophizing and untimely death. *Psychological Science* **9**, 127–130.

Piaget, J. and Inhelder, B. (1969) *The psychology of the child*. London: Routledge & Kegan Paul.

Pianta, R.C., Marvin, R.S., Britner, P. and Borowitz, K. (1996) Mothers' resolution of their children's diagnosis: Organized patterns of caregiving representations. *Infant Mental Health Journal* **17**, 239–256.

Pianta, R.C., Marvin, R.S. and Morog, M.C. (1999) The resolving past and present: Relations with attachment organization. In: J. Solomon and C. George (eds) *Attachment disorganization*, pp. 379–398. New York: Guilford Press.

Pilowsky, I. (1997) *Abnormal illness behaviour*. Chichester: John Wiley & Sons.

Plooij, F.X. and van de Rijt-Plooij, H.H.C. (1989) Vulnerable periods during infancy: Hierarchically reorganized systems control, stress, and disease. *Ethology and Sociobiology* **10**, 279–296.

Plsek, P.E. and Wilson, T. (2001) Complexity, leadership, and management in healthcare organisations. *British Medical Journal* **323**, 746–749.

Popay, J. and Groves, K. (2000) 'Narrative' in research on gender inequalities in health. In: E. Annandale and K. Hunt (eds) *Gender inequalities in health*, pp. 64–89. Buckingham: Open University Press.

Portegijs, P.J.M., Jeuken, F.M.H., van der Horst, F.G., Kraan, H.F. and Knottnerus, J.A. (1996) A troubled youth: Relations with somatization, depression and anxiety in adulthood. *Family Practice* **13**, 1–11.

Posner, M.I. and Rothbart, M.K. (2000) Developing mechanisms of self-regulation. *Development and Psychopathology* **12**, 427–441.

Powell, P., Bentall, R.P., Nye, F.J. and Edwards, R.H.T. (2001) Randomised controlled trial of patient education to encourage graded exercise in chronic fatigue syndrome. *British Medical Journal* **322**, 387–390.

Prout, A. (1988) 'Off school sick': Mother's account of school sickness absence. *The Sociological Review* **36**, 765–789.

Radke-Yarrow, M. (1998) *Children of depressed mothers: From early childhood to maturity*. Cambridge: Cambridge University Press.

Reid, I.C. and Stewart, C.A. (2001) How antidepressants work: New perspectives on the pathophysiology of depressive disorder. *British Journal of Psychiatry* **178**, 299–303.

Reite, M., Harbeck, R. and Hoffman, A. (1981) Altered cellular immune response following peer separation. *Life Sciences* **29**, 1133–1136.

Robbins, J.M. and Kirmayer, L.J. (1996) Transient and persistent hypochondriacal worry in primary care. *Psychological Medicine* **26**, 575–589.

Robertson, J. and Robertson, J. (1971) Young children in brief separation: A fresh look. *Psychoanalytic Study of the Child* **26**, 328–332.

Rolland, J.S. (1984) Towards a psychosocial typology of chronic and life-threatening illness. *Family Systems Medicine* **2**, 245–262.

Rolland, J.S. (1987) Chronic illness and the life cycle: A conceptual framework. *Family Process* **26**, 203–221.

Rolland, J.S. (1994) *Families, illness, and disability: An integrative treatment model*. New York: Basic Books.

Rollnick, S. and Miller, W.R. (1995) What is motivational interviewing? *Behavioral and Cognitive Psychotherapy* **23**, 325–334.

Rose, S. (1995) The rise of neurogenetic determinism. *Nature* **373**, 380–382.

Rose, S. (2001) Moving on from old dichotomies: Beyond nature–nurture towards a lifeline perspective. *British Journal of Psychiatry* **178** (suppl. 40), s3–s7.

Rosvold, E.O. and Bjertness, E. (2001) Physicians who do not take sick leave: hazardous heroes? *Scandinavian Journal of Public Health* **29**, 71–75.

Russek, L.G. and Schwartz, G.E. (1997) Feelings of parental caring predict health status in midlife: A 35-year follow-up of the Harvard Mastery of Stress Study. *Journal of Behavioral Medicine* **10**, 1–13.

Rutter, M. (1985) Resilience in the face of adversity: Protective factors and resistance to psychiatric disorder. *British Journal of Psychiatry* **147**, 598–611.

Rutter, M.L. (1999) Psychosocial adversity and child psychopathology. *British Journal of Psychiatry* **174**, 480–493.

Rutter, M. and the English and Romanian Adoptees Study Team (1998) Developmental catch-up, and deficit, following adoption after severe global early privation. *Journal of Child Psychology and Psychiatry* **39**, 465–476.

Sachs, L. (1983) *Evil eye or bacteria: Turkish migrant women and Swedish health care*. Stockholm: Studies in Social Anthropology.

Sachs, L. (1995) Is there a pathology of prevention? The implications of visualizing the invisible in screening programs. *Culture, Medicine and Psychiatry* **12**, 423–429.

Salmon, P., Peters, S. and Stanley, I. (1999) Patients' perceptions of medical explanations for somatisation disorders: Qualitative analysis. *British Medical Journal* **318**, 372–376.

Salovey, P. and Mayer, J.M. (1990) Emotional intelligence. *Imagination, Cognition, and Personality* **9**, 189–200.

Samuel, G. (1990) *Mind, body and culture: Anthropology and the biological interface*. Cambridge: Cambridge University Press.

Sandberg, S., Paton, J.Y., Ahola, S., McCann, D.C., McGuiness, D., Hillary, C.R. and Oja, H. (2000) The role of acute and chronic stress in asthma attacks in children. *The Lancet* **356**, 982–987.

Scarr, S. and McCartney, K. (1983) How people make their own environments: A theory of gene-environment effects. *Child Development* **54**, 424–435.

Schacter, D.L. (1996) *Searching for memory: The brain, the mind and the past*. New York: Basic Books.

Schama, S. (2000) *A history of Britain: At the edge of the world? 3000BC–AD1603*. London: BBC Worldwide.

Schore, A.N. (1994) *Affect regulation and the origin of the self: The neurobiology of emotional development*. Hillsdale, NJ: Lawrence Erlbaum Associates.

Schore, A.N. (1996) The experience-dependent maturation of a regulatory system in the orbital prefrontal cortex and the origin of developmental psychopathology. *Development and Psychopathology* **8**, 59–87.

Schore, A.N. (1997) Early organization of the nonlinear right brain and development of a predisposition to psychiatric disorders. *Development and Psychopathology* **9**, 595–631.

Scollon, R. and Scollon, S.W. (2001) *Intercultural communication: A discourse approach*. Oxford: Blackwell.

Scovern, A.W. (1999) From placebo to alliance: The role of common factors in medicine. In: M.A. Hubble, B.L. Duncan and S.D. Miller (eds) *The heart and soul of change: What works in therapy*, pp. 259–295. Washington, DC: American Psychological Association.

Taylor, G.J., Bagby, R.M. and Parker, J.D.A. (1997) *Disorders of affect regulation: Alexithymia in medical and psychiatric illness.* Cambridge: Cambridge University Press.

Taylor, R.E., Mann, A.H., White, N.J.: and Goldberg, D.P. (2000) Attachment style in patients with unexplained physical complaints. *Psychological Medicine* **30**, 931–941.

Taylor, S.E., Repetti, R.L. and Seeman, T. (1997) Health psychology: What is an unhealthy environment and how does it get under the skin? *Annual Review of Psychology* **48**, 411–447.

Teixeira, J.M.A., Fisk, N.M. and Glover, V. (1999) Association between maternal anxiety in pregnancy and increased uterine artery resistance index: Cohort based study. *British Medical Journal* **318**, 153–157.

Temoshok, L. (1990) On attempting to articulate the biopsychosocial model: Psychological–psychophysiological homeostasis. In: H.S. Friedman (ed.) *Personality and disease*, pp. 203–225. New York: Wiley.

Thompson, W.T., Cupples, M.E., Sibbett, C.H., Skan, D.I. and Bradley, T. (2001) Challenge of culture, conscience, and contract to general practitioners' care of their own health: Qualitative study. *British Medical Journal* **323**, 728–731.

Thoonen, B. and van Weel, C. (2000) Self management in asthma care: professionals must rethink their role if they are to guide patients successfully. *British Medical Journal* **321**, 1482–1483.

Tinbergen, N. (1951) *The study of instinct.* Oxford: Oxford University Press.

Tjomsland, O., Ekeberg, Ø. and Saatvedt, K. (2001) Placeboeffekt ved kirurgisk og prosedyrerelatert klinisk forskning. *Tidsskrift for Norsk Lægeforening* **121**, 2290–2293 (in Norwegian).

Toates, F. (1995) *Stress: Conceptual and biological aspects.* Chichester: John Wiley.

Torgersen, S. (1986) Genetics of somatoform disorders. *Archives of General Psychiatry* **43**, 502–505.

Torosian, T., Lumley, M.A., Pickard, S.D. and Ketterer, M.W. (1997) Silent versus symptomatic myocardial ischemia: The role of psychological and medical factors. *Health Psychology* **16**, 123–130.

Treasure, J. and Schmidt, U. (2001) Ready, willing and able to change: Motivational aspects of the assessment and treatment of eating disorders. *European Eating Disorders Review* **9**, 4–18.

Trevarthen, C. (2001) Intrinsic motives for companionship in understanding: Their origin, development, and significance for infant mental health. *Infant Mental Health Journal* **22**, 95–131.

Trevarthen, C. and Aitken, K.J. (1994) Brain development, infant communication, and empathy. *Development and Psychopathology* **6**, 597–633.

Trevarthen, C. and Aitken, K.J. (2001) Infant intersubjectivity: Research, theory, and clinical applications. *Journal of Child Psychology and Psychiatry* **41**, 3–48.

Trivers, R. (2000) The elements of a scientific theory of self-deception. *Annals of the New York Academy of Sciences* **907**, 114–131.

Tschudi, F. (1977) Loaded and honest questions: A construct theory view of symptoms and therapy. In: D. Bannister (ed.) *New perspectives in personal construct theory*, pp. 321–350. London: Academic Press.

Tucker, D.M., Luu, P. and Pribram, K.H. (1995) Social and emotional self-regulation. *Annals of the New York Academy of Sciences* **769**, 213–239.

Turner Cobb, J.M. and Steptoe, A. (1998) Psychosocial influences on upper respiratory infectious diseases in children. *Journal of Psychosomatic Research* **45**, 319–330.

Vaglum, P. and Falkum, E.J. (1999) Self criticism, dependency, and depressive symptoms in a nationwide sample of Norwegian physicians. *Journal of Affective Disorders* **52**, 155–159.

Vaillant, G.E. (1998) Natural history of male psychological health. XIV: Relationship of mood disorder and vulnerability to physical health. *American Journal of Psychiatry* **2**, 184–191.

Vaillant, G.E., Sobowale, N.C. and McArthur, C. (1972) Some psychologic vulnerabilities of physicians. *New England Journal of Medicine* **287**, 372–375.

Van den Bergh, O. (2001) 'Determinants of subjective health complaints: A dynamic perspective', Paper presented at the 16th World Congress on Psychosomatic Medicine, Gothenberg, Sweden, August.

van der Kolk, B.A. (1996) The complexity of adaptation to trauma: Self-regulation, stimulus discrimination, and characterological development. In: B.A. van der Kolk, A.C. McFarlane and L. Weisæth (eds) *Traumatic stress: The effects of overwhelming experience on mind, body, and society*, pp. 182–213. New York: Guilford Press.

van der Kolk, B.A., McFarlane, A.C. and Weisæth, L. (1996) *Traumatic stress: The effects of overwhelming experience on mind, body, and society*. New York: Guilford Press.

van Dongen-Melman, J.E.W.M. and Sanders-Woustra, J.A.R. (1986) Psychosocial aspects of childhood cancer: A review of the literature. *Journal of Child Psychology and Psychiatry* **27**, 145–180.

van IJzendoorn, M.H. (1995) Adult attachment representations, parental responsiveness, and infant attachment: A meta-analysis on the predictive validity of the adult attachment interview. *Psychological Bulletin* **117**, 387–403.

van IJzendoorn, M.H. and Hubbard, F.O.A. (2000) Are infant crying and maternal responsiveness during the first year related to infant–mother attachment at 15 months? *Attachment and Human Development* **2**, 371–391.

Van IJzendoorn, M.H. and Kroonenberg, P.M. (1988) Cross-cultural patterns of attachment: A meta-analysis of the Strange Situation. *Child Development* **59**, 147–156.

Van IJzendoorn, M.H. and Sagi, A. (1999) Cross-cultural patterns of attachment: Universal and contextual dimensions. In: J. Cassidy and P.R. Shaver (eds) *Handbook of attachment: Theory, research and clinical applications*, pp. 713–734. New York: Guilford Press.

von der Lippe, A. and Crittenden, P.M. (2000) Patterns of attachment in young Egyptian children. In: P.M. Crittenden and A.H. Claussen (eds) *The organization of attachment relationships: Maturation, culture, and context*, pp. 97–114. Cambridge: Cambridge University Press.

Vondra, J.I., Shaw, D.S., Swearingen, L., Cohen, M. and Owens, E.B. (2001) Attachment stability and emotional and behavioral regulation from infancy to preschool age. *Development and Psychopathology* **13**, 13–33.

Vygotsky, L.S. (1978) *Mind in society*. Cambridge, MA: Harvard University Press.

Waldron, I. (1997) Changing gender roles and gender differences in health behavior. In: D.S. Gochman (ed.) *Handbook of health behavior research 1: Personal and social determinants*, pp. 303–328. New York: Plenum Press.

Waldron, I. (2000) Trends in gender differences in mortality: relationships to changing gender differences in behaviour and other causal factors. In E. Annandale and K. Hunt (eds) *Gender inequalities in health*, pp. 150–181. Buckingham: Open University Press.

Walker, L.S., Garber, J. and Greene, J.W. (1994) Somatic complaints in pediatric patients: A prospective study of the role of negative life events, child social and academic competence, and parental somatic symptoms. *Journal of Consulting and Clinical Psychology* **62**, 1213–1221.

Walker, L.S., Garber, J., Smith, C.A., Van Slyke, D.A. and Claar, R.L. (2001) The relation of daily stressors to somatic and emotional symptoms in children with and without recurrent abdominal pain. *Journal of Consulting and Clinical Psychology* **69**, 85–91.

Walker, L.S. and Zeman, J.L. (1992) Parental response to child illness behavior. *Journal of Pediatric Psychology* **17**, 49–71.

Warren, S.L., Huston, L., Egeland, B. and Sroufe, L.A. (1997) Child and adolescent anxiety disorders and early attachment. *Journal of the American Academy of Child and Adolescent Psychiatry* **36**, 637–644.

Watzlawick, P., Weakland, J. and Fisch, R. (1974) *Change: Principles of problem formation and problem resolution*. New York: Norton.

Wellman, H.M., Harris, P.L., Banerjee, M. and Sinclair, A. (1995) Early understanding of emotion: Evidence from natural language. *Cognition and Emotion* **9**, 117–149.

Wheeler, M.A., Stuss, D.T. and Tulving, E. (1997) Toward a theory of episodic memory: the frontal lobes and autonoetic consciousness. *Psychological Bulletin* **121**, 331–354.

Wilkinson, S.R. (1986) 'Pretend illness': Analysis of one phase in the development of illness behaviour. *Family Systems Medicine* **4**, 376–384.

Wilkinson, S.R. (1988) *The child's world of illness: The development of health and illness behaviour*. Cambridge: Cambridge University Press.

Wilkinson, S.R. (2001) Developing practice on a ward for adolescents with psychiatric disorders. *Clinical Child Psychology and Psychiatry* **6**, 151–163.

Winson, J. (1993) The biology and function of rapid eye movement sleep. *Current Opinion in Neurobiology* **3**, 243–248.

Wood, B.L., Klebba, K.B. and Miller, B.D. (2000) Evolving the biobehavioral family model: The fit of attachment. *Family Process* **39**, 319–344.

Wright, S.M., Kern, D.E., Kolodner, K., Howard, D.M. and Brancati, F.L. (1998) Attributes of excellent attending-physician role models. *New England Journal of Medicine* **339**, 1986–1993.

Wuitchik, M., Bakal, D. and Lipshitz, J. (1989) The clinical significance of pain and cognitive activity in latent labour. *Obstetrics and Gynecology* **73**, 35–42.

Yamey, G. and Wilkes, M. (2001) Promoting wellbeing among doctors: We should move away from a disease model and focus on positive functioning. *British Medical Journal* **322**, 252–253.

Yellowlees, P.M. and Kalucy, R.S. (1990) Psychobiological aspects of asthma and the consequent research implications. *Chest* **97**, 629–634.

Ytterhus, B. and Tøssebro, J. (1999) Physical integration and social marginalisation in Norwegian nursery schools: Attitudes, rank ordering or situation dynamics? *European Journal of Special Needs Education* **14**, 158–170.

Zborowski, M. (1952) Cultural components in response to pain. *Journal of Social Issues* **8**, 16–30.

Zeanah, C.H., Keener, M.A., Stewart, L. and Anders, T.F. (1985) Prenatal perception of infant personality: A preliminary investigation. *Journal of the American Academy of Child Psychiatry* **24**, 204–210.

Index